CHEMICAL
COWBOYS

This book has a The Random House Publishing Group
... available ... American ... and full manuscript
... communication ... book ... and ...
... please call (800) 733-3000.

CHEMICAL COWBOYS

THE DEA'S SECRET MISSION TO HUNT DOWN
A NOTORIOUS ECSTASY KINGPIN

LISA SWEETINGHAM

BALLANTINE BOOKS • NEW YORK

2010 Ballantine Books Mass Market Edition

Published in the United States by Ballantine Books, an imprint of The Random House Publishing Group, a division of Random House, Inc., New York.

BALLANTINE and colophon are registered trademarks of Random House, Inc.

Originally published in hardcover in the United States by Ballantine Books, an imprint of The Random House Publishing Group, a division of Random House, Inc., in 2009.

ISBN 978-0-345-52115-6

Cover design and imagery: Henry Steadman

Printed in the United States of America

www.ballantinebooks.com

9 8 7 6 5 4 3 2 1

For Bodie

CONTENTS

PROLOGUE

TOWER AIR FLIGHT 31 from Tel Aviv touched down at the Los Angeles airport a little before noon on a Tuesday. Israeli nationals Ben Cohen and Nathan Hanan deplaned at gate 120, where a team of undercover agents dressed in jeans, T-shirts, and ball caps had been waiting. The agents slowly trailed the two Israeli targets as they walked through the terminal, brushing past hurried travelers and families getting an early start on the holidays.

Cohen and Hanan were met outside by a handsome, dark-haired thirty-three-year-old Israeli named Itzhak "Jackie" Cohen, who placed their bags in his Range Rover and took them to a Budget lot, where they rented a white Lincoln Town Car. The men drove in tandem toward the San Fernando Valley as DEA and U.S. Customs agents followed from a careful distance in unmarked vehicles.

It was a cool, clear fall day. Rows of top-heavy palm trees swayed in the Pacific breeze. The L.A. desert clime, whitewashed stucco homes, and gleaming high-rise towers had the familiar Mediterranean radiance of Cohen and Hanan's native Tel Aviv. Jackie led the men to a vacant single-family home at 6606 Whitaker Avenue, in a well-manicured neighborhood carved alongside the concrete L.A. River. For the next ten days, this was where Cohen and Hanan would carry out their work, unaware that agents were watching their every move.

In the last twenty-four hours, an Israeli National Police (INP) investigation team had received secret intelligence that Cohen and Hanan were traveling to Los Angeles to take part in a major narcotics transaction with Jackie's partner, Yehuda "Judy" Ben Atar. INP passed the tip to the L.A. drug cops who were investigating Judy's role in an Ecstasy distribution ring.

Judy Ben Atar was a thirty-four-year-old Israeli expat who lived in Sherman Oaks with his wife and children and kept close ties to leg breakers and mob bosses back home in Jerusalem. Judy had first caught the attention of LAX Customs agents four months earlier, when three women arriving from Paris were caught smuggling 140,000 Ecstasy pills hidden in false-bottom luggage and boxes of toys. Intelligence suggested Judy and his partners were behind the load.

The tip from INP was a good break for the Los Angeles drug cops, but only if they could catch someone holding the bag—picking up or dropping off cash or pills. A half-dozen undercovers were assigned to follow the suspects and report back any unusual activity or signs that the deal was about to go down.

Over the next five days, the surveillance team filled spiral notebooks with minute-to-minute observations about the dealers' meetings at a sandwich shop on Ventura Boulevard, late-night trips to public pay phones, and heated arguments in Hebrew, which none of the agents understood.

On November 29 at 1:35 p.m., a DEA agent was sitting in an unmarked vehicle a half block from the Whitaker Avenue house, when he saw an unknown suspect in a shiny black Lexus SUV pull into the driveway and go inside. Forty-five minutes later, someone—the agent couldn't see who—backed the suspect's SUV into the attached garage and shut the garage door.

Minutes passed. Nothing. At 2:35 p.m., the agent quickly slumped down into his seat to avoid being seen as the garage door opened and Hanan sped off in the Lexus SUV, with Cohen right behind him at the wheel of the rented Lincoln. The third suspect was nowhere in sight.

The agent called his teammates over the radio. It was time.

All units maintained constant radio contact as they followed the two Israeli targets onto the 101 freeway and then the 405 freeway heading toward West Los Angeles. A Customs Air Support helicopter hovered overhead, calling out the targets' positions. At 3:00 p.m. the chopper unit confirmed that Hanan had exited at Sunset Boulevard and was parking the SUV on Church Lane near the Holiday Inn tower, an iconic circular landmark that divided tony Brentwood from the smog-choked 405 freeway. Cohen pulled up beside him.

The car keys dangled from Hanan's hands as he got out of the SUV and slipped into Cohen's car. Two undercover agents followed the Israeli targets as they drove up the winding Sepulveda Pass through the Santa Monica Mountains back to the valley. The agents followed Cohen and Hanan into a supermarket in Encino and watched them purchase cleaning supplies, Gatorade, toilet paper, bleach, Coke, and eggs. Nothing special. All units were redeployed back to the abandoned SUV.

Cash or drugs. This was it. The vehicle had to be loaded with bundles of $20 bills or plastic bags filled with small white Ecstasy pills.

Shifts of two officers from DEA, Customs, and Torrance police maintained twenty-four-hour fixed and unobstructed surveillance of the SUV from unmarked vehicles on Church Lane and from an observation post inside room 906 of the Holiday Inn. The plan was to wait for the drug runner to come collect. They'd follow him, do a routine traffic stop, check his ID, find the load, and make an arrest. Or maybe they'd let the runner lead them straight to whoever was buying the pills or collecting the money.

Two days passed and the SUV sat undisturbed under the shade of the towering hotel. A thin layer of dust had settled on its cool black skin. Lead DEA Special Agent Michele Figura sensed that something was wrong. Brentwood was an unusual location for a drug drop. The ultra-wealthy neighborhood was known more for its palatial mountainside homes and elite private schools than covert drug deals. She started to worry that they'd taken a burn—that the dealers had spotted them and decided to abandon the load. Figura called DEA Special Agent Robert Gagne in New York for advice.

Gagne was the go-to guy of Ecstasy. Back in 1995, Gagne and his partners had led DEA's first major investigation into the so-called Love Drug when they infiltrated Manhattan's top nightclubs. While the agents in L.A. were babysitting the SUV, Gagne was deep into his own investigation of Judy's associate Oded Tuito, aka "the Fat Man," who'd made a fortune buying millions of the little, bright-colored pills—stamped with stars, hearts, and happy faces—for about $1 each from Dutch suppliers and reselling them to his network of distributors in the States for $6.

Gagne agreed with Agent Figura that something was amiss with the abandoned SUV. After years of watching Ecstasy dealers operate, Gagne knew they could get sloppy. Sometimes they'd be out all night partying at strip clubs and would wake up too late to pick up couriers. Other times the dealers would purposely switch their plans to throw off law enforcement. But nobody leaves drugs or money on the street for that long. Gagne checked in with his confidential sources—he had snitches from Boston to Bucharest—but no one had any further intel on Cohen and Hanan. Gagne knew it wasn't his place to tell them what to do, but if it had been on his turf, he'd have found a way to look inside that car and figure out if they were wasting their time.

On Wednesday morning, December 1, the two Israeli targets returned to the scene. The agents watched in anticipation as Hanan slowly walked around the SUV and peered into the windows. Seemingly satisfied, Hanan got back in the rental car, and Cohen drove them toward the airport to catch an afternoon flight back to Israel. DEA agents searched the Lincoln after it had been dropped off at the Budget office and secretly examined the contents of Cohen and Hanan's six checked bags at LAX. They found a pile of new clothes with the tags still attached—but no drugs, no cash, and nothing unusual.

On Friday, December 3, Agent Figura called Chris Kabel of DEA Special Operations Division in Virginia. Kabel headed Operation Rave, which managed the dozens of Ecstasy cases that had popped up in major cities across the country in the last twelve months.

"Chris, we've been watching this car for five days. Nothing," Figura said. "We're trying to decide what to do." Kabel advised her to find a legal way to open the car. Since the SUV had been abandoned for nearly a week, it would have been towed already if the agents hadn't been watching it. They could protect their cover by getting the Los Angeles Police Department to do the tow and perform a customary inventory of the vehicle's contents.

At 2:15 p.m. a tow truck pulled up. A police officer slipped a flat metal Slim Jim down the SUV's window well and pulled the tool up in short jerks, trying to trigger the locks.

Figura was on her cell phone with Agent Kabel when the door locks finally released.

Dope or money, dope or money echoed in her head as she popped the hatch release and the trunk door slowly rose. But it wasn't dope or money. Inside was a dead man, gray, bruised, and cold to the touch. He was naked and lying in a fetal position under the cover of a cargo shade.

"Shit!" Figura yelled.

A stream of dried blood had drained from the man's mouth and nose and was caked onto the cargo liner. His right hand was tucked under his right knee. A carton of Marlboro cigarettes was tucked behind his feet.

"Chris, it's a fucking body," Figura said. "Let me call you back."

Figura replayed Cohen and Hanan's moves in her mind, searching for signs they had missed. It didn't make sense. The agents had gone on a late-night trash run at the Whitaker Avenue house days earlier and found empty containers of bleach and laundry detergent and a small cluster of paper towels caked with blood, but they hadn't connected the dots.

Cohen and Hanan weren't dealers—they were hit men.

Bob Gagne was incredulous when he heard the news. How could they have watched a dead man's car for a week? They should have moved in sooner. Cohen and Hanan were long gone by now.

Gagne called his friend Gadi Eshed, the head of intelligence for the Israeli National Police's Central Unit in Tel Aviv. Israeli officers were already on their way to L.A. to assist Robbery-Homicide detectives in the investigation. According to Israeli intelligence sources, the deceased was a leg breaker named Allon David Giladi, who was linked to rival Mafia families in Israel that were suspected of overseeing gambling, prostitution, and extortion rings—as well as mob hits. Ecstasy dealing, however, had never been among their list of crimes. An autopsy later revealed that Giladi had been strangled to death.

Gagne and Eshed feared that the dead man in Brentwood signaled a dangerous turning point in the Ecstasy trade. Murder was typically the province of cocaine and heroin traffickers who hijacked whole villages in Central and South America to run their drug empires. The expat Israeli dealers had always governed over Ecstasy with the threat of violence more than actual deed. But if the top Mafiosos in Israel had caught wind of the easy money to be made, it was only a matter of time before they would start to move in on the action, and import their blood feuds along with the Love Drug.

KIDDIE DOPE

1 FEBRUARY 1995: NEW YORK CITY

"BOBBY, LISTEN. Ray's a little nervous," the informant whispered over the phone. "He just has to make sure that, you know—that you're all right."

"Okay," Gagne said. "Tomorrow morning."

Gagne heard the urgency in "Tommy's" voice. A few months earlier, the informant had introduced Gagne to Ray Solomon, a lanky ninety-pound Dominican dealer with a disarming three-toothed smile. Since then, Solomon had sold Gagne crack, heroin, cocaine, and two automatic Uzis with silencers. Solomon didn't know that "Bobby" and his partner "Jimmy" were really Robert Gagne and Matthew Germanowski, special agents with the Drug Enforcement Administration, investigating Solomon's involvement with a crooked longshoreman who was helping to bring guns and drugs into New York via cargo ships.

Drug traffickers have a choice of land, air, or sea when delivering product to American soil. Seaport routes are the slowest mode of transportation, but they carry the least risk of detection due to the tremendous volume of containers being moved in and out of American ports. Drug smugglers will take a container filled with typical imports—furniture, detergent, avocados—and hide millions of dollars' worth of drugs inside the goods or behind false walls of the container. But they still need an unscrupulous longshoreman to help move the contraband-laden containers past Customs agents. It's an easy job: the longshoreman simply hands the agent ninety-eight bills of lading for a shipment of a hundred containers—but he's already hidden the paperwork for the two containers loaded with the heroin. The Customs agent randomly pulls five bills of lading out of the ninety-eight and says: "Show me these containers." He inspects the five, they pass muster, and the entire shipment is approved to move out.

Gagne and his partner, Germanowski, figured that Ray Solomon's cohort was pushing about five hundred kilos of cocaine per shipment simply by pulling a couple of bills of lading out of a stack in the morning and then tucking them back in the stack at the end of the day. And for that ten seconds of work, he was paid roughly $5,000 for each drug-loaded container.

A good DEA agent arrests a target and keeps fishing, throwing the little fish back, hoping to bait a bigger fish. Gagne and Germanowski caught the informant Tommy, who was used to bait Ray Solomon, who could be used to bait the bigger fish—the crooked longshoreman and his foreign bosses who were supplying the drugs. But Solomon was feeling "a little nervous." Gagne knew he needed to build more trust with Solomon. He decided it was time to make a social call: no drugs, no guns, no deals, just cards, TV, and beer on a Saturday afternoon in Tommy's Sunset Park, Brooklyn, apartment.

All DEA operations—from buy to bust—are supposed to be conducted on the books, with official operating plans that include a team of agents standing in the shadows. Agents are not to go out undercover by themselves. Gagne knew this. But he was a gutsy agent, known for finding creative ways to bend the rules in order to get his job done. He didn't want to take his partner away from his wife on a weekend, and he certainly didn't want to pull together a full DEA team presence with twenty-four hours' notice just so the other

agents could spend their Saturday morning listening to
him play cards with Tommy and Ray Solomon.

The next morning, Gagne was sitting on Tommy's
couch when Solomon showed up.

"Hey, Ray," Gagne said.

The dealer strutted in, all wiry limbs and crazy smile,
walked straight up to Gagne, and pulled a loaded gun
from his waistband.

"What's up?" Solomon sneered as he pointed the
weapon at Gagne's head.

Every nerve in Gagne's body tensed as he trained his
focus on the black steel barrel of the .25 three inches
from his face. Tommy went pale.

Gagne could feel the butt of his own gun, a point-and-
shoot Glock, against the small of his back. He calculated
the time it would take to get his hands on his weapon,
three layers deep, past his checkered field coat, sweatshirt, and sweatpants.

I'm just not *getting to it,* he thought. *There's no way.*
He struggled to suppress the paralyzing tunnel vision
that made the barrel of Solomon's gun seem to get bigger, closer.

Easy . . . stay calm, he told himself. *He's testing me.*
Keep the cover. Keep talking.

Gagne leaned forward, looked Solomon in the eye,
and smiled. "Hey, what the fuck you got there?" Gagne
reached for the gun. There was an awkward pause:
Gagne's hand in midair, Solomon's eyes fixed on his.

Keep talking.

"That's a beauty," Gagne said.

Solomon was listening now. He glanced at the piece,
admiring its cold form, then looked back into Gagne's
eyes like a stray dog looking for signs of weakness.

"Is that a twenty-five?" Gagne put his fingers around
the barrel.

"Yeah," Solomon said. "I just got it."

Solomon loosened his grip and Gagne casually took the gun from the dealer's hands.

"No kidding?" He willed his fingers steady as the instrument traded hands. Any visible tremors would clue Solomon that he'd been bluffed.

"Yeah, this is nice." Gagne gauged the weapon's weight. "I'll give you three hundred bucks for it."

"Get outta here!"

"No, really! I'll give you three for it right now."

"Nah, I'm not selling it," Solomon said, betraying a shy, goofy smile as he accepted the gun back from Gagne and stuffed it down his waistband.

"No?" Gagne went to the kitchen to grab a beer out of the refrigerator for Solomon. "Change your mind"— he pulled out his wallet—"I got your money right here." There was $10 in that wallet.

Tommy was wan and mute from watching the near-disaster unfold in his living room. Gagne figured he had probably been racking his brain, trying to come up with an explanation he could give his drug-dealing buddies about how a dead DEA agent came to be found in his apartment.

2 BOB, MATT, AND JAY

THERE'S AN OLD SAYING around DEA: "Our best undercovers could talk a starving dog off a meat wagon."

Special Agent Robert Gagne was one of the best. He knew that if a target was listening to him, he couldn't act at the same time—he couldn't pull a trigger. It was talk or perish. Agent Gagne had had a lot of practice talking his way in and out of trouble. He grew up in working-class Pawtucket, Rhode Island, the second eldest child in a competitive brood of three boys and two girls.

Skilled undercover agents seem to fade into the scenery when surveilling a target. As a child, Bobby believed he had powers of invisibility. He would climb to the highest tree branch and watch the babysitter frantically search him out. He would tuck himself low on the floorboards of the green-upholstered backseat of "Old Betsy," his father's Chevy, and quietly stare at the back of his father's neck as he drove to work. Young Bobby wanted to be closer to his French Canadian father, René, to know what kind of man he was in the moments he believed he was alone. Problem was, Bobby didn't like what he saw. René had a part-time job pumping gas and a full-time job selling meat for Tarpy's Beef. When he wasn't at work, René was coaching his children in sports, hiding out at his girlfriend's place, or warming a seat at the bar and coaxing one more beer down his throat.

Gagne left his childhood hiding games for a life of hiding behind undercover personas and watching the "bad guys."

Agents and dealers share a common language. When a DEA agent says, "We had five bad guys up on a wire, scheduling loads, and then they all dropped their phones," the five suspects whose phone lines DEA was tapping literally chucked their Motorolas. When a drug dealer is arrested, his partners will say he's "sick" or he "got his legs broken." Sometimes he gets his legs broken by "our friends at the three letters." And when our friends at the three letters (DEA) talk in shorthand about arrests, it's all about taking down the bad guys while making sure that no good guys—agents and civilians— get hurt in the process.

Gagne saw his job in simple terms: arrest the bad guys. But sometimes, like in Ray Solomon's case, some-one else gets there first. Alcohol, Tobacco, and Firearms agents arrested Solomon a few weeks later on gun charges. (The crooked longshoreman was also later nabbed and pleaded guilty to weapons charges.) Gagne decided to pay Solomon a visit in his holding cell.

"I knew it!" Solomon said, shaking his head at Gagne's shiny badge.

"Ray, if you knew," Gagne replied, "you woulda shot me that day."

"You got me!" Solomon said, laughing. "You son of a bitch, you got me."

"The guys are gonna go get McDonald's, Ray. What do you want?"

Gagne felt like he owed Solomon a parting meal. He knew the dealer already had two prior felony convic-tions, which made him a three-time loser, facing a mandatory life sentence. Gagne had empathy for a lot of his targets.

Agents and the men they chase often have the same start in life. They are creative problem solvers, natural leaders with street smarts and an ability to anticipate their adversary's next ten moves. Somewhere along the way, guys like Gagne choose the law, and guys like Solomon choose crime. Gagne understood that there is a fine line between them, and he believed deeply in sticking to his side of the line.

Still, he knew his risk-taking nature irked his bosses. If Solomon had shot him that day in Brooklyn, Gagne would have preferred death to injury, because if he'd been shot and survived, his integrity would forever be in question. Even if DEA had let him keep his job, he'd be reassigned to special agent in charge of handing out batteries.

"Are you fucking cartooning me?" Germanowski had said when he learned about his partner's off-the-books meeting with Solomon. "Gags, you could have been killed—or worse, fired. That's really fucked up."

Gagne was always pushing the boundaries and pushing his luck. It irritated his partners. But it was what made him such a standout member of DEA New York's Group D-35.

DEA agents are typically assigned to groups based on their knowledge of a specific drug, their language capabilities, or their interest in a particular trafficking organization. Division 35 emerged in the early 1990s out of a thirty-four-agent-strong group known as D-31, which focused on money-laundering cases. The agents of D-31 slowly self-segregated into "inside" and "outside" teams. Inside agents wrote subpoenas and studied bank records and intelligence—the kind of work that gave them nine-to-five security and a clean shot at getting home in time to be with their families. The outside agents were a small corps of meat eaters—men who wanted to be on the streets, doing surveillance, putting their hands on people. They weren't afraid to get dirty, stay out late, work weekends.

When the front office decided D-31 was too large, they pulled a half-dozen meat eaters out of D-31 and formed Group D-35—an elite team of aggressive case makers. Special agents Matthew Germanowski and Jay Flaherty were Gagne's closest colleagues in D-35.

Jay Flaherty, twenty-eight, had wispy dark hair, gentle eyes, and an accounting background. He began his law enforcement career in 1988 as a special agent with the IRS Criminal Investigation Division. A year later the IRS rookie was assigned to work money-laundering cases with DEA agents. Flaherty liked the camaraderie and the fieldwork at DEA. He switched gears, entered DEA Academy at Quantico, and soon was chasing drug dealers alongside Gagne and Germanowski.

Matt Germanowski was twenty-six, tall, and barrel-chested, with biceps like bocce balls. He had an easy charm and a warm voice; he was the kind of guy who likes his beer from the bottle but always offers others a glass. Gagne called him "G."

Germanowski grew up in Pittsburgh, the son of Polish steel mill workers. A college baseball scholarship was his ticket out of a dreary life in the mills, and he even had a couple of tryouts with the Cincinnati Reds. But when a shoulder injury sidelined his sports-star dreams, he took an internship with the Pittsburgh police department and played on the police softball team for kicks. The drug agents on an opposing team convinced Germanowski to fill out an application for DEA, but he didn't give it much thought—he was determined to become a Pennsylvania state trooper. In early 1992, about a week before Germanowski was to report to duty as a state trooper, DEA called—his application was approved. He was torn, so he turned to his trooper friends for advice. *For the next five years you'll work the highways,* they told him. *You'll give moving-violation tickets, and with any luck, you'll work your way into a criminal investigator position.*

Germanowski knew that with DEA, he'd start as a federal investigator right out of the gate, with opportunities to travel to country offices around the world. In most federal law enforcement agencies, such as CIA or FBI, the positions are task-specific. But in DEA, agents are expected to take part in every aspect of a case: surveillance, undercover, intelligence, wiretaps, tactical operations, chemical analysis, trial testimony. Germanowski chose DEA.

Gagne was a handsome twenty-nine-year-old with hazel eyes, dark curly hair, and a faint scar that curled up the left side of his lip like a trigger—a painful reminder of his father. Like his partners, Gagne had gravitated toward law enforcement growing up, but he scoffed at the small-town cop beat. He wanted out of Pawtucket. He joined the Army National Guard at nineteen, and by twenty-two he was commissioned a second lieutenant, Military Intelligence, specializing in cryptologic tactical operations—conducting electronic warfare, intercepting transmissions, decoding conversations.

When Gagne wasn't training he was studying. He attended Southeastern Massachusetts University, dropped out because he felt the program was too liberal, and considered becoming a fireman. He took one EMT class at Rhode Island Community College and stayed on to earn his associate's degree in business administration with a concentration in law enforcement. At twenty-three, he enrolled at Northeastern University and majored in criminal justice.

When he wasn't training or studying, Gagne was working—sometimes holding two or three jobs at once. He taught martial arts, waited tables, caddied at a country club, and drove an ambulance. One spring, he invested in a meat truck with a friend and sold cheesesteaks on Friday and Saturday nights to the tipplers who stumbled out of Providence nightclubs. He would study in the ambulance when it was slow, hop the train to Boston to school, study more on the train, come home in time for dinner, and then work the meat truck until 3:00 a.m.

But selling meat like his dad was just a sideline. What Gagne dreamed of most was jumping out of planes, flying helicopters, and chasing the sound of bullets. He considered a path toward Special Forces, but that would mean more living in the woods, role-playing against a Cold War enemy, and another twenty years of hanging out with soldiers. His father hated the military, and as much as it would have pleased Gagne to pick a path that disappointed René, he didn't see himself as a soldier either, another cog in the wheel. He wanted to set himself apart.

Gagne earned his bachelor's degree from Northeastern just a few months shy of his twenty-fifth birthday and went straight into DEA Academy. He was assigned to DEA's New York Field Division upon graduation. Two years later he volunteered for a tour of duty in Honduras. By the following year, at twenty-eight, Gagne was on the front lines of the cocaine wars.

3 JULY 1994: PERU

OPERATION SNOWCAP, developed in 1987 by DEA and the State Department's Bureau of International Narcotics Matters, was based on the first Bush administration's "Andean Strategy," a plan that provided Andean governments with counterdrug assistance by increasing military, law enforcement, and economic aid. Snowcap operations were established in twelve countries, with a heavy focus on Bolivia, Peru, and Ecuador, where coca processing prevailed.

While DEA's main goal in Snowcap was to dismantle and disrupt cocaine trafficking operations, because drugs and terrorism are so intricately linked, the United States' counterdrug assistance often extended into counterinsurgency assistance. Peru, for instance, was reeling from the terrorist bloodlust of the notorious Maoist rebel group Sendero Luminoso, or Shining Path, known for hacking victims limb from limb with machetes. Shining Path's main rival was the Cuban-inspired Tupac Amaru Revolutionary Movement. Both insurgency groups sought to topple the Peruvian government and install Communist regimes. To fund their terrorist aims, they taxed cocaine traffickers and also provided security in exchange for weapons and money.

Snowcap was a coveted foreign operation, considered one of the most dangerous and demanding of DEA assignments. Street agents who successfully completed Spanish-language classes, intensive U.S. Army Ranger school, and Navy SEAL riverine training were dressed in camo and combat gear and dropped into the dusty villages and steamy jungles of Latin America.

Gagne's three-month tour of duty with Snowcap began in Peru. He was the youngest man on Mongoose, a team of three women and nine men. Mongoose was set up like a regular Special Forces A-team, which meant they had recruits from outside DEA—a communications officer who was former Special Forces, a medic, a heavy-weapons specialist, a demolition expert. The agents were also cross-trained on every specialty.

Snowcap had fifteen forward operating bases and a guarded safe house in Lima where the agents would take R&R breaks. Gagne and his Mongoose team were stationed at the Santa Lucia base in the Upper Huallaga Valley, where the Andes Mountains slope down to the Amazon River basin. It was a region almost entirely controlled by drug traffickers and insurgent terrorist groups.

Gagne's Snowcap duties were unpredictable. One day he'd have to fix the generator so they could take hot showers; the next he and his team would be raiding stash houses and blowing holes in the illegal landing strips that dotted the remote mountaintops and lower flatlands. Small twin-engine Piper Navajos and Beechcraft Barons were regularly flying into Peru from Colombia, landing at unregistered airstrips, refueling, and loading dope. Gagne and his colleagues would spot the airstrips during routine flyover missions. They'd touch down and blow giant craters, twenty feet wide by fifteen feet deep, into the strips. The agents would fly from one strip to the next, blasting holes until the airstrips looked like pockmarked battlegrounds. The smugglers would refill the holes days later. It was a constant cycle.

The most dangerous aspect of Snowcap was trying to determine who the bad guys were. Agents minimized the amount of information they gave to local cops. Aid them, work with them, but trust no one. Corruption among the Peruvian forces was so widespread that the police officers assigned to work with their American counterparts had to take monthly polygraphs to ensure they weren't playing both sides of the drug war.

Gagne was particularly fond of one officer named Luis Antonio Chilque Regalado, or "Lucho." Gagne bunked with Lucho for two weeks when he first arrived in Peru. Lucho liked to talk about his young wife and children in Lima. He seemed a little green and wide-eyed, but he was loyal and hardworking, and he never complained about their camp-style living. They slept in bunks and cooked meals on a small outdoor burner hooked up to a propane tank. Lucho's favorite meal was white bread slathered in butter and topped with pickles, washed down with thick espresso. He called it his version of pizza. It made Gagne nauseous. One day Gagne walked to town to buy groceries to show Lucho what a real Italian meal could be. He boiled pasta on the tiny burner and crushed tomatoes with his bare hands, throwing them in a pot with some olive oil, onions, and ground beef rolled in bread crumbs.

"*Es bueno.*" Lucho inhaled the spaghetti and meatballs. It would be his last home-cooked meal.

On July 27, 1994, DEA was tipped off by a CIA informant about the location of the base operations of the Cachique Rivera brothers, a notorious band of cocaine traffickers who had filled the vacuum left by Pablo Escobar's death the previous December. The brothers were sending roughly 1,000 kilos of pure cocaine hydrochloride and 20,000 kilos of its precursor, cocaine paste, every month to the Cali cartel in Colombia. Intel reports indicated that $2 million and 2,000 kilos of cocaine were sitting at the Cachique Rivera ranch in the jungles of Oxapampa. Their mission was to seize the cash, destroy the coke, and capture the Cachique Rivera brothers. They would be joined by a CIA agent, a Special Forces officer, a *fiscal* (judge), and a small team of Peruvian street cops, including Lucho. They would head out by daybreak.

Mongoose team supervisor Frank Fernandez Jr., thirty-eight, was apprehensive about the operation. They had only a crude hand-drawn map from the informant to guide them, and the place would be heavily guarded. Lucho seemed fidgety too. He hardly understood a word of English. But he had heard the name Abelardo Cachique Rivera, aka "the Lieutenant."

"El Teniente es muy peligroso"—dangerous, Lucho told Gagne later that night. He sheepishly revealed that he had never worked a jungle operation before. Gagne tried to calm the street cop's nerves. Lucho had only a small .38 pistol as a sidearm, so Gagne gave him his M4 assault rifle, a Special Forces version of the M16, but shorter and lighter.

"Do you know how to use it?"

"Sí, sí."

"This is auto, this is semi . . ."

"No, no, I understand," Lucho said confidently.

Gagne found one of his black-and-orange police vests—the kind DEA agents wore—and presented it to his friend. Lucho beamed with pride when he put it on. Gagne wanted Lucho to know that he depended on him.

At 5:00 a.m., the team scrambled into four Huey UH-1 helicopters and headed to the district of San Pedro de Longui. They flew for an hour over rivers and lush ground—the thunderous chopper blades announcing their approach—until they discovered a sprawling ranch house built into a carved-out mountain. A second home was under construction next to it. The Hueys set down on a small plateau and the agents quickly spread out, searching the two houses. Nothing. The place was deserted. The first thing Gagne noticed was the steam.

The main house's covered porch was encircled by a six-inch-wide railing, and all along the railing were small bowls, at least twenty of them, filled with steaming, half-eaten chicken soup. There was a large black cooking pot nearby, with a fire still smoldering.

"Frank," Gagne whispered to his team leader, "look at all those bowls." They triggered his memories of military drills in the mountains. "This is the army. It's soldiers."

"All right," Fernandez said gravely. He instructed the team to start looking for *caletas,* hiding places. Gagne signaled to Lucho.

"Listen, let's split up—I'm going this way." He pointed toward a small sentry post off in a cleared field. "You go that way, and we'll meet in the middle."

"Sí, sí. En medio," Lucho said.

It was one hundred degrees and humid. Gagne felt as if a thousand eyes were on him as he stalked the perimeter. As he reached the sentry shack he heard the sound of AK-47 fire—heavy and hollow, like a steel bar banging on a fifty-five-gallon drum. Enemy fire. He should have been hearing his teammates' M4s, like steel on a tin can. Gagne hit the ground in the middle of the open field, then began to run low, back toward his team. He heard screams and more gunfire. He found Special Forces agent Carlos Cruz and they both ran up a hill, toward the sound of the bullets. It was a sixty-degree grade, steep and slippery, and they had to huff it up on all fours. At the top of the embankment, Gagne nearly stumbled on Lucho's body, slumped over in a muddy pool of blood. They dragged him down the hill while Fernandez screamed for them on the radio. Gagne never heard him; his radio was accidentally switched off. When Fernandez finally caught sight of the agents, he motioned them to a ten-foot safe spot between the two houses.

"Where is everybody?" Gagne yelled.

Fernandez pointed down. Homes in the jungle were often raised about eighteen inches on stilts to prevent flood damage. When Gagne peered under the house, the first thing he saw was the *fiscal*'s .38 pointed at the sky.

"Get that thing out of my face!" Gagne screamed at the judge.

The judge and the Peruvian street cops refused to come out of hiding. Gagne was still holding Lucho. He was bleeding profusely from three bullets, one to the head. His body felt like a loose rag doll. There was no point in administering CPR. Gagne turned to Agent Cruz. They both wanted to fight, and they took off again, running back up the embankment to face whatever was on the other side. Stopping at a small perch, they started arguing about whether to lob grenades at the enemy or rake them with gunfire. Gagne noticed Cruz was only carrying a shotgun. Fernandez was shouting: "Get off the hill!" The helicopter pilots had taken off in fear. Everything was happening too fast. It was chaos.

The mission was aborted. The cocaine, the cash, and the traffickers remained untouched. Fernandez convinced the pilots to circle back to pick them up and everyone scrambled into the Hueys. As the big birds pulled up, the agents ripped the surrounding forest with M60s, grenades, and high explosives. Gagne drained his light machine gun, burning through two 100-round drums, before pulling out his Glock. The CIA agent was shooting a gun inches from Gagne's aching eardrums. Dark blood from Lucho's head pooled on the helicopter floor.

Gagne couldn't figure out why Lucho had climbed up the hill on his own. He must have heard something and wanted to chase after it, to prove his mettle.

A local newspaper reported that Shining Path assassins were claiming victory in Lucho's killing because they had believed he was a DEA agent. Gagne was haunted by thoughts of Lucho's last moments, alone on the hill, being watched by assassins who saw their prize in a DEA vest. His body was flown back to his family in Jalima, Colombia, where his wife and children laid him to rest in *el cementerio El Angel*.

It was just three weeks into a three-month tour of duty, and the team was spooked. Team leader Fernandez started having premonitions about his death. He stopped eating.

Gagne decided to put the incident out of his mind, turn it into a game. *It's not real.* Because if he let the fear consume him, he would lose his concentration, and there was no room for error in the jungle. "Adapt, improvise, and overcome" is the motto of many American soldiers, and it was a motto that Gagne lived by.

"I'm not dying in this country," Gagne boasted to Fernandez. "I'll be going home soon, Frankie. You can be with me or go do what you gotta do, but there's nothing here that I need to die for."

Fernandez liked the young agent's bravado. He told him, "You're my good-luck charm."

A month later, Gagne was on R&R in Lima when he was knocked out by food poisoning—bad ceviche. He suffered sweats, chills, a 103-degree fever, and dysentery. By Friday he had recovered and was well enough to take part in a flight with his team on Saturday, but then he got an invitation to a birthday party in Lima from a pretty girl. Fernandez agreed to let him extend his R&R just one more day. They spoke Saturday morning, August 27, for the last time.

"Are you eating?" Gagne asked.

"Yeah, I'm eating," Fernandez said.

"You're so full of it. If I'm here in Lima and you're there at the base, I know you're not eating."

Fernandez laughed and told Gagne he didn't like going out that day without his good-luck charm at his side. It was a routine flyover mission in the Upper Huallaga Valley, looking for clandestine airstrips to blow up. Agents Juan "Carlos" Vars, thirty-two, and Frank Wallace Jr., thirty-seven, were in the pilot seats of the Casa twin-engine plane. Agent Meredith Thompson, thirty-three, sat between them in the jump seat. Team leader Fernandez and Agent Jay Seale, thirty-one, rounded out the group.

The morning canyon fog cleared as the afternoon winds picked up and whipped through the steep mountainsides. Air traffic control lost contact with the agents shortly after 1:00 p.m.

Gagne was trashed on Peruvian moonshine and dancing with pretty Peruvian girls when he got the call that his teammates were missing. He sobered instantly and rushed back to Santa Lucia to join the search. The Peruvian Air Force later spotted the crash site from the air, but heavy rains slowed the recovery efforts, and it took two days to reach the wreckage under the layered canopy jungle. The dead agents were still buckled into their seats.

Gagne was in a shaky Russian-made helicopter, four feet above the ground on a cushion of thin air and hovering on maximum power. He felt like the bird was on the edge of falling out of the sky. He lifted five black zippered body bags into the helicopter. The smell of gas mingled with the overpowering stench of decomposing flesh. His hands shook as he unzipped one bag and saw the face of his team leader, Frankie Fernandez. The heavy chopper blades vibrated his bones and were so deafening that even if he had screamed it would have sounded like a whisper.

Operation Snowcap saw two more teams of agents, the last two tours of duty, before it was officially terminated. The program had been on the chopping block since Bill Clinton took over the White House, but the plane crash was the nail in the coffin. More DEA agents died in that crash than in any other incident up to that point in the agency's history. An investigation would later determine that the plane had been flying too low and too slow. The hot summer air in the jungle, with its low density, didn't give the propeller blades enough to bite into. It was simple pilot error. The black box revealed that the agents knew they were going down.

Gagne lost six friends to a senseless mission. For a time, he wanted to quit DEA. He went back home to Pawtucket, Rhode Island, to try to clear his mind. But after a couple of weeks he missed the work, the streets, the rush of his job. He decided he would return to New York. But he never wanted to do another cocaine investigation again if he could help it. It was too painful. DEA was obsessed with cocaine interdiction in the mid-1990s, but Gagne made a vow to himself that he would seek out a new battle in the drug war. He would follow his instincts and carve out a different path.

4 THE NEW YORK FIELD DIVISION

IN 1973, President Richard Nixon declared "an all-out global war on the drug menace," pushing legislation in Congress that gave birth to the Drug Enforcement Administration. This "superagency" would put a single administrator—appointed by the president and approved by Congress—in charge of federal drug law enforcement, maximizing the coordination between investigators and prosecutors.

The phrase "war on drugs" has lost favor with top brass because it denotes a battle that has a beginning and an end—and that can be won or lost. Experienced drug cops know that the war is ongoing and involves more than just locking up dealers. It also involves treatment, education, and an evolving dialogue with youth about the dangers of drug use—issues that are the primary concern of a number of different agencies that have come into being since 1973.

DEA, however, is the nation's only single-mission agency, and that mission is to enforce the federal drug laws. To this end, DEA works with the United Nations, Interpol, and other international organizations on matters of worldwide drug control. Its agents are stationed in eighty-seven foreign offices in sixty-three countries. In the States, DEA has 227 offices that are overseen by twenty-one field divisions nationwide. After headquarters, in Arlington, Virginia, the New York Field Division, or NYFD, is the largest DEA office in the world: In 1995—when Gagne returned to New York from Snowcap—the total cash and assets DEA seized in drug busts across all fifty states was about $244 million. Seizures in the New York Field Division alone accounted for $29 million (or 12 percent) of the nationwide total.

Any challenge faced by an agent in small-town America has already been dealt with by the agents of New York. The technology advances, legal strategies, and group problem-solving skills put in practice by the New York Field Division are copied by other divisions. NYFD evolved into DEA's most innovative division because New York has a long history as a drug trafficking epicenter, owing to its busy seaports and airports, diverse populations, and thriving cultural and financial centers. Just as legal products are brought into New York from around the globe, so it goes with illicit commodities. New York City is often the first stop from the source countries. Heroin, cocaine, marijuana, Ecstasy—and a wide range of illicit drugs—is imported to New York, stored and sold in New York, and then smuggled from New York to D.C., Boston, Atlanta, Detroit, and destinations beyond. A long list of organized crime networks—be they Dominican, Colombian, Jamaican, Pakistani, Afghani, Italian, Chinese—live among the densely populated neighborhoods of New York's five boroughs without ever appearing out of place.

"There's no better city, from a drug enforcement standpoint, than New York, because it has it all. If you want to work cocaine cases, they're here. Heroin cases, they're here. Traditional organized crime? It's here. Money laundering? You got it. It's all here," says DEA New York Special Agent in Charge John Gilbride. "You don't have that in other cities. In Miami, you'll have tremendous cocaine cases, but you won't have the heroin cases that you have in New York. Chicago: you'll have some cocaine and heroin, but it will be Mexican heroin. In New York, you have Southwest Asian heroin at times, Southeast Asian heroin other times, right now it's South American heroin—and it fluctuates."

Gilbride began his career in 1981 as a co-op intern at NYFD, graduated first in his Basic Agent class, and rose up the ranks, earning top awards and a DEA Purple Heart for getting shot in the head yet continuing to chase down a cocaine trafficker on the streets of Brooklyn in 1988. Now, as special agent in charge of NYFD, Gilbride is the top agent in New York and calls the shots over divisional offices in Rochester, Syracuse, Plattsburgh, Buffalo, Albany, and Westchester, and on Long Island.

Agents hone their skills in New York, in part, because they are constantly negotiating the inherent frustrations of the city. Sometimes traffic was so bad it would take Gagne and his partners almost two hours just to drive to Queens to watch a target's apartment. Other times it's the vertical challenge of New York that puts agents in danger—like when a dealer who is a known weapons hoarder is on the twenty-eighth floor of a thirty-story apartment building, there are lookouts watching from every corner, and the agents have to figure out how to get in, get up, control the situation as fast as possible, and make the arrests.

DEA investigations today focus on the highest-level narcotics trafficking organizations. But it wasn't always so. Retail-level dealers were fair game in SAC Gilbride's day, back when the city provided a beggar's banquet for drug addicts. Gilbride wore his canvas PF Flyers to work because he knew that each day promised, as the saying went, "a kilo, a gun, and someone was gonna run." Agents kept folding lawn chairs in the trunks of their "G-rides" (government vehicles) because it could take twenty hours at central booking to get an arrestee processed. Sometimes they didn't go home for days and would sleep in bunk rooms or on couches at NYFD, keeping extra clothes in their cars. An agent could spend hours driving around town, making arrests, and stuffing thousands of dollars in seized cash and drugs in the trunk, because there wasn't time to get it all back to the evidence vault before the next takedown.

"It was the Wild West up in Washington Heights," says Special Agent John McKenna. He was twenty-three years old his first day on the job in 1987, thrilled to have a gun and a badge—"like a kid in a candy store."

"We used to average three hundred fifty arrests in one year in just one group, and we took guns off these guys all the time," McKenna says. "I was in three shoot-outs my first four years."

On a typical day, McKenna and his team would drive a surveillance van up to Washington Heights, seize five kilos of cocaine and arrest five Dominican dealers, put them in the van, and then drive to Queens, where another deal was about to go down. They'd lock up a few Colombian dealers, throw them in the van too, and then go to the Bronx for another hit.

"We'd come back at night with like twenty people under arrest, three different cases. This was every single night," McKenna says. "We were hitting them so hard in Washington Heights they knew our group number— 'Oh, those thirty-three guys,' all the informants would say, 'They're scaring the dealers up there.' "

By the time Gagne and Germanowski were on the scene, DEA operations had evolved to higher-level targets—suppliers and cartel heads. Today, a twelve-agent group in NYFD averages between fifty and seventy arrests a year. The Wild West atmosphere slowly gave way to more complicated drug conspiracy cases. DEA's 1992 "Kingpin Strategy" refocused agency resources on targeting kingpins and their organizations. Evolution also brought about stricter policies on conduct, evidence handling, and case operations. For instance, the two-man rule requires that all evidence be immediately transported to evidence custodians by no less than two agents—no more running around town all day in a paddy wagon and then stopping off for a quick beer, letting the perps, cash, and coke cool in the van.

NYFD, like all DEA field divisions, is organized pyramid style. Below the SAC are several associate special agents in charge who oversee administrative operations, the divisional offices, the Diversion Unit (which polices doctors and pharmacists), the Unified Intelligence Division (a mixture of DEA, NYPD, and New York State Police, who gather intel to support investigations), and the New York Drug Enforcement Task Force—the oldest and largest drug task force in the nation, best known for its work on heroin cases, as dramatized in the film *The French Connection.*

Below the associate SACs are ten assistant special agents in charge, or ASACs. Each ASAC oversees a division and each division is made up of five enforcement groups, which are run by a group supervisor, or GS.

GS Lou Cardinali was responsible for special agents Gagne, Germanowski, Flaherty, and their teammates in group D-35—the so-called gun carriers at the bottom of the pyramid. Gagne and his undercover partners didn't write drug policy or speak at press conferences. They wore jeans and T-shirts to the office. And their office was a multipurpose tan brick building at 99 Tenth Avenue in a filthy corner of Manhattan.

Whenever Gagne pulled up to the office in the midnineties, he was met by the usual parade of hustlers, prostitutes, and drug dealers who lined the streets. The block was so crime-ridden, burglars would break into every unattended vehicle and DEA secretaries had to be escorted to their cars at night so they wouldn't be mugged or worse.

Gagne couldn't park without a hooker—usually of the

transsexual variety—jumping in the passenger side of his car and offering a blow job. "Out," he'd say with the casualness of one who has tired of the daily routine. The area was a petri dish of cheap sex, drugs, and carnage. In fact, the DEA building previously had held a meat-packing outfit. The abandoned elevated train tracks that once operated above Tenth Avenue still divert at 16th Street and tag the building's façade. Animals were brought in by boxcar, hoisted up by pulleys, and slaughtered on the top floors of the building. The floors were slightly sloped, with the highest point at the center, and the walls were free-floating so that blood and viscera could be hosed down from the top floors and wash down along the walls, floor to floor, until it reached the bottom.

DEA took over the lease in 1991 and turned the butcher block into NYFD command central. The floating walls have been shored up and the slaughterhouse remnants are long gone, but there are small reminders of its past: if a chemist in the lab accidentally spills liquid on the ground, it will slowly roll toward the walls.

Just as agents have to keep a low profile on the job, the NYFD building is an edifice of undercover style. The structure has no identifying signs or official seals. The twin front entrances—Tenth Avenue for visitors and 17th Street for employees—are sheltered by plain red awnings marked "99." The windows and glass entrance doors are shatterproof and dark-tinted to protect the identities of the undercover agents and confidential informants inside. There are some forty closed-circuit television cameras in and around the building monitored 24/7 by base operations and the guards inside the lobby and at the loading docks. X-ray machines monitor every package that comes through. Armed guards control access to the parking garage.

NYFD operations today are aided by high-tech

resources, such as audio recording devices the size and shape of shirt buttons. Surveillance teams can slap a GPS device under a target's vehicle in less than five minutes, so an agent can monitor his moves by computer, cell phone, and public surveillance cameras. But when Gagne and his teammates were chasing after drug traffickers in 1995, it was a low-tech era. There was no GPS. The agents shared a green-screen, blinking-cursor-style computer. Report of Investigation forms, or DEA-6s, were done in carbon triplicate on electric typewriters.

When the agents weren't on the street, they worked at cubicles on the eighth floor. Gagne's cubicle was decorated with photos of missions with his teammates in Peru and the latest shots of him with his D-35 teammates during their annual Columbus Day weekend golf trips.

Germanowski's cubicle was tidy. He taped his calendar to his desk so it wouldn't slide askew every time someone walked by and nudged it. Tacked to his corkboard was a photo of a half-naked Jennifer Aniston (until Group Supervisor Lou Cardinali made him take it down) and a Pittsburgh Steelers license plate. He kept a photo of his two-year-old son front and center. Germanowski had five rules he tried to live by and would pass on to his children: "Don't lie, cheat, steal, or quit, and be nice when you have a chance, because you never know when it will be the last one."

Germanowski was married, but not happily. Gagne could hear the coldness in his partner's voice whenever he called his wife to say he was working late. In marriages that endure, spouses of DEA agents tend to be patient about the long hours, the unexpected calls to duty, the last-minute cancellation of vacation plans, and finding themselves suddenly dateless for graduations, weddings, and recitals.

In the summer of 1995, Gagne was still single at

twenty-nine and living in a tiny apartment next door to the cacophonous Lincoln Tunnel. He paid $300 a month for a small one-bedroom, with a washer and dryer, all utilities included. But he was hardly ever there. NYFD was home, and Germanowski and Flaherty were family. Sometimes in the evenings, after the office emptied out, the agents would set up a golf course around the cubicles for miniature golf tournaments. In the mornings, they'd meet for target practice in the small seventh-floor shooting range or they'd lift weights in the fifth-floor gym.

The one place at NYFD where Gagne steered clear—perhaps the pain of Snowcap was still too fresh—was the Hall of Honor. At the entrance to the fluorescent-lit hallway is a dedication "to those brave men and women who made the ultimate sacrifice, lest we forget." A blue carpet, blue velvet ropes, and plastic flowers line a corridor filled with seventy-five portraits—seventy-five deaths—that date as far back as 1921, when Prohibition agents Charles Wood and Stafford Beckett were killed by whiskey smugglers near the El Paso/Mexico border, and as recently as 2004, when Milwaukee Task Force officer Jay Balchunas was gunned down by assailants as he walked to his car. Six New York agents are among the dead.

The most famous face in the gallery is number thirty-eight, Special Agent Enrique "Kiki" Camarena. Camarena was born in a poor Mexican barrio and moved to the United States as a boy to pick plums to earn money. Kiki became a naturalized citizen, a Marine Corps officer, a fireman, and a policeman before he devoted his life to DEA, fighting the flow of drugs from his native country into his adopted country. Camarena worked undercover in Guadalajara, Mexico, investigating a multibillion-dollar drug trafficking network that implicated officers of the Mexican army, police, and government. The thirty-seven-year-old father of three was on his way to meet his wife for lunch on February 7, 1985, when masked gunmen kidnapped him in broad daylight. Camarena was bludgeoned and subjected to sadistic cruelty over the next twenty-four hours. A physician injected him with stimulants to keep him conscious through the torture. On March 5, his body was found in a shallow grave on a ranch about seventy miles from Guadalajara. His eyes were taped shut, his hands and feet were bound, and his body was wrapped in plastic. His jaw, nose, and cheekbones were broken; his windpipe and skull were crushed.

Mexican authorities destroyed his clothing and other evidence. The U.S. government, through its own sources, obtained videotapes of the torture session—tapes that Mexican officials denied existed. Camarena could be heard pleading with his abductors, "Don't hurt my family."

In 1990, the DEA hired Mexican bounty hunters to kidnap the alleged physician-torturer and extradite him to the States for prosecution. His trial ended in an acquittal. Mexico eventually convicted more than two dozen people, including police and drug kingpins Ernesto Fonseca Carrillo and Rafael Caro Quintana. Six men were convicted in the United States, but some conspirators were never brought to justice.

Gagne was a year out of high school when Camarena was murdered. DEA wasn't even on his radar yet, but he knew about the murdered agent. It marked a turning point in the war on drugs and enlightened the nation on the brutality of drug traffickers. TV movies and documentaries dramatized Camarena's hopeful life and brutal death. National Red Ribbon Week in October was instituted in his honor, to educate schoolchildren about the dangers of drugs. An elementary school in La Joya, Texas, bears his name.

Camarena was the first DEA agent to be tortured and killed as a symbolic gesture to America that the "bad guys" weren't putting up with interference in their business. But instead of turning the agents into shrinking violets, it seemed to embolden them.

"Bottom line, we will never surrender to the drug traffickers," New York SAC John Gilbride says. "You will not scare us off. You're gonna hurt us, you may kill some of us, but we're not going away. We'll just come back stronger and harder. We'll keep going. That's why agents raise their hands to go to the jungles of South America. It's a lot more dangerous than any city in the United States, but they'll do it because they want to be as close to that source of supply and those major drug traffickers as possible—to have an impact."

On the wall in the Hall of Honor opposite Camarena's photo is a separate memorial for the five agents who perished in the plane crash in Peru during Operation Snowcap. No matter what time of year it is, invariably a prayer card left by a family member can be found tucked under the portrait of Special Agent Frank Fernandez Jr., the Snowcap leader who died without his lucky charm at his side.

5 THE ECSTASY DEALERS

IT WAS A HOT August summer night in 1995 when two men named Israel Hazut and Michel Elbaz hailed a livery cab after an evening of club hopping in Manhattan. As the chatty Lebanese driver slowly steered them home toward Queens, he asked the men where they were from and what they did for a living. The tall lanky one said that he and his brother had recently moved to New York from Israel and they were making a fortune selling Ecstasy in the nightclubs. The driver nodded his head coolly, as if he knew what Ecstasy was.

The dealer handed the driver a fat white tablet that was scored on one side.

"Try it—on the house," he said. If he liked it, they were $20 apiece.

"Anything you need," he said, "we can get it for you."

The driver thanked them for the free sample, took down their beeper number, and dropped the men off at their apartment in Queens. Then he dialed Bob Gagne.

The next morning, Gagne and Jay Flaherty met with the livery driver, a confidential informant named "Charlie," to pick up the drug sample. Gagne placed the pill in a clear plastic evidence bag and delivered it to the New York Field Division's on-site Northeast Regional Laboratory, where it was marked exhibit number one, expedited analysis requested.

Gagne didn't know much about Ecstasy. He had heard vague references to its use at all-night rave parties, but no one at NYFD had ever opened a major case on it.

DEA's resources were focused on the action: heroin and cocaine. But when everyone else turned right, Gagne was the type to turn left. He dug into the archives and came across an article about a New Jersey teen who'd died from taking one Ecstasy pill; that was enough to get him worked up. Gagne wondered if Ecstasy was that new path he was looking for—something that seemed solvable. It intrigued him. But he would still have to convince his partner.

"Dude, this is the next big thing," Gagne said with the confidence of a sledgehammer. "We'll go out, we'll make a buy, we'll make another buy—order up and knock 'em up."

"Wait a second," Germanowski said. "Cocaine's falling out of the sky right now, and you want to go after Ecstasy pills?"

"It'll be fun," Gagne said. "No wires, no heavy-duty surveillance—real simple."

Germanowski knew it was futile to argue.

"Listen, Gags, this is sort of bullshit, but it might be something different. Let's try it."

"Hey," Gagne offered, "you can do the undercover."

"Yeah, I'll do the undercover."

But when the sample pill Charlie had procured came back from the DEA lab analysis as NCSD, or "no controlled substance detected," the agents had nothing more than a couple of cough syrup peddlers in their sights. The pill was 23.6 grams of pure dextromethorphan hydrobromide—the active ingredient in Robitussin DM.

"Charlie, I want you to call them back," Gagne ordered his informant over the phone. "Tell them you're not falling for the banana in the tailpipe trick."

6 CONFIDENTIAL INFORMANTS

AN EASTERN EUROPEAN DRUG trafficker named "Joel" once told Gagne that the only difference between them was the law. Joel took care of his family and plied his trade with passion. But eventually he got caught, and like the guy who baited him, he saved himself by switching teams.

"He who makes the laws ·wins," Joel said of his predicament. Joel became a confidential informant and provided Gagne with valuable information that led to the arrests of several notorious Romanian drug traffickers.

Confidential informants like Joel and Charlie are the necessary interlopers who walk the line between both worlds. At some point in the late 1990s, DEA started calling informants confidential sources. It was semantics, really. Appeasement of the criminal mind. No snitch wants to be called an informant—but somehow "source" went down easier. Either way, they perform the same role and veteran agents tend to use the old nomenclature.

Confidential informants can be divided among three main types. There's the *regular informant,* the kind who wants to keep the law apprised of the crime going down in his or her neighborhood. Everybody is happy with a regular informant, a do-gooder. They hold up nicely on the witness stand. Then there's the *defendant informant.* This is the guy (sometimes the girl) who's looking at serious charges—the dealer who decides to help the agents reel in a bigger fish in the hopes of receiving a lighter sentence. The *restricted use informant* is typically someone who is on probation or parole or has a history of violent crime. It takes a criminal to catch a criminal, and a convicted murderer can be a valuable informant—but use him sparingly and keep him away from the witness stand if at all possible.

A fourth breed, more interesting and rare, is the *protected use* or *protected name informant*. Most agents will never encounter them. They tend to be foreign government officials or figures in overseas criminal organizations. For instance, a money launderer for a Colombian cocaine cartel who is in over his head might provide info to derail the cartel, but if it ever came to light that he spoke to DEA, he and his entire family would be slaughtered by the cartel. Protected use informants are never called to testify. New York has had at least one such informant and that person's file was kept in its own separate safe.

DEA agents have to develop and verify every piece of information they receive to make sure it can stand up in a court of law. And every piece of negative information about an informant must also be reported. The case law—*Brady vs. Maryland* (1963) and *Giglio vs. U.S.* (1972)—that Gagne and other agents learn in Basic Agent class says that if you use the CI at trial, the defense must be made aware of any prior convictions, drug or alcohol abuse, failure to pay taxes, or general double-dealing that puts an informant's credibility in question. Same for any benefits the informant receives for his cooperation, including plea agreements, charge bargains, immunity, assistance with immigration, free meals, phone calls, or cash payments for information.

Depending on their active involvement, informants might collect payments from $250 to $2,000. If they provide information that leads to a major cash seizure, case agents can request that the informant receive anywhere from 2 to 25 percent of the money. DEA is under the purview of the Department of Justice, which oversees the Asset Forfeiture Fund, and is the ultimate decider as to how much an informant receives. While it is extremely rare, there are million-dollar informants. A San Diego CI who helped DEA track down some of the men responsible for the murder of Special Agent Camarena was a million-dollar informant.

Protecting the source's identity is imperative. At NYFD, the Confidential Source System database is kept in a separately alarmed, combination-protected office. The 250-square-foot room is stacked wall to wall with fireproof steel-gray safes that contain the names, photos, and personal stats of every informant who works for NYFD. Only the confidential source coordinators have the combination to the room, and on any given day they maintain the files of roughly four hundred active informants. (Incidentally, some of the best informants are real estate agents—because who else would be the first to know about a home buyer who wants to build a chemistry lab in the garage or a renter who uses his apartment as a stash house?)

Charlie was a defendant informant who was arrested for trying to buy five kilos of heroin and flipped to save himself. Gagne thought Charlie was a good guy as far as confidential informants go. He had reliable information and he enjoyed the opportunity to work with the agents. As much as Gagne and Germanowski needed their informants, they could never really trust them. The CI-agent relationship is a psychological land mine. An agent starts spending time with the CI, driving him to deals, meeting for lunch, and after a while he starts to like his informant. The CI is helping to make his case. It's human nature. Even harder if the agent is single and lonely and the CI is an attractive woman.

A couple of hard-and-fast rules. Rule number one: Agents are forbidden from socializing with informants. Personal relations with confidential informants are grounds for termination. To ensure no lines are crossed, a DEA inspection team makes surprise visits and the informants are rounded up for questioning: *Have you accepted or given gifts to your handling agent? It says here you received $250 on March 3; did you actually receive that payment? Have you been seeing the agent socially?*

Rule number two: Use an informant, but do not be used by him. The CI coordinator, like a mother hen, is watchful of the agents' relationships with their informants, always reminding them of potential pitfalls: *Expect that the CI has ulterior motives and that those motives will change frequently. Never discuss your family. Don't leave magazines in your car that have your address on them. Expect that your informant is recording your conversations.*

Gagne and Germanowski worked their informants for all they were worth, an art form that takes patience and a well-tuned bullshit radar. Even experienced agents can get burned, because informants are professional liars.

Charlie, however, was a buff—the kind of informant who longed to please the agents. Gagne thought he bore a striking resemblance to Al Pacino. He worked out religiously and wore tank tops in the summer that revealed asymmetric pectoral muscles. Charlie was always trying to write himself into the operations. He'd present Gagne and Germanowski with a phone number and a lead on a dealer, then he'd propose a fantastic *Mission: Impossible*-style scenario, with Charlie in the Tom Cruise role, jetting off to Monaco, deep undercover, to aid DEA in foiling the bad guys. They humored Charlie's ambitiousness but kept him on a short leash.

7 "JIMMY" MEETS "GHEL"

ON AUGUST 24, Charlie pulled up to the corner of 97th Street and Queens Boulevard in Rego Park, Queens, at 4:40 p.m. and dialed Israel Hazut from a pay phone. Bob Gagne and a half dozen backups were watching the buy operation from unmarked cars parked on Queens Boulevard. Matt Germanowski waited in the backseat of Charlie's car. He wore a KEL recorder around his waist, a bulky device that sometimes overheated and burned the bellies of sweaty, nervous informants.

Hazut arrived by foot in a white T-shirt, red-and-blue checkered shorts, and sandals. He was twenty-eight, six foot one, 165 pounds, and clean-shaven, with close-cropped black hair. Hazut was born in Tel Aviv, just sixteen days after the final battle of the Six-Day War. He was lanky and fierce and had an eagle tattoo on his right shoulder.

"Who's the guy in the car?" Hazut asked. Charlie, the ambitious buff, led Hazut back to the car to meet his "friend."

Germanowski introduced himself as "Jimmy," a club owner from Pittsburgh. Hazut introduced himself as "Ghel," a dealer of superb-quality X pills.

Agents rely on their ability to read people, and Germanowski read Ghel as a car salesman, chasing down the highest bidder, eager to get to the top. It should have been harder for Germanowski to get the introduction. The seasoned dealer plays it slow and coy: he's not interested in meeting the new guy and he doesn't talk money or drugs on the first meet. But Ghel let Charlie pull him in, and now Ghel was on Germanowski like a drunken prom date. It gave Germanowski the opportunity to be the one to play coy, to hold back first.

"What do you need?" Ghel asked. He had weak pills for $11 or the strong stuff for $22.

"I'm looking for the strong stuff," Germanowski said.

Ghel handed him two capsules filled with white powder.

"This is the stuff you want. People love this stuff. It's the best stuff in the city. I sell it in all the nightclubs." Take one, Ghel promised, and in fifteen minutes he'd be flying for the next four hours.

"I'll give it to you for $20 each. As a favor to Charlie," Ghel said.

Germanowski paid $40 for two pills and said he'd be in touch if they were any good. Ghel said he could get fifteen thousand more with just five days' notice.

Germanowski shrugged.

"Jimmy, don't worry," Ghel said. "Nobody knows me, and I only met with you because you look and seem like a good guy."

At 5:15 p.m., the undercover team followed Ghel to his residence at 99–32 66th Road. Fifteen minutes later Gagne bagged and tagged the two pills, marked exhibit number two, and placed them in NYFD's overnight evidence vault for analysis.

Two pills for $40. That was the fruit of their first undercover buy.

The backlog of drugs to be analyzed at the lab meant the agents would wait several weeks for results. Just to be sure they weren't still chasing after cough-syrup pushers, Gagne requested a quick field test. The pills tested positive for MDMA—just how much was subject to further analysis.

Gagne was getting tired of seeing the blank stares

whenever he had to defend their new case to the other agents.

"What the hell is Ecstasy?" was a common refrain. "Guys are up on wiretaps seizing a hundred, two hundred kilos—and you guys are running around buying two pills?"

Ecstasy was a joke—"kiddie dope." Gagne decided to keep his mouth shut and focus on keeping Germanowski interested. He read everything he could about the drug's history. DEA had banned Ecstasy a decade earlier after learning about its widespread use in clubs and bars in Texas and California. But Gagne couldn't find any major case investigations on Ecstasy in DEA records. He wondered how this drug had completely fallen off DEA radar since it was banned. Even his brother Ronnie knew about Ecstasy.

"Yeah, it's getting really big out here," Ronnie told his brother that summer. Gagne knew if Ecstasy was a trend in small-town Pawtucket, then it was already flourishing in New York. He was onto something new. Something bigger. He could feel it.

8 THE GODFATHER OF ECSTASY

WHEN 3, 4-METHYLENEDIOXYMETHAMPHETAMINE, or MDMA, was outlawed by the DEA in 1985 through an emergency measure of the Controlled Substances Act, it sent shock waves through a tight-knit circle of Ecstasy advocates—psychiatrists, chemists, and mental health experts who believed MDMA was a tool with unparalleled therapeutic potential.

MDMA remains one of the most hotly debated psychotropic drugs in existence. It was a chemical reaction sprung from good intentions when it was used in couples counseling sessions in the 1970s and '80s by therapists who juggled the acronym and renamed it "Adam." But Adam escaped the therapist's couch for the streets. Renamed "Ecstasy" by opportunists, it was sold to the masses—with little regard for safety or chemistry—to disaffected youth and weekend escape artists, until the law caught up. Ecstasy became a permanent Schedule I drug by 1988. Since then, DEA has granted Schedule I licenses for two restricted studies of MDMA-assisted psychotherapy for patients suffering from post-traumatic stress disorder and for terminally ill cancer patients who have less than a year to live. Those studies are still under way, their results unknown.

German pharmaceutical giant Merck first synthesized MDMA at the turn of the century. According to researchers from the Department of Psychiatry at the University of Ulm, Germany, and the Department of Corporate History at Merck, the earliest mention of the chemical compound for MDMA was in patent 274350, filed by Merck on Christmas Eve 1912, and granted two years later. While the patent did not mention MDMA by name, it described a series of newly developed chemical formulas, including MDMA, that Merck hoped to use in the creation of blood-clotting agents. The formula, referred to as "methylsaframin" in Merck's 1912 annual report, reappeared fifteen years later when a Merck chemist conducted the first pharmacological tests with MDMA, calling it safryl-methylamin. Research was halted due to price increases, and the formula was never fully developed or tested by Merck.

MDMA resurfaced in the mid-1950s in controversial experiments funded by the U.S. Army Chemical Center and conducted at the University of Michigan. Researchers tested MDMA, mescaline, MDA, and other compounds on rats, mice, guinea pigs, dogs, and monkeys, examining toxicity levels and behavioral effects. MDMA was given the code name EA1475—the "EA" stood for the Edgewood Arsenal in Maryland, where the chemicals were synthesized. The CIA and Department of Defense admitted years later to conducting secret experiments using LSD and other psychoactive drugs on soldiers to uncover chemical weapons that could be used to incapacitate enemy soldiers. However, it doesn't appear that MDMA was ever tested on human subjects in the Edgewood Arsenal experiments or the University of Michigan studies, which were declassified in 1969.

By the late 1960s, MDMA's chemical cousin, MDA, hit the Haight-Ashbury scene as a popular love drug. When the 1970 Controlled Substances Act made MDA illegal, MDMA quickly filled the void, and a gray-haired University of California at Berkeley professor named Alexander "Sasha" Shulgin championed its experimentation.

Shulgin, nicknamed "the Godfather of Ecstasy," is a former DEA consultant and the author of *Controlled*

Substances: A Chemical and Legal Guide to Federal Drug Laws, which was a law enforcement reference desk mainstay for years. Alexander Shulgin was born in Berkeley, California, in 1925 to strict high school teacher parents. (Shulgin's father once left the boy's dead dog on the front porch to rot in the sun so little Sasha could observe the decay of flesh and bone.) Shulgin went to Harvard on a full scholarship at sixteen but dropped out to join the Navy during World War II. He worked at Dow Chemical while earning his Ph.D. in biochemistry at UC Berkeley.

Shulgin wasn't a hippie, but he was a believer in better living through chemistry. Inspired by such self-experimenters as Aldous Huxley, Shulgin took a massive 400-milligram dose of peyote in 1960. It was a religious experience, as he later wrote: "I understood that our entire universe is contained in the mind and the spirit. We may choose not to find access to it, we may even deny its existence, but it is indeed there inside us, and there are chemicals that can catalyze its availability."

Soon after, he made Dow a fortune with his invention of Zectran, one of the world's first biodegradable insecticides. In return, Dow gave its eccentric chemist free rein to pursue his own interests—which included developing psychedelic compounds and publishing his findings in *Nature* and the *Journal of Organic Chemistry.*

By 1967, the chemist and the corporation had parted ways. Shulgin worked from his home lab, making new drugs and consulting to research labs and hospitals.

While Shulgin and his counterculture contemporaries extolled the virtues of drug-induced mind expansion, many others were drowning in addiction. "Heroin Hits the Young," the cover of *Time* magazine declared on March 16, 1970—and not a moment too soon. A week before Christmas, Harlem had mourned the heroin overdose death of Walter Vandermeer. He was just one of roughly eight hundred people who died from heroin in

New York City that year—but Walter was only twelve years old, the youngest victim on record. When his eighty-pound body—with scar tissue on his arms—was found on the bathroom floor of a rooming house, he was wearing a Snoopy sweatshirt.

In 1970, Congress passed the Controlled Substances Act (CSA), which established five schedules, classifying drugs in decreasing order of danger. Heroin, LSD, and marijuana were classified as Schedule I, deemed to have a high potential for abuse and no accepted medical use. On the opposite end, Schedule V drugs—such as cough medicines with small amounts of codeine—were deemed to have accepted medical use and to exhibit a low potential for abuse. (Although federal law applies to all states, the majority of drug prosecutions occur in state courts, and some states have reclassified certain substances, such as marijuana, to create autonomy in how they handle drug offenses.)

DEA was formed three years later to enforce the Controlled Substances Act, and Alexander Shulgin initially enjoyed a good relationship with DEA. He held a Schedule I license, allowing him to synthesize and analyze illegal substances in order to offer expert testimony in criminal trials on the effects of such drugs as amphetamine and cocaine—substances he has characterized as "false" and "a complete waste of time." Shulgin's testimony was based on personal experience, as he typically tested his chemical creations on himself. He would start by ingesting an amount well below the active dose of a chemical's closest analog and then road-test the dosages upward. If he liked it, he'd give it to his wife, Ann. If Ann liked it, he'd give it to his research group of a dozen or so chairs of university departments, scientists, writers, and M.D.s. As classical music played softly in the background they would take a chemically induced trip, holding glasses of juice and notebooks to record their experiences.

In 1976, at the suggestion of a student, Shulgin synthesized and road-tested 3,4-methylenedioxymethamphetamine. He likened it to a "low-calorie martini." His research group soon nicknamed it "empathy" and "penicillin for the soul." They shared it with colleagues. Many of them would become witnesses at DEA's administrative hearings on the scheduling of MDMA, defending the drug's potential to help patients get in touch with feelings and repressed memories. MDMA induced a hand-to-God empathic effect on its early experimenters. Therapists who administered the drug to couples in counseling reported that their patients were able to drop their superfluous shields of fear and self-doubt, allowing for more open lines of communication.

According to Ecstasy historians, two early MDMA groups emerged: the proselytizers and the elitists. The proselytizers believed MDMA should be spread to the masses, as the drug held the power to make the world a better place. The elitists believed MDMA would be muddied by casual recreational use and that educated use in the context of a therapeutic setting would preserve its integrity. In the end, market forces would set the drug's course. By 1981, recreational use of MDMA had expanded from California to Texas. According to MDMA historian Bruce Eisner, a dealer in the early 1980s renamed it "Ecstasy" because he knew it would sell better than something called "empathy." "Empathy" might better describe the drug's effects, the dealer told Eisner, but how many clubgoers knew what the word meant?

From 1983 to 1985, an aggressive network of Ecstasy dealers and distributors known as the "Texas Group" devised a pyramid referral scheme that rivaled Amway. The drug was mass-produced and sold openly in bars and discos in Austin and Dallas, where it could be purchased with credit cards, and bar owners paid sales tax.

Its users were often yuppies, college students, and gay men, who would go out "X-ing" on the weekends.

A therapeutic-level dose of MDMA was about 100 milligrams, but in San Francisco, drug abuse clinics began to see teenagers stumbling in to detox after using ten to fifteen 100-milligram hits a day of the powder. Ecstasy seemed to follow a law of diminishing returns, whereby more was less, and users kept taking excessive dosages and bingeing in an attempt to return to the intensity of their first time.

How does the first time feel? Barring any adverse physiological reactions, tainted chemicals, and unexpected crises, the user may sense a gentle warmth flowing through his body as the drug begins to take effect and the mind slowly glides into a peaceful alertness, with feelings of happiness, security, and empathy. There is a heightened physical sensitivity. Simple cues—the touch of velvet, the sound of David Bowie's voice, the smell of freshly shampooed hair—flood the senses in richer depth and texture. There is often an afterglow and a desire to recall the feelings of self-esteem and forgiveness that permeated the experience.

But for some, Ecstasy is not so forgiving. MDMA was associated with only eight emergency room admissions between 1977 and 1984. It represented just .03 percent of the total number of drug mentions from 1986 to 1988. But by 1995, when Gagne and Germanowski were chasing after Ecstasy dealers, there were 421 emergency room mentions of Ecstasy, and the numbers would only rise, reaching 5,542 by 2001. Adverse reactions reported prior to the drug's outlaw status included involuntary teeth clenching, anxiety, delirium and hallucinations, partial leg paralysis, muscle tension, chills and sweats, increased susceptibility to various ailments including sore throats, colds, flu, herpes outbreaks and bladder infections, burnout and depression, and in rare cases, paranoid psychosis.

In the years since it was outlawed and its use became rampant in rave culture, further studies cited evidence of hyperthermia, seizures, stroke, kidney and cardiovascular system failure, possible permanent damage to sections of the brain critical to thought and memory, and in some extremely rare cases death after a single dose.

A study by researchers at Boston University in 2006 found that four doses over eight hours affected the blood-brain barrier in rats, leaving their brains susceptible to potential invasion by viruses and other pathogens. A study in 2003 by the Food and Drug Administration's National Center for Toxicological Research found that rats exposed to a single dose of MDMA suffered neuronal degeneration, and concerns were raised by researchers that human users who take doses high enough to produce hyperthermia may suffer from irreversible neuron loss. In 1999, researchers from Johns Hopkins and the National Institute of Mental Health reported persistent memory impairment in the brain of heavy Ecstasy users and damage to serotonin reuptake sites. Serotonin affects memory, impulse control, sleep patterns, and mood, and some Ecstasy users described a "suicide Tuesday" syndrome—a depressive period that hits several days after the initial high as a result of serotonin depletion. Long-term physical effects of MDMA point to recurring depression and anxiety in some users.

In the early 1980s, law enforcement estimated that thirty thousand doses of Ecstasy were being distributed in one Texas city each month. Sensing that a drug epidemic was under way, DEA proposed in a July 27, 1984, Federal Register notice its intentions to place MDMA into Schedule I. The administrative hearings lasted two years, with affidavits and testimony from dozens of witnesses.

DEA witnesses included a pharmacologist who took part in the secret University of Michigan studies in the 1950s. He testified that during his studies in animals, he found MDMA less toxic than MDA but up to six times more toxic than mescaline. Medical researchers testified that MDA and MDMA affected the brain in a similar manner, and since it was shown that MDA could cause brain damage, MDMA was likely to do the same.

On the opposite side were MDMA advocates, mostly therapists, who claimed that the drug had helped their patients to overcome traumatic experiences, such as rape and incest, and had helped some terminally ill patients to reconcile themselves to the idea that they were dying. They lobbied to have MDMA placed under Schedule III, where drugs such as hydrocodone and ketamine now sit, available by prescription.

DEA took a stopgap measure while hearings were in full swing, temporarily outlawing the drug on July 1, 1985, to curb abuse until the administrative process was completed. It was the second time in history that DEA used its temporary emergency scheduling authority. (The first was in March 1985 against a form of synthetic heroin.)

When the hearings concluded, DEA's chief administrative judge, Francis Young, recommended a Schedule III placement, agreeing that MDMA had potential medical use and finding minimal evidence of significant abuse. But DEA administrator John Lawn rejected the judge's recommendation and ordered MDMA's permanent placement into Schedule I.

Many therapists who found their licenses and careers at stake grudgingly abandoned the clinical use of MDMA. However, Sasha Shulgin determined to make his chemical children available to the masses. In 1991, the Shulgins self-published *PiHKAL*, short for "Phenethylamines I Have Known and Loved." PiHKAL was divided into two sections. The first is a love story, describing a vaguely fictional account of Sasha and Ann's lives, their courtship, and their drug experiences. The second part is the chemical story, with recipes and descriptions of 179 phenethylamines that Shulgin has synthesized and imbibed, including Number 109, MDMA.

Two years later, DEA agents raided Shulgin's lab looking for illicit substances, fined him $25,000 for violating the terms of his Schedule I license, and eventually rescinded his license.

On September 5, 1995, as Gagne and Germanowski were starting to build a case against the Israeli Ecstasy dealers, and on the same day that Germanowski had his second undercover meeting with Ghel, the *Los Angeles Times* published an interview with seventy-year-old Sasha Shulgin.

"A lot of the materials in Schedule I are my invention," Shulgin said. "I'm not sure if it's a point of pride or a point of shame."

9 SEPTEMBER 1995: GAGNE MEETS THE DEALERS

GHEL WAS AN ATTENTIVE salesman. He gave "Jimmy" (Germanowski) his pager number and told him to use the code 018 so they could quickly identify each other. He called periodically to see how his new client was enjoying the pills. And he promised to procure china (heroin) at a better price than the $87,000 per kilo Germanowski claimed to be paying his supplier.

Ghel believed that Germanowski was a Pittsburgh nightclub owner, and every extra flourish the agent could finesse made his undercover story that much more palatable. Sometimes Germanowski would return Ghel's calls from a pay phone near the airport. He would sit and watch the planes, and figure the intervals between landings and takeoffs—about thirty to forty seconds apart. Then he'd dial Ghel and leave a message:

"Hey, I just landed at the airport, I got your message and . . . sorry, hold on a second." Jets roared overhead. "Sorry about that. So, I gotta take care of some things, but I'll call you this afternoon."

Germanowski quickly built up confidence with Ghel. It was time for Gagne to join the story.

On September 12, Charlie pulled up at the corner of 99th Street and Queens Boulevard. Germanowski sat in the front; Gagne was in the back. Ghel walked up to greet them with a small black bag over his left shoulder. He seemed nervous. He wanted to exchange the pills and cash in the car, but who was the new guy?

"He's safe, he works for me," Germanowski said.

Ghel got in, sat next to Gagne, and told Charlie to drive around the block so they wouldn't attract any police attention. He reached into his pack and pulled out a clear plastic baggie filled with white capsules.

"Are these as good as your first samples?" Germanowski asked.

"Don't worry about it," Ghel said. "My friend, they are 100 percent MDMA, you are going to love them."

Gagne removed $4,000 in $20 bills from a green duffel and handed it to Ghel.

"Do you want to count it?"

"No, I trust you guys," Ghel said. "You are good businesspeople."

Ghel promised a price on heroin soon. When he got out of the car, he slipped Charlie $400 and thanked him for introducing such good clients. Charlie gave the cash back to Gagne when Ghel was out of sight. Charlie knew the risks: losing his CI status and gaining criminal charges for stealing money from the United States government.

That night, 179 capsules—drug evidence—were taken to the lab.

10 EVIDENCE

DEA HAS NINE FULLY accredited laboratories across the country that perform drug and evidence analysis. The New York Field Division's Northeast Regional Laboratory (NERL) is one of the largest, serving not only DEA but also NYPD, Customs, FBI—the entire northeastern United States.

The thirty bench chemists who sit in the fifty-thousand-square-foot lab work with millions of dollars' worth of machinery to perform analysis on drugs, gunshot residue, and fingerprints. There is even a special biohazard processing area to retrieve the kind of evidence—usually heroin—found inside the slimy latex balloons passed by couriers known as "swallowers."

Whenever Gagne took the elevator to the seventh floor to drop off drugs at the lab, he felt like he was walking up to a bank teller window at Fort Knox. The evidence custodian sat behind a bulletproof, bombproof glass window in the reception area. Gagne would hand her a completed DEA-7 evidence form and place the drugs in a sealed bag through a small one-way cabinet. She would retrieve his deposit, give it a number (today it's a bar code), and hand Gagne a receipt, and that was the last he saw of it. But from there the pills were carried to room 719, the permanent vault, where evidence in white bins is stacked high and as far back as the length of the building.

"A secure area within a secure area within a secure area" is how the architecture of NERL security is sometimes described. Just to get to the permanent vault, the evidence custodian has to use key and combination passes to unlock several layers of double-locked doors. The 179 capsules Gagne turned in would remain in the permanent vault until the chemist assigned to case number C1-95-0390 collected them for analysis. No other employee is ever allowed to touch the drugs except the assigned chemist. No one has access to the permanent vault except for lab employees. Cameras monitor their every move.

Lab employees, like all DEA employees, are subject to random drug tests. No one is exempt, not even the special agent in charge. On testing days, an independent team comes in unannounced, the bathroom is cordoned off, and each employee provides a urine sample in front of an analyst. Any trace of drugs in an employee's system is grounds for immediate termination.

Drug evidence housed at NERL is destroyed when a case is closed, but the paperwork, sign-offs, and checklists to close a case can take years to complete. Back in the 1980s, the vault overflowed with army duffel bags packed with thousands of kilos of cocaine evidence. Cases weren't being closed fast enough, so DOJ enforced a threshold amount. Drugs beyond that amount—for instance, ten kilos of cocaine and two kilos of heroin—were destroyed in each case after ninety days. The drug-destroying method at DEA is top-secret. New York City streets are blocked off as the evidence is delivered to the incinerating location, which is never disclosed. The drugs are lowered into an incinerating furnace and special iron markers are placed on the hopper—one marker before the drugs go through and one after—to ensure nothing is whisked away by opportunists during the incineration. Evidence destruction happens a couple of times a year. Only the chemists are allowed to touch the evidence. No one else. Ever.

11 ON SET

GHEL QUICKLY WARMED TO "Jimmy" and "Bobby." In a handful of subsequent meetings that September, Ghel shared small clues about the men in his circle who supplied the drugs. Ghel affectionately called these dealers his "brothers," although they were unrelated. Over lunch one day, Ghel told the agents he had a brother in Los Angeles with the heroin, a brother in Miami with the Ecstasy, and another brother "in the apartment," named Michel.

If Ghel was the Ecstasy car salesman, Michel Elbaz was the loan manager, slower to trust, more likely to walk away from a deal. The twenty-seven-year-old was born in Tel Aviv and raised by his mother. He had dark brown eyes and black hair that he wore in a Caesar cut. While Ghel relied on his imposing physical presence, Michel, at five foot six and 140 pounds, relied on his instincts.

The agents began to meet with Ghel and Michel about every other week to chat and talk product. Germanowski would argue dispassionately about price as if it mattered, like a move in a chess game. Negotiating gave the agents an opportunity to better understand where the dealers were positioned on the food chain: were they little fish desperate to unload merchandise or did they have the power to wait until the right number came up? They seemed like hungry little fish.

The "set" for meet operations was the Tower Diner, across the street from Ghel's apartment. Backup undercovers would arrive beforehand, ghost the agents from nearby booths, and leave after the meeting dispersed. Surveilling agents in parked cars would monitor conversations via Germanowski and Gagne's KEL body transmitters. Everyone got a copy of the written operational plans beforehand, which included descriptions of Ghel and Michel, the nearest police station (the 112th Precinct in Forest Hills), the nearest hospital (St. John's on Queens Boulevard), the type of operation (undercover meeting and acquisition of free sample), personnel assignments (GS Lou Cardinali in the blue Cougar, Jay Flaherty in the black Olds), the preplanned distress signals, both audio ("My friend is not going to like this") and visual (hands up above head), and the NYPD-designated color of the day. Informants and undercovers on set are supposed to wear an article of clothing in the color of the day, say, orange, so that if all hell breaks loose, the local authorities can visually spot the good guys in orange. It was a formality, really—a plan B if cover was compromised. Gagne and Germanowski never lost their cover. Most of the time, they acted more like mischievous brothers than stiff feds.

"Don't put your water glass on my napkin," Germanowski would snap at Gagne.

"Move your elbow over," Gagne would gripe at Germanowski.

One afternoon at the Tower Diner, as Michel was ready to hand over the next load of Ecstasy pills, a pretty blonde walked by outside the window and Gagne was fifteen years old again.

"Look at her." Gagne nudged his partner.

"She's not that hot," Germanowski said dismissively. He had a weakness for Salma Hayek–type brunettes.

"What's wrong with you?" Gagne said, shoving his partner.

"Don't touch me," Germanowski said. "Stop touching me."

The agents bickered for the next five minutes about the superiority of blondes versus brunettes.

"Guys." Michel rolled his eyes. "Guys, hello? I have your stuff here. I have it."

"Shut the fuck up. We're not through here," Gagne snapped at Michel.

Germanowski liked to say that if he had a dollar for every time Gagne said "Shut the fuck up," he wouldn't be working, he'd be golfing. Sometimes the arguing would end in ribbing; other times they came just short of blows. But the second anyone attempted to interrupt the sibling rivalry, the agents would quickly turn and cut down whoever dared enter their marriage. For the most part, targets never suspected the partners were DEA, and informants longed to play a role in their little family.

12 PURE MDMA

ON SEPTEMBER 19, the lab results for exhibit number two, the capsules Germanowski bought from Ghel at their first undercover buy in Charlie's car, were finally revealed. Gagne had opened the case nearly a month ago and he was anxious to learn more about exactly what they were buying off the Israeli dealers.

According to the forensic chemist who signed off on the analysis, the two pills weighed twenty-three grams apiece and contained 3,4-methylenedioxymethamphetamine hydrochloride—unadulterated Ecstasy. In bold type, the chemist noted an especially high purity level. Ghel's pills measured in at 84 percent MDMA, a rarity. It was great news for Gagne. They were on to something new and untapped. If the levels had been weak—more of the same Robitussin recipe—there was no way he could have defended keeping the case going. They just didn't have the resources.

Germanowski got a call from a supervisor shortly after the lab results came out. Seemed the front office also had taken notice. Even if Ecstasy was kiddie dope, this was dope straight from the source.

"Guess what?" Germanowski broke the news to Gagne. "They want us to go up on a wire on these guys."

13 DUTCH APPLES

"I'M SORRY FOR NOT being able to provide the capsules promised," Michel said as he slipped into their regular booth at the Tower Diner. He reached across the table and handed Germanowski a plastic dime bag decorated with red hearts. Inside were two white pills stamped with apple logos on one side. "This is the best X anyone can get anywhere," Michel said.

For a thousand pills, it was $20 each, Michel told them. Order ten thousand or more and it'd be $15 a pill.

Gagne and Germanowski did the math. Ten thousand pills equaled $150,000 in government funds. Dropping a couple thousand dollars in buy money here and there was no big deal, but the price for ten thousand pills was prohibitive. If they showed up with a sack of $150,000 in government cash, it meant the bad guys were one hand-off away from arrest—and that cash wasn't going anywhere. It was October 17, only their fifth meeting with the dealers. It was too early to take the case down. They still needed to weed out the source of supply, and they were just days away from getting court approval on the wiretap so they could start listening to the dealers' phone calls.

Michel must have sensed skepticism, because he proceeded to give the agents an Ecstasy-business primer.

As Pittsburgh nightclub owners, they should be taking a tip from the New York nightclub scene, Michel told them. What made the clubs in New York so popular? The music, the crowd, and the drugs.

"The clubs are a great market for Ecstasy," Michel said, adding that Ghel was delivering five hundred Apples to an employee at the Limelight nightclub in Manhattan that very hour.

It was true—one dealer could easily unload five hundred hits of Ecstasy on a busy night at Limelight, double his money on the young ravers who dropped $25 to $50 a pill, and expect repeat business if the pills were good quality.

"The best Ecstasy in the world comes from Holland," Michel said, and Apples were the best-quality X because they came directly from Amsterdam. Michel said his "brother" in Miami had a source in Holland who could supply "any amount of Apples needed."

Michel trusted these men, he said, because he knew them from his "motherland," Israel. Even the apple logo on the pills was a nod to Israel, oft referred to as "the apple of God's eye." Michel could get them bushels of Apples, and if the Apple supply ran low, he had a cheaper and slightly weaker pill called Blue and Whites. (Another nod to the motherland, in the colors of the Israeli flag.)

"Blue and Whites are fairly popular at the nightclubs," Michel said. He advised "Jimmy" to buy Apples in bulk to keep his nightclub patrons coming back.

"I only need one or two days' notice to have an order sent," Michel went on. "For the weekends, however, it's best to order by midweek."

The agents thanked the dealer, said they'd try the Apples, and let him know if they wanted more.

"The next time you guys come to New York," Michel said, "I want to take you both to a few of my favorite nightclubs. You can meet some of my people."

A month later, Germanowski received a memo from the DEA attaché in The Hague country office. Dutch police were investigating local Ecstasy traffickers and had heard talk on a wiretap about the purchase of large quantities of strong Ecstasy pills referred to as "Apples."

14 ON THE WIRE

ANYTIME THE U.S. government arrests you, searches your home, or listens to your phone calls, it is violating your civil liberties, your constitutional right to privacy. The Department of Justice's job is to protect the Constitution. As such, DEA wiretap requests, or Title III affidavits, are highly vetted for probable cause at DOJ's Office of Enforcement Operations (OEO) before they ever reach a federal judge's attention. This is how the system works for DEA agents, and in the best-case scenario, this is how it should work with every federal agency. (Post-9/11 revelations about the National Security Agency's warrantless wiretaps have shown that in cases of potential terrorist threats, the constitutional standard hasn't always been so vigorously applied. However, standard DEA wiretaps are another story—the process is tedious and there are no shortcuts.)

DEA agents work closely with their district's U.S. attorney's office and its prosecutors who are responsible for trying federal drug cases. In most field divisions, DEA agents have to write their own T-III affidavits, which can run up to 120 pages. But in New York, the assistant U.S. attorneys, or AUSAs, are dogged and efficient—they get their hands dirty and take on precedent-setting cases. They also write up all DEA wiretap requests. It's just cleaner and quicker to have an attorney do it.

A DEA wiretap can take several weeks or months to push through. In comparison, wiretaps in Israel can get court approval in a day. In the Netherlands, a judge can approve a wiretap in twenty minutes based on a prosecutor's three-paragraph-long request.

On October 25, 1995, a thirty-day T-III intercept was approved for the residential telephone of Michel Elbaz. It was the first DEA wiretap initiated specifically to snoop on Ecstasy dealers. Estimated cost for thirty days: $35,000. The next step was to send out the tech specialists.

Back in the days of POTS—plain old telephone service—DEA Investigative Technical Specialist Glen Glover would send out three or four undercover trucks a day to install secret recording equipment on landlines. Now, Glover gets one POTS job every other month. Dealers today purchase blocks of prepaid cell phones, ten or more at a pop, that the entire organization will use for two or three weeks. Just as the agents start to figure out names, sources, and scheduled drug loads, all at once the dealers drop their phones and everybody starts talking on new phones. It takes time for the agents to figure out the new numbers, and OEO is so backlogged with paperwork that by the time they get wiretaps approved for the second round of phones, the network is already using a third round of new cell phones.

Michel's phone was a simple POTS job, which meant that Glover or one of his tech specialists put on a lineman's uniform and drove out to Queens in a fake NYNEX truck. A tech specialist in those days would strap on a tool belt with a fat phone receiver, bluff an authoritative nod to the doorman (if there was one), and saunter down to the basement to find the phone board. The phone company *might* provide the block and pin number of the target's line, but everything would be mislabeled and jury-rigged, so Glover would have to plug his receiver into the phone board, wait for a dial tone, and start dialing 958 on every line until he found the right one. (Pick up a single POTS line anywhere in the country, dial a designated three-digit code, and a recorded voice will cite the number you're calling from. Every state has a specific code. New York's is 958.)

Once Glover found the target's phone, he'd attach the wire to a cylinder-shaped device called a slave. Then he'd hide the slave near the phone box and pray it wasn't discovered. A slave resembles a small black pipe bomb topped with multicolored wires, and it's what connects the target's line straight into the DEA.

Sometimes real linemen would show up in the middle of a job asking questions: "Who are you? What are you doing?" Linemen knew everyone who worked their areas. They'd test the tech specialists all the time—maybe ask to borrow a specific tool.

"Sorry, don't have that on me today," Glover would say, trying not to blow his cover.

"Oh, no?" the lineman would deadpan. "That's because it doesn't exist."

Glover was more tech nerd than steely undercover, but he could bluff with the best of the street agents. Once he was cornered in the basement of an apartment complex controlled by a Spanish street gang.

"What are you doing, man? You tapping my phones?"

"Nah," he said. "You want me to fix your phone or not? There's problems with this whole building."

The gangsters sat on tattered couches, drinking Coronas, never removing the bandannas covering their faces as they watched Glover work. He left with the slave in his pocket, and the job was rescheduled around the gangbangers' sleeping hours.

Today, the NYFD's seventh-floor wire room, or Title III Operations Center, is equipped with thirty-five listening cubicles or "pods." Calls come in through computer systems that digitally record the targets' conversations. Translators—who work from 8:00 a.m. to midnight every day—are assigned to cases based on their language proficiency: Spanish-speakers cover Colombian and Mexican cocaine and marijuana cases, while Chinese-speakers proficient in a variety of dialects work Chinese wires, which usually means heroin. Agents work closely with translators, who are about half men, half women. But when Gagne and Germanowski were chasing after pill pushers in 1995, the translators were mostly young Spanish-speaking women, who are fondly remembered by the male agents for their tendency to wear tight pants, loose blouses, and red lip gloss.

Agents and translators have to sign lengthy rules-of-minimization forms, which state that interceptions must be turned down and listening must cease during calls that are considered privileged. Privileged conversations include those between attorney and client, parishioner and clergyman, physician and patient, and husband and wife. The caveat is if the target also has a third person on the line during a conversation with his lawyer or his wife, the call is no longer considered privileged. Experienced drug traffickers know these rules too. They engage in seemingly mundane conversations about a certain "lady" (code for cocaine) or "boy" (code for heroin) who is scheduled to arrive in "the Twins" (a pre-9/11 code for New York).

When Gagne and Germanowski started the Ghel and Michel Ecstasy wire, they didn't have the digital technology of today's Title III ops center. In 1995, wiretaps at DEA were conducted in the Stone Age, which was located in room 582 on the fifth floor. Gagne and Germanowski spent thirty days in a windowless seven-by-eight-foot workspace with a table and three chairs. Cheap blue carpet was laid in small multicolored sections so that if an agent spilled coffee or dropped a lit cigarette, pieces could be ripped out and replaced with new blue squares. Gagne tacked surveillance photos of Ghel and Michel on one wall made of white corkboard that had yellowed from years of cigarette smoke.

Michel and Ghel's phone calls were intercepted through a line monitoring system, or LMS kit, a box about the size of a forty-inch-square TV, which opened up to reveal a three-reel tape deck. An orange light blinked whenever Ghel or Michel picked up the phone to make or receive a call, triggering all three tapes to record in unison. Scotch-taped under each cassette were labels to remind them which tape was the work copy, which was for the AUSA (assistant U.S. attorney), and which was the original. As the reels spun out to the end, the trick was to quickly pop all three out and slap in three new tapes at the same time without missing too much of the call. But sometimes one tape wouldn't play or the tapes would break because the gears hadn't been oiled.

A dialed number recorder, or DNR kit, sat next to the LMS, spitting out phone numbers like ticker tape. The agents would track the phone numbers and write them in thick black marker on five-by-seven index cards, trying to figure out the caller's name and what they were buying or selling. DEA intelligence analysts could subpoena subscriber information for those numbers to help the agents establish identities. The index cards were kept in a plastic file box, and when a call came in, they could see the number on the DNR, flip through the cards, find the matching digits, and identify who was on the line.

Ghel and Michel weren't as sophisticated as their Colombian counterparts in the cocaine trade. They didn't speak in code. They didn't drop their phones. They did deals openly and brazenly at all hours of the day. The agents could stimulate the wire—get the dealers to call their sources of supply—with a single well-timed phone call.

On October 25, the first day of the intercept,

Germanowski called Michel to say he was ready to place an order for Apples, starting with a six-hundred-pill deal. Then he and Gagne sat back and waited for the orange light to start blinking.

At 5:28 p.m. Michel made a call to the "brother" in Miami to tell him it was time to make another delivery to New York.

"Is it a done deal?" the man asked Michel.

"Yes."

15 "WHEN YOU COME DOWN, YOU COME DOWN NICE AND SLOW"

TAL SHITRIT HAD ONLY met Ghel and Michel in September, but they quickly became steady buyers and he had already sold them several hundred pills, sent in FedEx overnight packages. When Shitrit got Michel's call on October 25, he decided it was time to personally deliver a load. The next morning, Shitrit dialed Michel back with his flight information: he was arriving at JFK that evening, at 11:10 p.m., Carnival Airlines flight 182 from Miami.

"Bring everything," Michel told him.

Gagne and Germanowski were listening to the call from wire room 582. As soon as the dealers hung up, Germanowski's undercover phone rang. It was Michel.

"I can only get you four hundred fifty of the six hundred pills you want, but I will have them tonight," Michel said.

At 11:20 p.m., a DEA undercover observed Shitrit arriving at the TWA terminal. Shitrit wore a brown leather jacket, white jeans, and cowboy boots, with his strawberry red hair in a ponytail. Michel hugged him and said hello.

Michel drove Shitrit to his apartment in Rego Park, where Ghel was waiting inside. A second undercover agent was waiting outside in an unmarked vehicle.

At 11:50 p.m., Ghel and Michel left the apartment and were seen getting into a blue Pontiac.

At five minutes past midnight, special agent Jay Flaherty

watched the blue Pontiac park outside the Mélange Grill and Café on Austin Street in Queens.

Ghel and Michel entered the café and saw their pals "Jimmy" and "Bobby" waiting at a booth. They apologized for being late.

"My friend with the X was late arriving at the airport," Michel said. And he had only 400 pills now, not 450. Ghel unsnapped a black leather fanny pack from around his waist and laid it on the table. Gagne casually picked up the pack, fastened it around his waist, and headed to the men's bathroom. He stepped into a private stall, locked the door, and unzipped the front of the pack. Inside was a clear plastic sandwich bag, plump with small white pills stamped with apple silhouettes. Gagne felt the weight of the bag in his hands, nearly a quarter pound. He held the bag up to the light to get a better look. Four hundred pills was the most they had ever purchased. He shoved the pills down his waistband and stuffed $6,400 cash ($16 per pill) into the empty pack.

Back at the booth, Michel was schooling Germanowski on the chemical effects of Apples.

"When you take them you feel them very quickly," he said. "But the Apple is slower. When you come down, you come down nice and slow."

Gagne slid in next to his partner and placed the fanny pack back on the table. Ghel snatched it up and fastened it back around his waist.

"I'll need another ten thousand to twenty thousand Apples next time," Germanowski said. "And what about your brother with the china?"

"Two weeks for the pills," Ghel said. "The guy with the china—he wants to meet you guys. He wants you to come to Los Angeles."

As the men parted, Ghel told the agents: "You guys should buy a nightclub in New York."

16 THE BROTHERS FROM THE MOTHERLAND

OVER THE NEXT MONTH, Gagne and Germanowski sat in wire room 582, slapping in tape after tape and gathering incriminating evidence. They pinpointed the dealers' sources in about two weeks.

The "brother" from Miami, Tal Shitrit, was a green-eyed twenty-six-year-old Israeli national who ran a business that supplied plants to large retailers, such as Kmart. A surveillance photo of Shitrit meeting with Michel at JFK airport was tacked up on the wall next to Michel and Ghel's photos.

Based on the dealers' phone calls to California, the "brother" from Los Angeles with the heroin was identified as a thirty-six-year-old Israeli named Mordi Barak, who sold watches and lived in an apartment in West Hollywood. They'd get Los Angeles DEA to deal with him later.

Besides what they sold to DEA, the majority of the Ecstasy that Ghel and Michel distributed seemed to be heading straight into the city's nightclubs. Gagne and Germanowski were pub-and-grill types. The New York club scene was completely foreign to them. Gagne knew that would have to change.

17 THE VIP

ON A WEDNESDAY AFTERNOON in early November, Germanowski and Gagne were lifting weights in the fifth-floor gym, getting a quick workout before their 3:30 p.m. appointment with a new potential informant.

Gagne was religious about his daily workouts. At twenty-nine, the five-foot-ten drug cop was about 190 pounds of muscle and could bench-press 300 pounds on a good day. Gagne had his father René to thank for his unceasing physical discipline. Like his brothers, Ronnie and René, Bob played baseball, hockey, and football from as early as he could grip a stick. His sisters, Susan and Sherrie, played basketball and softball. Their father skewered them as failures if they weren't the fastest, the strongest—if they didn't make varsity as freshmen. Trophies and ribbons filled two wood-and-glass cases in the living room by the time the last Gagne child had graduated from high school.

Gagne would say that the most valuable thing he learned from his father was the kind of man he did not want to be. But he also learned how to deflect all self-doubt about his physical and mental boundaries—a trait that got him through his grueling military training. In 1985, at nineteen years of age, Gagne was three weeks shy of completing basic training when he caught a case of poison ivy so severe it covered three-quarters of his body, blistering his skin from his eyelids to his heels. His drill sergeant warned that if he went to the medic, they'd likely admit him to the hospital, where he'd go on sick call and have to be "recycled." That meant five weeks down the drain. Gagne decided against medical care and went back to training. On the last day, he powered through low-crawl drills, scraping his body against the red clay ground. His skin was on fire and the red clay felt like a flamethrower to his abdomen. But he finished.

At twenty-six, when Gagne was three days shy of passing Ranger Assessment—the training he needed to be accepted into Snowcap—his big toe throbbed from an ingrown nail that shot piercing jolts of pain up his foot and made walking excruciating. The medic warned that if he were to cut it the way it needed, Gagne wouldn't be able to walk for a week. He decided to endure the pain. He almost quit during a timed twenty-five-mile road march in searing heat, carrying a rucksack filled with eighty pounds of sand. It took almost seven hours to walk twenty-five miles without stopping, and he started to hallucinate in the home stretch. He thought his feet had fallen off and that he was walking on bloody stumps. He finished, of course, because quitting equaled failure.

Germanowski knew his partner was a little crazy. But having been a baseball star in college, he understood and complemented Gagne's competitive nature.

Gagne took a break between reps and walked over to the giant picture windows of the fifth-floor gym. Their three-thirty appointment was early. He was walking up Tenth Avenue just as Gagne peered out the window.

"G, you gotta come over here and see this," Gagne said.

Sean Bradley was a 120-pound, five-foot-four, nineteen-year-old runt with bleach-striped blond hair that was shaved on the sides and pulled back in a ponytail. He wore jeans that looked ten sizes too big, a dog chain that looped from his waistband to his knees, glow sticks around his neck, and an oversized backpack. Bradley was a VIP at New York's most exclusive clubs.

"Are you kidding me?" Germanowski said. "Dude, if that's how I gotta look, it's not happening."

Finding Bradley had been a stroke of luck. A DEA group supervisor had been cutting his grass when his Secret Service neighbor mentioned that they had recently arrested a teen who was passing counterfeit twenties at the Woodbridge Mall in New Jersey. Bradley got caught using the fake bills to buy shoes at Foot Locker and a Genesis CD at Sam Goody for his six-foot-tall stripper girlfriend. Bradley had a history of young-thug mischief—including criminal trespassing and possession of controlled substances—and he had become an errand boy for counterfeiters who paid him in fake cash. The Secret Service couldn't use him because he didn't know anything about the money printers. But he claimed to know everything about drug distribution in the nightclubs.

On November 8, at 3:30 p.m., Bradley had his first interview at DEA.

"Hey, guys-th-th," he greeted Gagne and Germanowski in the lobby. The agents detected a repetitive *clink-slurp-clink* sound echoing inside Bradley's mouth. His nervous habit of lightly running the stud in his tongue piercing across his teeth would soon unnerve them. They took him into a private interrogation room on the lobby floor.

"All right, what do you know?" Germanowski asked.

Bradley said that New York's most popular nightclubs—Tunnel and Limelight—were drug markets and everybody knew it. In fact, Bradley used to personally sell drugs in the clubs as a "house dealer," but the work had temporarily slowed after the police raid.

The agents knew that Limelight, on Sixth Avenue and

20th Street, had been the site of a botched NYPD raid in September. Undercover narcotics cops had made seventeen cocaine buys at Limelight that fall, and one officer noted in an indictment that drug dealing and use were carried out with a remarkable business-as-usual attitude at the club. But when NYPD hit Limelight on September 30 with warrants to arrest thirty suspected dealers, twenty-six of the suspects were nowhere to be found and the place was virtually clean of drugs.

NYPD suspected that the club owner, Peter Gatien, had an insider who'd alerted him to the raid ahead of time. Limelight was briefly shuttered under the public nuisance laws, and Gatien was forced to pay a $30,000 fine, post a $160,000 bond, and provide authorities with a list of club employees as well as signed statements promising they would not take part in the sale of narcotics and would report any illegal drug sales. Limelight was reopened in a week's time.

According to Bradley, the list that club management handed over to authorities did not include the names of two employees: Michael Caruso and Michael Alig.

Michael Caruso, aka Lord Michael, was a successful promoter and manager of techno DJs. Michael Alig was the infamous king of the "Club Kids," who reinvigorated the nightlife scene with campy fashion and regressive hedonism. At Limelight and Tunnel, Alig's parties attracted a predominantly gay crowd, while Caruso had a straight following.

Bradley told the agents that party promoters like Caruso and Alig had their own personal house dealers who moved through the crowd and made sure guests had a constant supply of a wide variety of narcotics. Dealers made money from their drug sales and the party promoters got a percentage of the door fees.

Limelight management had curbed the amount of

Ecstasy being sold since the raids, Bradley said, but word was that things had quieted down and dealers could get back to work in another two to three weeks.

The agents weren't ready to sign Bradley on as a full-fledged confidential informant yet. They had to get to know him a little better, try to get into the clubs on their own first to see if Bradley knew what he was talking about. If his information panned out, then they would rethink his role, maybe enlist him to open doors, make introductions.

"How do you think we should dress if we want to get into the clubs?" Gagne asked.

Bradley knew that the two agents would never pass as Club Kids: they didn't sport waifish physiques and designer clothes, and Germanowski was reticent to heed Bradley's fashion advice.

"Okay, well," Bradley said, "you guys could try to go as a couple of, like, you know, stylish guineas from Staten Island."

18 DECEMBER 2, 1995: TUNNEL NIGHTCLUB

THE BLACK STRETCH LIMOUSINE turned down 27th Street toward the Hudson River, slowly approached the crowd outside Tunnel, and stopped in front of the red velvet ropes. Gagne stepped out in black leather loafers and a *Miami Vice*–style double-breasted club suit, his short black curly hair gelled up slick, his beard shaved in a reverse goatee. Germanowski was equally sporty in tapered slacks and a black mock turtleneck under his club jacket. *Stylish guinea,* Germanowski had thought to himself as he looked in the mirror at the locker room at DEA.

The agents knew they could easily be spotted as the kind of guys who preferred sports bars and beer on tap to VIP lounges and bespoke cocktails, so they went the extra mile and borrowed the undercover limo. (*Hey, big spender!*)

Tunnel was housed in a former train depot along the West Side Highway, and at forty thousand square feet it was the largest club space in Manhattan. There was no formal line outside Tunnel, just a morass of bodies inching up to the entrance. The agents strutted up like two roosters and waited to be noticed. The Hudson-chilled wind whipped past the highway, cutting through their summer-weight suits. Winter overcoats would have clashed with their threads, so they went coatless, shivering martyrs to style. Twenty minutes later, they were still waiting.

"I'm fucking freezing," Germanowski whispered.

Ten minutes later they were up against the ropes, next in line, in plain sight of party promoter Darryl Darrin, a heavyset man with a slight voice. Darrin gave the agents a pitiful glance as he let in the clubgoers behind them and announced in their general direction: "If you've been here for any length of time and you haven't been picked, just go home. There's nothing here for you."

"C'mon," Gagne said, motioning to his partner. They changed their location along the ropes. "This'll throw the guy off."

The backup team tonight included their group supervisor, Lou Cardinali, on surveillance from the limo parked nearby, and Special Agent Jay Flaherty, who showed up minutes later by cab with Sean Bradley and two other agents. The men would ghost Gagne and Germanowski inside the club. The first thing Gagne noticed when the backup team arrived was that they were still in their work clothes, blue jeans and collared shirts.

"Jesus," Gagne said to his partner through chattering teeth. "They're never gonna get in."

Sean Bradley, who usually showed up with his stripper girlfriend and her scantily clad pals, had spent so much of his (counterfeit) money inside the clubs that Darrin seemed willing to overlook Bradley's nattily dressed guests this evening. Darrin plucked them from the crowd and let them squeeze ahead. Flaherty shot Gagne and Germanowski a sly wink as their group was shepherded past the velvet rope.

"Are you kidding me?" Gagne said. "This isn't happening. Now we have to get in!"

Gagne would later learn that entry for unvetted clubgoers was decided primarily on appearance and there was a clear pecking order. The clubs reduced patrons to A-crowd, B-crowd, and C-crowd. A and B got in; C was filler—but you didn't want too many guys in your C-crowd, you wanted more girls, because girls brought in the A-crowd guys—even if they were C-crowd girls.

The agents were probably pegged as D-crowd—the kind of guys who are likely to start a fight if they don't find female companionship within a certain amount of time.

Germanowski was cold and impatient. He had a bum shoulder that was still recovering from reconstructive surgery, and he had more grief waiting at home. It was his wife's birthday, and she wasn't pleased that he was spending it in a nightclub. Bob didn't want to hear about it. He had a herniated disk and was scheduled for major back surgery in a month.

Darrin made a second announcement: "If there's anybody here that I have seen and did not let in, go away. There's nothing here for you."

A guest-list girl showed pity on the agents and handed them passes to Limelight. Gagne felt embarrassed to even be acknowledged.

"Let's go," Germanowski said.

"No, no," Gagne insisted. "Just wait. We're getting in."

A young up-and-coming party promoter named Joseph "Baby Joe" Uzzardi had briefly stepped outside and Gagne latched onto him.

"Hey, why can't we get in?"

Uzzardi leaned back, gave Gagne a once-over, and offered a meek excuse: "Sorry, but it's gay night," Uzzardi said. "You're not getting in. Just go to Limelight."

"Bob, let's get the fuck outta here," Germanowski pleaded.

"Fine," Gagne said. "Fine! Call for the limo."

"I am not calling for the limousine. I just want to get out of here."

"Look, I came in the limousine. I'm leaving in the limousine."

Gagne sulked the whole three-block walk to a gas station, where he and his partner sat on the curb and waited. As the limo pulled up, the doors opened and a cloud of cigar smoke escaped into the cool air.

"You two fucking morons got all dressed up!" Lou Cardinali's cackling laughter drowned out the sound of empty beer bottles clanking on the limo floor. "You think you're cool-shit badasses. Nothing made me happier than watching you two stand outside freezing your ass off."

"That's it," Germanowski said. "Whatever it takes— if I gotta wrap my body in Saran Wrap and put a green horn on my head—done. I'm getting in this fucking place."

19 "DID YOU RECEIVE THE PRESENT YET?"

GHEL AND MICHEL HAD started their fledgling Ecstasy business in the summer of 1995 and by winter the dealers were making steady cash profits from their stable of nightclub buyers. As Gagne and Germanowski listened to the dealers on the wire, they could practically track the dealers' evolution from small-time peddlers to ruthless profiteers.

In December, shortly after the DEA agents were barred from clubland, Ghel and Michel made plans for a trip to France. It was to be a working vacation, with a visit to an old acquaintance who had an antique store that was said to be filled with millions of dollars' worth of jewelry and furniture. The dealers' brilliant plan was to bludgeon the owner to death, steal his valuables, and split the profits. The fresh influx of cash could be used to invest in larger Ecstasy deals. They revealed bits of their plan over the phone as Gagne and Germanowski were listening. NYFD authorities immediately contacted the DEA's Paris country office to alert French police and to warn the *vendeur d'antiquités* of the alleged plot against his life.

At the same time that Ghel and Michel were making vacation plans, Tal Shitrit, the Miami supplier, got an infusion of drugs—ten thousand hits of a new kind of Ecstasy from Holland, which he called "Rabbits." Shitrit needed to unload the Rabbits fast, so he decided to front Ghel and Michel 4,700 pills, worth $47,500, and send them same-day package delivery.

On December 11, 1995, at 9:15 a.m., Shitrit's girlfriend walked into Pakmail on Kendall Drive in Miami and approached the manager with a brown box. The manager, out of courtesy, informed her that same-day FedEx service would cost $179, but she could send it next-day air for half as much. Cost was unimportant, she said. The package was for her boyfriend's mother, and it had to get there today. She paid cash and left. The package was addressed to a false name, "Jaco Nastoros," at Ghel and Michel's Rego Park address.

What the dealers didn't know was that FedEx required same-day packages to be inspected before the company would take receipt. When the FedEx driver arrived, he opened the box and found a tan ceramic vase with flowers. It looked good to go. But the driver was suspicious—this was Miami, after all—so he took the flowers out of the vase, removed the foam core, and found several plastic bags containing small tan pills with a Playboy bunny imprint on them. The store manager called Miami Metro-Dade police.

At noon, Shitrit's girlfriend called Pakmail for a tracking number but the manager bluffed and said he didn't have one yet. She called again at 1:00 p.m. At two-thirty, Shitrit called. He called again at three. The manager politely suggested to Shitrit—at the instruction of the police detective standing behind him—that he should drop by the store to get the tracking number.

"That is not necessary," Shitrit said. He hung up and called Ghel.

Gagne and Germanowski, who weren't aware yet of the FedEx fiasco in Miami, were listening on Ghel and Michel's wire when Shitrit called.

"Did you receive the present yet?" Shitrit asked Ghel. "No."

"It's hot," Shitrit warned. "Do not sign on it, don't do anything." They agreed not to speak for a few days.

It was bad timing for Gagne and Germanowski. They

wanted stronger evidence before taking the case down—more buys before they went in for the bust. But now Ghel and Michel had good reason to leave for Paris as quickly as possible, to avoid being linked to the Playboy pills. The agents couldn't let them get on a plane and disappear. It was time to move in for the arrest.

The next day, on December 12, a team of special agents, including Jay Flaherty, descended on apartment K at 99–32 66th Road to arrest Ghel and Michel for conspiracy to distribute MDMA. No cash or drugs were found in the apartment. Israel "Ghel" Hazut and Michel Elbaz were advised of their rights and brought to NYFD, where Gagne and Germanowski were waiting.

As a safety measure, undercover DEA agents never take part in the arrests of the targets they've been meeting with, because if they've played their roles well, the dealer won't believe the agent is really a drug cop. The dealer's first impression when he sees the guns come out is that he is about to be robbed, and he's likely to pull out his own weapon to defend himself if it only means killing another drug dealer.

Ghel and Michel were in a holding area when "Jimmy" and "Bobby" walked in to introduce themselves as Special Agents Germanowski and Gagne. Ghel seemed happy to see them.

"Jimmy!" Ghel said. "They got you!"

"Ghel, I'm an agent," Germanowski said, showing him the gold badge on his belt.

"No, Jimmy, it's okay," Ghel said. "It's okay, you're not."

"No, Ghel—I really am. And I'm going to have to testify against you."

"No, you won't, Jimmy! You can just get an attorney," Ghel persisted. He was certain that "Jimmy" had been arrested and then set up by the DEA to trick him into talking.

But Michel had no doubts about who "Jimmy" and "Bobby" really were. They'd been duped. He started yelling at Ghel in Hebrew.

"Okay," Ghel finally said in English. "I understand. You guys did really good."

20 DOWNLOADING THE DEALERS

GAGNE LOOKED AT HIS watch. It was after 5:00 p.m. The agents had been with the dealers at NYFD all afternoon, and Ghel and Michel had finally agreed to take a plea bargain and cooperate. For the first time, Ghel downplayed his role as a drug dealer. He wasn't a large-scale trafficker at all, he said. The largest amount of drugs he'd ever sold was the four hundred pills to the agents. Gagne wanted to sign them up as defendant informants and use them to learn more about the Ecstasy networks in the nightclubs. The courts were closed, but he figured they could bring Ghel and Michel to jail, get them arraigned in the morning with public defenders, and then out on bail.

But the assistant U.S. attorney didn't see it that way. She informed Gagne that even with Ghel and Michel's promise to cooperate, they would never get bail because of their immigration status and the alleged murder plot. Their supervisor, Lou Cardinali, had more bad news: the front office was hot to do a press conference in the morning. Gagne imagined the headlines: "DEA Identifies Drug Traffickers in Murder Plot." With that kind of press, he knew, Ghel and Michel would never talk.

Gagne felt the pinch. He hadn't come this far just to throw the dealers in jail. It was imperative that they debrief them and get as much intelligence as possible while Ghel and Michel still had the impetus to cooperate. So he came up with a plan—an unorthodox, highly unusual plan—which he proposed to his cohorts, Germanowski and Jay Flaherty.

"You want to do what?" Cardinali was stunned. Gagne, Germanowski, and Flaherty were standing in his office, announcing that they wanted to spend the night with two drug-dealing potential killers.

"Lou, we only have a small window of opportunity to really debrief these guys. We gotta download them before we lose them," Gagne said. "So we'll do it all in one shot—tonight, at their apartment."

Gagne made it sound easy, but Germanowski would later claim his partner had employed Jedi mind-trick powers to convince him to go along with the sleepover, and to persuade the front office to hold off on the press conference. Cardinali was nervous about the whole thing. Gagne's crack ideas had helped to make his boss a two-pack-a-day smoker.

"Nothing better happen," he barked at the agents as they left. "And you hammerheads better have them at the U.S. attorney's office at eight tomorrow morning!"

As they drove Ghel and Michel home, Gagne, Germanowski, and Flaherty played it like they just needed to hang out with the dealers overnight and then bring them back to court for their appearance in the morning.

"We'll go over everything then," Germanowski said. The agents couldn't tell the dealers that there was zero chance of a judge granting them bail in the morning. These were men who would bludgeon an old friend for his baubles. The agents had to assume that if Ghel and Michel knew jail was imminent, then they would do whatever necessary to escape.

So for one strange, cold night in December, three New York DEA agents had a slumber party at the tiny apartment of two Israeli Ecstasy dealers. They kept Ghel and Michel up all night, chatting them up in the living room like old college buddies, and casually questioning them about their suppliers and the Ecstasy scene in New York's nightclubs.

Ghel said they'd first met the "brother" from Los Angeles with the heroin, Mordi Barak, when they all lived in Israel. When they learned he was selling MDMA in the States, they reconnected with Barak by phone and he sent them ten capsules by overnight mail in August 1995. He sent more pills in September—including the 84 percent pure capsules they'd sold the agents. But Barak's supply wasn't always reliable, and in late September, they met Tal Shitrit at Tunnel nightclub. The ponytailed dealer got his MDMA directly from a supplier in Holland. Ghel and Michel would buy Shitrit's pills for $12 or $13 apiece and resell them for $30 to $50 retail in the clubs or in bulk at $16 to $22 to buyers like "Bobby" and "Jimmy."

When the supply of strong, good-quality Ecstasy was low, the dealers had a stash of fake Ecstasy pills called "Bullets" that they could sell in the clubs for extra money. Bullets were small, fat pills that were scored on one side. Club Kids who danced until daylight to thumping techno music under an endless hallucinogenic laser show were so high they didn't know that the Bullets were just the cough suppressant dextromethorphan.

While Ghel and Michel talked, the agents carefully scanned the apartment in a covert search for weapons. They devised secret plans in their heads of how to kill the dealers if it became necessary. Flaherty caught Germanowski's eye and motioned to the space above Germanowski's head. Two giant samurai swords hung on the wall above him.

When it was time to sleep, Gagne took the couch and Flaherty took the floor. Germanowski got stuck keeping watch on first shift and was relegated to a small cushionless chair in the corner.

"No, no, it's okay," Germanowski said to Gagne, who was stretching out on the couch. "Because when they come out of that room looking to kill us, the couch is the first thing they're going to come across. Even though I'm awake, they'll kill you before I can kill them. So you sleep on the couch and sleep well, my friend."

"That's really fucked up," Gagne said. "When I'm sleeping I'm trusting you to keep me alive."

When Gagne awoke the next morning, Michel was in the shower, Flaherty had gone to NYFD to get his own shower, and Ghel was nowhere to be found.

"Where's Ghel?" a sleepy-eyed Gagne whispered to Germanowski.

"Huh? Oh, he went out for coffee."

"Oh. Okay."

Two minutes later, Flaherty walked in, saw the agents passed out, and asked the same question. Gagne and Germanowski always thought of Flaherty as the most levelheaded one.

"What?" Flaherty was incensed. "We've been here all night and you let Ghel go?"

Just then Ghel walked in the front door carrying bags filled with coffee and muffins for everyone.

After breakfast, they got in the undercover patrol car and headed to the Brooklyn federal courthouse. Germanowski finally broke the news: "Sorry, guys, but you've got to go to jail." Ghel was furious.

On December 15, Tal Shitrit was arrested in Miami pursuant to New York warrants. Gagne and Flaherty questioned Shitrit at DEA's Miami Field Division. Shitrit claimed he had never heard of Ecstasy.

"Ever heard of Playboys?" Gagne asked.

No, Shitrit said, the only Playboy he'd ever heard of was on videos. The Ecstasy pills Shitrit had tried to send to New York in the intercepted FedEx package were later tested by the NYFD lab and turned out to be nothing more than caffeine and ephedrine—diet pills. Tal Shitrit was sentenced to eighteen months in prison based on the load of Apples he'd delivered in October. The brother from Los Angeles, dealer Mordi Barak, was sentenced to time served after completing five months' home detention.

Michel Elbaz and Israel Hazut were each sentenced to time served after spending eleven months in jail. The Queens dealers weren't involved in heavy-volume trafficking and there were no sentencing guidelines at the time for Ecstasy distribution.

Gagne was satisfied with the outcome. He knew the case against Ghel and Michel was just a launching pad that opened his eyes to Ecstasy's prevalence. Nobody at New York DEA had ever chased after the so-called love drug, but Gagne was determined to follow Ecstasy into the clubs now and see where this thin strand of a lead would take him and his partner.

In wire room 582, a box of index cards contained the names and phone numbers of several dozen people overheard talking with the dealers on the wire. Tacked on the corkboard were the photos of the final targets in the Queens Ecstasy case: Israel "Ghel" Hazut, Michel Elbaz, Tal Shitrit, and Mordi Barak. They were little fish. But they had one tenuous link that Gagne and Germanowski missed.

In the same box, there was a single index card that contained the name of a man the Israelis must have called at least once. Jotted next to the words "bullet supplier" was a New York phone number for drug dealer Steve Hager. His card was copied along with all the other cards, tucked away deep inside the case file, and completely forgotten. It would be years before Gagne would hear that name again. Hager was the one who'd sold Ghel and Michel exhibit number one, the fake Ecstasy—the dextromethorphan Bullets. Hager was an independent Ecstasy dealer who sold, at most, a few hundred pills a week—some real, some fake. But very soon Hager would become a high-volume drug trafficker, making millions of dollars a year by working for the world's most prolific Ecstasy distributor, Oded Tuito.

"LIFE IN THIS CITY IS LIKE LIFE IN PETER GATIEN'S CLUBS"

21 TUITO'S AMERICAN DREAM

HIS LIEUTENANTS CALLED HIM "the Big Guy" and sometimes "the Fat Man," but not to his face. At six feet tall and 200 pounds, there was no denying he was large, but Oded Tuito carried his heft with authority, as if his paunch was a symbol of power.

Tuito had brown eyes, close-cropped black hair, a scar on his forehead, and a larger scar across his forearm. Girlfriends—and he had a few—noticed more scar tissue all over his trunk and legs. He'd had to kill a neighbor in Israel once, in self-defense, he'd say by way of explanation. Israeli National Police have no record of such an incident.

In late 1995, when Gagne and Germanowski started investigating Ecstasy, a handful of Israeli dealers were selling just a few hundred pills a week. That would change when Oded Tuito discovered the kiddie dope.

Oded Nissim Tuito was raised in the coastal farming village of Zerufa, not far from the cosmopolitan port city of Haifa. In 1947, there were more than 870,000 Jews living in the Arab world who were subjected to persecution, anti-Jewish riots, and murder. Some 580,000 Jewish Arabs sought refuge in the newly formed State of Israel between 1948 and 1972. Tuito's family was among the uprooted Algerian Jews who first settled Moshav Zerufa in 1949.

Zerufa means "sown land" in Hebrew. Citrus fruits and field crops were sown by the small farming cooperatives in Tuito's hometown for decades before large companies bought out the small farmers and a real estate boom in the 1980s saw many city residents snatching up Zerufa property to build their outsized dream homes. Today, Zerufa is home to about 530 inhabitants, and the village has managed to retain its rural charm through the land-grab era. The older, boxy stucco homes nestled behind palm, fig, and olive trees still remain alongside the newer multilevel residences that were built in a mix-and-match parade of Mediterranean, Greek, Spanish, and Moroccan styles. Family names, burnished on dark wood plaques, hang roadside in front of every house in Zerufa. Nearly a dozen of the nameplates end in "Tuito."

Oded Tuito was born July 25, 1961, the fourth of six children. He married Aliza Malul and a son was born in 1983. Another boy and a girl would follow. Very little is known among law enforcement sources about Tuito's family or his criminal rise to power, but confidential sources say that Tuito's drug trafficking career began during his service in the Israel Defense Forces, when he was smuggling heroin from Lebanon into Israel.

In 1994, he was convicted of heroin trafficking and was sentenced to three and a half years in an Israeli prison. The judge granted Tuito's request to take a week to settle his affairs before beginning his sentence. A day before he was to report to jail, Tuito fled Tel Aviv using his brother Daniel's passport. He later settled in quiet, tranquil Woodland Hills, California, where he rented a single-level ranch-style home and sent for Aliza and the children to join him.

Tuito dressed thrifty, never flashy. He preferred track-suits and loafers to suits and dress shoes. His friends considered him to be a protective and loving father to his children, and his new neighborhood had all the trappings of suburbia: a wood swing set in the yard, teenagers with heavy backpacks walking to the middle school down the street, and the Motion Picture Retirement Home—senior living for the stars—just a few blocks away. In the summertime Tuito would host family-style barbecues in his backyard at least twice a week. He fed his guests homemade savory meatballs and garlicky Moroccan fish.

In America, Tuito continued to ply his trade. He bought cocaine in bulk from an unknown Colombian connection and marijuana by the pound from a Mexican dealer. Tuito paid $400 a pound for the weed and sold it for $1,000 to a burgeoning network of buyers in Los Angeles, Miami, New York, and Pittsburgh. A member of Tuito's crew would later estimate that he sent about two thousand kilos of cocaine and six thousand pounds of marijuana (the equivalent of about three million joints) to Pittsburgh alone between 1995 and 1997.

Tuito was known as a fierce competitor who muscled out middlemen and rivals. In February 1996, gunmen shot him in broad daylight as he was walking down the street in Los Angeles. Tuito ran for his life and escaped with only minor injuries. The incident was never reported, but the shrapnel scars on his right leg and buttocks would become identifying marks in his criminal record.

Tuito's L.A. ring included trusted friends and relatives who helped him to transport and distribute his drugs and collect the cash. They opened front businesses— Sami's Bakery and MGM Beepers—in a cramped strip mall in the San Fernando Valley. Every few months, Tuito would make personal visits to his buyers in Pittsburgh, Miami, and New York to tend to business and party in the strip clubs and nightclubs.

Tuito told his friends he would never return to Israel now that he was a fugitive. But he still sent money home to his family in Zerufa. Tuito could afford to help his family—business was good. But good is never enough. Tuito wanted legitimacy as an American businessman. And he needed to open a cash-heavy business to hide his drug money behind. A Laundromat or hole-in-the-wall take-out joint would have sufficed for his needs, but Tuito wanted something with cachet—a social spot, where he could invite friends and entertain women. He set his sights on Pittsburgh.

Agent Gagne had never heard of Oded Tuito, but he already shared curious parallels with the man who would one day become his number one target. Gagne and his partner had told Ghel and Michel that they were Pittsburgh nightclub owners, in order to hide their real jobs as drug cops. Oded Tuito wanted to be a Pittsburgh nightclub owner in order to hide his real job as a drug dealer. And Tuito's club-owning dreams were inspired by the glamorous nightclubs he had visited in New York—the very clubs that Gagne and Germanowski were now trying to infiltrate.

22 THE CLUB KING OF NEW YORK

NEW YORK HAS LONG been an electric cultural intersection, a place where artists and civilians come together to indulge in poetry and poison as they write the era's next social chapter, from Harlem's Prohibition-era speakeasies, drunk on jazz and bootleg whiskey, to the mournful heroin-steeped blues clubs of the Village in the forties and the bohemian hippies at Woodstock in 1969, who smoked pot and prayed for peace as they swayed to folk and rock music on a rain-soaked muddy farm. In the seventies, New York gave us disco.

New York's Studio 54 made $7 million in its first year, 1977, by courting celebrity and mastering the art of the velvet-rope rejection. At Studio 54, disco was the feather-haired muse of the lip-gloss set and cocaine coursed through the blood of the satin-and-glitter fashion victims on the dance floor. When the club's owners went to prison for tax evasion three years later, New York nightlife was ripe for the taking. Enter Canadian-born club entrepreneur Peter Gatien, who staked his claim just in time to cash in on the impulsive 1980s-era Wall Streeters and yuppies who believed in spending their hard-earned money in conspicuous fashion.

Peter Gatien was a six-foot-tall willowy figure who dressed in black, chain-smoked cigarettes, and wore an ominous black eye patch that covered a hollow socket. Gatien had lost his eye in a hockey game at the age of sixteen and used the $17,000 insurance settlement to open a discount jeans store. The young businessman soon realized that alcohol earned better profits than jeans. He could make $4 on a pair of $8 jeans or sell 25-cent beers for $1.25, a 500 percent markup. At nineteen, Gatien opened his first club in his hometown of Cornwall, Ontario. He took a dilapidated country-and-western tavern, painted the walls black, put up a disco ball, and transformed it into a rock-and-roll club, with Rush as the opening-night act. (Rush was also, incidentally, Bob Gagne's favorite band.) Gatien went on to open successful clubs in Hollywood, Florida, and Atlanta, Georgia, where patrons danced on a glass floor with live sharks swimming underfoot. New York City was the next frontier.

The Episcopalian Church of the Holy Communion on Sixth Avenue and 20th Street is a grand piece of architecture designed by Richard Upjohn in 1844 as a Gothic-inspired house of worship with fifty-foot-high ceilings and stained-glass windows depicting biblical scenes. The church attained landmark status in 1966 but fell on hard times and was deconsecrated in 1972. By 1983, when Gatien purchased the building, it was Odyssey House, a rehab center and refuge for recovering addicts. Gatien poured millions of dollars into its redesign: the main dance floor and stage area featured a high-tech sound and light system, and a half-dozen staircases led clubgoers to sprawling lounges, DJ booths, cozy alcoves, and VIP rooms.

On November 9, 1983, Gatien opened Limelight to an estimated ten thousand clubgoers. Andy Warhol, Billy Idol, and other celebrities were shepherded past the patrons, who were lined up for six blocks. Some guests arrived dressed as biblical figures. A Jesus impersonator, held aloft on a cross, was refused admission. Religious protestors, horrified at the hedonistic reimagining of a house of God, staged protests outside. Peter Gatien was seen standing on the steps of his church that night, watching the birth of his own American dream.

The same year Limelight was born, a seventeen-year-old Fashion Institute of Technology dropout named Michael Alig was working as a busboy at the club Danceteria on nearby West 21st Street. Michael Alig, like Peter Gatien, had business acumen. As a boy in South Bend, Indiana, Alig sold candy bars out of a shoe box he kept in his locker. He'd buy five for a dollar and sell them at a dollar apiece to classmates, who nicknamed him "Michael the Candy Man." Alig was a five-foot-eight waifish gay teen with soft brown eyes, charismatic energy, a sharp intellect, and a rapacious hunger for attention. Alig had left his small-town roots to reinvent himself in New York. He studied the club business until he became Danceteria's most successful party promoter. Alig would make phone calls all day, then hit the bars at night, handing out free admission tickets to attractive night crawlers. When Alig worked the door, if he thought you were sexy, it didn't matter if you were underage, you were in. And he made sure you had a good time—drink tickets, drugs, and sex were party favors.

Alig soon nurtured a burgeoning circle of suburban youth and trustafarians who delighted in his impromptu mischief. He was their puckish leader, the pied piper of the latchkey set. They embraced adolescence, wearing diapers and pigtails and sucking on pacifiers. They painted their faces with polka dots and dressed up like every night was Halloween. When Danceteria's owners bought the club Tunnel on the Westside Highway, Alig was let loose in the wide open space and his Club Kids followed.

The Club Kids experimented with a life-as-theater aesthetic. Their bodies were pierced and fish-hooked and tattooed like walking artwork. The grotesque was glamorous. Alig's cohort and fashionista staple Ernie Glam created wild outfits (seatless unitards and glittery headpieces fashioned from wires and tubes) that evoked sex, science fiction, and campy fantasy in one-off looks he described as "robo-mutant club freak" or "perverted-sex clown aesthetic."

"The outfits weren't just outrageous, they were just sometimes disturbing," *Village Voice* columnist Michael Musto said in the 1997 documentary *Party Monster.* "I mean, everything from oxygen masks to blood on the face and all these apocalyptic images. The aesthetic was one that was both embracing American capitalism and mocking it at the same time."

When Alig tired of the boundaries of a club space, he took his band on raucous field trips, or outlaw parties. He wasn't the first to throw them, but he made them famous. The inaugural outlaw party was on an abandoned railway bridge, overlooking 99 Tenth Avenue, the future site of NYFD headquarters. Alig and his posse once posted detour signs on the Williamsburg Bridge, handed out cocktails to astonished motorists, and partied in the traffic jam. He held massive outlaw parties inside packed subway cars, where painted clubgoers danced from car to car; and at a Burger King in Times Square, where Alig ordered a hundred burgers for his guests and danced on the tables, sloshing vodka from a plastic cup. He once rented an eighteen-wheel big rig, had it fitted with a sound system, liquor bar, and disco ball, and invited two hundred partygoers to take a ride inside the disco truck. Panicked partiers fainted as the truck reached sweltering temperatures, the sound system crashed to the floor, and the driver failed to hear them pounding to be let out.

In 1987, Alig was twenty-one years old and the most famous party promoter in America. Alig and his Club Kids were written up in the pages of *Time, Newsweek,* the *New York Times,* and *People* magazine. They were TV guests of Joan Rivers and Geraldo Rivera.

Alig's popularity as a promoter coincided with Peter Gatien's initial descent as a club owner. Limelight courted 1980s chic, hosting star-studded Academy Awards parties, William Burroughs's birthday party, and celebs such as Mick Jagger, Rob Lowe, Phoebe Cates, Melissa Gilbert, and Grace Jones. The club had even staged such rock luminaries as Pearl Jam, the Red Hot Chili Peppers, and Guns N' Roses. But a confluence of financially challenging events almost buried Limelight. In May 1985, former Studio 54 owners Steve Rubell and Ian Schrager rebounded from tax evasion to open a rival club, Palladium, luring Gatien's regulars away with free admission. In 1987, a stock market crash drew away the wealthy clubgoers who paid full-price door fees and bar tabs. The club's faithful gay patrons also seemed to be less interested in dancing and more focused on fighting the AIDS epidemic that was ravaging the community. Compounding lackluster attendance was the increasing gentrification of Limelight's former industrial-zone setting. The new next-door neighbors didn't appreciate the big bass beats of Prince's "Erotic City," powered by 14,500 watts through 130 speakers, rattling the windows of their loft apartments at 4:00 a.m. By 1989, Limelight was nicknamed "Slimelight."

But then Tunnel's owner made the mistake of cutting Michael Alig loose, believing the Club Kid scene was on its last legs. Gatien quickly scooped Alig up.

Gatien saw himself as a patron of fashion, art, and music, but unlike Studio 54's gregarious Rubell, Gatien seemed to have little interest in circulating. Alig, on the other hand, was charming and arrogant, the consummate party host, court jester, and people pleaser. Alig played the role Gatien would not. Gatien gave him cash, creative control, and carte blanche to reinvent Limelight. In turn,

Alig remade the Gothic church into a thriving, money-making epicenter of nightlife once again, a feat that officially crowned him king of the Club Kids.

By the early 1990s, crass yuppie materialism had burned out, giving way to the cult of disenchanted youth. The Club Kids' simple message to anyone who felt neglected, misunderstood, or less than beautiful was: "Be somebody." It was the same message of the reefer smokers and dealers in the clubs of Harlem during the Jazz Age who encouraged hipsters to "light up and be somebody."

"There's a place for you," is how Club Kid James St. James described the new scene. "If you feel like you're a freak, if you've got a hunchback, throw a little glitter on it, honey, and go out and dance and show the world that it's okay."

Every time Club Kids showed up on TV, new young converts from middle America would be inspired to run away to New York to join them. Alig let them believe that in his world, they could become freakish superheroes. It was liberating and boundless.

"There was a plan to take over the country by spreading that mentality to other cities," Alig's pal Walt Paper told *Time Out New York* years later. "But unfortunately, everyone got strung out on drugs and ruined it."

In 1991, Alig discovered twenty-two-year-old party promoter and techno DJ Lord Michael, who would herald a new era in Gatien's clubs by flooding the scene with suburban ravers, wannabe thugs, and a seemingly limitless supply of Ecstasy.

Lord Michael was a dark-haired, blue-eyed Italian American who two years earlier had been just Mike Caruso, a college dropout and deliveryman at Mike's Radiator Repair, his father's shop in Staten Island. When a car accident put Caruso out of commission, he took the advice of his DJ cousin and began promoting parties. Caruso got his nickname during a trip to the United Kingdom and Amsterdam with a group of DJs and tour managers. When he exchanged his entire budget of American dollars for pounds all in one shot, he was stuck carrying around a ridiculously large wad of cash. The other managers dubbed him "Lord Michael," and the nickname stuck.

During his trip abroad, Caruso met a blond Grateful Dead–loving British hippie in his late thirties named Meru, who handed Lord Michael his first Ecstasy pill and encouraged him to bring techno back to New York City. Techno was high-energy, aggressive dance music. Whereas regular dance music was about 115 to 120 beats per minute, Techno revved up the floor at 140 bpm. Caruso was energized by the London rave scene—the all-night parties, strobe lights, and thumping techno beats—and the serotonin rush of his first hit of Ecstasy. When he returned to the States, he gave a crateful of techno records to spinners Anthony Acid and DJ Repeat, who played gigs in Staten Island. Michael Alig's boyfriend, DJ Keoki, happened to catch one of Repeat's shows, and soon Repeat, Anthony Acid, and their manager/party promoter, Lord Michael, were working parties at Limelight.

Caruso's popular Thursday night "Inner Mind" parties in Limelight's chapel room attracted the same faithful bridge-and-tunnel crowd that attended his Staten Island gigs. Gatien couldn't have been happier, because the B&T kids from the outer boroughs paid full-price door fees and bar tabs, unlike the Club Kid divas, who didn't think they should have to pay for anything.

In the spring of 1991, Caruso's mentor, Meru, traveled to the States and paid him a visit in Limelight's chapel. Meru gave the new party promoter 150 Ecstasy pills—a free sample to seed the clubs. Caruso would later testify that he handed Ecstasy out at no charge at his "Inner Mind" parties and gave twenty doses to Peter Gatien as a show of respect. The pills were a huge hit. A few months later, Caruso made a deal with Meru for two thousand pills at $8 a pill and sold them for $20 each. Two months later, Caruso placed another order for six thousand pills.

In the summer of 1991, Caruso added a Friday night "Future Shock" party to his Limelight lineup. Record numbers of guests stormed the Gothic church when word got out about Lord Mike's free Ecstasy punch—a special recipe of cranberry juice, vodka, and $1,000 worth of crushed pills. Caruso would mix up the concoction before the club opened and then serve it from a plastic-lined garbage pail around 12:30 a.m., handing the spiked cocktail out in plastic cups from the chapel floor or behind the DJ booth where he spun records. Clubgoers lined up an hour early waiting for the frenzied handout to begin. The punch would be gone in five minutes. Caruso's techno sounds, combined with the club's laser shows and strobe lights, only intensified the Ecstasy-taking experience. A good Friday night saw about three thousand guests. Caruso's "Future Shock" Ecstasy parties could bring in more than four thousand people and $66,000 at the door, plus another $25,000 to $30,000 at the bar.

Limelight's resurgence gave Gatien financial power. By 1992, he had bought up his competitors Tunnel and Palladium and added a fourth spot, Club USA, to his collection. Alig helped to oversee the design of new theme rooms and lounges for his old stomping grounds at Tunnel, including a padded room filled with plastic balls, unisex bathrooms, and a lobby area where a wall of urinals filled with sand served as ashtrays. Alig's parties drew an eclectic mix of gay icons, performance artists, and marginal celebrities who enjoyed rubbing elbows with the fabulous Club Kids. Alig idolized drag queen

RuPaul and Lady Miss Kier of the band DeeLite, who were frequent guests. He threw campy glitter-fraught award ceremonies for actresses Donna Douglas (Elly May Clampett of *The Beverly Hillbillies*) and Tina Louise (Ginger from *Gilligan's Island*).

Alig's famous "Blood Feast" party at Limelight was an ode to the slasher films he grew up watching with his mother, Elke. The theme: dead Club Kids. They covered themselves in fake blood and screamed at guests from glass coffins. Club Kid James St. James wore a bloody white dress and fishnets, scraps of rancid, raw liver hanging from his body, as he writhed on a gurney. Alig—who arrived at his party with a fake bloody axe through his head—was depicted on the party flyers as a dismembered murder victim, with Club Kid doyenne Jennifer "Jennytalia" Dembrow sampling his brains with a fork.

Alig's Wednesday night "Disco 2000" parties at Limelight delighted in debauchery and questionable performance artists such as Ida Slaptor, who would spray champagne enemas onto cheering crowds and pull Christmas lights from her rump. Costumed exhibitionists went by such stage names as Clara the Carefree Chicken, Danny the Amputee, and George the Pee Drinker. Alig was known to urinate on people from the tops of stairwells and trick friends into drinking cups of the same.

Club Kids who doubled as drug dealers dressed up too, including Limelight's most visible dealer, Andre "Angel" Melendez, a Colombian-born hopeful actor who wore a harness of white angel's wings that spanned nearly six feet. The dealers at Limelight and Tunnel offered a variety of pick-me-ups, downers, hallucinogens, and aphrodisiacs. Clubgoers could choose from ketamine (an anesthetic used in animal surgery, which can cause schizophrenia-like symptoms), GHB (a liquid depressant sold by the capful or swig), Rohypnol (the so-called date rape drug), speed, cocaine, and marijuana.

But it was Ecstasy that defined the Club Kid era. Ecstasy induced self-confidence, hypersensitivity, a desire to touch and be touched.

At Alig's "Emergency Room" parties, a tent decorated with a medic cross—tilted to resemble a giant X—was set up on the chapel dance floor. Club Kids Junky Jonathan and Richie Rich dressed in nurse's uniforms and wrote out "prescriptions" for their favorite party-goers.

"I feel depressed."

"You need an Ecstasy prescription!"

"I'm too hyper."

"You need a K prescription!"

"Patients" brought the prescriptions to another area of the chapel where Club Kids in white lab coats would dispense the drugs like Pez candies into the patient's mouth.

Alig even took Ecstasy with his mother, Elke, at his birthday party at Tunnel. They arrived by limo and were escorted in by security as fans screamed, "Michael! Michael!" Alig led his mother by the hand through the club and danced with her on the main floor. Everyone wanted to meet Elke, the belle of the ball. Alig gave his mother a hit of X and told her it would take away her headache. She later told Geraldo Rivera on national television that she enjoyed Ecstasy, that it took away her headache.

At Peter Gatien's height he had a thousand people on his payroll and was making millions of dollars a month in combined revenues from Tunnel, Palladium, Club USA, and Limelight. By some accounts, his clubs earned up to $350,000 a night on cover charges alone. He branched out into movies, executive-producing *A Bronx Tale*, with Robert De Niro, in 1993. He funded several of Alig's creative projects, including *Project X*, a Club Kid magazine, and Klub Kid Kards, campy trading cards with photos, bios, likes, and dislikes. Michael Caruso's card depicted him at the DJ booth with a hit of Ecstasy on his tongue.

When Caruso became a promoter at Limelight in 1991, he made $100 a week plus $3 per guest. By 1994, he was a club director, making $1,400 a week and living his dream. Caruso was photographed, high on Ecstasy, with counterculture icon Timothy Leary. He hosted Moby years before the DJ techno stylist became a Grammy nominee and multiplatinum recording artist. Lord Mike's fame and drug consumption would soar at competing rates. At the pinnacle of his celebrity, he was snorting cocaine four to six times a week, smoking pot six to eight times a week, and swallowing two dozen to three dozen Valiums and Quaaludes a week.

Caruso would later claim he had been corrupted by his sudden success and spoiled by Gatien's passiveness. Club security and employees knew that "the two Michaels" were untouchable—if Alig or Caruso wanted to take bottles of liquor from the bar, throw people out, or comp admission for twenty strangers on a whim, it was best to fall into line. Peter Gatien took the two Michaels to private dinner parties, gave them cash and gifts, paid for trips to Europe, covered their rent when they were late. Caruso shopped for Versace shirts with Gatien's ex-wife; he was friendly with Gatien's daughters; he had personal conversations with Gatien about hockey, football, sex, music, and his relationship with his longtime girlfriend, whom Caruso wanted to marry. He felt like club royalty, the lord of Limelight, which was a far cry from his station a few years earlier, picking up auto parts for his dad's repair shop. Caruso believed that Gatien was a close friend, something Gatien would later deny.

In 1992, Caruso hired Robert Gordon, a small-time thug from Bensonhurst, Brooklyn, to be his personal Ecstasy dealer. He started out by giving Gordon a baggie with twenty-five pills to sell to his friends in the clubs. Soon it was a hundred pills and he could sell to anyone.

"Don't worry about the security," Caruso told Gordon. "Just tell them, 'I'm with Lord Michael.' "

Greed ruled Caruso's heart. He later estimated that he made about half a million dollars in Ecstasy sales from 1991 to 1994. But he didn't stop at drug dealing. He became an accomplished swindler, trying his hand at cellular phone fraud, ATM robbery, extortion, and the hustling and robbing of dealers and friends alike. In the summer of 1992, Caruso agreed to sell twenty thousand pills to a promoter/fashion designer/Ecstasy dealer named Goldyloxx, but when Caruso had trouble coming up with the drugs, he decided it was just easier to rob the guy. Caruso hired two friends to pose as cops and when Goldyloxx sent his assistant, Mr. Purple—known for his purple hair, makeup, and clothes—over to Caruso's Gramercy Park apartment to buy the pills, the "cops" jumped Mr. Purple from behind, pushed him into the apartment, and ordered him to drop his bag of cash and lie on the ground. They handcuffed Caruso to make it seem like a real police bust. After taking his cash, they put Mr. Purple in a cab and told him they were going to let him walk this time. Caruso gave his accomplices $50,000 and spent the remaining $130,000 on studio equipment, $600 dinners, shopping sprees ($1,200 shoes and designer suits), and a first-class trip to Germany with his girlfriend.

A year later Caruso ripped off his main supplier and U.K. associate, Meru, who had sent a sixty-year-old female courier to the States to deliver nine thousand pills. Caruso took the pills and told the woman to go home, that he'd already taken care of Meru's payment. She knew she was being conned, but what could she do?

Peter Gatien's club empire was slowly being overrun by wannabe thugs and drug-addicted divas. And yet

Caruso's status at Limelight never wavered, even when he installed criminals into Gatien's clubs and handed over more responsibility to his right-hand man, Robert Gordon. Gordon wasn't even a club employee, but he was ever-present and known to socialize with Gatien. Gordon and a half dozen or so of his friends became regular "house dealers" working under the protection of club security. Some of the dealers—Totally Todd, Desi Monster, and Gene the Rabbit—came from Club Kid culture, while others were ravers and toughs who just co-opted it, guys like Paulie "Sir Paul" Torres and Frankie "the Baker" Romano. Gordon took the nickname "Stacy," short for Ecstasy.

On any given night, there would be three or four different parties at Limelight specifically tailored to a gay or straight crowd. The house dealers knew that straight ravers liked to buy Ecstasy or ketamine and dance on the main floor, while gay Club Kids took everything from Ecstasy and speed to heroin, crystal meth, and Rohypnol, hanging out mostly in the Shampoo Lounge. A rope at the back of the Shampoo Lounge marked the division between gay and straight parties. There were even separate entrances. The straight crowd entered at the front door on Sixth Avenue and the gay crowd had a 20th Street entrance. The drug dealers worked both sides of the dividing line and didn't care whose money they took.

The nightly distribution of drugs was well organized under Robert Gordon's command. Each dealer was given a plastic zip-top bag of party favors with their initials on it. Frankie the Baker was responsible for cooking the ketamine and giving security drugs, just to keep them happy. And everybody had a station. Gordon sold drugs at the foot of Limelight's first-floor staircase on the gay side. On the straight side, Frankie the Baker was by the two phone booths along the south wall of the TV room. Totally Todd was on the main floor. Sir Paul took the chapel. Gene and a guy known only as "Vinnie" were under the staircase on the main floor. Clubgoers just handed over the money and palmed the drugs.

Dealers worked from 11:00 p.m. to 5:00 a.m. At the end of the shift, Gordon would cash out the dealers on the gay side and Paulie would cash out the straight side. If a dealer started out with a bag of twenty pills, he was responsible for twenty pills. Cash and remaining pills were collected, minus a cut of the profits. If Caruso or Gordon saw a rogue dealer in the club, they'd send someone over to shake the guy down and make him pay $300 or more just for permission to sell. Then they'd whisper to security to throw the guy out and steal his drugs. Sometimes they'd come out and beat the guy up for sport.

By the summer of 1994, trance music had supplanted techno. Trance was a synthesizer-heavy, melodic electronic sound meant to induce trancelike states during the peak of an Ecstasy high. Techno-centric Caruso had less control over the music and found his role diminishing. His drug dealing had also tapered off, and he decided to leave it behind altogether at the encouragement of his new best friend, Chris Paciello, a doe-eyed twenty-three-year-old who grew up in Staten Island and dated the daughter of Johnny Rizzo, one of mobster John Gotti's top soldiers.

Paciello was born Chris Ludwigsen, but he took his mother's maiden name at sixteen, in rejection of his father, a former bouncer and heroin addict who faced charges in the late 1980s for burglary, auto theft, and drugs. Paciello was tight with the Bensonhurst Bath Avenue crew, a gang that got its start robbing pet shops and video stores and paid the Bonanno crime family for the right to invoke its name for protection in disputes.

By twenty-one, Paciello had orchestrated a $300,000

bank heist in Staten Island. A year later, in 1993, he was behind the wheel of a Mercury sedan playing the get-away driver in a botched home invasion robbery in Staten Island that ended with the death of forty-six-year-old housewife Judith Shemtov. Paciello had heard that Shemtov's husband, Sami, a wealthy businessman, kept hundreds of thousands of dollars in a safe hidden somewhere in the house.

Judith Shemtov was sipping tea when she answered a knock at her door and three men with guns shoved their way in and ordered her to "open the safe." Sami heard gunfire and rushed in to find his wife shot in the face with a .45 automatic. The shooter was thirty-year-old Tommy Reynolds, a Bath Avenue soldier so reckless that he had nearly killed a Gambino crime family associate outside a Brooklyn bar two years earlier.

Chris Paciello needed a good reason to leave New York while police snooped around the unsolved Shem-tov murder. In August 1994, Paciello moved to Miami and bought Mickey's, a restaurant previously owned by actor Mickey Rourke, and managed by John Gotti's for-mer driver Carlo Vaccarezza. Paciello invited Caruso to join him as a promoter and club director.

Skipping town seemed like a good idea to Caruso. He had burned a lot of friends and was on the hit list of the Latin Kings gang over a brawl outside a rival nightclub. Caruso accepted Paciello's offer and agreed to put in $25,000 for club renovations in return for a 10 percent share of the profits. When it came time to tell Gatien he was leaving, Caruso lied and said he had run up a $40,000 gambling debt. Gatien wished him luck.

In November 1994, Caruso and Paciello reopened Mickey's as Club Risk. Attendance was lackluster. Pa-ciello lost faith in Caruso's promoting prowess, and Caruso grew increasingly frustrated at being frozen out of management decisions as Paciello took closed-door meetings with Gambino family associates Johnny Rizzo and John D'Amico.

Caruso's girlfriend, who stayed behind in New York, had just given birth to their son and wanted Caruso to come back home. But it wasn't until he found a murder fugitive in his Miami apartment that he decided to cut his losses. Paciello had given Gambino mobster Vinnie Rizzuto Jr. the okay to hide in Caruso's apartment while the FBI and the Columbo family were looking for him for the murder of a capo's son.

By February 1995, Caruso had fled back to New York and vowed to his girlfriend that he would uphold his New Year's Eve resolution not to drink, deal drugs, or be lured back into a life of crime. Caruso was fearful that Paciello would kill him just for what he'd seen and heard.

Fugitive Rizzuto, who was later caught using Caruso's name and identification, would eventually plead guilty to murder and be sentenced to twenty-five years. Club Risk mysteriously burned down weeks after Caruso's exit, and Paciello used the insurance money to open a new club that boasted such celebrity guests as Jennifer Lopez, Donald Trump, Niki Taylor, and Gianni Versace. The handsome nightlife impresario became a celebrity in his own right, dating supermodels and attending charity balls. But years later, the feds finally caught up with Paciello. In 2000, the twenty-nine-year-old club owner pleaded guilty to his role in the bank heist and Shemtov's murder as part of a cooperation deal and was sentenced to seven years. Tommy Reynolds, who shot Shemtov, got life in prison.

By the time Robert Gagne set out to infiltrate Peter Gatien's nightclubs in January 1996, the "two Michaels" were mostly absent from Limelight and Tunnel. Michael Caruso was promoting and producing musical talent and raising his son. Michael Alig was indulging in a heroin and ketamine habit that sapped his attention away from his Club Kids. But the legacy of drug use and dealing they left behind remained firmly in place, nurtured by a new coterie of promoters and dealers.

23 DEEP COVER

NEW YORKERS ENDURED A bipolar winter in 1996. A record-setting blizzard dumped more than twenty inches of powdery snow in Central Park on January 7—the second-biggest snowstorm in New York City history. Schools were closed, travelers were stranded, Broadway shows were canceled, and 26,528 tons of salt was spread on city streets. The icy crush was briefly followed by an unexpected thaw, when bone-chilling 6-degree lows turned to gentle 55-degree highs. Club Kids could return—without fear of frostbite—to the steps of Gotham's nightclubs dressed in skin-exposing lederhosen and peekaboo bustiers.

Gagne and Germanowski decided it was time to return to the scene of their chilling rejection: Tunnel. But if they were going to make it past the velvet ropes, they had to find a way to remedy their D-crowd status. They needed a style makeover.

"Couture" was the cure, according to fashion-savvy Sean Bradley, who was upgraded from "source of information" to full-fledged, cash-earning confidential informant. The agents shopped off the sales rack at the Gap, but Club Kids, Bradley explained, shopped at Patricia Field, a boutique in Greenwich Village that catered to a heroin-chic cross-dresser sensibility. They squeezed $1,000 in costuming cash from DEA and headed downtown.

As they walked down a flight of steps into the flashy East 8th Street boutique, Germanowski was struck by a scent that reminded him of his brother: the smell of designer clothes.

Germanowski had been eight years old when his eighteen-year-old brother, David, moved from Pittsburgh to New York to be a dancer. David was a committed bon vivant, no apologies, no regrets, and straight-up gay. He listened to Barbra Streisand, Judy Garland, and Queen (the one band he and his brother could agree on) and thrilled to the 1970s disco scene. Germanowski, on the other hand, played drums and imbibed a steady diet of Kiss, hair-metal bands, and later hard rockers Godsmack and Pantera. "For the record," Germanowski liked to say, "Scott Weiland, the lead singer of Stone Temple Pilots, should be granted an exemption from the president of the United States to be permitted to use heroin anytime he wants. He was a lyrical genius when he was on that stuff. He got clean and his music stunk." Gagne hated it when his partner said that.

David was thirty-four when he died of AIDS. He had moved back home in the last months of his life to be taken care of by his family. Sometimes Germanowski would put an empty pot in the front yard and let it fill with rainwater. He'd drop a cloth into the pot, soaking it through, and then lay the cool rag on his brother's pale, gaunt face so David could smell fresh rain and grass. He died in 1993, a year after Germanowski graduated from DEA Academy.

"Well, I'm definitely in a gay store," Germanowski said to Gagne as they strolled through Patricia Field.

"What do you mean?" Gagne said. "How do you know?"

"It's not a phobia thing. It's just—designer clothes."

"Can I help you?" a salesman named Kevin asked the agents with a tone of practiced kindness.

"We need trendy, fashionable outfits," Gagne said. "And money is no issue."

Kevin took a long look at the two misplaced muscle-bound gladiators dressed in American Eagle collared shirts, blue jeans, and Nikes. He accepted the challenge. For the next two hours, Kevin guided his guests through style dos and don'ts, with Gagne as his human mannequin. He schooled the agents on the proper selection of quality fabrics, how to coordinate colors, how to accessorize.

Germanowski watched the fashion show from a plush couch, nibbling cubes of cheese and sliced fruit and sipping white-ginger tea, occasionally posing questions like: "So you're saying I don't have to buy all my clothes at Dick's Sporting Goods?"

Kevin dressed Gagne up in seatless pants, Jean Paul Gaultier belly shirts, leather pants, a velvet handmade jacket with cashmere detailing. As he lectured the men on proper fit, Kevin would press his hands slowly along Gagne's muscular back and shoulders, flattening out and rubbing down any lumpy seams. Gagne held his breath and talked himself into a safe place (*Be cool, laugh, make jokes, go along with it*). He tried to act relaxed. Gagne had watched enough *Three's Company* to know how to be "light" (although he felt that Jack Tripper overplayed it sometimes). But he was miles from his comfort zone. He kept telling himself: *This is my job. This is what I have to do.*

"Hey, Kevin, what about that one?" Germanowski said, pointing to a white, puffy blouse with French cuffs. Kevin unbuttoned the shirt off a mannequin and handed it to Germanowski.

"How much is it?" Gagne asked.

"Three hundred dollars."

"Shut the fuck up!"

"No, I'm serious," Kevin said. "This shirt is handmade by two designers here in New York."

"I really want this shirt," Germanowski said to his

partner. "Remember how cool Tom Cruise looked in *Interview with the Vampire*? Dude, I can look that cool."

"No, you can't," Gagne said. "You will never be confused with Tom Cruise."

Kevin eventually left the agents alone with their pile of couture and went to help other customers. Germanowski was still coveting the vampire shirt.

"Okay. We'll get the shirt," Gagne said. "It'll be the marquee piece. We'll just accessorize around it."

The agents picked out their favorite pieces and thanked Kevin for his helpful style tips.

When they got back to 99 Tenth Avenue and opened up their shopping bags . . . disaster. They had blown their entire $1,000 budget on two pairs of pants and two shirts.

"We didn't even get any shoes," Gagne said, bewildered. "Christ—we still gotta accessorize!"

Buyer's remorse sank their spirits. They needed some time to heal and regroup. They went to the gym to lift weights.

"Okay, I have an idea," Gagne said. "We were there for a fashion lesson, and now we know how to dress. So let's take it all back, get our money, and get the same stuff at a thrift store."

Germanowski was quiet.

"Look, what are we going to do if we gotta be in the clubs for months?" Gagne said.

"Fine. We take it all back. But not my shirt."

The agents returned to Patricia Field a few days later. Kevin's steely silence as he rang up the return on each item was painful. They took their government cash out of pricy Greenwich Village and headed to the low-rent East Village, where they snatched up used clothing: a black fur coat with short sleeves, a fuchsia boa, a long black dress, pleather pants, black boots.

While other agents kept flak vests and holsters in their

gym lockers, Gagne and Germanowski's lockers held feathers and leather, giant cross necklaces, and goth makeup. They got their ears pierced. Gagne got a Caesar cut. Germanowski shaved his head and painted his nails black. They were as prepared as they were ever going to be for the mission at hand: infiltrate Tunnel disguised as gay ravers.

Late one night in mid-January, they ate dinner, lifted weights, showered, and suited up in the locker room. Gagne wore black boots, black pants, a tight black spandex shirt, silver double-hoop earrings, and a metal-link dog chain that connected to a leash dangling down his back.

By 11:30 p.m., Gagne was almost ready, applying the final touches: thick black eyeliner to his lids and black mascara to his long lashes. Germanowski was standing nearby, staring pensively at himself in the full-length mirror. Germanowski was wearing combat boots and a long-sleeved black A-line cotton dress that floated below his knees. The "G" tattoo on his calf peeked above black golf socks.

"Dude," Germanowski said, "I can't go out in this."

"What the fuck are you talking about, you can't go?"

"I can't go. This dress makes me look fat."

Gagne studied his partner's outfit. It was true. Germanowski's boxer shorts gave him a lumpy silhouette.

"Nah, it doesn't make you look fat," Gagne said. "We just need to accessorize."

Gagne sifted through their thrift store treasures and retrieved a matching chain-link collar for his partner. He suggested losing the bulky boxer shorts, which Germanowski did.

"Hey! You know what you need?" Gagne said. "You need a wrap."

Germanowski chose a clean black flannel shirt from

their thrift pile and Gagne brushed it down with a metal brush to give it a fuzzy texture.

"Here," Gagne said, helping his partner to place the cover-up around his frame just so. "Now, wrap that around you like a little shawl."

"Yeah," Germanowski said as he looked in the mirror. "Yeah, that really works."

A gruff voice suddenly startled them.

"Now I've seen it all."

A night-duty agent was standing in the doorway of the locker room.

"There's a lot of people that are not shocked by the shit you two do," he said. "But this? This takes the cake."

Most agents at DEA knew that Gagne and Germanowski were doing an Ecstasy case, but the partners had kept their interest in the nightclubs quiet. They didn't want to take any chances of a leak. Rumor was that the leak in NYPD dripped straight to club owner Peter Gatien.

"Look," Gagne said, "don't you repeat a word of this."

It was time to go. Germanowski slipped the dog collar around his neck, Gagne put a pair of dark sunglasses on his head, and the two men exited the gym.

A little after midnight, they rolled up in a cab to the velvet ropes at Tunnel. Darryl Darrin was working the door, the same gatekeeper who'd turned them back the last time.

Here we go, Gagne thought.

They shuffled up to the front, feeling slightly awkward in their outfits. Darrin spotted them immediately and pointed at Gagne.

"How many with you?" Darrin asked.

"Just two," Gagne said softly while holding two fingers in the air with an exaggerated bent wrist.

Darrin reached toward the elbow of the rope and with

a single magical flick of his thumb he opened the spring-clip lock and pulled back the velvet barrier. They were in.

Gagne couldn't believe it. He wanted to shout at Darrin, *Hey! Guess what? We're the same two guys you wouldn't let in last time, ya jerk!* but he kept his cover.

The agents paid $20 admission apiece and stepped through a long hallway, excited to finally pull back the club world curtain. Their senses were overwhelmed as they were swept up into a sea of bodies, swaying to the trance beats pounding through overhead speakers. Red and green laser lights pierced across the swinging flesh on display. The pungent aroma of pot escaped from private nooks. Patrons flitted by, casually opening small vials of drugs, pouring little bumps of ketamine and cocaine on the backs of their hands.

"You want to buy some E?" A stranger approached them at the bar, but it was too early to start buying drugs. They needed to get their bearings, create a mental map of the club geography. They ordered cocktails from the bartender instead, gawking at the $14 in damage, while trying not to gawk at the diminutive Asian man in Coke-bottle glasses go-go dancing on the bar in front of them in a skirt, fishnet stockings, and high heels.

The whole place was writhing with sweaty, glittering bodies in freakish getups. Clothing was optional. Within minutes of their arrival, Gagne was propositioned for a role in a gay porn film. He declined (but was secretly flattered).

"If you change your mind, I'd really like it if you'd come down for an audition," the recruiter said as he handed Gagne a flyer that the agent later pinned to his cubicle. It was a casting call announcement for "Leathermen, Chelsea Boys, Trannies, Glamour Gals, Cross-Dressers, Gym Bunnies, Club Kids, Ravers, Pier Queens, and Other Divas," with the pitch "Everybody Be Somebody."

The agents decided to look around the place and ventured up a flight of stairs. They walked down half-empty hallways, peeking into VIP lounges and jiggling the handles of locked doors. Germanowski noticed a master temperature panel that read 76 degrees. Stifling hot. He later theorized that club owner Peter Gatien was a modern-day zanjero, commandeering the precious water supply. Ecstasy dehydrates, especially if you've been dancing all night in an overheated nightclub. Clubgoers rolling on Ecstasy don't want alcohol, they want water—and water was a major commodity at Tunnel and Limelight. An 8.5-ounce bottle of Evian cost the agents about $8. There was no free tap water at the bar. Gagne was disgusted to discover that only hot water flowed in the bathroom. (Gatien's attorney would later deny such claims and maintain that both taps were always working.)

As he toured the cavernous space, Germanowski broke the numbers down in his head: Tunnel could hold more than four thousand people, and if they averaged $15 apiece at the door (taking into account reduced admissions), then Gatien was making roughly $60,000 in door fees on a good night before cashing out the employees. If just 25 percent of those overheated patrons bought nothing more than an $8 bottle of water at the bar, add an extra $8,000. That's $68,000 just for opening his doors and selling some water.

The agents were down at the main dance floor now, watching the scene. Men and women wearing little more than Ecstasy smiles tuned out reality as their pulses kept apace with the high-energy, aggressive beats.

Germanowski got lost in thoughts of his brother: *David, you would have really liked this music.*

He felt Gagne nudging him.

"Dude," Gagne said, "what's the deal with *that*?"

Standing on a speaker to Germanowski's right was a sinewy dancer in a skimpy G-string, his feet shoulder-width apart, and his hips gyrating back and forth as his penis slapped the entire length of his thigh. Germanowski's jaw dropped. As the happy dancer pranced on his stage, a couple nearby was smoking weed and making out on a couch. Behind them, a young man was giving a blow job.

The agents needed a break. Germanowski was feeling tense. They headed to a dimly lit second-floor bathroom, where they took a moment to relax, breathe, and drop their undercover personas.

"I just need to stand like a man for a minute," Germanowski said as he took a swig from his $7 vodka and orange juice. Gagne snickered at the sight of his partner standing like a man in a tight black dress and black lipstick.

"What?" Germanowski said. But he knew he looked ridiculous. In fact, now that he looked at Gagne's outfit, it wasn't even that outrageous. Gagne had just thrown on some tight black clothes and a dog collar. How did *he* end up wearing the dress tonight?

Fucking Jedi mind tricks.

Gagne was still laughing. Germanowski glimpsed his own black-nail-polished meaty fingers gripped around the plastic cup of booze and started laughing too. Soon they were both doubled over from body-shaking howls, tears streaming down their faces, mascara be damned.

"Will you pee on me?" a voice begged in the dark.

"Jesus Christ!" Germanowski jumped. A man was lying on the floor nearby, strung out, masturbating, and staring at Germanowski.

"I want you to piss on me!" he barked as he touched himself.

"That's it," Germanowski said. "Let's go."

"Okay," Gagne said, still cracking up. "But, I mean, here's your chance. When are you going to have the opportunity to piss on a guy ever again?"

"You know what? Hopefully never."

Gagne looked at the surly masturbator sprawled out on the sticky ground.

"Piss on me! Piss on me!" the man screamed. He couldn't have been more than twenty-three, totally wasted, and absent all dignity. It made Gagne angry. He had nothing more to laugh about.

"You're right," Gagne said. "C'mon, let's go."

24 FAMILY SECRETS

BEING A DRUG COP gave Gagne a deep sense of purpose. He knew the drug war was unwinnable. He couldn't stop people from trying drugs. But he believed he could rein in the opportunities. He believed in the mission because he'd seen the effects of drugs and alcohol on his own family. His sister Sherrie had been the first to fall.

When Gagne entered into duty as a DEA agent in February 1991, Sherrie was a senior in high school. In a class of 161 students, Sherrie graduated twenty-fourth and boasted many accomplishments: Rhode Island honor society, class treasurer, student council, captain of cheerleading, a star basketball and softball player. She smoked pot on the weekends. No big deal. But when she got to college, Sherrie lost interest in her studies. She wanted to have fun and party with her friends. She started hitting the snooze button, skipping class, and smoking weed all day. She dropped out by the end of the semester, moved back to Pawtucket, got a night-shift job as a cashier at a supermarket, and fell into a deep depression. One winter, she tried to end her life, swallowing sixty-nine sleeping pills and walking out to a snow-covered beach, where she lay down to die. As the pills began to take hold, Sherrie saw a quarter resting near a pay phone and decided it was a sign to call friends for help. She survived after her stomach was pumped. She moved in with her father and his new wife and tried to put her life back together, but she soon fell back into her old habits.

In 1992, Sherrie was arrested in Montreal. She had run away to Canada with a girlfriend and got caught at a check-cashing kiosk trying to pass checks she had stolen from her father. Gagne called the police in Montreal, and they agreed to let his sister go as long as a family member came to collect her and take her back to the United States. Sherrie's mother and sister made the drive to Montreal. Gagne and his siblings pressured their father not to press charges against Sherrie for the roughly $2,000 she had stolen from him. He left all of her belongings in trash bags on the front porch.

Sherrie agreed to enter an outpatient rehab center, but after six months inside, she met a man who introduced her to crack cocaine and the two of them left the program to spend their days getting high in his aunt's house. When their money ran out, she broke into her mother's house and stole a VCR to pawn. She also stole checks from her brother Ronnie, who reported it to the police.

At some point, Sherrie woke up next to her crack-addicted boyfriend, looked around at the mess they were living in, and decided this was not her life.

"I'm leaving," she told him. "I'm going to get help."

He put his hands around her neck and told her he would kill her before he let her go. Sherrie escaped and ran home to her mother, Irene, to ask for help. Irene was a rock. She never said no to her children.

It was 1994. Gagne had just completed Navy SEAL training on the Mississippi River, learning how to do river patrols and ambushes in preparation for a Snowcap tour in Bolivia, when his mother called: "I need to talk to you about Sherrie."

Gagne was practically on his way out the door to start his assignment. He turned around and called his supervisor, Frank Fernandez, who told him to go home and be with his sister; he could pick up the next tour in Peru.

Sherrie was facing jail time because breaking and

entering into her mother's home had been a violation of her probation on check forgery charges. When Gagne got home, he drove Sherrie to the courthouse for her hearing. He was barely able to contain his confusion and anger.

"What are you doing?" he barked at her in the car on the way. "Do you know what I do for a living?"

"Uh—yeah, I get that," Sherrie said sarcastically.

"I want suppliers. Who are you buying from?" Gagne said with the earnestness of a shiny new agent.

"Are you nuts? These people know where I live. Do you want to get me killed?" Sherrie said. "You want someone? Just drive around this area, Bob. They're on every street corner."

Gagne pictured his baby sister driving at night in dangerous neighborhoods, cruising past prostitutes and johns walking the buckled sidewalks, and rolling her window down to buy enough crack for her and her boyfriend. It shook him to his core.

At the courthouse, he made an emotional plea to the judge for court-ordered rehab.

"Listen, this isn't her. She's got a drug problem, she needs some help."

Sherrie spent forty-two days in prison and then entered an inpatient drug treatment program. It was what she wanted too. She was fighting for her life. She knew she couldn't wage that battle while living at home.

Jail and rehab sobered Sherrie and gave her a clean start. She became close to a man she met while in treatment—someone who had previously dealt drugs and was determined to leave that life behind. Relationships in rehab were forbidden, but that never seemed to stop anyone from falling in love. They fell—so deeply that they got married, raised a family, and stayed sober. Flourished, even.

Sherrie was tough. And she had siblings and a mother who constantly checked in, kept her close, and supported her recovery. Gagne knew that her success was the exception compared to a lot of the young people he encountered in his work who were struggling to overcome addiction. He was certain that 90 percent of the people in jail on drug possession charges were victims of absentee fathers and fractured families, or maybe they just didn't have anyone in their life who cared about them enough.

When Gagne infiltrated the club scene, he encountered more young people caught up in drugs and drug dealing than he had ever witnessed in his five years as an agent. But he understood why they indulged in it. They wanted to feel alive. They wanted to be somebody. Sometimes when Gagne looked in the mirror, all he saw was the son of a drunk meat salesman. Nobody special. He knew he could have taken that same road. But that would have been surrender.

25 INVESTIGATING THE CLUBS

GAGNE AND GERMANOWSKI COULDN'T rely solely on Sean Bradley's information about the alleged drug dealing at Tunnel and Limelight. They had to witness drug activity for themselves so that if the case went to trial, they could testify with firsthand knowledge. They needed to unravel the alleged distribution hierarchies and find out: Who were the main conspirers? How were the profits divvied up? How long had it been going on? Was club security in on it? Was club management involved? Was Gatien profiting from it?

Gagne and Germanowski would make more than a dozen visits to Tunnel and Limelight from January to May 1996 to try to answer these questions. Sean Bradley introduced them to suspected dealers, Club Kids with names like Victor Extraordinaire, Totally Todd, and Larry Tee. The agents traded government cash for Ecstasy pills and brown glass vials of ketamine during buy operations in the Asian Room, the Cha-Cha Room, the Library Room. Once in a while they would see Peter Gatien walking uninterested through the crowd or standing on a balcony stone-faced, watching the dance floor. He always wore black, always had a cigarette between his fingers, the black eye patch strapped around his head.

When Gagne and Germanowski worked the clubs, they carried no guns, badges, or IDs—just their undercover licenses and cash. Sometimes they would go alone, no backup and no buys, just trying to look like newbies to the scene instead of feds clocking the illegal activity.

Gagne reached deep into his undercover bag of tricks for excuses to avoid sampling the drugs offered to him: *I'm on probation and I have to pass my drug test tomorrow; I'm rolling on E and don't want to mess up my buzz.* Gagne's mother, Irene, a nurse, gave him special eye-drops that dilated his pupils for that drug-induced wide-eyed look.

The agents determined that drug consumption was most prevalent in the VIP lounges, which is also where they were at most risk of unwanted sexual advances. The trick was to keep moving. But Gagne always got tagged in the Police Room.

Club Kid Michael Alig had christened the Tunnel's Police Room in honor of the botched NYPD raid back in September 1995. The yellow caution tape and barricades left behind had been refashioned as decorative motifs. Stickers that read "Drug Use Will Not Be Tolerated" were stacked in such a way that the word "Not" was obscured. Gagne was impressed by Alig's creativity.

The Police Room gatekeeper was a towering drag queen named Gravity. Thin and strong, well into her thirties, Gravity was at least six feet tall barefoot, but she preferred platform heels. She always remembered Gagne and Germanowski on their return visits. Especially Gagne.

"There you are! I've been looking for you," Gravity said one night as the agents passed by. She was wearing a tight police shirt with a plastic NYPD badge and a police hat. A billy club hung from her waist. She grabbed Gagne by the arm while her other hand reached for his crotch. Gagne resisted the urge to roll his fist into a ball.

"I'm with somebody," Gagne said in a fake fey voice.

"Is he with you?" Gravity asked Germanowski.

"Not me!" Germanowski said as he blew a kiss at Gagne and walked away.

Germanowski enjoyed dangling his "boyfriend" out to Gravity like chum, watching him squirm as he got molested. Gagne employed his "keep talking" trick, engaging Gravity in conversation while evading her big octopus hands. Germanowski would eventually tire of the torture and come back to collect him.

"He *is* with me," Germanowski said. "I just wanted to give you a minute to enjoy him."

"Oh, thank you, child," Gravity purred.

"Dude," Gagne whispered to Germanowski, "I'm going to kick your ass later."

"All right," Germanowski said, pretending to flirt with Gagne in front of the other boys.

"Can't you play the jealous type?" Gagne would plead.

Their partner, Jay Flaherty, would join them on occasion, but Flaherty never dressed up or painted his nails.

"It's just a whole different world that I never knew existed," Flaherty said to his partners after a couple of visits. "It's different. I guess I'm not really crazy about the people. It's not like I can ask them what the score was in the Knicks game."

Their boss, Lou Cardinali, was supportive, but he pushed them to hurry and finish the case as he rushed through embarrassing payment vouchers for rubber clothes and makeup.

"How can I send this to the front?" he yelled at Gagne one day. "You're buying clothes for undercover at the pet store?"

Gagne scratched his head as he studied the receipt. "Oh, yeah! I had to buy a dog collar."

When Germanowski came to work with a dyed blond stripe down his head, Cardinali ordered him to wear a hat.

"And if you see anybody from the front, any executive staff walking around, turn around and run the other way," Cardinali said. "Go in the bathroom, the elevator, I don't care—just run."

Cardinali dropped into Limelight one night to see

what his agents were up to. He hung out by the bar and watched as a performer took the stage and sat down in front of an electric synthesizer. The man banged away on sound-effects keys—*crash! smash! bang!*—as he screamed at the top of his lungs into a microphone: "I fucking hate you! I fucking hate you!" and broke beer bottles over his head as a finale.

"What the hell is this?" Cardinali mumbled to himself.

A clubgoer sitting next to Cardinali turned to him and asked: "Man, is that talent or what?"

"You guys are outta your minds," Cardinali told the agents the next day. "Just get this case done."

Gagne and Germanowski were in uncharted territory, and every time they'd get a break, Gagne would declare: "See? It's a sign." Like the time they discovered that directly across from Tunnel was the FBI's car maintenance garage. The FBI agreed to let them use the corner lunchroom to set up surveillance equipment—a low-tech time-lapse video camera trained on the window of Gatien's office. His shades were typically closed, but on April 12, at about 11:00 p.m., the blinds were open and he was sitting at his desk. Germanowski and Gagne were watching from their FBI-sanctioned perch when Gatien appeared to lift a silver tray up to his face.

"Did you see that?"

"How could I see it? You have the binoculars. Gimme 'em."

"Hold on, hold on."

"Would you give me the fucking things?"

"He just did a fucking one-hitter. I saw him."

"I didn't see it. I could only see his head go down."

One of the agents believed he saw Gatien lean down to snort cocaine off the tray using a cylindrical "one-hitter" device. Gatien was about twenty to twenty-five feet from their surveillance post. They had no video to prove it. But Germanowski wrote it up in a report of investigation and Gagne would later swear to the one-hitter incident in an indictment.

Problem was, more than a decade later, each agent would recall the conversation clearly, but each believed that it was the other one who was holding the binoculars. Meaning that both agents saw Gatien with a tray and some kind of head movement, but neither agent could specifically recall seeing Gatien actually snorting drugs through a one-hitter. In retrospect, they would both admit it was a shaky observation, heightened by the fact that they were desperate to catch Gatien doing something illegal.

Confidential sources later told Gagne and Germanowski that Gatien carefully avoided all talk and personal use of drugs inside his clubs.

Outside his clubs, however, Gatien indulged in an expensive crack cocaine habit. Every few months, to let off steam, he would rent a $3,000-a-night, three-bedroom suite at the Four Seasons hotel and go on drug benders. He would invite Michael Alig, Michael Caruso, and other club employees to hole up with him. His credit card added up thousands of dollars' worth of room service, caviar, champagne, and hookers who accepted American Express. Michael Alig almost died during one of Gatien's hotel parties after he passed out and turned blue from a heroin overdose. Gatien denied ever having a serious problem.

"How am I supposed to be operating four clubs, managing 1,000 employees, and have a crack problem?" Gatien told *New York* magazine in 2006. "Have I partied every now and then? Yeah. It's been documented. Anywhere from zero to three times a year, I would rent a hotel room and do my thing. Am I proud of it? No. But there it is."

Among the "documented" evidence the government collected was a Dear John letter Gatien received from the general manager of the Four Seasons on March 23, 1996. The tone of the letter was civil but clear: Gatien had outlasted his welcome.

> Dear Mr. Gatien,
> As a result of your recent visit, the Governor Suite suffered damage which I have detailed in the attached breakdown. Unfortunately, this is not the first time that we have incurred damages following your visits. . . .

Gatien's final Four Seasons party had set him back nearly $18,000 for three nights' stay, room service, phone calls at all hours, gift shop purchases, and repairs to the carpets, silk panels, and entertainment center. A private note was filed in Gatien's guest history profile: DO NOT ACCEPT A RESERVATION UNDER ANY CIRCUMSTANCES.

Gatien's hotel bacchanals had reached a destructive crescendo only matched by the chaos in his club empire. In the days of Michael Alig and his merry band of Club Kids, Ecstasy dealing was the province of gentle artistic youths who gave away as much as they sold. But when Michael Caruso entered the scene, he helped to install a new league of pill pushers.

By the time Germanowski and Gagne infiltrated the clubs, it wasn't just wasted Club Kids passing out the love drug for free; it was also serious drug dealers standing in the shadows, not dancing, not drinking, not talking, not smiling. The agents didn't know it at the time, but the majority of Ecstasy in New York was brought in through Israeli organized crime networks. The Israelis sold the pills in bulk to a wide net of third-party dealers who had direct connections to clubgoers, party promoters, and select "house dealers" who could sell drugs under the protection of club security. The Israeli dealers had managed to evade detection by police and DEA by always working a few layers back, never directly selling in the clubs or on the streets. (The exception, of course, was rookie dealers Ghel and Michel, whose sloppy solicitation of a livery driver put Ecstasy in Gagne's sights.)

By May 1996, the agents were wiretapping the phones of three suspected house dealers: a carpenter and club bartender named William Civalier, a musician and clubgoer named John Charles Simonson, and promoter Joseph "Baby Joe" Uzzardi.

Uzzardi had attended his first Limelight party when he was a senior at North Caldwell High School in New Jersey. Now, at twenty, he was a New York University student and Ecstasy dealer who promoted his own parties at Gatien's clubs and appeared to be jockeying for the position of heir apparent to Club Kid Michael Alig. Baby Joe wasn't even old enough to legally drink, but he was deeply entrenched in the drug scene. Listening to Uzzardi's wire was sheer tedium—he received hundreds of calls a day from people wanting to be put on his guest list for reduced admission. Gagne began to better understand what it felt like to be in Uzzardi's shoes.

"He's really just, like, this dweeby kid with artistic flair," Gagne said to Germanowski.

"Yeah, so?"

"I mean, he's buying expensive clothes, making good money, everybody thinks he's fucking cool because he's a promoter. But listen to him: he's trying to do good in school and maintain some semblance of a student life, but people are calling him at all hours, he's up until four in the morning, banged out on E, and working his parties. You can just tell he's always tired."

"He's eccentric and pompous is what he is," German-

owski said. "Are you listening to this right now?" Uzzardi was placing a food delivery order over the wire.

"*I want one order of kung pao chicken, but very few
peanuts,*" Uzzardi said.

"*No peanuts?*" the hurried order taker asked.

"*No, I said very few peanuts. I want peanuts, just
very few of them. And I want two egg rolls, crisp but not
burnt. Also, I want the chicken to be mild, not spicy.*"

Gagne rolled his eyes. Point made. Germanowski
couldn't help himself—he put on his best Baby Joe
voice, picked up the phone, and dialed the Chinese
restaurant back. "Hi! I need to change my order. Did I
say mild? I meant extra spicy! The more hot sauce the
better. Thanks!"

26 "DON'T TRUST HIM"

ON FEBRUARY 25 AT about 1:20 a.m., Gagne, Germanowski, and informant Sean Bradley were at Tunnel, sitting on couches in the Police Room, watching the drugs go by. A dark-haired man with a pierced nose palmed three white pills into a buyer's hand; a woman passed a joint around; an Asian male inhaled white powder off his thumbnail. Baby Joe Uzzardi didn't seem too concerned, considering the bad news.

Uzzardi told Bradley to let his "friends" know that club management just got word that NYPD was sending undercovers to Limelight to catch people with drugs.

"As long as you guys stay in here, in my room, you'll be safe," Uzzardi said, believing his VIP lounge was impenetrable to narcs.

Club director Steve Lewis entered the Police Room at 4:05 a.m. and whispered into Uzzardi's ear. At forty-three, Lewis was one of the top bosses at Tunnel and Limelight and worked directly under Peter Gatien.

Uzzardi approached Bradley and the agents with a grim look.

"The police just arrested a few people at Limelight, and Steve wants you to leave in case they come here," he told Bradley, explaining that Lewis was making him kick out all his personal drug runners—including Bradley. "I told him you weren't selling drugs, that you were just a guest. But he said it didn't matter."

Germanowski and Gagne shot knowing looks at each

other. If club management knew that police were planning an operation at Limelight, then there had to be a snitch at NYPD. DEA didn't even know undercovers would be at the clubs that night.

Drug arrests never slowed down dealing in the clubs for very long. Five days later, on March 1, Gagne bought nine more pills from Uzzardi at Limelight for $270.

Between March 6 and 8, the agents listened to wiretap suspects Uzzardi, Civalier, and Simonson making deals for the purchase of thousands of Ecstasy pills with cute names like "Cat's Eyes," "Fruitloops," and "Toucans."

On April 30, Gagne was perched on scaffolding at East 51st Street and Madison Avenue with a camera equipped with a 200 mm telephoto zoom lens. He snapped shots of Civalier and two dealers meeting in the foyer of St. Patrick's Cathedral and trading cash for drugs.

Over the course of their investigations, Gagne and Germanowski learned that several dozen suspects sold and distributed Ecstasy in the clubs. It seemed as if everyone was getting in on the profits: from hardened cons, bartenders, and bouncers, to college-age clubgoers who lived at home with their parents and hid the drugs in their dresser bureaus, and a pretty twenty-eight-year-old financial analyst for Paine Webber who sold X on the weekends. Even Uzzardi's NYU roommate was overseeing business when Uzzardi was out of town.

Late one Friday night, March 29, Gagne and Germanowski were parked outside Uzzardi's NYU dorm while Sean Bradley was inside playing junior undercover narc. Gagne fiddled with the radio dial, looking for something with a country twang or classic-rock guitar riff. (His partner's preference for hard metal B-sides drove Gagne up the wall.) As he absentmindedly scanned the stations, Gagne was thinking about Bradley's most recent stupid move. Bradley had called the agents to ask "for a friend" how to beat a drug urine test. They knew Bradley had to stay clean as part of his plea agreement, which meant occasional drug tests.

"For your friend?" Germanowski had been at his desk, talking on speakerphone, with Gagne leaning over his shoulder.

"Um—one of Jessica's friends," Bradley mumbled, putting the onus on his girlfriend.

"Okay, here's the deal." Gagne shot his partner a *go-with-me* look. "There is one way. It's a special drink your friend has to make."

"Okay. What is it?"

"Well, first," Germanowski piped up, "you gotta mix one cup of warm olive oil with three tablespoons of Texas Pete's hot sauce."

"Olive oil?" Bradley said.

"Yeah. See, the olive oil will get right into her bloodstream and it's thick enough to stay in it for days, if not weeks, and then all the hot sauce will dilute whatever else is in her system."

"Olive oil and Texas . . ." Bradley was writing it down.

"Texas Pete's hot sauce," Germanowski said, trying not to laugh as Gagne nudged him.

"Wait," Gagne said. "You forgot the vinegar."

"Right. The vinegar, very important."

"After you mix the olive oil and the hot sauce," Gagne said, "then you gotta stir in eight ounces of vinegar and a handful of crushed almonds."

"Crushed almonds," Bradley carefully recited.

"Tell your friend to drink it all in one sitting," Germanowski said.

"And then immediately eat a glazed donut," Gagne added.

"Got it. Thanks, guys!"

As much as the agents enjoyed putting one over on their troublemaking protégé, Gagne sensed an incurable duplicity in Bradley. Something just wasn't right.

"Don't like him," Gagne told his partner in the car that night outside Uzzardi's dorm.

"C'mon, don't you feel bad for the kid?" Germanowski said. "No dad. His mother doesn't care about him. He'll latch on to anyone who pays attention to him. Nobody in the clubs likes him because he's Sean Bradley; they like him because he'll bring in counterfeit money and forty Ecstasy pills and give it all away."

"Don't trust him," Gagne said.

Germanowski didn't trust Bradley either. But he took him on in a personal way, tried to be a mentor to him, even spoke on his behalf to an admissions counselor at a junior college when Bradley decided he wanted to go back to school. Germanowski thought the kid just needed a chance.

At about 11:35 p.m., Uzzardi and Bradley exited the dorm and got into a brown Buick driven by another suspect. They drove up Third Avenue, stopped at 33rd Street, and pulled up next to a parked gray Mazda. The dreadlocked dealer in the Mazda nodded at them and then led the caravan to an apartment building on East 66th Street. Bradley and Uzzardi were told to wait in the car while the dealer and his posse went inside.

By midnight, the deal was done and the players and cars dispersed. Bradley told Uzzardi he was heading home, then he jumped in a cab to meet Gagne and Germanowski back at DEA. Bradley told the agents that the other dealers had sold Uzzardi 1,230 pills called "Golds," which they had just purchased from an individual who lived in the 66th Street apartment building. Uzzardi would sell three hundred Golds at Tunnel that same Friday night. The next day, Uzzardi's wire was burning up with bad news: the Golds were laced with LSD. "Everybody got sick last night . . . the whole Tunnel was sick. Tunnel is *not* a good place to do acid."

Uzzardi was furious. He wanted only *the best* Ecstasy at his parties. But there was little he could do about it. He knew he was buying drugs from people who boasted a history of assault charges. He wasn't about to go looking for the mysterious source at the 66th Street apartment. Gagne and Germanowski stayed focused on the clubs rather than spin off a separate investigation into the Golds dealer. They just didn't have the resources to follow every single lead. But if they had, they would have eventually discovered that the source of the LSD-laced pills was Oded Tuito's New York soldier, Steve Hager.

27 THE ECSTASY CONNECTION

STEVE HAGER KNEW THAT his presence intimidated people. At six foot four, he was the tallest member of his family. His T-shirts were XXXL, and he weighed over two hundred pounds. A thin scar ran along the left side of his face. He had a husky, thick-Hebrew–accented voice that would rise in anger at the slightest provocation. In truth, however, Hager was more bark than bite: the scar on his face was from a benign childhood accident and his menacing voice was betrayed by a slight lisp.

In 1977, when Hager was seventeen, his parents moved the family from Israel to America, hoping to give their children a life without war and the threat of violence. His attorney mother and rabbi father, who still call him by his given name, Zvi, settled in Brooklyn and became American citizens. Hager did well at yeshiva but he was more interested in chasing trouble. He thrilled to the first movie he saw in America: *Midnight Express,* the story of a hashish trafficker who fights his way out of a Turkish prison. His earliest job was to drive wiseguy Italians around his neighborhood. From that point on, he was a paid member of organized crime and knew to keep his mouth shut about it. He had a job in a restaurant ("nothing special") and in a clothing warehouse ("nothing much") and would never reveal what those jobs really entailed, except to say that "nothing was on the books."

In the early 1990s, Hager met an Israeli named Jacob Orgad on the beach in Fort Lauderdale. Orgad was born Yakov Ben Moha in Morocco, but everyone called him "Koki."

Hager and Koki reconnected in a Hollywood nightclub a few years later. By then, Koki was the owner of J&J Beepers and the self-proclaimed "Beeper King" of L.A. He had also become a close associate and bodyguard for Hollywood madam Heidi Fleiss, and he supplied Fleiss's high-priced call girls with beepers and drugs. Hager was impressed.

Koki had a close friend from Haifa named Itzhak "Jackie" Cohen, who moved to Los Angeles in the late 1980s and began selling Ecstasy in 1990 or 1991—just a few hundred pills here and there. It was Jackie who introduced Ecstasy to his inner circle of friends.

Steve Hager first tried Ecstasy with Koki and Jackie in Palm Springs in 1993 or 1994. The first pill had no effect on him. The second pill felt good enough to try more. Cocaine was Hager's real love; Ecstasy would become his living.

In 1994, Koki introduced Hager to an Indian nightclub owner named Rick Singh. Singh was making a fortune in Houston distributing fake Ecstasy pills (mostly made of caffeine and dextromethorphan). Young ravers, blissed out from dancing all night under strobe lights and glow sticks, often couldn't even tell they'd ingested the equivalent of a double-shot espresso. Hager bought batches of Singh's pills to sell to midlevel dealers in New York because he knew that fake pills were safer.

"Who is going to arrest me for selling diet pills?" Hager liked to say. But he would switch to pushing real Ecstasy after Koki and Jackie introduced him to Yehuda "Judy" Ben Atar, a Jerusalem native who had connections to hit men back in Israel.

Judy had been dealing small amounts of Ecstasy with Jackie in Los Angeles, but he was ambitiously seeking bigger profits. Judy knew that Hager had established buyers in New York. In 1995, Judy and Hager struck a partnership: Judy would procure the pills from an Israeli contact named Yosef Buskila, whose brother, David, aka "Dudu," was based in Holland and had chemist connections. Hager's job was to line up his stable of cash-on-delivery buyers in New York City, Boston, and Columbus, Ohio.

Getting the pills from Holland to America was simple—Dudu just mailed them. Hager went out one day and rented private mailboxes all over Manhattan under a fake name. Judy would order up a load of pills from Buskila, Dudu would send them from Holland, and pretty soon packages of fresh Dutch pills would arrive at Mail Boxes Etc. locations across the city. Hager and Judy picked up five thousand to ten thousand pills at a time from their private mailboxes. They'd buy the pills for about $7 each and sell them for $9 to $11 apiece. One shipment of ten thousand pills earned the partners a minimum of $20,000—all for the cost of a mailbox rental.

Judy brought Jackie in to help coordinate the New York shipments. Hager brought in a Canadian-born Israeli named Sean Erez to count and sell pills and do grunt work.

Sometimes Hager would fly to Amsterdam to bring Dudu cash payments. He'd wear women's exercise tights underneath his regular clothes and slip the bills between his skin and the snug body-hugging tights. He'd put more cash inside his cowboy boots. Hager could body-pack up to $50,000 per trip. But he never carried pills, he never met with Dudu's suppliers, he didn't know who the pill brokers or chemists were, and he didn't care. It was better not to know.

Hager still made occasional purchases from Rick Singh's bunk Ecstasy supply—like the Bullets that ended up being DEA exhibit number one in the Ghel and

Michel case, and the LSD-laced Golds that left Uzzardi's party patrons sick and tripping all night. But Hager didn't know any of the club dealers personally; they were naïve prey who paid cash up front.

Koki, Jackie, and Judy first met Oded Tuito in 1994 through their mutual chain of criminal contacts—but they had heard his name before. Tuito was known as a major dealer in Israel who came to the States with built-in connections. Tuito drew the L.A. dealers into his work and his personal life with invitations to his back-yard barbecues and family-style dinners during the high holidays. In turn, Jackie and Judy introduced Tuito to Ecstasy.

At the same time that Gagne and Germanowski were uncovering the Ecstasy networks within the clubs, Oded Tuito was injecting MDMA into his own drug distribution network. The thirty-four-year-old narcotics entrepreneur had made good money trafficking cocaine and marijuana, but Ecstasy made him better money, bigger profits. He sent a cousin to live in Belgium to coordinate pill shipments from Holland to the States and to oversee the drug couriers. His Pittsburgh buyers were more than happy to add X to their regular pot and coke orders. In Florida, Tuito partnered with Israeli nationals Meir Ben-David and Yosef Levi, who flooded the Miami clubs with his pills. Tuito was flush with cash.

In March 1996, while Gagne and Germanowski were spying on Club Kids in New York, Oded Tuito put up $170,000 for a building on the South Side of Pittsburgh. It would be the future site of the club Vertigo. He put the names of two trusted L.A. associates on the deed. Tuito imagined Vertigo as a swanky nightclub with a restaurant on the first floor, dancing on the second, and a VIP lounge on the third. He poured half a million dollars into building renovations and naïvely let his flaky drug-dealing associates oversee the work. Renovations dragged on. He needed more revenue.

When Tuito struck a partnership with Judy to sell Ecstasy to his New York contacts, Steve Hager suddenly became a de facto associate of the Fat Man.

Hager was selling Tuito's Ecstasy pills in early 1996, but he didn't actually meet the Fat Man in person until late 1996 or early 1997 at a nightclub in Miami.

"I'm a friend of Judy. And I know who you are," was all Tuito said to him.

Judy later told Hager that Tuito was "a good guy," which Hager took to mean "goodfella" in the Italian sense. Tuito's reputation preceded him. He was known as a vicious and brutal competitor. Everybody had heard the story about the man who fled to Holland after a deal with Tuito went south: the guy was later found in an alleyway, stripped naked and unconscious. Some claimed that Tuito or Judy arranged to have the guy kidnapped, injected with a mind-numbing dose of heroin, and left to die. The victim survived, but he refused to divulge the facts of his ordeal to authorities. Investigators later surmised from a review of hospital records that he was simply a junkie who had nearly killed himself, not the victim of drug warfare. But it didn't matter, because the more the story was retold, it became a part of Tuito's mythology—you don't cross the Fat Man.

Hager's profile hit a tipping point when he began selling Tuito's Ecstasy pills. He went from selling ten thousand pills a week tops to selling as much as two hundred thousand pills a week. He bought gold jewelry, wore Versace, and drove a Mercedes-Benz with black leather seats. He changed apartments at least once a year, partly out of a desire to keep moving and partly to keep people guessing at his whereabouts. He was thirty-five and he felt like he had finally made it. He modeled himself after the men in his favorite mob movies—partying like a wiseguy, dropping $100 bills on the valet, buying the right to trash the place and still be invited back.

When Koki, Judy, and Jackie would meet up with Hager in New York, Hager would bring them to his favorite restaurant, Baraonda, an Italian eatery on the Upper East Side that attracted a mix of Euro-riche men and women with a wild streak. Koki always brought an entourage of busty, bubbly girls. Hager had his own crew of dancers and other women who tripped into his life. The maître d', Bruno, would greet them warmly. Being a gracious host, Bruno never asked what Hager and his friends did for a living. They were loyal customers who stayed late and spent a lot of money. He had the chef make them special Mediterranean plates, fish that they would eat with their hands, Israeli style. Hager washed his meals down with Rémy Martin and an eight-ball of coke before they hit the strip clubs. Bruno knew Hager was a nice guy with a short temper. He'd seen him turn tables upside down if someone didn't say "excuse me" for bumping into Koki.

Hager spent most of his money on drugs and entertaining women. He had a crew of girls he liked to spoil—Carlie, Nikki, Max, and especially Jackie. Jackie Suarez was a twenty-six-year-old Puerto Rican beauty who smoked Parliament Lights and didn't need to fill the space between them with idle chatter—unless they were sharing coke, and then conversation was good.

Unlike most of the women in Hager's entourage, Suarez didn't strip—she was a receptionist at a construction company. Suarez's roommate introduced her to Hager one night, and the next day Hager took Suarez shopping for perfume at Barneys: a bottle of Chanel No. 5 for her mother and Allure for her. It was easy to see why Hager was drawn to Suarez—she was seductive and witty, but she also had a kind of melancholy loneliness about her.

Tuito would one day see the same in Suarez and want her for himself, changing Hager's life once again.

Suarez got Hager right away: he took care of the girls and paid their way, and the women kept him company. Suarez quit her job and spent her days hanging out in Hager's apartment. He was fun and exciting at first, like a giant child who had a ton of toys (drugs) and playmates (strippers). She didn't ask a lot of questions about his business. She thought of him just as he secretly thought of himself—like a character from a mob movie. He seemed to spend his days fielding international calls on four different cell phones, always yelling at someone in Hebrew and arguing in numbers. By midnight, she and Hager would hit the strip clubs, dressed to the nines. Hager would escort Suarez and his entourage of strippers to Tunnel or Limelight after hours, where the women liked to dance. Hager spent thousands of dollars on table service, bottles of liquor, drugs, and champagne. They never had to wait in line.

Gagne and Germanowski never saw Hager, Tuito, Koki, or any of the Israeli dealers in the nightclubs. But even if they had, none of the men would have particularly stood out in their minds. The agents were watching the dealers—the men in the shadows who were not dancing, not smiling, just waiting to make their next sale. And Tuito's associates never needed to sell Ecstasy hand to hand in the clubs. That was nickel and dime. Tuito and Gagne were on parallel tracks on opposite sides of the law. They would have to cross paths. But for now, they were worlds apart.

28 CLUBLAND ARRESTS

ON MAY 14, 1996, Gagne signed his name at the bottom of an eighty-page affidavit in support of arrest warrants for twenty-four individuals suspected of conspiring to distribute MDMA at Tunnel and Limelight. He put club owner Peter Gatien, director Steve Lewis, and promoter Joseph "Baby Joe" Uzzardi's names at the top of the list of suspects.

"As the owner and president of the nightclubs, Gatien sought to ensure that MDMA and other controlled substances were readily available to patrons, while ensuring that the distribution of controlled substances would not result in prosecutions of nightclub employees," Gagne alleged in his affidavit.

He described the Ecstasy buys that he and Germanowski witnessed and engaged in while inside the clubs, and he recited excerpts of drug-related conversations from about 110 different phone calls—a small sampling—that were intercepted. He noted that DEA received intelligence from seven different confidential sources who alleged that Gatien had an insider on his payroll alerting him to NYPD undercover activity at his clubs. Gagne also claimed that he and his partner witnessed Gatien doing a one-hitter of cocaine in his office.

A federal judge approved the warrants the same day. All the arrests had to be made at once.

Gagne, Germanowski, and Flaherty were the main three agents on the case, but other DEA agents as well as officers from NYPD and other law enforcement agencies would take part in the arrests in order to do them in one clean sweep.

At 6:00 a.m. on May 15, 1996, Jay Flaherty rang the doorbell at Peter Gatien's three-story town house on 10 East 63rd Street with a warrant in hand. Gatien came to the door and was met by two DEA agents, two NYPD detectives, and an IRS agent. Flaherty read him his rights on the way to the New York Field Division, where Gatien was photographed, fingerprinted, and processed. The forty-four-year-old club king wore his black leather eye patch in his mug shot photo, his arms crossed, his face belying a tired defiance.

At 7:45 a.m. he was transported to the federal courthouse in the Eastern District of New York, where he was charged with conspiracy to distribute MDMA. He pleaded not guilty and spent nearly two weeks in jail before posting $1 million bond.

At 9:00 a.m. Flaherty's team served a search warrant at Tunnel. Flaherty seized employee records, computer disks, tax documents, receipts, and notebooks from Tunnel offices. In the basement, agents collected several hundred empty plastic capsules that were scattered on the dance floor.

Earlier that morning, at 6:00 a.m., Germanowski and three other agents had arrived at Baby Joe Uzzardi's girlfriend's apartment on Houston Street with an arrest warrant for the twenty-year-old party promoter.

"I recognize you from the clubs," Uzzardi told Germanowski when he came to the door.

Uzzardi was cooperative from the start. He told the agents that in his two years working for Gatien's clubs he had learned from club director Steve Lewis that the two main requirements for successful parties were "good music and good drugs." The better-quality drugs they offered, the more money everyone would make. Uzzardi claimed that the promoters knew this, security knew it, and Gatien knew it too.

A team of agents searched Uzzardi's NYU dorm room and seized a metal Altoids box containing 165 pink pills and 23 more pills in a plastic bag.

Steve Lewis was at his girlfriend's house in Philadelphia when he got a 7:00 a.m. phone call from Gagne, informing him he was wanted on drug charges. Lewis didn't believe it. He had recently defected from Gatien to go work for a competitor, and he feared Gatien might be setting him up for some kind of reprisal. He called Gagne's supervisor, Lou Cardinali, who assured Lewis it was not a setup and he should turn himself in immediately. Lewis took the next train back to New York and surrendered to DEA.

Gagne and Germanowski played it friendly with Lewis. They told him that they knew he was "a good guy" and that they were really after Gatien. Lewis spilled puddles of gratitude and damaging information, according to DEA reports and court documents. Lewis told the agents that the drug dealing at Tunnel and Limelight had been going on for as long as the clubs had been open. He said he never sold drugs, but he purposely allowed certain "house dealers" to sell. He said he feared Gatien was attempting to have him killed because of everything he knew. Gatien had a lot of connections, Lewis said.

"What kind of connections?" Gagne asked.

Gatien paid people off for information and assistance, Lewis claimed. One week before the September 1995 NYPD raid, Gatien had a closed-door meeting with a detective from the Manhattan South division named Mitch Kolpan. Afterward, Gatien allegedly told Lewis "something was going to happen involving the NYPD," but not to worry because he would provide Lewis with an attorney and pay his expenses if he was arrested. The only thing Gatien asked in return, Lewis said, was that he tell the authorities that Gatien knew nothing about narcotics sales in his clubs. Gatien also allegedly told Lewis to make sure not to let any "house dealers" in the clubs. The dealers were absent during the raid and Lewis was not arrested.

Now Lewis was thanking Gagne and Germanowski for finally arresting him, saying he had wanted to "end all this," that he knew the drug dealing was wrong, and he had wanted to go to the police on his own, but he was apprehensive about a reprisal from Gatien. The agents thanked him for his candor.

A judge would later grant Lewis's motion to have his post-arrest statements suppressed because they were made without the presence of his attorney. Gatien's attorney has characterized NYPD detective Mitch Kolpan as a friend of Gatien's and a guest at his clubs but denied any knowledge that he ever passed any information to the club owner about NYPD activity. Kolpan retired immediately after Gatien's arrest and was never charged with any wrongdoing.

A few days before the agents took the case down and made their first wave of arrests, Germanowski was in the wire room, monitoring Uzzardi's line, when he heard a troubling conversation between Uzzardi and John Charles Simonson.

"You gotta come down here," Germanowski called over to Gagne. "We've got a problem."

Germanowski replayed the call for Gagne.

"*Your fucking friend Sean just ripped me off,*" Simonson told Uzzardi. "*Who does he think he's dealing with?*"

"No!" Gagne said. "Are you kidding me?"

The agents would never reveal to Bradley what the

next steps in their investigation were, but Bradley was sharp, and they must have slipped up somewhere. From what they could tell, Bradley had done one last buy with Simonson—off the books and without permission—of two hundred pills for $2,000. They met at a phone booth at 33rd Street and Eighth Avenue. Simonson left the pills in a bag inside the booth. Bradley took the pills and left behind an envelope of cash. By the time Simonson opened the envelope, flipped through the wad, and saw forty $1 bills rubber-banded in front of a stack of white slips of paper, Bradley was long gone, on a train to New Jersey. Bradley must have figured Simonson would be in jail soon and unable to come after him. But Bradley didn't know the agents had been tapping the dealers' phones.

"*Where does this guy live?*" Simonson went on.

"*What are you going to do?*" Uzzardi asked.

"*It doesn't concern you, but I'm going to find him and take care of it, so he'll never do that again.*"

Gagne sighed and told his partner: "We better find the little bastard first."

On Saturday, May 11, at 7:30 in the morning, Gagne, Germanowski, and Flaherty tracked Bradley down in an apartment next to a strip bar off Route 35 in Hazlet, New Jersey.

"Sean, we gotta talk," Germanowski said. Bradley invited them in. His girlfriend, Jessica, and three other strippers were half dressed, sitting around a giant glass bong in the living room getting high. The agents spoke to Bradley alone.

"Where are the pills, Sean?" Flaherty asked.

"I don't know what you're talking about," Bradley said.

"We know you ripped off John Charles for the pills," Germanowski said.

"No, I didn't, G! I would never do that!"

Bradley went back and forth with Flaherty and Germanowski, denying that he'd stolen drugs from Simonson, denying he had any pills. Gagne had had enough. He saw a tiny kernel of toast on the table, pointed to it, and began to speak in a low voice to Bradley.

"You see this crumb, Sean?" Gagne said. "This crumb is your life, and every time you lie to us, I'm gonna push this crumb closer to the edge of the table. And when it goes over the edge—you're done."

That is so corny, Germanowski was thinking. He and Flaherty exchanged arch glances.

"Where are the pills, Sean?" Gagne said.

"I'm telling you," Bradley said with big eyes, "I don't have 'em."

"I'll ask you again." Gagne dropped his fist on the table, pressed his index finger on the crumb, and slowly pushed it toward the edge of the table. "Where are the pills?"

"I don't know! I swear—I didn't do it!" Bradley's face was red, his breathing faster.

Are you fucking cartooning me? Germanowski thought. *How is this actually working?*

"This is your last chance, Sean!" Gagne lifted his fist, threatening to crush the tiny crumb and push it off into oblivion. "Where are the pills, Sean?"

"Okay! They're upstairs! They're upstairs!" Bradley cried, tears streaming. "I'm sorry! I just did it because John Charles is just such a jerk. I hate him!"

Bradley tearfully escorted the agents upstairs and recovered about five hundred pills from his jacket.

"Sean, you did not eat fifteen hundred pills last night," Gagne said. "Where are the rest?"

Bradley pulled more bags of pills out from hiding spots around the apartment. Before the agents left, they broke the bong and seized a small glassine envelope filled with marijuana, a film canister containing Blue and Whites, and

185 plain white Ecstasy pills—exhibit numbers thirty-five through thirty-seven—which were deposited in the DEA evidence vault.

Bradley was called into DEA on Monday, May 13. Gagne informed him that they'd tried to talk to the prosecutor, but there was nothing they could do. He'd already been given too many chances: in April he had been arrested for trying to sell ketamine and ephedrine pills he was passing off as Ecstasy to an undercover officer at the same mall where he was first busted for counterfeit bills. The agents had tried to help then, even speaking on his behalf at his court hearings. But now they were done with him. He was under arrest for distributing Ecstasy and lying to federal agents.

Bradley teared up as his former handlers processed his belongings and took his mug shot picture and fingerprints. Germanowski discovered a clear plastic jug in Bradley's backpack. It was filled with a liquid recipe resembling motor oil and crushed almonds. He shook his head and smiled. He had tried his best with Sean.

29 INVESTIGATING THE INVESTIGATORS

PETER GATIEN WAS OUT on bail, running his clubs and preparing for trial. He seemed to be fighting an uphill battle against a city that had once welcomed him. He was under investigation by the IRS for tax fraud, he was in danger of losing his liquor license, and club attendance was down 20 percent. He insisted he had no knowledge of drug use in his clubs and believed he was being unfairly singled out, a victim of his own success as the club king of New York.

"What standard do you think a club should be held to?" Gatien told the *New York Times*. "If somebody in the subway pushed somebody over the tracks, nobody comes down on a subway station. In a nightclub, it's 'Let's close them down.'"

The agents saw it differently. They knew Gatien wasn't selling or directly profiting from the drugs, but they believed he was actively supporting their sale and distribution—creating dangerous conditions—in order to maximize club attendance and profits.

At a press conference immediately following the May 15 arrests, the U.S. attorney told reporters that Gatien's clubs were "virtual Ecstasy supermarkets," and claimed the club owner had "installed a management structure at the Limelight and the Tunnel designed to ensure successful distribution of Ecstasy to nightclub patrons.

"We determined that the dealing of drugs at both of these establishments was not just a lucrative sideline but was really the centerpiece of the operation," U.S.

Attorney Zachary Carter told reporters. "To a certain extent, it can be fairly said that these clubs existed to distribute these substances. . . . The drugs were the honey trap that attracted these young people to the club in the first place."

Months later, Carter's hard-boiled quotes were the inspiration for an irreverent "Honey Trap" party—an obvious snub at law enforcement, a crack at the government's assault on nightlife.

But law enforcement had had enough of the drug use associated with the club scene. Mayor Rudolph Giuliani and Police Commissioner William Bratton were on a cleanup mission, putting more cops on the street and increasing arrests for even minor offenses such as drinking alcohol in public. When New York City's crime rate in 1995 registered its steepest drop in twenty-three years, Bratton credited police for taking on not just criminal behavior but outright seediness.

"We were probably the most permissive and tolerant city in America for social deviancy," he told the *New York Times*. "Now we're one of the least tolerant cities when it comes to the abuse of public spaces."

The failed police raid on Limelight in 1995 had been a sore spot in NYPD's quest to make New Yorkers safe from drug dealers and other "social deviants." When Gagne and his partners' investigations received heavy rotation in the press, NYPD gladly joined forces with DEA.

Giuliani and Bratton had already revived the city's nuisance abatement laws to successfully close drug dens, brothels, and illegal gambling operations. Under the same laws, city attorneys could get a judicial order to close the clubs if it was determined that drugs were rampant and sold in an "open and notorious" manner. Gagne and Germanowski lent their confidential informants to NYPD as part of covert buy operations inside the clubs. The DEA informants would be used to help bring undercover NYPD narcotics detectives into the clubs and help facilitate drug buys. Just three open and notorious buys would merit a judicial closing order— and it didn't take long to get there. But before police came in with the closing order, the agents made another round of arrests.

On August 20, 1996, at 3:45 a.m., seven DEA agents, including Gagne, Germanowski, and Flaherty, and several NYPD detectives arrested two bouncers at Tunnel for conspiracy to distribute drugs.

"What is going on here?" Gatien came out of his office to confront the agents.

"We're federal agents—" Germanowski began to explain.

"Right, right," Gatien interrupted. "I knew you were coming."

Gatien asked to make a copy of the arrest warrants. The agents insisted on escorting him to the copier machine, so he invited them up to his office.

Gatien turned and looked at Gagne as they walked up the stairs.

"Aren't you Gagne?" Gatien asked.

"Yes," Gagne said. He noticed that the club owner had pronounced his name "Gawn-yay," as Gagne's own French Canadian ancestors would have. Nobody called him "Gawn-yay."

"Why would you lie like that?" Gatien said, presumably referring to the one-hitter allegation in the affidavit—the shaky claim that the agents had observed the club owner snorting drugs off a silver tray in his office. "Man to man, I want to know why you would swear to something that was not true. Man to man, you should not do that. I do what I do, and you do what you do. If you are going to go after somebody and get them, you should be man enough to do it without lying."

"What you believe is true and what I believe is true are

two different things," Gagne said before feeling a nudge from his partner, who had been suddenly distracted by the strange scene just outside Gatien's office. Two men were sitting on the floor, counting money out of two industrial-sized black garbage bags. The bags were filled to the top, stuffed so tightly that they couldn't be drawn fully closed. As they pulled out crumpled wads of tens, twenties, fives, and ones and folded them into neat piles, neither man noticed that officers had just walked in.

"You are the other one that has been here?" Gatien asked.

"Yes, Matt Germanowski. I'm a special agent with DEA."

"I know what is going on in the other clubs. Why in the hell aren't you doing something with them?" Gatien said. "I know you are doing your job, but you shouldn't have to ruin somebody's life and turn it upside down like this to do your job. It's starting to become ridiculous."

Three days later, Tunnel and Limelight were shut down by the NYPD after DEA's informants had helped them to meet the requisite number of undercover buys. A spokesman for Gatien told the *New York Times* that the authorities had purchased illegal drugs a total of five times. "To get only five buys, Mr. Gatien should get a medal," he said.

Peter Gatien cut a deal in court: he agreed to pay $30,000 in fines to the State Liquor Authority, forfeit the $150,000 bond he'd put up after the police raid in 1995, and hire the consulting firm Kroll to monitor security in the clubs and develop a plan to ensure that preventing drug activity became a priority to club management. For this, Tunnel was allowed to reopen, but Limelight, his famed Gothic church, was ordered shuttered for a year as punishment for the rampant drug dealing.

It was a small victory for law enforcement, and the agents were pleased that their informants had helped to bring about Limelight's temporary closure. But it came at a cost. One of the informants who helped shut down Limelight was a twenty-four-year-old hustler named Sean Kirkham, who would soon bring a dark chapter into the agents' lives.

Kirkham first contacted DEA looking for work after reading about Gatien's arrest in the tabloids. Kirkham had been a party promoter for clubs in New York, the Hamptons, and Miami. He knew the scene and the players, and he checked out as a past informant for Miami DEA. He seemed legitimate to Gagne and Germanowski, so they signed him up as a paid source. Kirkham began arranging meetings and taping his conversations with Ecstasy dealers who sold in the clubs. He got doorman Darryl Darrin to talk about management's alleged knowledge of drugs in the clubs. But when Kirkham's usefulness waned, when his stories stopped adding up and the agents stopped calling—that's when Kirkham turned against his handlers. Unbeknownst to Gagne, Germanowski, and Jay Flaherty, Kirkham kept a recorder in his backpack and had been secretly taping the agents during their meetings.

Clubland author Frank Owen would later profile Kirkham for the *Village Voice*. In their jailhouse interview, Kirkham described himself as a Canadian descendant of Inuits who was orphaned as a child. As a teen, he traveled through Europe, working as a waiter in Paris, a tour guide in Salzburg, a doorman at a club in Greece. He said he was deported when his visa ran out, and he moved to New York at nineteen, where he slept on the streets and in homeless shelters. He attended NYU for two years and worked at Club USA in New York, where he first met Alig and Gatien. He moved to Florida and infiltrated the Miami Beach Russian Mafia and the South Beach nightclub scenes, rubbing elbows with nightlife celebrities and Colombian cocaine traffickers while feeding tips to law enforcement for cash.

Kirkham was a master at mixing truth with small lies. Kirkham also claimed to reporter Owen that the agents gave him a weekly clothing allowance to keep him in designer clothes and that they let him have his pick of costumes and accessories from the DEA wardrobe room. He said that Germanowski taught him how to detect and avoid surveillance by using reflective surfaces, à la *The French Connection*. He said that he and Gagne partied together in Miami at Chris Paciello's nightclub.

Kirkham was certainly paid cash for his information as an informant, but he never received a clothing allowance and there is no "DEA wardrobe room" (the agents had to wear the same thrift store duds for almost five months). Gagne recalled seeing Kirkham in Miami once, but they never went club hopping. And while Germanowski enjoyed imagining himself as a cloak-and-dagger undercover with mirrors in his pockets, he had to admit that he just wasn't that cool.

In the fall of 1996, Sean Kirkham placed a call to Peter Gatien and dropped a bombshell: he said he had taped proof of government misconduct by the agents. Gatien hung up and called Benjamin Brafman.

Brafman was a savvy defense attorney who got his start as an assistant district attorney in the Manhattan DA's office. As enticing as Kirkham's claims may have been, Brafman wasn't going to take the bait. He passed the information to the assistant U.S. attorney who was prosecuting the Gatien case, Eric Friedberg.

Friedberg knew that the Gatien investigation was a high-profile case, and if their DEA agents were guilty of using corrupt means to bring Gatien to prosecution, Friedberg needed to get a handle on the situation as quickly as possible. Instead of confronting the agents, he targeted them: a secret FBI investigation was opened on

Gagne, Germanowski, and Flaherty. As the agents prepared for trial, they had no idea they were getting the Chinese wall treatment from the federal prosecutors they spoke with almost daily.

Likewise, Sean Kirkham didn't know that Gatien was leading him straight back to the feds. In September 1996, in a bizarre collusion between the prosecution and the defense teams, Brafman arranged for Kirkham to meet a man named "Pat Cole," who was introduced as one of Gatien's private investigators. Cole was really FBI agent Pat Colgin, the lead investigator in the case against Gagne, Germanowski, and Flaherty.

Colgin pretended to buy Kirkham's tapes on Gatien's behalf. The FBI listened to the tapes carefully and got an earful of mundane debriefing meetings. Kirkham said he had more tapes. It seemed he was looking for a handout any way he could get it. FBI bought five more tapes and heard nothing amounting to misconduct. Maybe that should have been enough to clear the agents, but Gagne *did* have a reputation for being a maverick.

It was decided that—just to be sure—they would put the men to a test. In October 1996, Colgin asked Kirkham to set up a sting on his former DEA handlers.

Germanowski got a call shortly afterward. Kirkham was full of news, said he had an idea he wanted to share. Could they meet him right away?

"What's up, Sean?" Gagne said as he and Germanowski slid into the booth at a diner in Manhattan where Kirkham was waiting.

Germanowski noticed a man with gray hair sitting nearby. He had no setup at his table—no silverware, ice water, food, or menu. Germanowski thought it odd, but he tucked it away.

Kirkham told the agents that if they really wanted to nail Gatien, he had a plan: he would get Gatien alone in his office and secretly record their conversation. Then he would take the tapes to a friend who could edit them to make Gatien "say things."

"What are you saying to us?" Germanowski asked.

"I can make a tape of Peter," Kirkham said, "and if we can make it go to ten minutes, we can make that tape say *whatever* you want."

Kirkham was practically winking at the mysterious man in the next booth when he felt Gagne's sledgehammer fist in his chest. Kirkham's shoulders popped forward, his neck tensed, and his eyes bulged as he gasped for breath.

"Don't ever say that to us again," Gagne said in a contemptuous growl.

Germanowski stifled his laughter as Kirkham coughed for air.

"Sean, we're not going to arrest you," Germanowski said. "But you're done. Your day with us is over."

Back at the office, Germanowski's first call was to AUSA Eric Friedberg to tell him they had to drop Kirkham as an informant.

"I need you to get Gagne and Flaherty and come to my office right away," Friedberg said. "And bring your supervisor."

"Ooo-kay," Germanowski said. "But, Eric, do I need an attorney too?"

"Not anymore." Friedberg laughed.

When they arrived at Friedberg's Brooklyn office, the mysterious diner, Pat Colgin, was waiting for them. Friedberg introduced Colgin and explained that the agents had been targets of an FBI investigation on corruption allegations. But it was all over now, Friedberg said. Kirkham's tapes were bogus, and when they refused his offer at the diner, the agents were officially in the clear. (Colgin was kind enough to refrain from mentioning that Gagne had punched Kirkham.)

Gagne was stunned. Friedberg seemed to be in a cele-bratory mood. But the agents were stone silent. Their in-tegrity had been under attack based on the claims of a drifter con man. They had been working alongside Friedberg for three months, never knowing he was in on the secret. It was a crushing revelation, and it would damage their working relationship with the prosecutor through to the end of the case.

"Hey, listen, these are yours." Colgin offered Gagne Kirkham's audiotapes.

"I don't want them," Gagne said coldly. "You keep them."

On October 16, 1996, Sean Kirkham was arrested for lying to federal agents. He pleaded guilty, fled to Van-couver, and then turned himself in three months later. He was sentenced to fifty-seven months in prison. Kirkham was blacklisted in DEA databases, but it didn't stop him from trying. His name would come up again nearly a decade later, when he tried to sell the FBI infor-mation about the London train bombings and terrorist activity in Bulgaria. His information proved to be false.

30 THE CASE EXPANDS

GAGNE HAD A LASERLIKE focus on Peter Gatien. He couldn't rest until he'd questioned every witness, gathered every shred of evidence, and developed a complete picture of the drug dealing inside the clubs and Gatien's alleged role. The more Gagne learned, the more he wanted Gatien to go down. If the stories he was hearing from former employees and house dealers were to be believed, then the club owner had a Machiavellian grip on nightlife. Sometimes it was just petty accusations of Gatien's dirty dealings—like driving down business in rival clubs by sending people to start fights or making calls to the fire department to have competitors shut down for overcrowding violations. But then there were stories about young men and women, passed out from drug use, who were put out the back door, dumped into a cab with $20, and sent away—all in an effort to avoid unwanted police attention. (Gatien's lawyer has repeatedly deemed these characterizations "totally false.")

After debriefing dozens of witnesses, Gagne and Germanowski came to see that the drug dealing at Tunnel and Limelight had been at its height in the years prior to their investigation—the Alig and Caruso years. The U.S. attorney's office wanted to expand the case, and the agents got a new directive: conduct an exhaustive historical investigation into the clubs. It would help to enhance their charges against club king Peter Gatien. It also meant that Gagne and his partners would work on the case for almost two years before it went to trial.

31 THE KING OF THE CLUB KIDS

MICHAEL ALIG'S NAME WAS not on the original May 15, 1996, indictment that led to the first wave of arrests. Gagne and Germanowski never even saw the legendary Club Kid during their time inside the clubs. Alig was rumored to be in rehab, rumored to have killed his drug dealer. But Alig enjoyed stoking rumors, and nobody took him seriously when he joked that he had murdered and dismembered Andre "Angel" Melendez.

Melendez, the six-foot-tall Club Kid in angel wings, sold cocaine and Ecstasy as a house dealer for Alig, and he also delivered drugs to Gatien's hotel parties. Melendez disappeared on St. Patrick's Day, 1996. The police had no solid leads beyond rumors of Alig's involvement. *New York* magazine, the *Village Voice,* and the gay nightlife magazine *Next* wrote about Melendez's alleged demise that summer as if it mirrored the demise of New York nightlife.

"This is exactly the sort of lurid, nocturnal goings-on that even we don't enjoy discussing . . . the type of gruesome clubworld unpleasantness that makes us want to turn in our Roxy Gold Card and never again leave the house after dark," columnist Perry McMahon wrote in *Next.* "Oh, for those heady, carefree days when night-crawling was simply seedy and not potentially lethal."

In November, Gagne and Germanowski finally tracked Michael Alig down at the Chelsea Hotel, where he was crashing with a friend and planning his comeback to the club scene. He opened the door. He was thin, pale, and unshowered.

"Guess who we are?" Gagne said.

"I have no idea," Alig said. "You just look like a couple of regular beer-swigging, football-watching guys to me."

"Well, yeah, we are," Germanowski said, amused. "But more importantly, guess who else?"

When they identified themselves as DEA agents, the light left Alig's eyes. They spent the next hour telling him what they knew about his role bringing drugs into the clubs and about his rumored involvement in Angel Melendez's disappearance. They leaned on him, saying they were ready to arrest him right there on drug conspiracy charges. If he went to trial and lost, he could get up to twenty years in prison, they told him. Of course, the agents knew that there weren't even sentencing guidelines yet for MDMA, and even though the maximum for drug conspiracy was twenty years, it was more likely Alig would get closer to five to seven. But by the time they were done talking to him, Alig believed he was facing twenty to life and a possible needle in the arm for Melendez.

Alig shed a few tears as he considered his choices. If he was willing to cooperate in the case against Gatien, he might get a sentence reduction. He might even get off with probation. But it would mean betraying his friend and mentor.

"Okay, I'll talk."

Alig surrendered to DEA on November 18 and pleaded guilty to drug charges as part of his cooperation deal. He was given bail and would be sentenced at a later date.

Gagne liked Alig. The kid was artistic and bright. But he had to get clean. Alig had been on methadone, trying to kick heroin, and Gagne chastised him for trading one poison for another. Truth was, Alig was secretly using both with equal fervor. He couldn't get through one day without getting high on something. Anything. "You gotta go cold turkey," Gagne would say. But Alig couldn't do it.

Gagne, Germanowski, and Flaherty met with Alig regularly, sometimes at the Chelsea Hotel, sometimes in a park near the financial district—an area they knew no Club Kids inhabited. He led the agents through an oral history of the drug dealing in Tunnel and Limelight: how it started, who was involved, and what he believed Peter Gatien knew. He gave the names of his personal house dealers. He described how they advertised Ecstasy and ketamine on party flyers to get more people to show. He claimed that Gatien personally approved the flyers, and he sent the agents to a print shop near NYU where they found copies of old flyers with the initials "PG" on them.

Alig described Gatien's hotel parties in vivid detail, as if reliving his glory days. He told them about how he and his best friend, a pretty bleached blonde named Cynthia Haataja, aka Gitsie, would rip off the king-sized bedsheets and build a teepee in the living room. He and Gitsie would huddle in tight under the crisp white sheets and smoke crack cocaine together. Alig claimed Gatien once hired hookers and made them wear collars and leashes, walking naked on all fours, while barking like dogs. Another time, Alig claimed, Gatien ordered a girl down on her hands and knees and placed a mirror on her back so they could all take turns snorting lines off her body.

Alig never talked about Angel Melendez, and the agents didn't push. They were prosecuting a drug case. The murder case belonged to NYPD. But one day, as they sat on a bench near Battery Park, Germanowski turned to Alig and asked him point-blank: "Mike, why'd you kill Angel?"

"It didn't happen," Alig said. "It's not what anybody thinks. I didn't plan any of it."

To Germanowski, Alig seemed on the verge of breaking, maybe even confessing—if he trusted them enough. Not long after, during a routine debriefing, Gagne and Germanowski told Alig they wanted to show him a photo of an unidentified body that had washed up along the East River.

Alig fidgeted nervously.

"We just want you to study the photo," Germanowski said, "tell us if you think it's Angel."

Gagne laid the picture on the table. It was a crude, underexposed snapshot depicting the upper half of a corpse, lying on an orange police stretcher on the dirt, presumably just fished out of the river. The victim's wet, gray flesh had mostly slipped off—or been nibbled off—down to cartilage and bone. The arms had been severed at the elbow and stuck out like stiff drumsticks. The skull and hollow eye sockets were exposed. Kernels of loose teeth were still holding tight onto an angular jawbone. There was a steel collar around the victim's neck and chains around his trunk.

Alig laughed.

"That's not Angel," he said defiantly.

Gagne and Germanowski realized in that moment that Alig knew exactly what had happened to Melendez, and when he saw the photo of the only lead police had, he knew they weren't even close. He had won that round, and the agents had lost a little credibility. He didn't say any more about Melendez and they didn't ask.

Late one night in December, Gagne got a panicked call from Alig's new boyfriend, Brian. They had been staying at a Howard Johnson's in New Jersey, snorting heroin and watching TV, when NYPD pounded on the door at 3:00 a.m.

"Everything is going to be okay," Alig told Brian as he was taken away in handcuffs.

The thirty-year-old promoter was being charged with first-degree murder. Turned out there was a second corpse—a legless torso that had washed up on the shores of Staten Island back in April. It had recently been identified through dental records as Angel Melendez. (The other corpse was likely a mob hit, as evidenced by the chains.)

Alig denied any involvement in Melendez's murder. But the police had already arrested Club Kid Robert Riggs, aka "Freeze," earlier that week, and Riggs gave a signed confession to the killing, naming Alig as his co-defendant. Riggs had been in a holding cell for six or seven hours and in the clutches of painful heroin withdrawal symptoms when he signed the confession. He had been begging for drugs, methadone, medical attention—anything to make the pain stop. Which is why Gagne and Germanowski knew that Riggs's confession wouldn't stand up in a court of law. In a cold sweat and foaming at the mouth, Riggs would have told them he was Santa Claus just to get some methadone. It angered Gagne. He and his partners took their time with defendants because they knew they had one shot at getting a confession that would stick—one shot to do it right. And if they got a guy to confess under physical duress, then they were the same as the bad guys.

Riggs's confession should have been an embarrassment to the police. It wasn't going to stick. But Alig didn't know that.

Shortly after Alig's arrest, Gagne and Germanowski received a string of urgent phone calls from Alig's mother, Elke; his boyfriend, Brian; and his best friend, Gitsie. They begged the agents to go see Alig at Rikers. He wanted to tell them something. He trusted them. He refused to speak to anyone else.

Gagne knew Alig wanted to confess, and it was going to jeopardize their entire case. Alig could connect Peter

Gatien to the drugs, the cash payouts to house dealers, the drug budgets, and the hotel parties. But the details that Riggs had revealed to police were gruesome and gory. If Alig had really murdered Melendez the way Riggs had claimed, then there was no way their play-it-safe prosecutor, AUSA Eric Friedberg, was going to let them put Alig on the stand to testify against Peter Gatien.

32 THE CONFESSION OF MICHAEL ALIG

ON DECEMBER 9, 1996, four days after Michael Alig's arrest on suspicion of murder, Gagne, Germanowski, and Flaherty slowly drove out to Rikers Island. Slowly, because they weren't certain they'd make it there before they got cold feet and turned the car around. Gagne seemed to be struggling most with the decision. His cell phone rang. It was one of the attorneys assigned to their case. Germanowski could hear screaming through Gagne's cell phone.

"You guys are going to fuck this whole case up! He's our best witness!"

The attorney urged them to go back. *Wait until after the trial to get your murder confession,* the attorney pleaded. *We can get him on the murder, but one thing at a time.*

Gagne had heard enough.

"What's that? I can't hear you . . . I think I'm losing you." He closed his phone.

The agents sat in the parked car outside Rikers for a few minutes, staring at the gates.

"What do you think?" Germanowski said.

"You know what Alig's gonna say when we go in," Gagne said. "You know what the fucking guy's gonna say."

"If Angel was my brother, I wouldn't want anyone to wait," Flaherty said.

"Right. Okay. Let's do this," Gagne said. Whatever

fallout resulted, they would just deal with it. Gagne knew it was only bad news waiting for them inside.

"This is huge for Peter," Gagne said. "This is gonna be great for him."

Alig was hungry to confess when he saw the agents.

"Michael, everything you say," Flaherty told him, "nothing good is going to happen for you."

"You know that whatever you tell us," Germanowski said, "as much as we like you as a person, this information is going to be used against you. You understand this, right, Mike?"

It was important to them that Alig declare beforehand, with the prison guard as a witness, that his confession was at will and that he was not being coerced. It had to be clean.

Alig understood. He refused the presence of counsel. He said he needed to talk and he knew the consequences.

Vivid details spilled from his mouth. He had been carrying the dark images in his mind for nearly nine months and they had been eating away at him. He couldn't get the words out fast enough.

"Slow down, Michael," Germanowski said. "Slow down."

33 THE MURDER OF ANGEL MELENDEZ

ON ST. PATRICK'S DAY in New York, green beer flows by the gallon at pubs and bars from the Bronx to the Bowery. Crumpled plastic cups and green vomit are washed off the sidewalks and subway platforms the next morning. In 1996, Alig and Riggs got a day's head start on the holiday partying at Tunnel, snorting coke, heroin, and ketamine, and getting as wasted as possible. The next morning, Sunday, March 17, they stumbled into Alig's apartment at 560 West 43rd Street around 7:00 a.m. Angel Melendez arrived two hours later.

Melendez had fallen in love with the Club Kid scene in the early 1990s and garnered minor celebrity as Alig's personal drug dealer. The twenty-six-year-old lived in New Jersey, but most weekends he crashed at Alig's Manhattan apartment.

Alig treated Melendez shabbily. He stole from his stash of drugs and cash. He derided him as a hanger-on who never really got the Club Kid aesthetic—mocking Melendez's giant wings, which were always knocking things over.

Melendez was fed up with Alig's abuse. The club scene had lost its shine and he wanted to get out and move on. But he was still owed money, and when he arrived that Sunday morning at Alig's apartment he was in a dark mood. According to Alig, Gatien paid cash fees— so-called appearance fees—to some house dealers, and Gatien allegedly owed Melendez money for selling drugs exclusively at Tunnel and Limelight.

"Peter knows he owes the money. But the more you bother him the longer you'll have to wait to be paid," Alig told Melendez. (Gatien, on the contrary, would deny that he ever owed Melendez drug money, or that he ever paid fees to secure the services of house dealers.)

Frustrated but exhausted, Melendez napped on the couch while Alig and Riggs cooked up more "Special K" (ketamine) in the oven, heating the liquid anesthetic into a powdery form that they could snort to achieve an out-of-body numbness. As they waited for the drugs to cook, they rifled through Melendez's pants pockets and stole small amounts of cocaine.

"We should just kill him and take his dope," Freeze joked before heading to the bedroom to relax.

Melendez arose by noon, still angry about the debt owed him. Alig agreed to call Gatien to ask for the money in an attempt to placate Melendez. But when Gatien's wife, Alessandra, answered the phone she refused to put Gatien on.

"Peter wouldn't want to talk on the phone, especially about anything concerning *that*," Alessandra allegedly said before hanging up on Alig.

"I want my money. What are you going to do about it?" Melendez screamed. According to Alig, Melendez's anger quickly escalated to physical violence. He slammed Alig through a large glass cabinet and pinned the 155-pound junkie on his back. Alig bit Melendez's chest and grabbed a shirt off the floor, stuffing it into Melendez's face to try to break free.

Riggs was rustled from his nap by the sound of breaking glass and Alig's screams. He ran out from the bedroom to find Melendez shaking Alig like a twig and yelling: "You better get my money!"

Riggs grabbed a hammer from the kitchen table and slammed the back of Melendez's head—one, two, three times. Alig put his hands around Melendez's neck and squeezed until Melendez's eyes rolled over. Alig couldn't be sure whether it was the choking or the third hammer strike that had made Melendez finally go limp.

Alig and Riggs stared at Melendez's still body. One of them thought to check for a pulse, but neither knew how, so they put a spoon under Melendez's nose, waiting for it to fog up.

Nothing.

In a junkie haze, Alig took Drano—or maybe it was air freshener, he couldn't be sure—and poured it down Melendez's throat, believing it would abate the smell of internal decay. Riggs helped Alig undress Melendez down to his white underwear and drag his heavy, lifeless body into a bathroom in the spare bedroom. They dropped him into the tub, poured ice over him, and left the apartment to find heroin and get high as quickly as possible.

Alig eventually called Gatien again.

"Why do you want to talk to Peter?" Alessandra asked. She always kept a wall between her husband and trouble.

The problem with Melendez had become much worse, Alig said. Alessandra hung up. Fifteen minutes later, she called back to inform Alig that neither she nor Gatien had any idea what he was talking about but that he had better take care of it.

Alig went to see Gatien at Tunnel. The Club Kid hemmed and hawed about "a problem" with Melendez but he wouldn't say what it was. Alig would later claim that Gatien acted paranoid and pretended not to know anyone named Angel. Gatien allegedly handed Alig $160 in cash and told him that whatever the problem was, "take care of it and I'll call you later." Alig used the money to buy heroin and get high with Riggs.

Alig had a decision to make. He had been planning to throw a small party for several weeks, but now he had a dead body in his bathtub. Alig had grown up on slasher flicks—it wasn't beyond his imagination to simply pour a little more ice on Melendez, lock the door, and send his guests to the spare bathroom. The party continued as planned. Gitsie noticed a faint smell of decay coming from the back of the apartment, but she was too kind to say anything.

Melendez had been dead for eight days. According to Alig, that's when he finally returned to see Gatien, broke down in tears, and admitted his crime. Alig said he begged for help and guidance and that Gatien berated him for causing a "huge problem" for everybody. Alig claimed that when he told Gatien he was considering going to the police, because it was an accident, and they would have to see that, Gatien said that would be the worst thing he could do—after the NYPD raids of September 1995, they didn't need any more police interest. According to Alig, Gatien counseled him to get rid of the body and then get out of town as soon as possible. Alig would later tell DEA that he received about $4,000 in cash from Gatien over the next week, never hand to hand but from assistants who passed the money down surreptitiously. (Gatien's attorney has countered that Gatien never spoke of Melendez's murder with Alig, and no money was ever given to Alig specifically for the purpose of leaving town. Gatien was never charged with anything related to the murder.)

On March 26, Melendez's corpse was ten days cold when Alig sent Riggs to Macy's to buy a new TV and a set of culinary knives. They got high before they entered the bathroom.

Alig began. He selected a serrated knife and pressed the blade to Melendez's thigh. As he began to saw through the leg, he felt faint and welcomed the opportunity to mentally detach, to go slightly unconscious. But it was no use trying to get numb. The task required his full strength and attention, as Melendez's body was in extreme rigor mortis. Alig felt like he was filing away at cold steel blocks. The acrid smell of flesh was unbearable. He sliced through the first limb until he heard a sickening noise that reminded him of the sound of a chicken wing snapping. He wanted to vomit. He felt dizzy and nauseous. Riggs cut through Melendez's other leg while Alig tugged and twisted until the same snapping sound was achieved. They placed the two legs in two layers of thick garbage bags, walked to the Hudson River at 42nd Street, and threw the bags into the water. Then they scored more heroin and stayed out all night.

The next day, Alig and Riggs stumbled back to the apartment to finish what they had started. They stuffed Melendez's torso into a trash bag and dumped the bag into the empty television box. Together, they wrapped several rolls of gray packing tape around the TV box and then pushed it into the elevator and out the lobby of Alig's apartment building. Once outside, they hailed a yellow taxi, and headed sixteen blocks due south toward Tunnel.

When the cab dropped them off, Alig must have had a shudder of a glimpse at how far he had fallen. He was a month shy of his thirtieth birthday. How many birthdays had he spent at Tunnel? It wasn't so long ago that he'd brought his mother here to celebrate with him. They had stepped out of the limo, bathed by the blinding flash of cameras. Clubgoers had lined up to pay their respects and strangers blew kisses on Alig's cheek, telling Elke she looked "fabulous." Now Alig was just a junkie and a murderer, pushing a corpse in a box along the West Side Highway.

Alig and Riggs hoisted the heavy cardboard tomb up and over the railing, letting it drop into the Hudson River. It smacked hard against the water and was briefly swallowed up by the current. Alig panicked when the box rose to the surface as it floated downstream.

In the days and weeks that followed, Johnny Melendez, Angel's brother, would file a missing-person report with the police and put up flyers offering a $4,000 reward for any information that would help the Melendez family find Angel.

Alig's way of dealing with the murder was to joke about it: "I did it! I couldn't stand Angel anymore. He bored me, so I killed him!" He knew that no one really believed it.

It was time to get out of town. He put his belongings into storage and set out on a road trip to visit his mother in Indiana, and then on to Denver, Colorado, where he planned to quit drugs.

Gitsie had previously saved his life by giving him CPR after he passed out from a near-fatal heroin overdose at one of Gatien's hotel parties. Alig asked her to join him on his road trip to sobriety. They had five bags of heroin to share for the entire five-week trip. They went through it all in less than a week. When they got to South Bend, Alig was shaking and suffering through cold flashes, diarrhea, and vomiting. His muscles and bones ached. Elke tried to hug her son but he pulled away.

"Please, Mommy," he begged. "Don't touch me. I hurt too bad."

In June, Alig returned to New York—addicted to both heroin and methadone—and was taken in by a friend who was living at the Chelsea Hotel. A few months later he met the DEA agents when they knocked on his door. He trusted them enough to share his ordeal with them. He felt relieved to have finally confessed. That was all he had to say.

Germanowski still had one question.

"Mike, what'd you do with Angel's testicles?" he asked. "What did you do?"

"Nothing," Alig said.

The coroner's report on Angel's torso noted a clean incision in the scrotum, with both testicles missing. The agents had heard rumors that Riggs and Alig were so high they may have ingested them.

"Mike, they were surgically removed," Germanowski pressed. "It wasn't a thing where you were cutting the leg and the knife hit the scrotum and gouged it or ripped it or sliced it. This was a straight incision and both testicles were cut off. So where are they?"

"I have no idea what you're talking about," Alig said soberly.

Germanowski let it go. It was irrelevant. Maybe it was too dark even for Michael Alig to revisit.

Gagne, Germanowski, and Flaherty had three separate interviews with Alig about Melendez's murder. His recollections were lucid and unwavering. Germanowski recited the interviews in graphic detail in his DEA-6 reports.

Gagne tried to forget a lot of what he heard. Alig had been a talented young artist who had helped make Peter Gatien millions of dollars. As far as Gagne was concerned, Gatien was one more person in Alig's life who let him down by letting Alig fall apart, letting him drown in his own recklessness and addiction to the point where he became a murderer.

34 "THE ISRAELIS CAN WAIT"

IN THEIR THIRTY-MONTH investigation, Gagne and his partners secured guilty pleas and cooperation deals with some thirty defendants—drug dealers, bouncers, promoters, and directors—who played different roles in the drug-dealing hierarchy. They all agreed to become potential witnesses in the case against Gatien for a chance at leniency at their own sentencing hearings. Only three defendants pleaded not guilty: Peter Gatien, Steve Lewis, and a bouncer named Ray Montgomery, who was later acquitted.

The government amended its indictment against Gatien to include Racketeer Influenced and Corrupt Organizations Act, or RICO, charges, alleging Gatien was the mastermind behind a well-organized and well-funded drug-dealing hierarchy, and that he rewarded top employees with invitations to his hotel parties—which he paid for with his corporate credit card.

Getting the DEA and the media to take a closer look at Ecstasy and the rising abuse of club drugs would come to define Gagne's hard work on the Gatien case. But his drive to bring Gatien to justice clouded his judgment in two ways that would deeply affect his career.

His first mistake was pushing aside the bigger picture: the Israeli suppliers. In debriefings with defendants, it was the same story again and again—Club Kids used to supply the drugs, but it was the Israelis now, they were bringing the pills from Holland by the tens of thousands.

Wiretap target John Charles Simonson described to the agents drug deals he took part in with nameless men: "I don't know where they're coming from, I don't know where they live, but they set up a deal, I walk outside my apartment at four a.m., and they're right there."

Germanowski knew that was the sign of a pro: "I know where you are, and I know where you live, but you know nothing about me."

Baby Joe Uzzardi said he heard talk about a major supplier known as Israeli Steve, Big Steve, or Fat Steve. It was obviously a reference to Tuito associate Steve Hager, who'd sold the LSD-laced Golds. But Hager might as well have been a ghost—Gagne and Germanowski had nothing on "Big Steve."

Germanowski became increasingly interested in the Israeli supply network. "This is bigger than we know," he would say. If it had been up to him, they would have chased the Israeli suppliers from the start, back when they had arrested Ghel and Michel and were just learning about the "brothers from the motherland." But they didn't have the support to conduct a historical investigation on the clubs *and* open a new case against the mysterious Israeli suppliers. They had to pick one direction, and Gagne was focused on Gatien from the start. He knew that arresting an Israeli drug trafficker with an unpronounceable name might be a page-five blurb in the *Post*. But going after a multimillionaire club owner made front-page headlines and exposed the out-of-control drug use—especially Ecstasy use—in New York's nightclubs. Gagne wanted the club king.

"The Israelis can wait," he would tell Germanowski. "I promise you, we'll come back for them."

Gagne's second mistake was chasing down Robert De Niro.

35 "NOT VERY FUCKING FUNNY"

ALIG'S DECEMBER 1996 MURDER confession meant the loss of another important witness to severe credibility issues. But there was still an unexplored aspect of the Gatien case, a link the agents had yet to fully investigate: Mitch Kolpan.

Germanowski was at home with his wife and son when he got an angry phone call from his supervisor late one Sunday night in January 1997.

"Where the fuck are you?" Cardinali barked.

"I'm at home, Lou. You just called me here," Germanowski said.

"Where's Gagne?"

"I don't know."

"You two are together all the time. Where is he?"

"Lou, I'm telling you," Germanowski said. "I don't know where Gags is."

"Well, can you explain to me why I just got a call from the SAC, who got a call from the SAC in L.A., who got a call from Robert De Niro's attorney, who said Gagne's in L.A. waiting to interview Robert De Niro?"

Germanowski laughed. That was the craziest thing he'd heard his partner do in a long time, maybe crazier than the sleepover at Ghel's apartment.

"Not very fucking funny," Cardinali said as he slammed the phone down. The front office was all over Cardinali for not keeping his agent on a short leash.

Gagne had gotten a call earlier that week from the U.S. attorney's office. The prosecutors wanted him to go to Los Angeles to question De Niro about NYPD detective Mitch Kolpan. According to Steve Lewis's post-arrest statements, which were later suppressed, the retired cop was allegedly leaking information to Gatien about planned drug stings at the clubs. Kolpan was never charged with any wrongdoing, but the prosecutors wanted to know if De Niro had any information linking the cop to the club owner.

De Niro's connection to both men was thin. His 1993 directorial debut, *A Bronx Tale,* about a boy torn between his working-class heart-of-gold father (played by De Niro) and a murderous paternal mob boss (played by Chazz Palminteri), was based on a one-man play written by and starring Palminteri—who used to work for Gatien at the clubs before he became a movie star. Gatien executive-produced *A Bronx Tale,* and Mitch Kolpan had a small part as a detective. Kolpan went on to more bit roles in *Casino* and *Money Train.*

Gagne and Germanowski had already questioned Palminteri in New York. It was a bust. As far as both agents could recall, Palminteri put on an Oscar-worthy charm offensive: *I don't remember. I'm so sorry to see Peter caught up in this. Drugs are a problem. You guys are doing a great job. Hey, you know—when you're going undercover, you're acting for real. I wouldn't mind calling on you guys sometime, you might have a legitimate shot at my business.*

Still, the prosecutors hoped that De Niro might have information that would bolster the club owner/cop angle. Phone records indicated Kolpan had called Gatien's home 36 times and Limelight 290 times in the months leading up to and after the NYPD raid. Maybe De Niro could confirm a suspiciously close relationship between the cop and the club owner.

Gagne was game to go to L.A. to question the actor, but he had to pull together last-minute travel approvals to make the trip happen. In the interest of seizing the opportunity, steps were missed: the special agent in charge of New York didn't know about the trip, Cardinali had been out of the office and hadn't been in the loop, and Los Angeles DEA didn't get a courtesy call about Gagne's visit to their district.

Gagne rented a car when he got to Los Angeles and drove to Culver City, where De Niro was working on the set of *Wag the Dog*. De Niro's lawyer had already gotten a call from the federal prosecutors and had agreed to set up the meeting.

A friendly assistant led Gagne over to De Niro's trailer.

"He's very busy shooting. But he'd like to meet you and then reschedule to talk this evening," she said.

De Niro came out of his trailer.

"Hello, how you doing?" The actor cordially shook Gagne's hand. He apologized for not being able to talk on the set. He invited Gagne to meet him at his house later. He was renting Paul Newman's place, by the way. Gagne felt like he was being schmoozed.

Their interview that night, just like Palminteri's testimony, went nowhere. De Niro said he couldn't remember anyone named Mitch Kolpan. He didn't know anything about any drug dealing in Gatien's clubs. He didn't know anything about crooked cops. He was sorry he couldn't be more helpful.

On his drive back to the airport, Gagne got in an accident when someone slammed into the rental car and totaled it. A fitting end. Gagne was tired and frustrated. He felt like the entire trip was a waste. He went home with nothing for his troubles, but the bosses at DEA would repay him for it a month later.

In February 1997, Gagne was in the field with Germanowski when his supervisor called.

"You're getting transferred to S-eleven," Cardinali said.

That's a stupid joke, Gagne thought.

"You'll start Monday."

Gagne felt his heart pounding. S-11 was support staff—intelligence work. A desk job. Intel agents didn't chase dealers or work undercover; they analyzed phone records and bank statements. Gagne was a meat eater, not a nine-to-five fact finder. He didn't understand what Cardinali was saying.

Cardinali tried to soften the news: the front office was shaking things up, creating a whole new intelligence unit, and Gagne was being pulled off group D-35 to be a part of this new unit. Cardinali didn't come out and say it then, but the truth was this was punishment for Gagne's trip to L.A. He had a reputation for testing the boundaries, and he had pushed them too far. The new assistant special agent in charge in New York got yelled at for the De Niro episode, and from then on he had it in for Bob Gagne.

Being sent to Intel, away from Germanowski and Flaherty, felt like a death to Gagne. The shame and confusion was crushing. He quietly hung up the phone.

"What? What did he say?" Germanowski asked.

"I'm going to S-eleven."

His words hung heavy in the silence.

"Dagger to my heart," was all Germanowski could say.

On Monday morning, Gagne packed up his desk and moved down to the fifth-floor Intel Unit. He would continue to work on the Gatien case; trial was a year away. But after that, he'd be stuck in the office doing support work while his family was three floors up, carrying on as usual. It was a dark time. Gagne had promised Germanowski they would come back for the Israeli traffickers. But nothing was certain now. He put the disappointment and anger out of his mind. Pushed it down. Forgot about it.

36 "THE PARTY IS OVER"

MICHAEL ALIG SPENT Christmas Day 1996 at Rikers Island. He wore a gray jumpsuit, sweat socks, and plastic sandals for his mother's visit. Elke hugged him tight and kissed his hands.

By the spring of 1997, unbeknownst to the DEA agents, Alig was receiving jailhouse visits from Gatien's attorney Ben Brafman. Alig told his mother he was busting to tell her some exciting news but had been sworn to secrecy. By summer, Alig's exciting news had hit the papers: Brafman had received a signed affidavit from Alig in which the Club Kid recanted his statements against Gatien to the DEA. Gagne and Germanowski, Alig claimed, "attributed information to me that was simply not true. They would take part of what I said and add to it in order to make Peter appear to be personally involved in activities that I knew he had nothing to do with."

Even worse, Alig claimed the agents had helped him to score drugs and let him snort heroin in the backseat of their official government vehicle. Both agents vehemently denied the accusations. Gagne had always wanted Alig sober. Not just for his own health—but because he'd be a better witness on the stand.

On October 1, 1997, Alig and Robert Riggs were transported to the New York State Supreme Court at 100 Centre Street to be sentenced for the first-degree manslaughter of Angel Melendez. They waited together in a holding pen outside the courtroom, catching up while Riggs smoked a cigarette. Alig hadn't seen Freeze in a while and noticed how common he looked without his makeup and bleached blond hair. A prisoner in a cell across the way recognized Alig and wanted to know if they were "those Club Kids—the ones I saw on TV who killed that guy." Alig thought the inmate was cute, so when the guy pestered Riggs for a cigarette, Alig made him pull out his penis and jerk off for them first. A guard came to collect Riggs and Alig moments after the inmate finished. Riggs tossed the guy a cigarette as they were led to the courtroom.

Half a dozen of Alig's friends were sitting in the gallery, for moral support. But Alig wasn't worried. He felt assured, based on conversations with his lawyer, that his sentencing date would be held over, that he was going to get a slap on the wrist, and that this hearing was merely a formality.

The judge asked Riggs if he had anything to say. Riggs stood and read from an impassioned statement he had penciled on several sheets of yellow legal paper. Alig was dumbfounded.

"I endeavor to understand the aspects of myself that led me down such a gross and destructive path, but I have yet to come to any definite conclusions," Riggs said. "What I am certain of is that all of us involved—myself, Michael Alig, Daniel Auster, and Angel Melendez—are victims of the same hideous evil, whose name is drugs."

In the last year, it had come to light that there was a fourth person in Alig's apartment when Melendez was killed—Daniel Auster, the son of renowned novelist Paul Auster. Alig and Riggs had never mentioned Auster in their confessions, perhaps trying to protect him. Though cleared of any involvement in the murder, Auster would later plead guilty in 1998 (when he was twenty) to having stolen $3,000 from Melendez after he was killed.

"Drugs are, of course, the problem, but they cannot be the excuse," Riggs went on. "There is no excuse. I know that. However, there are reasons why so many young people end up drug-addicted, drug-dealing Club Kids, and various outcasts of society. And I for one am committed to finding out those reasons in myself."

Alig was panicked. It was almost his turn to speak and he had nothing prepared. Riggs's speech was long and heartfelt and ended with Hallmark-card recollections of the night he and Melendez had laughed as they first glued feathers onto his cardboard angel wings.

"Wherever you are," Riggs concluded, "I hope that you are flying in peace on the real wings that you deserve."

The judge praised Riggs for his newfound remorse but still sentenced the twenty-nine-year-old to the requisite ten to twenty years' incarceration for first-degree manslaughter.

Alig's lawyer requested a postponement of Alig's sentencing, pending a psychiatric evaluation, but the judge denied the motion.

"Do you wish to be heard?" the judge asked Alig. Nervous and bewildered by the turn of events, Alig stood up and fumbled his way through a rambling nonapology.

"I came here today not prepared to accept my sentence, so I didn't come with a speech because I was told we were going to postpone for another week, two weeks, or something like that, I don't know," Alig said. "All I know is that I've been told lots of different things by lots of different people."

Alig claimed he had been "used by the feds" and then "railroaded" by people who lied to him to get him to accept a plea bargain. But he knew as the words fell from his mouth that he was only making his situation worse.

"You are the victim?" the judge asked Alig.

"In a way, yes."

"In a way, you are the victim?"

"Yes."

"I don't think that you are the victim," the judge said. "I think that Angel Melendez is the victim—"

"He is *also* the victim," Alig interrupted.

"He is the victim of your selfish, uncontrolled ego that has yet to be harnessed, that has yet to face reality." The judge made his final remarks: "For you the show is over, the party is over. Mr. Alig, you are sentenced to ten to twenty years."

37 HAPPY NEW YEAR

THE JUDGE HAD SEALED Alig's fate, officially heralding the death of the Club Kid scene. And on that same day, in the same hour, some twenty-five hundred miles west of the Manhattan criminal courthouse, along a tree-lined street in a quiet suburban San Fernando Valley neighborhood, LAPD narcotics detectives were preparing to deliver a similar fate to Ecstasy dealer Oded Tuito.

Tuito had been puttering about in his ranch-style home all week while a task force surveillance team had been watching his front yard through binoculars, waiting for the right moment to descend. It was the start of Rosh Hashanah, the Jewish New Year, and he and his wife, Aliza, were planning to host dinner with friends. Tuito had been trying to tie up loose ends before the holidays—making phone calls and readying drug packages for shipment. He was unaware that an anonymous tipster had recently alerted cops to his drug dealing.

On September 30, police had followed Tuito as he drove his gray GMC Yukon to his cousin's beeper store in North Hollywood, picked up a box, and then delivered it to a FedEx in Canoga Park. The package, marked "motorcycle parts," was destined for a warehouse in Pittsburgh. Inside the box was a brick kilogram of cocaine (worth about $25,000 on the street) wrapped in fabric softener and duct tape. The cops had decided to do a controlled delivery—to let the drugs reach the intended recipient but secretly follow and control the shipment every step of the way.

On October 1, while Michael Alig was being sentenced, a police officer posing as a FedEx employee was delivering Tuito's cocaine to the Pittsburgh warehouse. The men who accepted the package were immediately arrested and the facility was raided. Pittsburgh police arrested six suspects, seized $47,980 in cash, and collected seven plastic baggies filled with "X-files" pills, in addition to the cocaine.

That same evening in Woodland Hills, Tuito and Aliza were entertaining guests when narcotics task force officers started banging on the front door, arrest warrants in hand. Judy Ben Atar was supposed to be at Tuito's house, but a fight with a girlfriend had delayed him. Jackie and Koki also had been invited but were out of town. In the end, police rounded up four of Tuito's Los Angeles associates and charged them with drug trafficking. Four kilos of cocaine, five kilos of marijuana, 525 Ecstasy tablets, and three bags filled with $64,268 in cash was seized. Also collected were a Colt rifle, a pump-action shotgun, a semiautomatic 9 mm Beretta found under a bedroom mattress, and a small handgun belonging to Aliza.

The Fat Man, however, had escaped. Tuito had heard a disturbance on his front lawn that day and glanced out his window. When he saw drug cops in flak vests running up his grassy front yard, past his son's swing set, guns drawn, Tuito quietly slipped out the back door—and disappeared.

38 "HE LOST EVERYTHING. MY GOD"

IN DECEMBER 1997, a couple of months after Michael Alig's sentencing, Bob Gagne got an unexpected phone call from Alig's mother.

"Does Michael know you're calling me?" Gagne asked.

"No, Michael has no idea."

Gagne taped their conversation. He wanted to get to the bottom of Alig's betrayal.

"I know Michael wants to turn his life around and start with a clean slate," Elke said as she ruffled through letters her son had written from jail. "He's talking future. He's talking about what he wants to do when he comes out. And he knows that he has been *had*, he has been had by a very rich man."

"Did he tell you that in the letters?" Gagne asked.

"I have something in writing, in front of me, that was addressed to an attorney that we want to hire, but we haven't been able to hire him sufficiently because of lack of money," Elke said. She read out loud from her son's longhand notes.

According to Alig's letter, he believed that his attorney, Gerry McMahon, had colluded with Gatien's attorney, Ben Brafman, to help Gatien's case while letting Alig's case suffer. He was accusing his attorney of a conflict of interest. He was also worried about his upcoming federal sentencing—the reason for Elke's call.

Alig had already received ten to twenty for Melendez's murder. But he still hadn't been sentenced on the federal drug charges, and the U.S. attorney's office had torn up his cooperation agreement after he signed the affidavit recanting his statements against Gatien. No one on the fed side was going to bat for Alig now. And even though he was looking at no more than seven years for drug conspiracy, if the judge decided to throw the book at him, he could be forced to serve his two terms consecutively.

Elke was emotional and scattered as she spoke. She was having trouble concentrating. Her son was in prison and she was desperate to protect him. Gagne tried to bring her back around.

"I have to understand what happened between Michael and his attorneys," Gagne said. "The affidavit concerns specifically myself and Matt. And there's pretty strong allegations in there."

Elke said the answers were in Michael's notes. She continued to read:

" 'Instead of discussing my case . . . we constantly discussed Peter's case, what the feds may have done that was unorthodox—to discredit them and have Peter's case possibly dropped—and my signing many papers for Peter's benefit, some taking much of the blame off of Peter and attaching it to myself. Other papers I signed were sworn statements on unethical moves made by the feds, which turned them subsequently against me.

" 'All of this was done, or so my lawyer told me, so that Brafman would "speak to his friends at the DA's office," since he used to be one himself, and he'd do something to reduce whatever time they would otherwise be giving me. Shortly thereafter, my lawyer, Mr. McMahon, told me not to be surprised'—and listen to this Bob!—'not to be surprised if I hear or find out that he has received a lump sum of dollars from Brafman, because he, (a) has done a service for Brafman, (b) has not received enough money from me.' What do you think about that?" Elke said.

"No comment. Keep going."

"You're thinking something, Bob. You're just as human as I am."

Gagne wasn't going to tell Elke that Alig's betrayal had wounded him and hurt their case immensely. He hadn't seen or talked to Alig since. But still, he felt something for the kid. He imagined Alig—spacey from all the medications he was on for his depression and withdrawal symptoms—signing away on meaningless pieces of paper and thinking he'd be back with his clubland family. Alig was a little fish swimming with sharks.

Alig would later file a complaint with the appellate court about his lawyer's alleged conflict of interest. In his response to the filing, Gerry McMahon denied ever receiving any money or benefits from Brafman. He also claimed that he had counseled Alig not to sign the affidavit.

"In truth," McMahon wrote, "Mr. Alig signed the affidavit for Peter Gatien because he loved being in the limelight and seeing his name in the newspaper."

Elke believed that it was McMahon who was trying to make a name for himself, by currying favor with Brafman. Alig had told his mother that before his sentencing, he was promised by the attorneys that Gatien would come visit him in jail—the club owner had allegedly offered to pay Alig to redesign Limelight while he was behind bars.

"I'm kind of not following you," Gagne said to Elke. He followed, but he needed her to be very clear about what she was saying. "They wanted Michael to redesign the Limelight?"

"Yeah. And they sent Michael blueprints," Elke said.

"They sent him blueprints?"

"Yeah. And you know Michael . . ."

"Yeah, he gets excited about that, because he's good at that stuff," Gagne said.

"You're right," Elke said. "And he was really excited about it and the sum of fifty thousand dollars."

"The sum of fifty thousand dollars?" Gagne said, pushing Elke to clarify.

"Uh-huh. Which never, you know, was paid. Shortly after that Michael was moved to Rikers; he couldn't start on the blueprints. He lost everything. My God."

Alig claimed that after he signed the affidavit against the agents, he'd never heard from Brafman or Gatien again.

"Now, was the fifty thousand dollars—I mean, I can understand the fifty thousand dollars, they wanted him to redesign everything," Gagne said. "But was part of the deal to say bad things about myself and Matt?"

"The fifty thousand dollars that was offered to pay for redoing the Limelight was just a bribe for Michael to do the affidavit," Elke said.

"Right," Gagne said. "That was my question."

It was hearsay. Brafman would vehemently deny that Alig had ever been promised money for anything. But at the time, it gave Gagne some small peace. Trial was a little over a month away. He numbered the tape as an exhibit and tucked a copy into the evidence file for safe-keeping.

39 JANUARY 14, 1998

BEN BRAFMAN PACED CONFIDENTLY in front of the jury, delivering his opening statements: "This trial is going to show that life in this city is like life in Peter's Gatien's clubs."

Gatien watched from the defense table as his attorney set the stage for the most important public moment of his career. His personal finances, his struggles with addiction, and the drug-infested environs of his club empire would soon be revealed in lurid detail. Reporters sat elbow to elbow with Club Kids and Gatien supporters in Judge Frederic Block's packed Brooklyn courtroom. Several in the press would note in their stories the next day that Gatien had ditched his signature eye patch for tinted sunglasses, possibly as an attempt to soften his image. Gatien's wife, Alessandra, and his daughter, Jennifer, sat in the front row of the gallery with earnest expressions.

It had been twenty months since Peter Gatien was awakened that May morning in his town house and arrested on drug conspiracy charges. In the lead-up to trial, New Yorkers were fed sensational tidbits in the local rags—allegations of government misconduct competed for column inches with stories about Gatien's lascivious hotel parties. Two days before trial began, government witness and Alig's best friend, Cynthia Haataja, aka Gitsie, was found dead in her apartment of a heroin overdose. The fragile twenty-two-year-old Club Kid had once promised Alig she would smuggle in enough heroin for him to kill himself if he got life in prison.

The Club Kids were in the throes of a nasty hangover, a cultural regression only compounded by the bleak national headlines of the last twenty months: a six-year-old beauty queen was murdered on Christmas Eve in her parents' basement; Heaven's Gate cultists committed mass suicide in a San Diego mansion; a fame-obsessed serial killer murdered fashion designer Gianni Versace; Princess Diana died in a fiery car crash while being chased by paparazzi.

Just days after Gatien's trial began, the nation would be rocked by a new scandal and subsequent details of President Clinton's blow jobs and cigar play in the White House with a twenty-two-year-old intern. Sex and sin led the news. The glamorous had become grotesque. Reality TV superstars, paparazzi millionaires, and willfully insouciant heir-heads were just around the corner. The nation seemed to have collectively lost its impulse control.

Gatien was feeling the sting of backlash. For a decade, his clubs had dominated New York nightlife. But megaclubs were a dying breed under Mayor Giuliani's quality-of-life edicts that cleaned the city of broken windows, visible homelessness, and anything that was unfriendly and unsafe to commerce, tourism, and families. The forty-six-year-old club king now had just one of his four clubs, Tunnel, in operation; he was facing tax evasion charges for skimming millions of dollars in profits from his business; and if the jury before him now found him guilty of drug conspiracy and racketeering charges, he could get up to twenty years in prison.

"Some people used drugs in our clubs despite our best efforts," Brafman said to the jurors. "Some of the millions of people who came to the clubs in the six years in this case came for drugs. But it was not a part of a criminal conspiracy by Mr. Gatien."

The government's charges, Brafman claimed, were based on fabricated evidence and the coached and researched testimony of low-life criminals and drug dealers who would lie on the stand to save themselves.

Gagne, Germanowski, and Flaherty sat at the prosecution table with assistant U.S. attorneys Eric Friedberg, Lisa Fleischman, and Michele Adelman. In her opening statement, Adelman told the jury that the government was not charging Gatien with directly selling drugs or taking a cut from the drug sales in his clubs. Gatien, the feds alleged, was the mastermind and financier of a well-organized employment hierarchy, and he encouraged drug distribution to maximize his own profits from door fees and bar sales. Gatien rewarded top employees, Adelman alleged, with gifts and invitations to his infamous hotel bacchanals.

At his clubs Tunnel and Limelight, Adelman said, "thousands of young nightclub patrons would take hallucinogenic pills as if it was candy at Halloween and drug dealers dropped cocaine powder into the hands of club patrons as if it was sugar."

The jury of seven women and five men were mostly middle-aged and working-class. They included a truck driver and a retired factory worker—not the types one would meet snorting cocaine in the Police Room.

Michael Caruso would be the government's first witness. Gagne and Germanowski had arrested Caruso in early 1997 in Staten Island, where he was living with his girlfriend and infant son. Caruso had turned a corner by then. He'd come clean about his role in bringing Ecstasy into Gatien's clubs, he'd given up his former cohorts, and he'd admitted to a long list of crimes—fraud, robbery, identity theft—that he'd never gotten caught for and had no good reason to admit, other than full disclosure. Gagne had believed Caruso when he said he was done with all that. He'd liked Lord Mike from the start and would continue to check in on him over the years.

When Caruso took the stand in Gatien's trial in 1998, he hadn't worked Gatien's clubs in years, but he had an insider's perspective. AUSA Eric Friedberg shot a series of probing questions at Caruso in an awkward (and painfully straightlaced) attempt to teach the jury about the nightlife scene.

"What were Club Kids?" Friedberg asked.

"They were basically flamboyant club categories who worked in nightlife only—mostly, I should say," Caruso said like a freshman anthropologist. "They had shocking outfits from time to time that they wore, like high platform heels, makeup on their faces, sometimes high designer wear, sometimes homemade designer wear, piercings."

"Was there a leader of these Club Kids?" Friedberg asked.

"Michael Alig was the Club Kid king."

"What characterized the behavior of the Club Kids at the club?"

"They were nightlife party people that, you know, partied pretty heavily, and anything that was hip, great, cool, was considered fabulous."

"You mentioned this term 'fabulous.' What does that mean?"

"Hip, great, cool, over the top."

"Was that a term the Club Kids used themselves?"

"They used it to describe a night; the night was fabulous, that outfit was fabulous."

The government put up a large Velcro photo board as a kind of visual who's who of the racketeering and drug conspiracy hierarchy. At the top of the photo family tree was Gatien. Below him were the directors and party promoters—Alig, Caruso, Steve Lewis, Baby Joe Uzzardi, all responsible for making sure drugs were available at the parties. Below these were house dealers—guys like Rob

Gordon, Paulie Torres, Frankie the Baker, Goldyloxx. And at the bottom of the tree were the bouncers who permitted sanctioned dealers to enter the clubs.

In evidence were Gatien's financial records and club budgets. Caruso testified that he and Gatien had negotiated the cost of Ecstasy punches into club budgets during a conversation at Limelight in 1991.

"Basically, I was going to put a thousand dollars on the budget toward pills. Then Peter denied that, said he would only pay five hundred dollars, half of it," Caruso said.

"When you wrote out your budget, did the budget explicitly say 'Ecstasy Punch' on it?" Friedberg asked.

"No."

"What did it say?"

"'Special promotion,' 'goodies,' 'birthday parties,' 'favors.' We used a number of different things."

Defense attorney Brafman suggested that Gatien thought the clubgoers were lining up for Gatorade, because the punch was sometimes served from Gatorade jars—and what else would hot, sweaty kids who had been dancing all night want but free Gatorade?

Friedberg showed the jury party flyers, marked with the initials "PG," which made reference to the drugs that would be available that night—all the E's, K's, and X's in the flyers were set off in distinctive colors and fonts.

Caruso claimed that Gatien had had concerns about the brazenness of the ramped-up dealing in the clubs.

"[He] said, 'Hey, you know, you guys, you are going to get me locked up, you keep printing stuff like this on the invites. You can't do things like that,'" Caruso said.

"Did you continue to print them?"

"Yes."

"Did they continue to go out?"

"Yes."

"Did you pay for these invitations personally?"

"No."

"Who paid for them?"

"The club did."

Caruso claimed that Gatien knew about the house dealers he was bringing into the clubs.

"I had come into the office one day and basically Peter said to me, 'Do you have a crew of guys in here selling drugs for you in the club, in the Limelight?' I said, 'Yes, I do.' "

"What happened?" Friedberg asked.

"He then said to me, 'Well, you know, they're boasting and saying, "Hey, X, X, X, coke!" in the hallways. They can't be boasting out loud and yelling these things in the hallways to make their sales.' He said, 'Keep them, calm them down, and make sure they keep it to that crew, keep it to the crew of those guys.' "

Caruso's testimony seemed to bolster the government's claim that Gatien was focused on the money.

"There was a lot of competition with other clubs," Caruso testified. "Peter was talking about, 'Can you get some of your guys, Paul or somebody, to go up to Tavern on the Green, any of these clubs, and sort of sabotage their night,' whether they would beat the walls, clog the toilets so they flood out, so that people aren't comfortable and want to leave.

"And then within that conversation, I believe it was Michael Alig that came into the office and the subject of Ecstasy came up, how big our supply was and how what a great quality of drug that we had, and Peter stated, 'Can you make sure that Rob [Gordon] doesn't work any other clubs, that he only attends Limelight and works at this club and sells that X at this club?' and I said, 'That's no problem, I'll just tell Rob.' "

Rob Gordon was called to the stand as part of his cooperation deal with the government. The former drug dealer known by the club nickname "Stacy" testified that he had first met Gatien after Caruso had him deliver a pepper grinder (to pulverize rock cocaine) to his room at the Four Seasons.

Gordon told jurors he and Gatien had become friendly after that, and he described the Christmas gifts he'd bought the club owner: a $200 pair of Jean Paul Gaultier leather gloves one year, a silver box containing ten Ecstasy hits the next. Gordon said he once watched Gatien pick up the phone to call a fire department contact to get a rival club raided. He described writing up "86 lists" for Gatien—naming rogue dealers who were impinging on the house dealers' business—and then watching security run around the club on Gatien's command, kicking out everyone on the 86 list.

Gordon testified that he and Gatien bonded over hockey, and he gave Gatien a special code, 88, to use when paging him. It was the number of Gordon's favorite hockey player, Eric Lindros, of the Philadelphia Flyers.

Former club promoter Baby Joe Uzzardi told the jury that he had been drug-free until he began working at Tunnel. Then he'd begun taking massive doses of Ecstasy and LSD and heeding club director Steve Lewis's advice that "good music and good drugs" would make his parties more successful.

Uzzardi testified that in the summer of 1995, he told Gatien that they needed to organize the drug dealing because it was starting to get out of control. Uzzardi claimed Gatien replied, "I don't want to hear about drugs," and walked away.

Six different house dealers would testify to their experiences working for the clubs. Gatien was painted as the controller and financier of the drug dealing by virtue of the fact that he controlled the club budgets. However, they also testified that Gatien never spoke about drugs on the phone, collected money for drugs, or did drugs in his clubs. The government argued that it was a calculated self-protective measure on Gatien's part.

Clubland author Frank Owen sat through the month-long trial listening to days of tedious evidence about the club layout and secret drug messages in the party invitations. But like many reporters, he was waiting for some kind of startling admission or "freak show" fireworks.

"As the prosecution droned on I kept thinking 'Where's the beef? Where's the substance, the smoking gun, the missing part of the puzzle that will put Peter Gatien in prison for the rest of his life?' The odd thing was it should have been an open-and-shut case for the government," Owen wrote.

"Plus, Gatien's defense—that he was so screwed up on cocaine most of the time that he didn't know what was going on at his clubs—seemed less than compelling, even if it was true."

Gagne and Germanowski had convinced about thirty suspects to plead guilty for their roles in the drug-dealing conspiracy and to cooperate in the case against Gatien. It should have been a slam dunk. But they had underestimated the skill of Gatien's defense attorney—a five-foot-six-inch forty-nine-year-old bulldog in designer suits.

Defense attorney Benjamin Brafman had started out in 1976 as an assistant DA in the Rackets Bureau, handling political corruption, white-collar, and organized-crime cases. He lost one case in four years, and decided to hang out his own shingle in 1980. He quickly built a name for himself winning acquittals for members of the Gambino crime family—the kind of defendants he used to prosecute—and his former bosses at the DA's office were irked to see their protégé in a front-page photo in the *New York Post* in 1985, paying his respects at the funeral of Paul Castellano, the mob boss gunned down in front of the Sparks steak house.

In 1991, Brafman had represented Salvatore "Sammy the Bull" Gravano, the underboss who teamed with John Gotti to kill Castellano, securing Gotti's position as the new don. But when Gravano decided to cooperate with the feds against Gotti, Brafman distanced himself from his client-turned-rat, making sure to state in open court that he had nothing to do with Gravano's decision. In 1997, as Brafman was preparing for Gatien's trial, *New York* magazine named him the number one criminal defense attorney in the state.

On the opposite side of the courtroom, federal prosecutor Eric Friedberg was going on nine years with the U.S. attorney's office and was known for doing clean cases, no tricks up his sleeve. It infuriated Gagne and Germanowski. Every day after court they would meet to recap and discuss the next day's witnesses. Sometimes Brafman would call Friedberg and make a case for why the prosecution shouldn't call certain witnesses—including Michael Alig and Sean Bradley. He promised to vigorously cross-examine witnesses about their troubled pasts and to bring up the myriad allegations of government wrongdoing. Gagne and Germanowski would listen quietly as Brafman planted the seeds of doubt.

"Well, he does have a point . . . ," Friedberg would say, dropping another witness from the list.

The agents urged Friedberg to push back.

"Look, Brafman's a dirty street fighter," Gagne argued. "If he gets the chance, he'll kick you in the balls and run away. He's fighting like he's in an alley, you're fighting like we're in an Olympic boxing match, and we're gonna get clobbered."

"No," Friedberg would say. "We're the U.S. government. People expect more from us."

Friedberg had reason for his apprehensiveness. Brafman had brilliantly maneuvered every angle behind the scenes in the lead-up to trial. In 1997, Brafman filed court papers accusing Gagne and Germanowski of fabricating evidence. In his filing was a ten-page "Dear Judge" letter from Sean Bradley—the original informant who was arrested for an illegal Ecstasy buy. After being sent to jail, Bradley switched sides and claimed the agents had coerced his statements, taken drugs, and given him a secret recipe to beat his own drug urine test.

"Bradley accused us of having sex with his girlfriend. His attorney basically called me a Gestapo agent, a homophobe, and gay-basher," Germanowski later said. "I tried to help the kid as much as I could. Until he screwed me over. Then he can burn in hell like everybody else."

Bradley ultimately refused to testify to his allegations for fear of perjury charges.

Sean Kirkham, the con man with the fake tapes, also came back to throw another barb at the feds: Kirkham claimed he and prosecutor Friedberg had been engaged in a secret sexual relationship. Brafman wrote up Kirkham's salacious allegations in a pretrial motion requesting that the judge force the government to turn over Kirkham's confidential informant file.

"It is disheartening," Friedberg wrote in his legal response, "that you have used this meritless request as a way to publicly air what I am sure you know are false and potentially libelous allegations."

An investigation by the DOJ's Office of Professional Responsibility found Kirkham's claims to be false, again.

That was all just a preview. When they got to trial, Brafman was in full force, masterfully drawing out the criminal pasts of the prosecution's witnesses and marring their credibility during forceful cross-examinations. Michael Caruso, who had been stoic through nearly four days of testimony, broke down in tears when Brafman suggested he had murdered his roommate Damon Burrett.

In March 1993, Caruso had come home to find Burrett shot in the head in their loft apartment. Burrett had tried to commit suicide before, and police believed he had succeeded this time. Still, Caruso's shifty past played into rumors that he was somehow responsible for Burrett's death.

Brafman was a deft showman who injected *Law & Order*–style gotchas into the proceedings, and Rob Gordon fell into the same trap when he was cross-examined about his history of credit card theft and identity fraud.

"Now, the cloned phone—the fraud with the phone—same thing, right? You talk and talk and someone else pays."

"Yes," Gordon said.

"That was sort of your way of life? You commit the crime, and someone else pays?"

"Objection!" the prosecutor shouted. But the jury heard Brafman's message loud and clear: the bad guy was the one on the witness stand, not the one at the defense table.

Gagne sat at the prosecution table measuring the increasing fatigue in the jurors' faces and watching the case slip away from them. Every witness told the same story: the drug dealing in Gatien's clubs was open, obvious, and encouraged by upper management. But on cross-examination, their criminal misdeeds were easy fodder for Brafman. These witnesses had lied in the past, went the argument, so there was no reason to believe them now. Gagne wanted to scream: *Of course these witnesses had criminal pasts! Who employs Boy Scouts to be drug dealers?*

"We lost them," he said to Germanowski. "They're not even listening anymore. It's like they're thinking to themselves, 'Oh, shit, did I turn off the coffeepot this morning? God, I gotta pick my daughter up at four'—I mean, this is what they're thinking about."

At the same time, Friedberg was starting to worry about putting the agents on the stand. Brafman was threatening to trot out the misconduct affidavits. It wasn't going to look good.

"Are you kidding?" Gagne said. "The affidavits are crap. And we've got the tape of Alig's mother—you could even bring her in as a rebuttal witness.

"Look, we're gonna take some dings, but that's it," Gagne said. "You get us talking about how we interviewed all these guys for two years and independently they all say the same story—you can't preclude us from doing this."

Germanowski tried to stay positive, convincing Friedberg that they could bring it all back around once they got a chance to tell their side.

One evening, as the two attorneys were having a typical end-of-day call about the following day's witnesses and the agents were silently listening on speakerphone, Brafman made an unusual request.

If you rest right now and don't call your agents, Brafman told Friedberg, *then I won't put on a defense. And I won't have to dirty up your agents with those misconduct allegations.*

Oh, my God. He's really going to do this, Gagne thought.

Friedberg asked Brafman for his personal guarantee that in his closing arguments he would not say anything negative about the DEA agents.

Germanowski was furiously writing on sticky notes:
Mistake.
Mistake.
Mistake.
Brafman said he'd give it to him in a stipulation in

writing. They struck a deal. (Brafman would neither confirm nor deny the characterization of their conversation. Eric Friedberg did not respond to repeated attempts for comment.)

Up until that point, whenever Brafman would call to bully their AUSA, Gagne would bite his tongue and leave the room. But now, he was so worn down, he felt like he was floating through a bad dream. The fire left him.

The government rested its case without a word from Gagne, Germanowski, or Flaherty. Brafman kept his promise and did not call a single witness or put on a defense. It was an incredibly risky move.

Eric Friedberg delivered his closing argument with a workmanlike pitch. "For every person that came in to get a pill of Ecstasy thrown in their mouth by Michael Caruso or a glass of Ecstasy punch . . . for every person that came in and bought a bag of cocaine . . . a little bump of ketamine or Rohypnol at the 'Emergency Room' party, handed out to them for free . . . what did Peter Gatien get? He got twenty dollars at the door for every person that came in," Friedberg told the jurors.

"Having made millions of dollars off all these kids that are coming in and buying drugs—not directly through the drug sales, but through the gate, through the bar—now having made that money, Peter Gatien wants to walk away from this and say, 'I don't know about this. I didn't have anything to do with it. What they were doing they were doing despite management's best efforts,' " Friedberg said. "This is just absolutely not true."

As Brafman began his closing, he told the jury he was "mad as hell," sitting there for the past three and a half hours listening to Friedberg "try and pull a fast one" on the jury. He penned giant X's over the faces of the government's witnesses on their Velcro board, slaughtering their credibility one by one: "involved in suicide," "drug dealer," "armed robbery."

He asked the jurors to show "courage and integrity."

"We live in a time when everything is driven by the media: by television, by the movies. Everything is a problem. Everything is a concern. There is a concern about drugs. There is a concern about regulating them, whether they should be legalized or not. That's a debate we can have until the cows come home. That's not what this trial is about. It's not a referendum. Don't let the current that's out there affect your decision," Brafman pleaded with jurors. "I'm asking you to help me because you know and I know, and you heard the testimony and I heard the testimony. There isn't a juror here who I believe honestly can go home tonight and say, 'Brafman is wrong.' "

On February 11, 1998, after seven hours of deliberations, the jury reached a verdict: not guilty.

"In my heart, I felt I couldn't convict him on the evidence that was brought out," one juror, a sixty-two-year-old tractor-trailer driver, told the *Daily News*. "I really didn't get anything out of the government witnesses. I didn't think their testimony was credible."

When the judge adjourned and left the courtroom, dozens of Club Kids in the gallery, many who worked for Gatien, jumped out of their seats, overcome with joy, and danced in the aisles as they cried and hugged one another.

The prosecutors wanted to head out the back door of the courthouse, but the agents insisted on walking out the front.

"I got nothing to hang my head about," Germanowski said.

The agents passed Gatien and Brafman on their way out, past a horde of reporters, brandishing notebooks, microphones, and TV cameras.

"They went out for me any way they could," Gatien said. "This was an evil, mean-spirited prosecution. Right now, I'm just grateful to God. I want to go to church."

Brafman called the verdict a "categorical rejection" of the prosecution's case and the "sweetest victory" of his career.

"It was crystal clear to us that Peter Gatien knowingly allowed the dealing to go on and profited from it," Flaherty would later say about the case. "But the jury just didn't see it. I'd like to bring the jury to the clubs."

The bosses at DEA were supportive of the agents despite the loss—after all, they had succeeded in bringing attention to a class of drugs that specifically targeted youth and had previously been ignored by DEA and the press—the so-called club drugs Ecstasy, Rohypnol, GHB, and ketamine. More Ecstasy investigation cases were being opened as a result, and Gagne and Germanowski had become the resident experts, getting calls from across the country from reporters and drug cops who wanted to understand MDMA.

After the Gatien trial, Gagne returned to his cubicle at Intel, back to analysis and paper pushing and lending desk support to the street agents who were doing what he loved and missed the most—chasing bad guys. It was a bitter end to a case that had taken nearly three years of his life. He had fought so long and so hard that the verdict felt like a body blow—an affront to his sense of right and wrong. He would stop trying to make sense of it. Just close the door. Try to forget.

III "I'M THE BOSS. DON'T FUCK WITH ME"

40 ON THE RUN

ODED TUITO'S MOST IMPORTANT buyers and distributors in Pittsburgh had been arrested in the October 1997 warehouse raid. Unlike the arrests in Los Angeles, none of the Pittsburgh crew was family. It made Tuito paranoid and restless. He thought about whom he'd have to call a hit on, who needed killing, because it was only a matter of time before someone in Pittsburgh became a snitch, divulged Tuito's identity, his network, and his plans for Vertigo, which was still under construction.

Tuito had fled to a safe house in Miami after slipping away from Los Angeles police. He met up with his lieutenants in Florida—Meir Ben-David and Yosef Levi—and reached out to his L.A. and New York crews, keeping things under control as he planned his next move. Even without Pittsburgh, he was still in the drug game. But now he was wanted in Israel and America, and he refused to live in hiding in the States. He lay low for a few weeks, collected debts, and procured a new false ID to travel with.

Instead of calling a hit, Tuito decided to leave the country and walk away from his half-million-dollar nightclub investment. Vertigo was abandoned before the doors ever opened. His next base of operations would be Brussels, Belgium, and he would send for Aliza and the children once he settled in. In Belgium, Tuito could reconnect with Israeli expats and develop new criminal partners. The best part: he was just a border's drive from the source of Ecstasy supply—the clandestine Dutch labs.

41 THE CHAIN OF TRUST

IN THE 1980S, Ecstasy was so popular in Holland, Dutch drug dealers with pagers delivered pills like pizza, running promotions of buy five and get the sixth free. By the mid-1990s, Dutch law enforcement took a hard look at their synthetic drug problem and reluctantly admitted that the Netherlands was to Ecstasy what Colombia was to cocaine. Even worse, it soon became apparent that Dutch police had inadvertently helped to spread Ecstasy production and expertise among the very organized-crime factions they were trying to dismantle.

Every country has its share of organized crime, and the Netherlands is no different. Since 1991, Amsterdam has been the site of at least twenty-nine gangland hits, or "eliminations," in feuds among Dutch and ethnic criminals. The most famous Dutch drug lord, who emerged in the late 1980s, was Klaas Bruinsma, the son of a soda company CEO. Bruinsma began selling hashish in high school. By thirty-five, he was Holland's "Dutch Godfather" and the reigning kingpin of a multimillion-dollar organization that imported hash and cannabis to the Netherlands. When Bruinsma suspected his bodyguard, kickboxer André Brilleman, was stealing from him, the boxer's body was soon found encased in concrete and dumped in the river Waal. In 1991, Bruinsma was shot to death in front of the Amsterdam Hilton by a former police officer who was working for the Yugoslavian Mafia.

A combination of liberal drug laws, geographic accessibility, and an extensive chemical industry had turned the

Netherlands into a haven for drug traffickers. The first gift to traffickers was the Dutch Opium Law of 1976, which decriminalized use and distinguished between hard and soft drugs. Whereas the United States has five schedules, the Dutch have List 1 hard drugs (cocaine, heroin, LSD, Ecstasy) and List 2 soft drugs (cannabis and hashish). Mushrooms, if they are fresh and just picked, are List 2. But if they are dried and used in baked goods, they become List 1.

Drugs are not legal in the Netherlands, but just about any adult can walk into a hash bar in Amsterdam—taking care to note that "koffee" shops are for drinking coffee while "coffee" shops serve drugs—and order up a hash brownie or a cannabis cigarette. Enjoy it in private without causing a public nuisance and it is considered "nearly legal" and is tolerated. Coffee shop owners may not advertise or offer drugs. It's also illegal for them to purchase drugs, but they can have about a pound in the store without repercussions. It's "legal on the front door and illegal at the back," as they say.

The Dutch model is based on harm reduction: protect the public health, provide treatment options to users, and let law enforcement focus efforts on high-level drug producers instead of the drug users. As a social experiment, the Dutch people have benefited, with abuse rates significantly lower than those seen in the United States. In fact, immigrants and narcotourists account for the majority of abuse and distribution in the Netherlands. But the Dutch police have come to realize that soft drugs don't equal soft crime. Amsterdam has suffered for its role as the drug-dealing capital of Europe.

Commander Gadi Eshed of the Israeli National Police is a witness to the Dutch and Israeli Ecstasy connection. Eshed joined the police force in 1979 after serving three years in the army and studying international politics and cinema at Tel Aviv University. In 1985, the twenty-eight-year-old officer traveled to The Hague to take part in an Israeli heroin case. Dutch drug traffickers made good money in the 1970s and '80s importing cheap, clean heroin from Thailand, and Eshed found that Israeli criminals were importing that same heroin from the Netherlands to Israel. Eshed was so excited about his first international case that he gave up his hotel room, preferring instead to sleep on the floor in the wiretap room at the police station in The Hague for five weeks—just so he wouldn't miss any important phone calls between the dealers. It was a small operation, netting just two kilos of heroin, but Eshed loved the work, and he would return with his family in 1991 for a special four-year assignment as the Israeli representative in The Hague, aiding Dutch investigators in Israeli-related cases.

Today, Eshed's passport is filled with stamps from nearly every European country, parts of Africa, South America, and the United States. He speaks perfect English, Romanian, and Hebrew. His colleagues describe him as having an encyclopedic knowledge of organized crime. In Eshed's thirty years as an officer studying criminal networks around the world, he has come to recognize an enduring theme among traditional Israeli crime networks—a model he calls the chain of trust. Most chains involve men who grew up in the same impoverished neighborhoods in Israel, skipped out on army service, and spent time in jail, or "the academy," as Eshed sometimes calls it. It's where they learn who's a snitch and who's trustworthy by observing which prisoners receive better conditions.

The Netherlands, which maintained an open-door policy for immigration, was home for some 140,000 Jews when it was occupied by Nazi Germany in 1940. Resistance movements were futile. By 1942, the Nazi attempt to make Holland *Judenrein* (clean of Jews) had resulted in mass deportations to Auschwitz, Sobibor, and the Holland-based Westerbok camp. Some, including emblematic diarist Anne Frank, stayed in hiding in Amsterdam. In 1946, there were 30,000 Jews in the Netherlands, just 20 percent of the prewar Jewish population.

By the 1970s a renewed Jewish diaspora had reached Amsterdam and the border-close communities of Brussels and Antwerp in Belgium. Mixed among the hardworking and law-abiding Jewish citizens who settled in the welcoming Dutch and Belgian neighborhoods were small-time crooks. Burglars, extortionists, drug dealers, and auto thieves found they could take advantage of the idyllic communities where houses and cars were left open and unalarmed. In those days, street-level drug dealers could buy about ten grams of heroin for a pittance, take a train to Germany to sell it, and then hop on the next train back to Holland. They'd save enough to buy a hundred grams and sell that for a fivefold profit to buyers in Paris.

"They started with cocaine and heroin, and then this magic happened to all of them when they found this very cheap Ecstasy," Eshed says. "And all it cost was a phone call from Antwerp or Brussels, because until 1993, it was illegal for police to listen to phone conversations in Belgium, so you didn't even have to use codes. And besides, who would understand Hebrew?"

Ecstasy was first introduced to the region by 1980s jet-setters who thrilled to their first MDMA experience in Ibiza, Spain; Goa, India; and the United Kingdom and then spread the drug through house parties and raves in Amsterdam. MDMA was imported at first, but in time it would become a major Dutch export thanks to innovative amphetamine pioneers.

In the 1970s, Dutch criminals in the southern provinces of Limburg and North Brabant created clandestine amphetamine labs and established well-worn trafficking routes to Scandinavia, the United Kingdom, and Germany. They forged criminal links just across the border in Belgium with the thriving mom-and-pop bootleggers who slowly transitioned from liquor into amphetamine cooking. Decriminalization of drugs in 1976 only emboldened the entrepreneurial spirit of these synthetic drug traffickers.

As Ecstasy demand proliferated in the 1980s, the freelance amphetamine cookers switched to MDMA, using the same labs, chemical expertise, and relationships they had used for amphetamine production. About 10 percent of their investment was in lab hardware and 90 percent was in precursor chemicals. Obtaining the raw chemical materials was easy for them because the Netherlands is home to some 2,400 legal chemical companies. The main precursor for Ecstasy, PMK, already had legitimate uses in everything from perfumes to insecticides and was not even licensed by the Dutch until the July 1995 Prevention of Abuse of Chemicals law. Even then, Dutch criminals could turn to corrupt chemical facilities or simply import the precursors from China and Eastern Europe.

The liberal Dutch drug laws did little to discourage production because prison sentences were so light. Key members of an organization, such as chemists who possessed production knowledge, faced an average of four to six years' incarceration if caught and convicted. But the majority of unskilled traffickers received, at most, up to a year in prison, where they made new contacts and resumed their place in the illicit networks upon release.

The Netherlands made MDMA illegal in 1988, but by 1991, when Gadi Eshed began his assignment in The Hague, high-quality pills were being produced by Dutch chemists and distributed by established underworld criminal organizations. In February 1992, Dutch police dismantled a major MDMA production facility run by a group of former hashish traffickers. The group owned labs, imported precursor chemicals from Belgium, and produced millions of pills. One of the main organizers of the network was a Belgian physician named Danny Leclère, aka the "Ecstasy professor," who had learned the trade from southern amphetamine cookers. Leclère was "eliminated" in 1993 by an unknown assailant who shot him dead in his car on the Amsterdam ring road. Police found the MDMA formula in Leclère's vehicle.

Gadi Eshed was witness to one of the most damaging crises in the country's law enforcement history: in the early 1990s, police had unwittingly helped drug traffickers further expand and heighten MDMA production. It began when Dutch prosecutors and police responded to the new tolerance for cannabis by reprioritizing their investigative efforts to target hard-drug producers. They turned a blind eye to the trafficking of soft drugs, ultimately allowing dozens of tons of cannabis to be imported into the Netherlands. The injection of riches that the organized crime syndicates made in cannabis trafficking gave them the capital, the contacts, and the gumption to branch into hard drugs. Their high-end amphetamine labs soon gave way to Ecstasy labs.

But it wasn't just turning a blind eye that made law enforcement culpable. The Dutch police took part in long-term secret investigations, whereby undercover officers and informants infiltrated the ground levels of criminal organizations and worked alongside the lower ranks in an attempt to build credibility all the way up to the targets: the drug lords. But the undercovers had entwined themselves so tightly with the organizations that it became unclear who was in control—the police or the criminals.

In one case, a criminal undercover known as "the Snail" learned how to produce MDMA from a southern amphetamine cooker. When the cooker was arrested, the Snail taught the other members of the network how to produce Ecstasy. He also supplied precursor chemicals and lab equipment, and made repairs to the equipment over a four-year period. His criminal cohorts nicknamed him the Snail because he was slow to respond to their trafficking propositions. They didn't know it was because he was waiting for instructions from his police handlers at the Criminal Intelligence Division.

The Snail helped to bring down several southern Ecstasy barons, but many of them were later released when an investigation into Dutch policing methods determined there had been a rampant use of undercovers and informants that was judged illegal. The crisis was only compounded by the culture of secrecy that Dutch police had been working in. The country had twenty-five different policing districts, with a twenty-sixth national police unit—and yet each district worked as if it was independent, keeping separate databases and intelligence files. The districts failed to share information, allowing corruption to breed.

Meanwhile, Israeli criminals had partnered with Dutch chemists to become astute Ecstasy pioneers, quick to exploit the vulnerabilities of the Dutch legal system and reap the benefits of smuggling in the Benelux region. There were already easily accessible smuggling routes by land (vehicle border checkpoints were slowly fading with the increasing integration of the European Union), by sea (Rotterdam was Europe's largest port and a major transit point for chemical products), and by air (drug couriers in a pre–September 11 world could easily hide drugs in their suitcases on direct flights from Amsterdam to New York, Los Angeles, and Miami with little worry).

With one phone call to a New York contact—a link in the chain of trust—a dealer could line up capable Israeli buyers and distributors in the States, where Ecstasy consumption was skyrocketing among nightclub denizens. Israelis almost never ran Ecstasy labs. They learned it was smarter to stick to what they were good at—overseeing distribution chains—and let the Dutch traffickers and their networks of chemists handle production.

Slowly, the Israeli traffickers in Amsterdam reached out to their relatives and old neighbors in Israel, inviting them to join them. They learned the language, they married Dutch women—many who were from the red-light district—and their wives widened the chain of trust to local Dutch criminals who had access to drugs.

One of the most well-known interlopers among organized crime factions was the Israeli Edmond "Eddie" Sasson, who married a Dutch woman and lived in Amsterdam for twenty years. Sasson trafficked cannabis with an Egyptian man who was active in prostitution and human trafficking in the red-light district. Sasson's Maya restaurant and jazz club, on the Leidseplein, was known by Dutch police to be a thriving nightspot for underworld figures.

Oded Tuito and his drug-smuggling friends would visit Maya when in Amsterdam. Another notable Maya patron was a tough Israeli con from the north named Jacob "the Dog" Elchik. Like Sasson, Elchik had moved to Holland and married a Dutch woman. But Elchik also spent fourteen years in a French prison for drug trafficking. He padded his stable of criminal contacts while behind bars, and at the end of the 1990s, when Elchik was released, he returned to Amsterdam to reconnect with his Dutch partners, who were now running Ecstasy labs.

During Gadi Eshed's tenure in Holland from 1991 to 1995, the Israeli MDMA networks in the Netherlands were of the freelance, loose-knit variety. They distributed thousands of pills a week and very little of it was destined for the United States. As far as Eshed could tell, there were no Israeli kingpins or Mafia monopolizing the trade. The change came when the Fat Man moved to Belgium in 1998.

One of Jacob "the Dog" Elchik's most important acts after he was released from French prison was providing introductions to Oded Tuito that put the Fat Man in direct contact with Ecstasy labs that could produce half a million tablets a day, made to order.

Tuito had made thousands of dollars a month selling heroin in Israel and marijuana and cocaine in the States. But when he abandoned those drugs for Ecstasy trafficking, he made millions, and America became his most valuable customer.

42 ADAPT, IMPROVISE, AND OVERCOME

AFTER SEVEN YEARS AS a drug cop, Bob Gagne never imagined he'd be burning out at a desk job at the age of thirty-two. The key to his success as a street agent was building relationships with people. The key to success in Intel was embracing numbers. It seemed to Gagne that everyone was wading through reports and raw data, searching for the magic statistic to send up to their boss that would pinpoint the next big success, trend, or crisis in the drug war.

As a street agent, his work hours were unpredictable and dictated by the movements of the drug dealers he was shadowing. As an Intelligence agent, Gagne got into the office by 8:30 a.m., worked out in the gym until ten, did analysis at his desk all day, and left by six. He hardly saw his two best friends anymore. The other Intel agents were at a place in their careers where they wanted to relax. Gagne wanted to work. He would train hard in the gym until he was so physically exhausted that he was too numb to feel his emotional exhaustion. He wouldn't show his anger at the office. He didn't want to be *that* guy—the one who walks around telling people how miserable he is. But on the drive home alone, he couldn't escape the nagging thought: *Tomorrow will be exactly the same.* Gagne wanted to quit DEA, and he hadn't felt that way since Snowcap. He knew he was suffering a crisis of confidence. He decided to get married.

Kristen was a pretty fitness instructor Gagne had met through a friend in 1995. She was smart, blue-eyed, blond, not a hair out of place. After enduring men in drag with octopus hands and having to squeeze into tight pants and black lipstick, Gagne was desperate for normalcy. Kristen looked like an angel to him. She came from a loving home. She didn't touch drugs. She smiled at him like he was someone special. She felt like the answer as he trudged into a second depressing year at Intel. They moved into an apartment on Long Island together.

Gagne's family had trouble warming to Kristen. Gagne's family was working-class. Kristen's vacationed on Martha's Vineyard. Germanowski saw Gagne's courting of Kristen as another wedge between them.

"Bob, she's like a Kennedy," Germanowski said one day. "Look, my dad was a steelworker, my mom was a secretary. Yeah, I think it would be cool to be a Kennedy too. But I'm not. And Gags, this isn't you."

Gagne didn't want to hear their concerns. He had grown distant from his own family and felt alienated from his DEA brothers in group D-35 since being sent downstairs to S-11. He wanted to start a family of his own now.

Gagne proposed to Kristen in the Hamptons after first receiving her father's permission. They would marry in the fall of 1998 and save up to buy a house in suburban Long Island. Gagne wanted children right away.

At work, he set his mind to adapt, improvise, and overcome. He would make Ecstasy his intelligence specialty. If he shared his knowledge with the enforcement groups handling MDMA cases, maybe he could convince the bosses to let him go out on some of their operations. *It's always easier to apologize than it is to get permission,* Gagne thought. He'd just tag along until someone told him it couldn't be done.

43 JACKIE SUAREZ

ODED TUITO WAS ALSO feeling amorous. Tuito had left behind several courier girlfriends in Pittsburgh and he needed new mules. Steve Hager, who was promoted to courier recruiter, handpicked the new stable from his entourage of strippers and party girls.

Hager had asked his dark-haired muse, Jackie Suarez, to go to Brussels for him to pick up Ecstasy on a few occasions. All she had to do was carry the pills back in her suitcase and she'd receive $10,000 plus travel expenses. Suarez always said no. It was too risky and she didn't really need the money when Hager was paying her bills. But by the summer of 1998, Suarez was starting to tire of Hager. His temper constantly flared over the smallest perceived slights, whether real or imagined. She felt like property. He belittled her in front of his friends. She put up with it because she was addicted to the glamour and ease of the life, and to cocaine, which Hager liberally supplied. But $10,000 could give her some independence. In July 1998, Suarez finally agreed to do the job.

Hager sent Suarez to Tuito on a Delta/Sabena Airlines flight to Brussels after they spent a string of drunken, cocaine-shot nights together. She was dehydrated and exhausted, and her nasal passages felt like Swiss cheese. She took pills to sleep on the plane. When she arrived in Brussels, she got a room at the Ibis Hotel and called Hager to check in. She was peeved when he didn't answer. She called her mother and lied that she was spending Independence Day on the Jersey shore. Then she heard a knock at her door.

Tuito was over six feet tall and about 220 pounds, with black hair and brown eyes. He spoke muddled English and introduced himself as "Daniel" (his brother's name). He told Suarez that she would be moving to a new hotel in the morning.

"I'll have to check with Steve."

"Forget about Steve," Tuito said, annoyed. "I'm the boss."

Suarez thought Tuito was rude. She began to have regrets about accepting the assignment. She spent the evening alone at the hotel bar, next to Belgian barflies and tourists who were transfixed in front of the TV set, cheering wildly as they watched the World Cup soccer finals.

When Tuito came for her the next morning he had softened. He helped her with her bags and took her to lunch with his lieutenant, David Ben-Amara, whom he introduced as "Gingi." Gingi was a thirty-four-year-old Israeli fugitive who oversaw Tuito's American and Israeli couriers. He should have been handling Suarez himself, but Tuito always wanted to meet the women Hager sent him.

After a few glasses of wine, Suarez began to see a kindness in Tuito's eyes. They chatted about New York. He knew about her relationship with Hager, but she wasn't sure how or what he had been told. He also knew about her relationship with cocaine. He looked her in the eye and told her unequivocally that anything that "fucked with business" was unacceptable, which meant that doing cocaine on company time was not going to cut it. Alcohol and Ecstasy were fine—in fact, Tuito had a tremendous appetite for both—but he didn't want his girls to be cokeheads. Suarez agreed to meet Tuito later that night to sample some of the Ecstasy she was about to smuggle back to the States for him.

When it was time for Suarez to return to New York, Tuito had a proposition: come back in ten days with a delivery of cash, he would make all the arrangements, and then he would take her to Nice for pleasure, no business.

She said she would think about it.

Back in the States, she made it safely through Customs at JFK, where a stranger was waiting for her. He took her bags and dropped her off at Hager's apartment.

There was something about Tuito that moved Suarez. He was generous. He seemed a little vulnerable. He also had gunshot wounds and knife marks covering his legs and arms. Any other woman might have taken that as a sign to run. But Suarez was intrigued. She accepted Tuito's proposal. As instructed, she kept it a secret from Hager. Suarez was Tuito's courier now. She felt strong and independent and grew to resent Hager for having treated her so shabbily. She decided she didn't need him anymore.

Hager, who was deeply stung by Suarez's sudden departure from his clique with no explanation, was too proud to act like he cared.

Tuito had a dependable soldier in New York named Ronen "Tuff Tuff" Dayan, who sometimes coordinated shipments with Hager and Judy Ben Atar. Tuff Tuff was told to look after Suarez—check on her, take her out once in a while, and keep her away from cocaine. For her first assignment for Tuito, Suarez was sent to a man in Queens who gave her two suitcases filled with $250,000 cash hidden in false-bottom bags. She would carry the money to Belgium. Before she got on the plane she popped into the bathroom to do some blow. Just a quick pick-me-up.

Suarez passed, with no snags, through airport security in Brussels. A driver was waiting on the other side. He took her straight to Tuito's apartment, where she was greeted by the Fat Man with kisses and bottles of wine. He cooked her dinner and then took her to Carré, a nightclub just outside the city, to meet his friends. Everyone took Ecstasy that night and Suarez got lost in the cacophony of techno music, streaming lights, and the swirl of different languages being spoken around her. When Suarez was with Tuito, people looked after her comfort and listened when she spoke. Tuito took her back home and they had sex for the first time. He was a giant, hairy teddy bear of a man, and not the most sensitive or skilled lover. But it wasn't his prowess in bed or looks that kept her around. He made her feel special.

The next day they flew to Nice and took a room at the four-star Le Meridien, where they spent wine-drenched nights making love with a moonlit view of the Mediterranean Sea. They wandered up the coast, eating shrimp, drinking more wine, listening to jazz. They walked along a marina where Tuito shared his dream of buying a fishing boat one day, so he could spend more time on the tranquil sea. He also talked of having killed men—in self-defense, he said. He spoke of his love for his mother, his children, and his wife. He made jokes at his own expense about not being the best Jew. Tuito had a rapacious appetite for food, booze, drugs, and sex. He had trouble staying kosher and was regretful that at his son's bar mitzvah, he'd struggled through prayers he should have known. As far as Suarez could tell, he took care of his employees and he sent money home to his family in Israel. Suarez never suspected Tuito was the world's biggest Ecstasy trafficker. They spent twelve days together on the French Riviera, some of her best days.

Before Suarez returned to the States, Tuito sat her down to talk business. He told her that all he knew was being a criminal. This was all he had to offer her. And then he asked her what she wanted—what part of his business she would like to stake her claim in. His trust in her cemented her loyalty. From then on, Suarez would handle New York with Tuff Tuff.

44 "CLARE"

BY AUGUST 1998, Gagne had been so instrumental in providing intelligence support for a crystal meth and Ecstasy case out of Long Island that he had convinced the enforcement group to let him do the undercover buy/bust of one of the targets—an Ecstasy dealer named "Clare."

Clare could have been any number of troubled defendants who stumbled into the drug trade and got lost. She was a stripper who got caught selling a handful of pills in a nightclub; she was addicted to coke, X, and gin; she had an absentee father and a mother whom she drove to chemotherapy appointments each week.

"Yeah, you guys got me. Go fuck yourself," Clare greeted Gagne the first time he visited her in her holding cell.

Gagne took his time with Clare.

"Look, I know you're dealing with the Israelis and you're probably afraid of them," he said. "But I also know that your mother's very sick."

She gave Gagne a cold stare and said nothing.

"This is your second offense. I'm not going to ask you to cooperate. I'm not going to tell you what to do. Because I think you need time to think about it for yourself."

Five minutes after Gagne left, he got a phone call to come back. Clare was asking for him.

"All right," she said. "I'll talk to you."

Gagne had been burned by confidential informants enough times to know whom to trust and whom to walk away from. Dealing with sources was a constant dance of control: be light; casually nod in agreement and pretend to know more than you do, because it keeps the source talking; don't lie, because if they catch you in a lie, everything else that comes out of your mouth will be met with suspicion.

Gagne built trust with sources by never making promises he couldn't keep. And for some, keeping a promise of confidentiality was a matter of life and death.

It took months for Clare to begin to divulge small crumbs about the Ecstasy networks in New York and Holland. The first piece she gave Gagne was a Manhattan dealer named Steve Hager—it was the first time Gagne had heard his full name.

Hager recruited dancers from Scores, Ten, and VIP to mule pills, Clare said. The money was good: $10,000 per trip plus travel expenses.

Gagne knew from Clare's travel records that she had flown to Belgium at least once, likely to mule pills for Hager, but Clare denied it. She claimed she could never mule pills because she had white-knuckle panic attacks on airplanes, and that didn't bode well for someone aiming to deflect attention. Clare said she preferred to sell pills for extra cash and had purchased several thousand hits of X from Hager in the past year.

Gagne had a problem. Clare gave him the first real link he had ever encountered to the Israeli networks, and she was willing to set up undercover buys—but Gagne was S-11 and Intel agents couldn't open cases. He'd have to convince a street agent to do it, and then insinuate himself into the operations.

Since Clare's arrest was out of Long Island, Gagne asked special agent Roger Bach of the Long Island

Division Office, or LIDO, to start a file on Steve Hager. Bach would be the official case agent, but Gagne would do as much legwork as he could get away with.

For Clare's first undercover buy with Hager, she wore a recorder on her body. Gagne later listened to his voice on the tape: Hager had a deep, hurried accent, a slight lisp. His pills tested positive for MDMA. Clare arranged for a second buy/walk of a thousand pills for $8,000. It was a low-ball purchase in Hager's world, but just squeezing that kind of cash out of DEA was a challenge for Gagne. His solution was to share the case with the Office of the Special Narcotics Prosecutors, an agency exclusively dedicated to the investigation and prosecution of narcotics felonies in the five boroughs. For Gagne, it meant Hager's case would be handled in state, not federal, courts—and he would lose some control. In return, OSNP would chip in a major portion of the buy money.

On October 22, Clare geared up for the final buy/bust. The agents searched Clare's black Mitsubishi 3000 GT for drugs, issued her a KEL transmitter, and sent her to 33rd Street and Third Avenue, where Hager had asked her to meet him. Special agent Robert Yoos watched across the street from a black undercover Nissan 300ZX. A few minutes after five, the surveillance team saw Hager exiting his building on East 34th Street carrying a small shopping bag.

"He's on the corner," Yoos called on the radio once Hager was in sight of the staging area. "Okay, he's walking across the street."

But something wasn't right. Hager passed Clare's car.

"Where is he going?" Gagne said. The agents were burning up the radio: "Did he see us?"

"He's walking right toward me!" Yoos said. "I'm going off air!"

Yoos dropped his handheld radio just as Hager opened the passenger-side door of the Nissan and got into the car. The other agents held their breath, waiting for a signal to move.

"You're not Clare!" Hager said.

"Uh, no."

"Sorry, sorry." Hager dialed Clare's cell phone as he scrambled out of the car. "Where are you? Oh, I see you. Okay, I'm coming."

When Hager was out of earshot Yoos picked up the radio.

"You're not going to believe this," he told his team. "He got in the wrong car."

Clare kissed Hager hello, they laughed about his absentminded mix-up with her car, and then she looked in the shopping bag: large zip-top bags swollen full of small white pills.

"Okay," she said. "I just need to get the money from the trunk."

She stepped out and popped open the trunk—the prearranged arrest signal—and the agents circled.

Hager stayed calm as he was read his rights and Agent Bach took custody of his shopping bag. Inside were three thousand pills stamped with a "Tweety Bird" logo. In Hager's front-right pants pocket was $8,238. Two of the $100 bills matched the serial numbers of the buy money Clare had paid him a week earlier, further implicating Hager. The agents asked him to sign a release to search his apartment and Hager began to sweat and shake. He seemed to be stalling. He claimed to be diabetic, which was true. Hager was eight days shy of his thirty-eighth birthday and in the worst shape of his life, a bloated 240 pounds from excessive indulgence in cocaine, Ecstasy, alcohol, rich foods, and a lifestyle that was slowly killing him. He eventually handed over the keys to apartment

19G. Inside, Gagne and Yoos found another four thousand pills in a safe. On the living room coffee table was a cocaine grinder and a suitcase filled with $14,700 in $100 bills. Gagne seized Hager's address books, papers with scribbled numbers, his passport, and several photographs. But what he had missed was a quarter of a million Ecstasy pills that had been whisked away minutes earlier by Oded Tuito's New York soldier Ronen "Tuff Tuff" Dayan. Hager had wasted just enough time for Tuff Tuff to notice he had been gone too long. Sensing something was amiss, Tuff Tuff grabbed the pills and took off.

Hager was charged with sale and possession of MDMA. He spent a few days in jail and was released on bond. He turned to his younger brother, Isaac, for help, while begging Isaac not to tell their parents. Their father had been a rabbi in Israel, their mother a lawyer—it would be too shameful. He had managed to keep his drug business a secret from them for this long; his arrest was just one more little secret to add to the charade.

Hager hired a top attorney and let his case drag through the state court system for as long as possible. Gagne kept close tabs on him, studying his address books, his phone records, and his movements. Hager knew he was being watched and it put a crimp in his business. But he continued to spend his money on copious amounts of cocaine and girls. He couldn't resist the girls.

Clare moved back home to be closer to her sick mother. She thought about going back to school. She quit the strip club, but her girlfriends still called. She hated it when they bragged about being wined and dined in Europe: champagne, drugs, and luxury hotels. She knew that wasn't always the case. Sometimes a girl was left to wait in a cheap, dirty room for two days without a word. Sometimes the dealers took her bags, dumped her clothes, and made her change hotel rooms in the middle of the night. Sometimes she was treated like an actual mule instead of a woman.

Clare gave Gagne the next piece of information, and it was more than a crumb: the big guy, his name was Tuito. She said his lieutenants used a travel agent in midtown to buy the girls' tickets and that the suitcases all the mules carried had Velcro strips along the inside seams at the bottom of the bag. Just lift the strip and there was a hidden compartment underneath for the pills.

In fact, the false-bottom design had been around for years, originally created for Antwerp's diamond dealers. The Ecstasy traffickers simply adapted its use from diamonds to pills.

45 "NOBODY EVEN KNEW WHERE ECSTASY WAS COMING FROM"

DEA TURNED TWENTY-FIVE in 1998, and like any entity reaching the quarter-century mark, it was taking stock. Up until then, the majority of DEA's time and cash had been earmarked for cocaine and heroin interdiction. But Ecstasy trafficking had reached unprecedented levels. Fewer than 200 tablets were mixed in among the drugs DEA seized nationwide in 1993. By 1997, more than 68,000 pills had been confiscated by DEA agents; U.S. customs agents reported an additional 370,000 pills seized at borders, seaports, and airports.

Drug trafficking was also changing, thanks to the streamlined efficiency of globalization. The same developing technologies that had fomented legitimate international commerce were also creating paths to wealth for illicit commerce. Traffickers could be in four corners of the globe, in constant contact through cell phones and e-mail, utilizing legitimate shipping and transport companies, and coordinating millions of dollars in drug loads around the world. In Europe, cooperation among EU countries was a boon for traffickers. The Schengen Agreement—a plan that allowed free movement between EU countries—meant that drugs could be driven from the Netherlands to Belgium and Paris without a single border stop. DEA headquarters had decided it was time to take a closer look at Europe.

A DEA intelligence bulletin on Ecstasy trafficking in Western Europe had noted a sharp rise in MDMA demand in 1997 among fifteen- to twenty-five-year-olds.

Bad pills were flooding the market to fill the gap between supply and demand. In Scotland, police had seized half a million tablets that were really dog-worming pills. British police found purported Ecstasy made of heroin and horse steroids. Germany reported fifteen deaths attributed to Ecstasy use.

Seizures and arrests were on the rise in Belgium, France, Ireland, Italy, Spain, Austria, and Croatia. Interpol estimated that 396 million Ecstasy tablets had been seized in Europe in 1995, with the Netherlands as the top source country. By the end of 1998, the United States was the top importer of Dutch pills.

Around the same time, four DEA agents stationed in different parts of the world found themselves at similar junctures in their careers. Each was in a new city with a new assignment and looking for ways to distinguish himself. Gagne would soon come to know these men—Ecstasy would be their common denominator.

In late 1997, Special Agent James Chris Kabel was sent to Special Operations Division in Virginia, a purse-controlling division of DEA. SOD was suits-and-ties territory, but Kabel was a rugged young agent who had spent six years in the jungles of Thailand, eluding armed insurgents and dismantling heroin labs as part of Operation Tiger Trap.

When Kabel got to SOD, they dumped a pile of teletypes on his desk and said, "Here ya go, you've got Flashback."

Operation Flashback was a special enforcement program begun in July 1997 to target the domestic distribution of LSD and hallucinogens, and later MDMA. It was an umbrella program that supported field division investigations, so street agents interested in LSD or MDMA could raise the priority of their smaller cases amid the sea of heroin and cocaine cases that dominated most field divisions' resources.

As the keeper of Flashback, Kabel had access to GES-CAN, DEA's automated message handling system. Every day he would type in "MDMA" and "Ecstasy" and the system would spit back hits from every international DEA teletype. Kabel was getting an unprecedented one hundred teletypes a day. It seemed that none of the field divisions were actively sharing Ecstasy intel.

"At that time, nobody even knew where Ecstasy was coming from," Kabel says. "From the DEA perspective it's a club drug, kiddie dope. But we were starting to see common names, Israelis importing Ecstasy from Europe. We were tracing phone tolls back to the same locations—Miami, Los Angeles, New York, Holland, Belgium, and Germany."

Officers from the Bundeskriminalamt, German federal police, or BKA, were visiting the office one day on a separate matter and happened to mention to Kabel that they were studying MDMA distribution as well, and would he like to see their data?

"They break out this flowchart and it's the mirror image of our flowchart—it's the same guys. They had the exact same assessment that we had," Kabel says. "It was an affirmation for us that we were on the right track."

Special agent Stephen Luzinski became DEA's country attaché in Brussels in October 1998. The Brussels office is significant today because of its proximity to the offices of the European Commission, the executive branch of the European Union. But when Luzinski came on in 1998, it was a struggle to justify the office's expensive existence—nestled among crumbling Old World buildings, chocolatiers, and antique shops—especially when foreign operations were focused on heroin- and cocaine-producing countries.

Luzinski dug into the Brussels files looking for interesting cocaine cases—after all, Antwerp had one of the biggest ports in Europe. To his surprise, he found memo after memo from local drug cops calling about Ecstasy. The information had gone nowhere.

"We were literally at ground zero in terms of Belgium being a major producer and major transshipment point," Luzinski says. "I started finding that our Belgian counterparts had tremendous intelligence into Ecstasy operations but no one was bridging the gap and getting that information into our U.S. offices."

Next door, in the Netherlands, Special Agent Don Rospond arrived in November 1998 as an assistant country attaché to The Hague.

"We estimated that 80 percent of the drug was produced in Holland and that America was the primary consumer," Rospond says. "It really exploded around the time we got here."

By then the Dutch authorities were painfully aware of their Ecstasy problem.

"They were starting to realize they were the source country for this stuff and they really didn't want that label," Rospond says.

And while Gagne was just starting to investigate Tuito's New York network, he had no idea that another agent had spent the last year digging up evidence on Tuito's Pittsburgh crew.

When police arrested Tuito's partners in the warehouse raid of October 1997, DEA picked up the case for federal prosecution and rookie DEA Special Agent Gregg Drews took the lead. Drews figured he had a marijuana and cocaine ring on his hands, but after several months of debriefing the suspects, all anyone talked about was Oded Tuito and Ecstasy. Drews learned everything he could about both. He clipped newspaper articles, kept meticulous case notes, and studied intelligence flowcharts that depicted Western Union transfers to Tuito's networks in Israel and Los Angeles.

Just as Tuito had feared, one of his former lieutenants

in Pittsburgh eventually became a snitch in order to save his own skin. In November 1998, the guy was back in touch with Tuito and secretly taping their phone calls to hand over to Drews and his partners.

"*I want you to find someone to buy Vertigo,*" Tuito. was overheard ordering the informant.

"*How much do you want to sell it for? A million?*" the CI asked.

"*Too much. A half million is good.*"

Before they hung up, Tuito told the CI to go and "put a mark" on the face of a dealer in Pittsburgh who owed Tuito money, and to please pass along his new pager number to a stripper in Pittsburgh named Angel. And while he was at it, could he also "find a bitch" to send to him in Belgium—"not for work, for vacation."

Agent Drews had big plans. He wanted to bring an undercover into the relationship and he imagined his undercover making buys in Pittsburgh, wending his way into Tuito's network, flying to Belgium to meet the top soldiers, and eventually bringing down the entire ring. Even if Drews could pull it off, it would be a time-consuming and expensive operation: travel to Europe, $40,000 drug buys, wiretaps. He wasn't going to get that kind of support from his bosses just to go after kiddie dope. But if he could bring agents from around the country together to share intel, maybe it would drum up more resources and support for the Tuito case.

Drews called Chris Kabel at Special Ops, who was still reviewing international teletypes on Ecstasy intel. Kabel agreed: Ecstasy was big, and they needed to host a strategy conference and coordinate their efforts on this thing.

Drews was excited, but to get more money for his case, he had to share, and sharing meant he might lose his case. Drugs enter the United States primarily through

El Paso, Miami, L.A., New York—which is why those DEA field divisions get the most press coverage and target the biggest drug lords. Drews didn't want to see one of the big cities—where the majority of Tuito's pills were landing—steal the Fat Man out from under him.

The Fat Man was like a romantic mystery to Drews. When he first got ahold of Tuito's local cell phone number, he dialed it a few times and it always went straight to voice mail. After that, he must have called a hundred times just to listen to Tuito's muddy hard-bitten English on the outgoing message. It was just seven words: *"I'm the boss. Don't fuck with me."* Beep.

46 TWEETY

IN NEW YORK, Gagne was punching up names and numbers from Hager's phone records and address book looking for connections. He ran an AutoTrack check on Hager's home address and an interesting lead came up: a guy named Sean Erez had once used Hager's address to apply for a New York driver's license. Clare remembered Erez. Said he used to sell pills in the clubs, but last she heard he had been arrested by NYPD and she hadn't seen him since. Police confirmed that Erez and his girlfriend, Diana Reicherter, were picked up in July with a hundred tabs of X. Charges against his girlfriend were dismissed. Erez was charged with intent to sell, reckless endangerment, and resisting arrest, but he copped a plea deal, got time served, and had been released from jail on October 8.

Another lead: Hager's phone records showed that he had been constantly dialing the number listed to a Jackie Suarez at 814 Tenth Avenue for months, and then nothing since August. Clare said she didn't know any strippers named Jackie. Gagne did a DMV lookup and found a Jacqueline Suarez in New York. She was pretty, with dark eyes and hardly any makeup.

As Gagne sought out the New York links, he noticed an increase in Ecstasy teletypes from Europe. The French police seemed to be knocking off couriers left and right.

On November 17, 1998, a fax came from the DC Interpol office: France was reporting the October seizure of 36,330 Ecstasy tablets at the Charles de Gaulle airport in Paris from a thirty-year-old Israeli from Haifa who was on his way to JFK. The Tweety pills—hidden in two false-bottom duffel bags—matched the type of pills seized from a female courier in September out of Zaventem airport in Brussels. A third courier, a New Yorker named Christina Ridgeway, would be arrested in November attempting to board an American Airlines flight from Paris to Miami.

Ridgeway was interrogated in a French prison for three days. The twenty-seven-year-old singer/model said she danced for extra cash at private parties when she was broke, which was often. At the time of her arrest she had just $60 to her name. A stripper named Jennifer had recruited her to mule pills for Israeli dealers, saying it was an easy $10,000. Ridgeway flew to Brussels, checked into room 336 of the Ibis Hotel, and was met by three Israelis who called themselves "Terry," "Gingi," and "Sam." They partied that night with other women she had never met but suspected were also mules. Some of them took Ecstasy with the dealers.

On Sunday morning, Gingi called Ridgeway's room and told her to step into the lobby. At the elevator, he handed her two soft travel bags and then left. Alone in her room, she peeked into the bags but saw nothing. Terry called next and instructed her to go outside, where he was waiting in a small black European car. He handed her a train ticket to France and told her to check in at the Select Hotel in Paris. When she arrived, another Israeli man took her to the airport and left. Suspicious Customs agents took it from there. Ridgeway never made her flight.

"I regret having been so naïve as to allow myself to be drawn into that business," Ridgeway told her questioners through tears.

The police showed her a photo spread.

"That's the one I call Sam," she said, pointing out Oded Tuito. "I recognize his smirk."

Gagne studied the arrest details. Ridgeway was carrying almost thirty-four thousand Ecstasy pills in her bags, all of them stamped with the Tweety Bird logo.

It clicked. Tweety—Tuito.

He was building his signature brand.

Operation Snowcap made close friends of DEA agents Frank Fernandez, Jr., Jay Seale, Robert Gagne, Linda Miller, and Meredith Thompson. A plane crash in Peru shortly after this photo was taken would devastate the team and forever alter Gagne's personal mission in the drug war.

Robert Gagne with his D-35 brothers Jay Flaherty and Matthew Germanowski

Michel Elbaz
(Courtesy DEA)

Israel "Ghel" Hazut
(Courtesy DEA)

Michael Alig, left, at an East Village club in 1989, the same year Peter Gatien hired the party promoter to revitalize his club empire
(© Catherine McGann / www.catherinemcgann.com)

Alig, center, with his mother, Elke, at his twenty-third birthday party in 1989
(© Catherine McGann / www.catherinemcgann .com)

Peter Gatien at Club USA in 1993, with DJ Merritt and Marc Berkley
(© Catherine McGann / www.catherinemcgann.com)

After being rejected at the velvet ropes, Germanowski and Gagne went undercover in makeup and thrift store finds, hoping to pass as gay ravers.

Gagne and his partners arrested Alig in November 1996. The Club Kid gave the agents insider information about drugs in the nightclubs—and a chilling murder confession. *(Courtesy DEA)*

Former party promoter Michael Caruso told jurors how he'd lured thousands of patrons to Limelight by giving out free cups of Ecstasy-laced punch. *(Courtesy DEA)*

Oded Tuito and his wife, Aliza, in an undated photo from DEA case files. *(Courtesy DEA)*

By late 1998, Oded Tuito was believed to be responsible for 80 percent of the Ecstasy supply in the United States. His signature "Tweety" pills were known for their high MDMA content. *(Courtesy DEA)*

Seizures of MDMA in Belgium and Netherlands increased 925 percent from 1998 to 1999. The pills were often produced in secret makeshift labs like this one discovered by Dutch police.

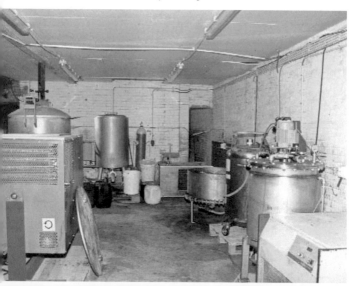

Agents expected to find pills or cash in an SUV abandoned in Bel Air in December 1999. Instead, they discovered the battered body of an alleged Ecstasy dealer and hit man. *(Courtesy LAPD Robbery-Homicide Division)*

Sean Erez broke ranks with Tuito and started his own Ecstasy ring in Amsterdam, charming young ultra-Orthodox Jews into being his mules. Erez and girlfriend Diana Reicherter enjoyed a lavish lifestyle until Dutch police started tapping their phones. *(Courtesy DEA)*

In July 2000, Customs agents at LAX inspected sixteen boxes marked "clothing" off a commercial airliner. They found 2.1 million tablets worth $41 million—the largest seizure to date. *(AP Photo / Nick Ut)*

Mob turncoat and Witness Protection dropout Salvatore "Sammy the Bull" Gravano was busted in February 2000 for heading a family-run Ecstasy ring in Arizona. Gravano got his pills from the Israeli distributors. *(AP Photo / Michael Ging, POOL)*

By 2000, Ecstasy use had skyrocketed in New York, Los Angeles, and South Florida—aka "The Party Triangle." U.S. Customs Commissioner Raymond Kelly addressed the MDMA problem at a Capitol Hill hearing in July before the Senate Caucus on International Narcotics Control. *(Courtesy U.S. Customs and Border Protection)*

By 2001, some eighteen members of Sean Erez's ring had pleaded guilty to drug conspiracy charges. It was the largest takedown in New York State to date. *(Courtesy DEA)*

AUSA Linda Lacewell made a name for herself prosecuting the Ecstasy dealers and was later tapped to join the executive staff of New York Attorney General Andrew Cuomo as counsel for economic and social justice.

In 2001, Gadi Eshed and his INP colleagues shared secret information with DEA at an Ecstasy conference in Tel Aviv, which would set an aggressive new course of cooperative investigations into the dealers.

INP Commander Yosef Sedbon and Eshed were privately troubled by the rising tide of public sympathy and fascination for their number one target and suspected mob boss Ze'ev Rosenstein.

Oded "the Fat Man" Tuito was placed on the U.S. President's Drug Kingpin List in 2002. Prosecutors never found the millions in drug money he was suspected to have hid away for his family. *(Courtesy DEA)*

Israeli police believed Ze'ev "the Wolf" Rosenstein was involved in murder, extortion, gambling, and prostitution rackets. In the end, it was the Ecstasy charges brought by the Americans that led to his arrest in November 2004. *(AP Photo / Brennan Linsley)*

In 2006, INP handed Rosenstein over to U.S. marshals at the tarmac of Ben-Gurion airport. He was the first Israeli crime boss to be extradited to the U.S. *(Courtesy DEA)*

Gadi Eshed, John McKenna, and Avi Noyman were among the recipients honored by the Department of Justice in August 2007 with a Best International Coordination Award for their work on the Rosenstein case. *(Courtesy DEA)*

47 "YOU CAN'T MAKE THAT KIND OF MONEY ON WALL STREET"

DEA'S FIRST INTERNATIONAL ECSTASY strategy conference was held in secret in an austere hotel conference room in Philadelphia on a cold December morning in 1998. Chris Kabel, section chief of Special Operations Division and his boss, Ken Dinino, section chief of Domestic Operations West, cohosted the conference with the Philadelphia SAC and case agents Drews and his partner, Andrew Petyak.

After a round of introductions of top brass, Gregg Drews took the podium with a PowerPoint presentation describing MDMA, its effects, street names, and prices.

Bob Gagne looked around the room. The tables were arranged in a giant square and he counted about forty people—DEA agents, Customs officials, and law enforcement from Boston, Los Angeles, Miami, and Pittsburgh, and foreign drug officers and attachés from Belgium, France, Germany, and Israel. Everyone wore sports jackets and ties. Gagne looked down at his Top-Siders, khakis, and button-down shirt. A teletype had been sent out a month in advance inviting any case agents with Ecstasy investigations to participate—but Gagne, being an Intel agent, was the last to hear about it. He had thrown a duffel bag in his car and driven to Philly the night before. He may have been the driving force behind New York's nascent MDMA investigations, with more Ecstasy experience than any DEA agent in that room. But on paper, he wasn't really anybody anymore.

Drews began to outline Oded Tuito's cocaine, marijuana, and Ecstasy activity. He described their attempts—so far unsuccessful—to make direct contact with Tuito through a former lieutenant, their CI snitch.

But the best intelligence anyone had on Tuito at that time wasn't from Drews's CI, it was from a girl named Ursula Koppenheffer. She was intelligent and had a keen recollection of details. The petite, twenty-five-year-old brunette met Tuito on July 4, 1997, during a boat ride with her Israeli boyfriend, one of Tuito's main buyers. She dumped the boyfriend and started moving Ecstasy, marijuana, and cash for the Oded Tuito organization. Tuito paid her bills, bought her clothes, and furnished her apartment. She believed she was his number one girlfriend. She agreed to marry him to help secure a green card and was even converting to Judaism to be closer to the Fat Man.

Among the Israeli dealers it was known that there were mules one might take a special interest in and maybe even take care of. But a woman you loved—a girlfriend, a wife—you just didn't bring them into the business. That would be putting them in potential danger.

When Tuito fled the country, Koppenheffer made two trips to Brussels. And then she got arrested by Miami Customs in April 1998 with forty thousand hits of X in her suitcase. She was left to fend for herself in jail, and eventually the veil of her misguided emotions lifted.

When Koppenheffer decided to talk the floodgates opened. She identified Tuito's associates in Florida, Pittsburgh, California, and New York. She even identified the guy who had provided the crew with false driver's licenses. She knew how much Tuito paid for pills ($1 to $2) and how much he sold them for ($7 to $13). She knew his code words for Ecstasy ("bonbon" or "candy") and cash ("paper" or "paperwork"). She described bringing Tuito $140,000 in drug money to Belgium and watching him pay his soldiers in $10,000 stacks of cash. She believed he dealt directly with a lab somewhere between Brussels and Amsterdam because it would only take him a few hours to leave and return with pills.

Agents Mike Mancuso and Edward Alvey of Fort Lauderdale had regular jailhouse debriefings with Koppenheffer and were keeping tabs on Tuito's Florida lieutenants: Meir Ben-David and Yosef Levi. According to their sources, Ben-David was the brains behind the Florida post—a smart businessman who rarely partied, avoided socializing with the strippers, and wisely invested Tuito's money in safe houses and real estate. Surveilling the men was difficult, because they were always watching their backs, dropping phones, firing couriers. The men started using aliases as a rule: Ben-David was Benny or Michael Anton; Levi was Khubi; Tuito was Daniel or Simon.

When the conference presentations wrapped up, discussion was opened to the floor and one by one the drug cops went around the table, sharing their case information and common links to Oded Tuito. The Ecstasy problem was larger and more entrenched than any of the American agents had realized before that day. And business wasn't just flourishing, it was evolving.

The Dutch had formed a National Unit Synthetic Drugs (USD) in 1997 specifically to coordinate MDMA cases with domestic and foreign law enforcement. USD had discovered twenty-eight labs in 1998 and the traffickers were starting to separate responsibilities. The acquisition of precursor chemicals, powder production, tabletting, distribution, and disposal of chemical waste was all being handled by different groups, often in different locations, to reduce the risk of discovery and lost profits. And profits were staggering. One chalky white pill could be made for less than five cents. A good-sized lab could produce fifty thousand tablets a week. One five-cent pill fetched $25 to $50 in American nightclubs. That's as high as $2.5 million per week from as little as $2,500 worth of product—a 1,000 percent profit. Of course, everybody got a cut along the way. Since moving his base to Europe, Tuito had begun to send millions of pills to the States, pushing mules through Zaventem, Schiphol, and Charles de Gaulle airports like revolving doors.

With so much product moving, Tuito took careful note of the tastes of his American buyers. He had already seen how pills stamped with Mercedes and Louis Vuitton logos were marketed to hip city kids, or peace signs and doves for disaffected suburbanites. Tuito wanted his brands to stand for quality. His Tweety and Star of David pills were known for delivering a strong and long MDMA high, which is why copycats were producing knockoffs with cheap fillers—making it impossible for law enforcement to know if all the Tweetys seized were from the Fat Man's organization. German and Dutch authorities were in the process of perfecting ballistics-style pill analysis that studied tool markings on the tablets to match them back to specific machines and pill labs, to help pin drug loads to specific trafficking groups.

Belgian and Dutch drug cops had also become increasingly concerned about the dump sites associated with pill production, which were a serious environmental hazard. One kilo of Ecstasy could generate thirty kilos of toxic waste—chemicals, filters, powders. The waste runners in the South of Netherlands would drive two hours from the lab to the northern region of Belgium and dump jerry cans filled with toxic sludge out in the countryside. Eventually, the runners would get lazy and dump closer to base, so the Dutch USD started tracking dump patterns on a map. Like a game of hot-cold, over time the waste sites brought them closer to hidden labs.

As the strategy conference began to wind down, Special Ops piped up: *Well, we've heard from just about everyone. What does New York have to say?*

Gagne had ridden out a lot of criticism over the years for going after the "kiddie dope." He hadn't come armed with a formal presentation or visual aids. He had a mint and a pad of hotel paper in front of him. It was clear that everybody in the room, Gagne included, wanted Oded Tuito. But the Gatien case had taught Gagne that MDMA wasn't solely the province of organized crime. They were dealing with the nascent stages of a free-market drug trade. It was unlike anything they had ever seen with cocaine and heroin, where competing drug lords viciously monopolized the raw product. With Ecstasy, even day traders and college students were cashing in.

"Look, let's talk about Tuito, let's talk about the common links. But let's keep in mind it's not about Tuito, it's about Ecstasy," Gagne said. "You can go to a club, sell three hundred pills, and make yourself ten grand a night. You can't make that kind of money on Wall Street.

"Unlike heroin and cocaine, there are no barriers to the Ecstasy business. Ecstasy crosses all social and economic barriers, regardless of race, creed, color, or religion," Gagne went on. "Anybody who goes to Bogotá, gets off a plane, and asks where they can buy some cocaine would be kidnapped, held for ransom, and eventually killed. With Ecstasy, the market's wide open. Hell, anyone in this room can fly to Amsterdam and in fifteen minutes and five thousand dollars in your pocket, you can score ten thousand pills. That's why Ecstasy is a serious, growing problem."

Gagne was on a roll, feeling confident. He went out on a limb: "And that's why Sean Erez is on his way to Europe right now looking to become the next Oded Tuito."

48 SEAN EREZ

ABOUT A MONTH BEFORE the Ecstasy conference, Gagne had pulled together all the Dutch calls from Steve Hager's phone records and dialed up the American Embassy in The Hague to see if anyone at DEA could investigate the numbers, see what names might come up. Gagne knew the Netherlands was ground zero for MDMA production—maybe Tuito was in the Netherlands? Assistant country attaché Don Rospond said he'd ask the Dutch police to check it out. A few days before the Philly conference, Rospond had called Gagne back with a surprising lead—and it wasn't Tuito.

One of the numbers was traced back to the Okura Hotel in Amsterdam, where Sean Erez had been checked into room 1703 with a female guest from November 21 to 28. He'd made several phone calls to the States, France, and Belgium while he was there. The hotel staff was under the distinct impression that Erez and his female companion were making plans to permanently relocate to Amsterdam in the near future.

Sean Erez was a businessman. In his late teens, he owned an ice-cream parlor in Tel Aviv. At twenty-one, he had a frozen yogurt company in Montreal. By twenty-five, he was co-owner of SoHo Jeans, running three 500-square-foot retail stores in Manhattan. At twenty-eight, Erez dumped the jeans business for the better profit margins of the Ecstasy business.

Erez first met Steve Hager at his ice-cream shop in Tel Aviv. They reconnected again in the 1990s at Scores strip club when Hager's Ecstasy business was booming from the infusion of Tuito's pills. Hager recruited Erez to do grunt work—counting pills, picking up couriers—for Tuito's network. Erez eventually met Tuito and Koki while partying with the crew in Miami.

Erez was six foot one, with meaty arms and legs, thick brown shoulder-length hair, and sometimes a goatee. He had dual Canadian and Israeli citizenship and a raspy New York accent. Even when he was speaking in Hebrew, it was a slangy stream of "dude," "bro," and "how ya doin', baby?"

Everybody said Erez was ambitious. And greedy. All he had to do was look at Tuito's life—homes in Israel and Europe, respected and feared by his soldiers—to realize that selling pills retail was chump change. The closer he could get to the source of supply, the more money in his pocket.

While DEA was in Philly trading Ecstasy secrets, twenty-eight-year-old Erez was lining up Dutch pill brokers in the Netherlands. He was calling buyers in the States—like Steve Hager—who could receive and sell his pills. His twenty-year-old girlfriend, Diana Reicherter, packed up the contents of her Franklin Square apartment and Erez's First Avenue pad, dropped it into a $160-a-month Moishe's Mini-Storage container, and then joined Erez in Amsterdam. Erez rented a spacious apartment at 528 Herengracht, a canal house on the ring, surrounded by seventeenth- and eighteenth-century ornate gabled mansions with tilted façades. They were close to the flower markets and antique shops, a stumble from the red-light district and casinos.

He was settled in and his new business venture was ready to roll. All that was left was recruiting the couriers. And for this, Erez had a special plan.

49 "WHO'S IN CHARGE?"

SPECIAL OPS WAS INUNDATED with Ecstasy intel after the Philly strategy meeting. In New York alone, thirty new cases involving Ecstasy were being tracked. Operation Flashback spun off into Op Rave, focused solely on MDMA trafficking.

DEA soon determined that about 90 percent of the Ecstasy smuggled into the United States was being commanded by a loose-knit network of Israeli criminals, and their distribution chain defied the traditional hierarchy. It was a system that mystified the top brass.

In every major drug trafficking organization until then, agents could rely on a predictable power structure: there was the top guy, and below him were his lieutenants and soldiers. Everybody had a position, everybody had a role, and everyone knew his place in the organization. But Ecstasy wasn't like that. There was so much demand for Ecstasy that the Israeli dealers could buy, sell, and partner up with one another and their competitors without having to battle over territories.

The old-school DEA agents had gotten so used to looking at pyramid charts that when Gagne would pull out something that was circular, they didn't get it. "Wait— who's in charge?" they'd always ask. Oded Tuito used fear and threats to enforce a pyramid style in his own organization. Loyalty was important to him. But there was so much Ecstasy to go around that he didn't need to kill a guy to make his point: he'd just rip him off, steal his drugs, and have him beaten good.

By January 1999, Tuito was living in France and building a formidable presence in the United States. Gagne's best lead on Tuito so far was Jackie Suarez. Her international travel records revealed at least nine trips since July 1998, entering the States from Brussels, Nice, and Paris. Gagne subpoenaed her phone records, which provided the probable cause to obtain a pen register. Pen registers, like wiretaps, are secured through court orders but the legal standard is much lower because it reveals only a list of numbers dialed from the target's phone. It's a way to study links. For instance, Suarez had a high volume of calls to Miami, so Gagne put in an official request for Miami DEA to cross-reference those numbers with their cases to find potential criminal associates.

Gagne discovered Suarez was using three different calling cards on her landline and cell phone connecting her with Tuito in France and Germany and with Ben-David in Florida. He wanted to do a wire on Suarez, but he kept tripping over Pittsburgh agent Gregg Drews.

Drews had brought in an undercover narcotics agent from the Pittsburgh Bureau of Narcotics Investigation to try to infiltrate Tuito's network. When the BNI agent left messages on Tuito's cell phone, hoping to start a buying relationship, Tuito had Suarez return the calls.

Suarez spoke warmly to the new potential Pittsburgh client the first time she dialed him. She explained that "the big guy" asked her to call. She gave the narc her cell phone number and told him to call her if he was traveling to Manhattan.

Pittsburgh DEA was hot to get Suarez to travel to Philly to sell them Tuito's pills, but Tuito told Suarez not to go—the new client should come to her. That was no good for Drews. It was a venue problem: they couldn't press charges in Pittsburgh if she sold them pills in New York.

Gagne knew that Pittsburgh was trying to lure Suarez and it pissed him off. Suarez was a New York dealer, handling Tuito's New York business, and Gagne was already investigating her. His bosses proposed a compromise to Pittsburgh: New York would apply for a T-III wiretap on Suarez's phone and Drews could come to Manhattan to be the affiant on the wire.

But Drews wasn't interested in sitting in a wire room for thirty days and sharing the evidence, only to let New York run with his case.

Pretty soon, Suarez stopped returning the narc's calls. Drews took a gamble and got an intermediary to ask for her home number from Gagne.

When Suarez picked up her phone that day and heard the pushy Pittsburgh "client" on the line she panicked: how had he gotten her home number? She quickly hung up. She was on to them. And that meant she was going to start watching herself, talking less on the phone, taking more care in how she conducted business. Gagne was furious, but he had no game. DEA was made up of quarterbacks who all wanted the ball, and not so they could go three and out—they wanted to go all the way, to win. Gagne felt like the guy on the sidelines who kept the stats—nobody cared about stats unless they needed to prove a point or support a theory.

Gagne tried to come up with another play, another way to get to Jackie Suarez. But he was feeling ineffective and increasingly distracted by reminders of his past failures: Peter Gatien was in the news again.

50 CHEMICAL COWBOYS

IN A SURPRISING TURN, Peter Gatien had pleaded guilty on January 8, 1999, to tax evasion charges. Adding to his troubles, the State Liquor Authority was threatening to take away his liquor license. On January 12, *Village Voice* reporter Bill Bastone wrote a scathing article about Gatien's continuing claims that he knew nothing of the drug dealing in his clubs, that he was the victim of a government vendetta, persecuted by dishonest prosecutors and DEA agents. The reporter suggested liquor officials take a peek at Steve Lewis's suppressed statements to the feds about document shredding, hush money, house dealers, and a crooked cop on Gatien's payroll.

"Three years and one acquittal later," Bastone wrote, "and Gatien still desperately needs everyone to believe that he was, in fact, operating in the dark."

A smile had crossed Gagne's face when he read that article. But then there was only bleak news from clubland.

On January 23, a waifish teen named Jimmy Lyons celebrated his eighteenth birthday at Tunnel by taking Ecstasy with ketamine, a common club-drug cocktail. A little after 3:15 a.m., someone pulled Lyons into the bathroom, or maybe he stumbled in on his own—dizzy, hallucinating, dehydrated, foaming at the mouth. Word was he tried to get a drink from the faucet, but all that came out was hot water.

Jimmy Lyons suffered the symptoms typical of Ecstasy-related overdose: chills, sweats, fever, teeth-rattling seizures. Around 5:00 a.m., emergency medical technicians found Jimmy on the street near a loading dock outside the club's back door. His body was bruised from flopping on the pavement like a landed fish, seized by uncontrollable convulsions. He was pronounced dead on the scene. Three hours after his death, he should have been cold to the touch, but his body temperature was 104 degrees, still baking from the inside out.

Regret and anger ate away at Gagne. Even if Gatien's claim that he was unaware of drug dealing in his clubs were true, did it make him innocent? Gagne didn't think so. A fool on the throne isn't absolved from responsibility simply because he is a fool. Jimmy's death was the second drug overdose at Tunnel in January alone and Gatien's reps had countered with a specious claim that Jimmy really died from steroids he had taken earlier that day. A medical examiner told the *New York Post* that Jimmy's toxicology results were negative for steroids, that his death was a result of "acute intoxication by the combined effects of MDMA and ketamine." Jimmy's friends said they'd seen him buy two hits of E inside Tunnel.

In 1993, there were just 68 mentions of Ecstasy in emergency room visits nationwide, but by 2000, Ecstasy would land 4,511 people in the ER. High school students would soon cite Ecstasy as one of the easiest drugs to obtain next to marijuana.

Gagne knew there were more dangerous drugs, but Ecstasy was like a wolf in sheep's clothing. It was called the "love drug" because that was how dealers marketed it to suburban youth. While heroin traffickers branded their product with names like "Instant Death," "Red Devil," or "Lightning Bolt," Ecstasy traffickers made aspirin-sized tablets in Froot Loops colors, stamped with happy faces, peace signs, dolphins, the initials HP

(Harry Potter), Pokémon, and Scooby-Doo. If Flint-stone's chewable vitamins were good for you as a kid, Ecstasy looked like the sexy upgrade.

Sometimes Gagne felt like he was swimming up-stream, fighting the Ecstasy machine in a society that embraced hyperconsumption of the new and improved. Wait a couple of minutes, and a better TV, computer, or cell phone would be ready for purchase. He worried about the wholesale embrace of drugs that promised a new and improved life. It was as if no one had the forti-tude to endure the mental challenge of self-doubt or human imperfection anymore. To make varsity, there's steroids. To make kids behave, there's Ritalin. To feel special and connected to other human beings—just take a pill. There's plenty of Ecstasy to go around.

People would talk about Generation X or Generation Y, but Gagne didn't know what to call this new generation. They could be vegan yoga fanatics, totally passionate about the environment, and yet they treated their bodies like toxic dump sites.

"They'll do two hits of X, a couple bumps of K, a cap-ful of GHB," Gagne says, "but they're very concerned about air pollution, water pollution, and won't go into a Burger King or McDonald's. But come fuckin' Satur-day night they're like the chemical cowboys."

51 SECRETS AND LIES

IT WASN'T EASY BEING the boss. Tuito was supplying New York, Miami, and Los Angeles and every day he had to ride his lieutenants and soldiers, make sure they were keeping the money flowing and the pills moving. With the recent spate of courier arrests, Tuito needed to keep a stone's skip ahead of the law. So he left Brussels for Nice, and put his right-hand man, David Ben-Amara, aka "Gingi," in Frankfurt. When his New York lieutenant Tuff Tuff moved back home to Israel to be with his family, Tuito promoted Jackie Suarez to keeper of pills and cash.

Suarez had been selling Tuito's pills for $7 to $8 and, with his permission, tacking on an extra 25 to 50 cents kickback for herself. She had a safe in her Tenth Avenue studio apartment invariably filled with as much as $100,000 of Tuito's money. She started suffering from paralyzing panic attacks, making it difficult to breathe, impossible to sleep. She kept it a secret from Tuito. She was handling too much money and too many drugs to lose it in front of the boss.

In February 1999, Tuito sent for her. She would stop over in Miami, meet with Yosef Levi to pick up cash, and deliver it to Tuito in Frankfurt. It had been months since she'd seen him. He came to her room at the Omni hotel, woke her from a deep sleep, and spent the next ten days romancing her as best he could in a city that Suarez found to be cold and antagonistic.

The night before Suarez was to return to New York, she lay in bed next to Tuito. Something was dark in his manner. He seemed tense and unhappy. In the eight months she had known him, he was constantly on the move. He seemed tired. She never knew when he might disappear for good. Tuito had promised Suarez that if she ran off one day, married someone, and started a family, he would always be a friend to her and look out for her. But she wanted to be his protector in that moment as he fell asleep next to her.

When she awoke, she quietly dressed, not wanting to wake him, and took a taxi to the airport.

52 HEARTS

POLICE AROUND THE WORLD were waiting for Oded Tuito to make a wrong step. Israeli police were tapping phones of his Israeli associates; the German BKA police were tapping Gingi's phones in Germany; the Dutch were on the lines of suspected pill brokers in Amsterdam. Tuito was living in Nice with Aliza and their children, where the French essentially left him alone.

The BKA investigation, dubbed Operation Twingo, revolved around surveillance and scrupulous attention to Gingi and Tuito's calls. The dealers spoke daily, in barely coded conversations about money and women and flaky male couriers whose messy hair and frumpy clothes made them unfit for scrutiny by Customs agents. Tuito nagged Gingi over every detail—did he check and double-check flight arrangements, did he confirm everything with the travelers, was he out so late that he missed an important phone call or pickup?

Tuito's moods were never hidden. Sometimes he would lash out in anger and promise retribution for dealers who were slow to pay for loads they had already received. Other times he could be heard bemoaning his pet dog, who unfailingly ignored his commands: "Sit! Lie down! Sit, I say!"

When Tuito had reached the end of his rope with someone, he would order Gingi, "Tell him the Fat Man said so . . . tell him that's it."

The BKA knew that Tuito had a half dozen couriers in the Frankfurt area awaiting orders to smuggle pills into the States, but to find them, the police needed names, flight times, airlines. They got a break late one Saturday night in February.

"When is Yakov traveling?" Tuito asked.

"Tomorrow," Gingi said.

"What is he taking?"

"He's taking the hearts. Sixty." Gingi had sampled the hearts himself.

"I ate from it yesterday, their work is much better. Like the butterfly."

Gagne got a call at 4:30 a.m. from Gregg Drews. He grabbed his cell phone from the nightstand and snuck out of the bedroom so as not to wake Kristen. Drews told him a Tuito courier was headed to New York.

Gagne called the DEA attaché in Berlin and learned that two men from Israel had checked into the Ibis Hotel in Frankfurt and were seen receiving luggage from Gingi. One of them got on a Lufthansa flight Sunday morning, February 7, en route to JFK. Gagne looked at his watch; the plane was scheduled to arrive in about eight hours. He'd have to get the case agent up if he wanted to meet that flight.

"What are you doing?" Kristen was sleepy-eyed and wondering what her husband was up to.

"I gotta go into the city later," Gagne said. "We gotta arrest a guy. I should be back in time." She sighed and went back to bed. They were supposed to spend the day together, maybe go to the mall. She knew he wouldn't be back in time.

A little before 1:00 p.m., Gagne and case agent Roger Bach watched as Yakov Ariel picked up two Samsonite bags off the carousel and timidly shuffled toward the Customs line. An inspector asked him to open his bags. The inspector would later report that hidden under Ariel's "21 shirts, 9 pairs of pants, 8 pairs of underwear, 1 book, and 2 religious items" were secret flaps, and under the flaps were 59,298 round, grayish pills bearing a raised logo: heart-stamped pills, just in time for Valentine's Day. Ariel's belongings were inventoried and sent to the Customs warehouse at the World Trade Center.

Gagne attempted to read Ariel his Miranda rights, but the courier pretended not to understand. Only Hebrew, he said. He refused to sign anything and asked to speak to an attorney. He told the agents in broken English that the bags were not his. A girl he met in Brussels had had so many bags that she'd asked him to take these for her, he said. But in time, like the others, Ariel would reveal his story.

53 THE ACCIDENTAL COURIER

YAKOV ARIEL WAS A twenty-eight-year-old from Haifa who worked for a moving van company and owed $7,500 in gambling debts to the Russian Mafia. The man he owed the debt to made him an offer: *Do a job for me for some friends abroad and we'll call it even.*

A few days later, Gingi knocked on Ariel's door, gave him an envelope of cash, and told him to buy a ticket to Frankfurt. When Ariel arrived in Germany, Gingi put $150,000 in his luggage and sent him on a plane to Nice. *When you get there,* Gingi told him, *walk across the street to a rental car agency, where you will meet a fat man.*

The Fat Man drove Ariel to a hotel, where he stuffed the cash in a room safe and shoved the key to the safe in his pocket. The Fat Man told Ariel he'd done good, and he had another job for him: *Now you will bring pills back with you to the States.* Ariel started to sweat.

Later that night at a club, Ariel slipped into the restroom, tossed his passport into the trash can, and told Tuito he couldn't make the return trip because it seemed he had lost his passport. Tuito was livid. He sent Ariel to the police station to file a lost passport claim, and waited for him outside the station.

Ariel returned to Israel in deeper trouble with his Russian loan shark. For his nonsense in Europe, he was being fined an extra $200 and would have to get a new passport and do the whole trip again. A month later, Ariel was back in Frankfurt. Another courier, thirty-six-year-old Yalon Scheps, bunked with him at the Ibis Hotel. Scheps told Ariel not to worry so much—he had done the trip many times, with twice as many pills, with no trouble.

Gingi gave Ariel two Samsonite bags with secret compartments and Scheps gave him two sedatives: one to take before he checked in at Lufthansa, and one to get him through U.S. Customs.

"If the police arrest you," Scheps said, "just tell them that a girl gave you the bag because she had too much luggage."

Gingi picked Ariel up on Sunday morning and drove him to the airport. He instructed Ariel to look for a young dark-haired woman named Jacqueline, who would meet him at JFK.

"If you don't see her," Gingi said, "go to the nearest Holiday Inn and check in and she will find you."

Ariel told Gagne that he assumed Jacqueline had been waiting for him on the other side of Customs. Sure enough, records indicated that Suarez's cell phone had pinged at the JFK cell tower. In fact, Suarez may even have seen Gagne that day. She was waiting in a car out front when she saw her courier pickup being escorted by federal officers.

Jackie Suarez stepped on the gas, speeding as far away from the airport as she could get. Her heart was pounding. She tried to concentrate.

She would call Tuito. Then she would get out of town as quickly as possible. She had about a thousand pills and $7,000 in her safe at home.

Suarez thought about all the weed and Ecstasy she had sold since meeting Tuito. A nice sum of cash, but she had little to show for it. She had to get her life straight. But first, she thought, she would go to Miami and party like the feds were about to bust down her door.

54 FRANCE PRESSES CHARGES

BKA POLICE ARRESTED GINGI and Scheps as they were on their way to the Frankfurt airport. Scheps had 65,000 pills—"Butterfly" and "e" brands—hidden in his two bags. Another 20,000 pills were seized off Gingi.

A week later, a twenty-five-year-old Brooklyn Israeli was arrested at JFK with about 54,000 Hearts and e's in his bags. Next came a twenty-year-old Israeli girl from Miami, with 63,000 hits of a new brand—"Clovers," for St. Patrick's Day.

Tuito was losing millions of dollars' worth of pills and Gingi, his top lieutenant, was in a German jail. Israeli police were tapping the phone of one of Tuito's cohorts when they overheard Tuito confide to the man that he was considering leaving France, another move to seek "safe haven." They couldn't let him escape again. The Israelis passed the tip to the French Office Central pour la Répression du Trafic Illicite des Stupéfiants, or OCRTIS.

On February 24, at 5:30 a.m., OCRTIS officers arrested Tuito at his home in Nice and charged him with conspiracy to smuggle Ecstasy from France to the United States. They seized $10,000 and 50,000 francs in cash, cell phones, an address book, and personal documents. They froze two bank accounts holding $250,000. But it took police a couple of days to confirm Tuito's true identity, because he gave the name and fake passport of an Eliyahu Mamo.

Pittsburgh agent Gregg Drews was disappointed in the turn of events. He had twenty-five recorded undercover phone calls between Tuito and his associates. He had hoped to work the case longer and eventually see Tuito extradited and brought to prosecution in Pennsylvania. Now he'd have to wait to see what the French were going to do.

As far as Gagne could tell, the French did whatever the French wanted. But, like Drews, he didn't think they had enough: two couriers had been arrested at Charles de Gaulle with a collective seventy-two thousand pills, all of it destined for New York City.

Whether or not the French charges stuck, Gagne knew that Tuito's partners would reorganize to keep the pills and cash flowing. Nobody was going to throw in the towel. The American cases would continue while the French figured out their game plan.

Tuito had escaped charges in Tel Aviv, Los Angeles, and Pittsburgh. He had moved four times in the last year. Now he was on ice in a Fresnes prison while French officers studied the documents seized from his home. Everything was in Hebrew and had to be translated. Slips of paper inside Tuito's phone book revealed visits to the Savoy Hotel in Munich. There was a phone number for Suarez in New York, one for Koki in Los Angeles, and a recipe for lentil pea soup. His list of to-do items included "Give money to the snake."

Next to some phone numbers, Tuito had written code names—"the pious one," "the butcher," and "susa." A Hebrew translator noted that while "Sosa" or "Sus" may be a legitimate last name, when the word "susa" has an accent on the second syllable it means "mare." It appeared that Tuito used the word as code: mare = horse = mule.

All of the susás in Tuito's phone book were women.

Civilians and strippers. Those were the couriers. That's how it was always done.

55 THE DUTCH WIRE

"BOB, YOU SHOULD HEAR this." Don Rospond was calling from The Hague. "They've got an American on the line."

In March 1999, the Dutch police were investigating a drug trafficker named Wyste Lijklema when they heard an unexpected English-speaker on a wiretap. He had an accent that the Dutch guessed to be "strong New York/New Jersey."

Dutch police are forbidden from soliciting drugs from dealers, using informants, or tape-recording meetings with a suspect. Such methods are considered an affront to civil liberties. However, police can get judicial approval to tap a phone line based on mere suspicion. And when the Dutch police started listening to Wyste Lijklema's phones, they spun off dozens of new wiretaps on his suspected criminal associates and *their* associates, including the mysterious American. Gagne had a hunch it was Sean Erez.

From what the police could tell, the American had started an independent Ecstasy network in Amsterdam and was sending couriers to the States through airports in the Netherlands, France, and Belgium. He was overheard checking his balance—nearly a million dollars—in a bank account in Luxembourg. His source of supply was a man named Michel Denies, who was an associate of Wyste Lijklema.

Gagne faxed a copy of Erez's DMV picture to Don Rospond to give to the police. A Dutch surveillance unit in Amsterdam bicycled past the home of the wire suspect, snapped shots of him leaving his Herengracht apartment, and verified his identity—it was Erez.

Gagne knew that the Dutch police couldn't care less about Sean Erez. The Dutch work on projects, with targets of interest, and that's it. Sean Erez was not a project target. But Wyste Lijklema and Michel Denies were.

Lijklema allegedly sold plastic explosives and fully automatic weapons in addition to drugs. Denies was thought to be one of Oded Tuito's backup Ecstasy suppliers. The Dutch believed Denies and Lijklema took part in the exportation of millions of pills a year, but they were having trouble getting evidence.

Sean Erez's phone tap was under the Dutch unit that investigated organized crime—the Interregionaal Rechercheteam Noord en Oost Nederland, unit Noord, or IRT for short. Gagne needed to convince IRT to stay up on Erez's phones and then share that wire with him in New York, to be used in Erez's prosecution. If Gagne could catch Sean Erez, maybe he could flip him and use him to help the Dutch catch Denies and Lijklema. That was what he would offer the Dutch in return for their help.

It was a tall order and as far as Gagne could tell it had never been done before with the Dutch—a cooperative international wiretap, conducted contemporaneously on an American. Erez wasn't even an American; he had dual Canadian and Israeli citizenship. But his drugs were hitting American soil and that was crime enough in a court of law. The 1983 treaty between the United States and the Netherlands on mutual assistance in criminal matters made it completely permissible for the Dutch to share the wire evidence. But a treaty meant nothing if the Dutch police decided they had better things to do. In America, if an informant walks in off the street and says, "Hey, I know someone who's selling drugs," the DEA agents are out the door chasing that lead, that potential target of opportunity. But in the Netherlands, if an informant calls the police station and says, "There's a truckload of cocaine parked in front of the police station," they are likely to reply: "Thank you very much, that's nice. Have a nice day." The Dutch are dogged investigators who do tremendous casework. But their work is project-specific.

Gagne would have to gain their trust and respect. He needed to fly to the Netherlands to meet the Dutch officers—get to know them, have a beer, discover their commonalities—so that any time of the day he could pick up the phone and call in a tip, ask a favor, or share intelligence and they would be happy to hear from him. Gagne knew their policing styles were different, their drug policies were at odds, their whole way of life was different—but bottom line, they were united in their desire to take down Ecstasy dealers. And what Gagne needed most to take down Sean Erez was the Dutch wiretap.

But he was getting ahead of himself. He couldn't even open a case on Erez without handing it over to another agent—a street agent. He could barely get time on the streets of New York, let alone Amsterdam. He desperately needed to catch a break.

56 "DON'T BULLSHIT ME, BOB"

"JACKIE SUAREZ—WHAT DO you got?" Chris Kabel of Special Operations Division was on the line. It was April 1999, and the Oded Tuito case had essentially come to a standstill since his February arrest by French authorities. SOD was still interested in breaking down Tuito's network and Kabel knew that Suarez was a critical piece of Tuito's entire operation.

"Gagne, you going up on her phone or what?" Kabel asked.

"Listen, I can't do this from Intel," Gagne said. "No one's interested in the case out on Long Island except Roger Bach, but he's been promoted, so he's gone."

Gagne wanted Bach's now-vacant spot. It would put him back on the streets—and closer to home—and give him the authority he needed to really go after Suarez and Sean Erez.

"Look, I'm doing this half-assed because I'm doing it from here. You get me out there and I'm telling you it will get done and it will get done right."

"Well, I don't know," Kabel said. "I don't know if we can do anything."

Gagne worried he had pushed too much. The last thing he needed was to alienate his bosses.

"Chris, if somebody takes the case over in Long Island, that's all well and good, and I'll walk them through it, tell them everything I know, help them out to the best of my ability. But you know as well as I do, I can never sit down with someone and explain everything so that they'll get it and get behind it the way I would."

"Okay," Kabel said. "Let me see what I can do."

The next day, Gagne got called into the office of one of his supervisors, Assistant Special Agent in Charge Gary O'Hara.

That was quick, Gagne thought.

As he walked toward O'Hara's office, he figured this was headed one of two ways: *Who the fuck do you think you are, getting SOD to take you out of here?* or *Pack your desk, you're going to Long Island.*

Gagne liked O'Hara. He got what Bob was trying to do. He'd even started running monthly meetings on club drugs after Gagne got back from the Philly strategy conference in December. O'Hara was the last person Gagne wanted to piss off.

"Sit down, Bob," O'Hara said. He was reading through stacks of memos and reports on his desk. "I got a call from SOD. They think that this Ecstasy case you're working out there would be better served if you worked it from Long Island."

O'Hara put his papers down and looked at Gagne.

"All you agents are so full of shit. Don't bullshit me, Bob. Tell me the truth: can you work this case better here or in Long Island?"

"Sir, I will not bullshit you. I can work the case better in Long Island." Gagne felt a tinge of guilt. Truth was, he knew he could work the case anywhere as long as he was a street agent again—he could run it from Pittsburgh if he had to. But he was thinking of his wife, and starting a family, and he needed to be closer to home.

"All right," O'Hara said. "If that's what you're telling me."

Two days later, Gagne got the official memo. He was being transferred to Long Island, effective in one week. He had a lot of work ahead of him. He wanted to prove himself again, show his bosses that putting him back on the streets hadn't been a mistake.

On the Friday morning of his last day at NYFD, instead of going to the gym, Gagne took a last long walk through the building. It was quiet and practically empty.

He passed through the locker room where he and Germanowski used to costume up. He walked down the main agent floor and glanced over at his old cubicle, where he used to break out his clubs and challenge Flaherty to miniature golf tournaments. He lingered for a while inside the Hall of Honor, where he studied the photos of fallen agents, and for the first time, he read through the tributes for his old Snowcap teammates. He let the memories sink in.

57 THE HIT MEN

ON APRIL 15, a Dutch judge approved the opening of a case project on Sean Erez in order to keep the wiretaps and surveillance of Erez ongoing. On April 26, Gagne flew to the Netherlands to meet the IRT agents and finalize protocol on the wiretap transfer.

Although the average Dutch citizen is under the impression that DEA spy helicopters are watching them like Big Brother and agents are manipulating Dutch drug cops in Situation Room–style meetings, in truth the cramped four-person DEA offices at the American embassy haven't been upgraded since the embassy was built in the 1960s, and the employees work more like information liaisons than street agents. They share intelligence and hope for reciprocal interest. They are an important part of the collective diplomatic pressure. But they have no authority. DEA agents can't carry guns in the Netherlands, they can't initiate investigations, and they can't arrest Dutch citizens. Which is why Gagne knew it was a gracious gesture when the Dutch cops invited him to tag along on an Ecstasy case surveillance operation.

Dutch wire intelligence suggested that Ecstasy trafficker Michel Denies was at war with a guy who refused to pay for thousands of dollars' worth of pills.

Gagne and the Dutch officers were sitting in a car in a quiet suburb about fifty yards from the dealer's home. The police knew from listening to his phone that he was expecting visitors that evening: two pill buyers. It was almost quitting time, but the police figured they'd wait and see if the buyers showed up, take some notes, then head out for beers with Gagne. They hadn't counted on the excitement to come when the garage door opened and two unidentified men drove off in the dealer's car.

Gagne readied for what was certain to be his first Dutch car chase. But nobody moved. The officers spoke calmly to one another on their radios. Gagne watched the suspects drive away.

"Um, don't we want to follow that car?"

After much hand-wringing, the officers eventually agreed to split up—one team stayed at the house and a second team (Gagne's group) would follow the assailants. It was the most polite car chase Gagne had ever taken part in, replete with anxious glances at the clock (the officers' shift was coming to an end), anxiety over the sudden change of plans, and trepidation over crossing into another police district's territory.

"Oh, we really should be going back."

"Maybe, just follow them," Gagne said, "and if they go anywhere we're not supposed to go, then we'll turn around."

When they caught up to the two men at a gas-and-go shop, twenty minutes from the German border, Gagne had to convince his hosts to approach the men.

"What, are you crazy? We don't do that, we are just surveillance."

"Okay, look—you need to write a report on this later, right?"

"Yes, of course."

"Then, just ask the guy for ID so at least you can identify him in your report."

That did seem logical to the officer.

After a haphazard ID check and halting conversation with the suspects, the police soon realized they had nabbed two hit men—guys who allegedly worked for Denies and Lijklema. In the trunk of the car were a hundred thousand pills they had just stolen from the dealer.

The hit men had snuck in through a back entrance of the dealer's home while Dutch surveillance sat outside waiting for the real pill buyers to show up. The hit men stole the guy's pills but didn't kill him. When police found the dealer inside, he was tied up with extension cords. Sharp kitchen knives were lying on the counter next to him. Police figured the hit men must have fled after hearing a message being left on the dealer's answering maching in the middle of their home invasion. It was a call from the real pill buyers. They apologized for being late and promised they were just minutes away.

Gagne later heard that one of the men was an Albanian grifter and ruthless contract killer who was eventually extradited to Germany, where he was wanted on murder charges. (Dutch police rejected several interview attempts and would not comment on this operation or any of the Ecstasy cases.) According to Gagne's sources, the guy would kill just for pocket cash and traveling expenses. It didn't matter if the target was a drug dealer or a businessman. He'd wake up, have a bowl of cereal, go out and kill someone, have lunch, read the paper. He never bought a gun or got caught holding a weapon. He was known to slip in, use whatever was handy to beat, stab, bludgeon, or strangle his target to death, and then slip out, whistling down the alleyway as he left. Gagne always remembered him as the MacGyver of hit men.

58 LINDA LACEWELL

MATT GERMANOWSKI AND Jay Flaherty were preparing for the trial of former nightclub director Steve Lewis. They wanted Gagne to work the case with them, together like old times. But Gagne didn't want to look back. He was older, a little gun-shy. Besides, he had a full plate working the Dutch angle on Tuito's former underling Sean Erez and collecting intel on Jackie Suarez. Gagne didn't want to lose this time and he would play everything by the book. But he needed a new partner— a strong assistant U.S. attorney. He wanted AUSA Linda Lacewell.

Lacewell was a whip-smart prosecutor who'd studied law on a full scholarship at the University of Miami and put time in at two boutique defense law firms in New York, handling tax and white-collar cases, both civil and criminal.

When she decided to play for the opposite side, she started out in the Eastern District of New York working in General Crimes, where her caseload was mostly drug traffickers stumbling through JFK airport. It was always cocaine, heroin, cocaine, heroin, cocaine, and then all of a sudden it was Ecstasy, Ecstasy, Ecstasy. Lacewell knew that JFK's Ecstasy problem represented a microcosm of what was happening in the rest of the country. When she moved next, to the Narcotics division of EDNY, she got her hands on broader investigations, prosecuting drug distribution rings.

As a federal prosecutor, Lacewell felt she had more discretion: she didn't have to prosecute every case, and the decision about whom not to prosecute was sometimes more important. She could be aggressive and dogged, but she deeply believed in the maxim that the government wins when justice is served, regardless of the verdict.

Lacewell's first assignment in Narcotics was the drug conspiracy cases of Steve Lewis and former club bouncer Ray Montgomery, who were tried together. She read the Gatien transcripts, learned from the mistakes of the past, and let Germanowski and Flaherty guide her through the blind spots.

The trial ended in early May 1999. Ray Montgomery was acquitted; Lewis was convicted and later sentenced to a year in prison, with three hundred hours of community service and $15,200 in fines. Even with the mixed result, Germanowski couldn't say enough good things about Lacewell to Gagne. The thirty-five-year-old prosecutor had a no-nonsense, commanding presence in the courtroom. She did a clean, short trial. She didn't overplay her hand or suggest that Lewis and Montgomery were some kind of drug kingpins overseeing an empire. She told the jury that they had roles to play in the conspiracy, just like everyone else.

Gagne went looking for Lacewell the next day at her office.

"Congratulations," he said. "Now we need to do the Sean Erez case."

"Bob, I just did a trial. I'm exhausted. Leave me alone."

"Linda, we have to do it now. Erez is in the Netherlands. There's a wiretap on him, and the Dutch are willing to cooperate. But if he leaves, we won't be able to track him. You're the only one I want on this. We can do this. I need your help."

Lacewell felt like she was being smooth-talked, but she also knew from Gagne's partners that Gagne was a tireless, hardworking investigator. Plus the latest courier arrests at JFK revealed that Erez had stooped to new lows in the drug trade, exploiting a vulnerable coterie of mules who just hadn't seen it coming.

"Okay," Lacewell said. "Let's do it."

59 PILGRIMS WITH PILLS

THERE IS A PICTURE wall along a corridor of the New York Field Division laboratory—a kind of smugglers' hall of fame. The photos depict case exhibits: heroin smuggled inside food-tray carts on airplanes; lollipops with drug-filled centers; a funeral urn made of cocaine; a Christmas-tree skirt—decorated in green wreaths and gold ribbons—with drugs sewn into a hidden layer; plastic green bananas mixed with real green bananas, but pull one of the fakes by the stem and the banana opens like a change purse to reveal the cocaine inside.

The most famous New York DEA press release was about the arrest of Medellín-based heroin traffickers who had crudely implanted packets of liquid heroin into the stomach linings of Labrador retriever puppies destined for the United States. The story broke all records for Web site hits, press interviews, and personal calls from concerned animal lovers wanting to know the fates of the puppies. A few of the dogs had died from the crude surgeries, but Colombian police found homes for the surviving animals. One of the puppies, Heroina, is now a drug-sniffing dog for the Colombian national police.

Ecstasy traffickers sometimes hid pills on slow-go freighter shipments of Dutch tulips, antique furniture, bread machines, auto parts, and once in the hollowed-out frame of a poster of Rembrandt's *Night Watch*. But when millions of dollars are tied up in each load, time is of the essence, and the fastest way to get pills in the hands of buyers abroad is to send them with human couriers.

American strippers and Israeli citizens were the Ecstasy standard. Agents at JFK airport's Narcotics Smuggling Unit caught on quick to the stripper mules—attractive, flirty women just back from "shopping trips" in Paris and Brussels. But nobody would have guessed that ultra-Orthodox youth, with dark clothes and curled side locks, returning from "a youth tour" in Europe, were smuggling thousands of Ecstasy pills in their suitcases.

After Gagne ID'd Sean Erez back in March, the Dutch police started watching him more closely, and noted several meetings with young men in religious dress at the airport. It seemed unlikely that Erez was seeking spiritual guidance. Gagne and his partners passed along word to Customs agents out of JFK to be watchful.

On March 11, a twenty-year-old Erez courier named Brenda Mendelovits was arrested at JFK with forty thousand clover-shaped pills.

Joel Gluck, eighteen, of Williamsburg, Brooklyn, was arrested on March 24 with thirty thousand "Yin-Yang" pills concealed inside rolled-up socks.

Like the others, twenty-four-year-old Benjamin Gratt's trip began in Brussels. He stayed at the Hotel Le Plaza, not far from the temptations of the Grand'Place central market's breweries and alfresco cafés. On a notepad in his hotel room, Gratt scribbled a 917 area code phone number, the same number that Mendelovits had written on the inside of her airline ticket sleeve. On March 23, Gratt took a Delta flight to New York (confirmed kosher meals), picked up his bags off the carousel, and was arrested by the Narcotics Unit with thirty thousand Yin-Yangs inside thirty socks. He had been given an airline ticket, $400 for expenses, and the promise of an additional $1,000 at the completion of the trip.

While Tuito paid his couriers $10,000, Erez promised little more than $1,500 and an economy-class ticket to Europe. His couriers were naïve and unaware of the dangers. And Erez had devised an inspired scheme to prey on their faith: the young pilgrims were told they were smuggling diamonds for the Holy Land.

60 SEAN EREZ'S CREW

GAGNE WORKED BEHIND THE scenes to convince his Dutch counterparts to turn over their evidence on Sean Erez. AUSA Linda Lacewell worked the legal channels, with help from the Netherlands liaison at the Department of Justice's Office of International Affairs. By late May 1999, the Dutch sent everything they had on Erez: audio recordings, written reports, logs of wires on six different cell phones and one landline. The wire packages arrived almost daily on zip disks and CDs containing countless hours of phone calls. Gagne sat in Lacewell's office for weeks, listening to the tapes, trying to piece the conversations together.

Sometimes it was all too surreal for him. With a normal wire, everything happened in real time, with case agents on the street, ready to move with the bad guys. But with Erez, the deals and the meetings and the money handoffs—everything was happening overseas and a week ago, and there was nothing he could do about it. Gagne and Lacewell would get punchy from the tedium but remained unceasing in focus. They grew close over the ensuing weeks. She was his new Germanowski.

Most AUSAs had a way of talking about the agents—it was always "Let me call you back, my agent is here," or "I'll have my agent do it," or "I'll ask my agent to pick it up." It was hard enough to run a case for months knowing that the prosecutor was eventually going to take it over—let alone to be treated like the prosecutor's assistant. But Lacewell never once called Gagne "my agent." They were partners. Sometimes they worked fourteen-hour days, six days a week.

Kristen didn't like that.

"You could be having an affair and I wouldn't even know," she said one Saturday morning as Gagne was on his way to the city.

"What?"

"You spend a lot of time with her. I wouldn't even know about it."

"Trust me, you have nothing to worry about," Gagne said dismissively. He didn't have time to talk about it, and besides, having an affair was the last thing on his mind. Securing the Dutch wire was a major coup, but only if it led to real evidence. Each call was like a small piece of the big picture, and every day he and Lacewell were getting closer to locking those pieces in place. He was finally starting to see Erez's network.

In the States, Erez depended on three key distributors: Goombah, Tiny, and GQ. Twenty-three-year-old Giacomo Pampinella, aka "Goombah," handled New York. Richard Berman—nicknamed "Tiny" for his six-two, 215-pound frame—was a twenty-nine-year-old stock trader who took care of Miami with cohort Yves Cesar Vandenbranden III, a confident twenty-four-year-old green-eyed model whom Erez called "GQ."

In the Netherlands, Erez had a seventeen-year-old gopher named Shimon Levita, aka "Shimi," who was raised in a Bobover Hasidic community in Borough Park.

Erez's crew was an eccentric group and their antics on the wire were like a study in Keystone criminalia for Gagne and Lacewell. Erez's plans were continually stymied by Goombah's lazy indifference, Shimi's naïveté, and his own inability to control every step.

Just coordinating a load of twenty thousand pills into New York through Canada almost put Erez in a padded room: Shimi couldn't find his cell phone, Goombah didn't bring the right ID to get across the border, GQ waited at the Ritz Hotel for two hours because Tiny took down the wrong room number.

"You guys are stupid! You guys are really fuckin' stupid!" Erez was overheard on the wire. "It's room six-two-one, is that so fuckin' hard? It's three numbers!"

Tiny suggested they give up the suicide mission and liquidate at fire sale prices, $4 a pill, to the Hell's Angels who controlled the market in Montreal.

As Gagne and Lacewell got to know Erez's voice on the wire, they could hear the dealer's increasing paranoia after Customs agents started picking off his Hasidic couriers in the States. Tiny once had the nerve to suggest to Erez that his phone might be hot.

"I never call you, ever, from a fucked-up phone!"

"Okay, okay," Tiny said.

Erez was under the mistaken assumption that he was safe in the Netherlands from federal wiretaps and American justice, but he still kept a half-dozen cell phones, using a different number for every supplier. His sources of supply were many, but Michel Denies seemed to be the constant. Erez called Denies "Papa."

Michel Denies cut a smart figure in the Dutch underworld. He was thirty-two, six feet, and thin, with a thick scrub of dark brown hair. He wore stylish dark-rimmed eyeglasses that gave him an intellectual flair, the look of someone who might spend his days at a café on the Leidseplein reading Spinoza in the sun. He owned such a place in Marbella, Spain, called Café Saxo, which Erez and his girlfriend, Diana Reicherter, had visited.

In the six months since they had moved to Amsterdam, Erez and Reicherter had taken first-class trips to Israel and Spain, rented luxury vehicles and homes, bought white-gold rings with diamonds and Rolex watches. Reicherter was overheard on the wire making an appointment for Erez for a liposuction and tummy tuck consultation. Erez was overheard planning a whirlwind summer vacation on the French Riviera. They lived well on drug money.

61 GADI ESHED

ECSTASY TRAFFICKING FROM EUROPE was exploding. In 1997, Customs had seized about 350,000 Ecstasy tablets. That number increased to 750,000 a year later. In 1999, Customs would seize a record 3.5 million pills. International trafficking had become so intense that Interpol established an Ecstasy desk just to take calls and collect data.

The only way drug cops around the world could hope to keep up was to use the same kind of chain of trust that the criminals used. Gagne checked in with his foreign counterparts daily. They shared tips on new phone numbers, suspected couriers, developments on wiretaps, and busts at airports. And somewhere along the chain, Gagne was put in touch with the head of intelligence at Israeli National Police's Central Unit in Tel Aviv, Gadi Eshed. A number may have been passed along, a suggestion they share information—neither man could be certain when they first spoke, because their connection became seamless. They talked several times a week.

Sean Erez was a name Eshed had not heard before. The new mules were also a surprise. In Eshed's experience, it was rare to find criminal activity among the *haredim* (ultra Orthodox) communities in Israel.

"He recruits them from two places," Gagne told Eshed. "Borough Park and Monsey—two very large Hasidic communities."

"There is a reason why they use Hasidic couriers," Eshed said. "To the Customs agent, it looks like here is a friend of God, very innocent and very naïve, and no way in the world those people would dare to do something wrong."

Eshed and Gagne didn't believe that all of Erez's couriers really thought they were smuggling diamonds. Some seemed to have been swayed by the excitement of the easy money and free travel.

"The average Hasidic young Orthodox prefers to spend his day at the yeshiva, to pray and to study," Eshed explained to Gagne. "So the ones that are not the best students and the ones that maybe feel stuck in an extremely religious community—they are the ones that may stray, choose to take the wrong way from their normal way of life."

Gagne liked Eshed. They had both served in the military, were passionate about their countries and their callings, and yet quietly suspicious of dogma in all forms. Eshed was sharp and disciplined (he arose at 4:45 every morning to swim laps), but he also had a warm sense of humor. He was a family man with two preteen daughters that he doted on and a beautiful wife he called "boss." And Eshed understood just as well as Gagne that Ecstasy was a wide-open market.

The magic of the Israeli Ecstasy networks was that if someone dropped out, the drugs still flowed because there was always a new link to slip into the chain, someone to take receipt of pill loads or fulfill lost orders. There was so much supply, and even more demand, that the Ecstasy traffickers existed in relative peace and prosperity, forming loose coalitions of joint ventures.

Case in point: Earlier that year, on January 22, 1999, the day before teenager Jimmy Lyons overdosed at Tunnel, Dutch police confiscated two hundred thousand pills at Schiphol airport that were secreted inside the false-bottom drawers of antique desks. The pills were destined for a buyer in New York who was taking his orders from Judy Ben Atar. The Dutch cops determined the pills were being supplied by Maya owner Eddie Sasson in Holland. German police overheard Tuito's right-hand man, Gingi, discussing the shipment over wiretaps with Sasson's associates in Amsterdam. Sasson was a known associate of Ecstasy dealer Yosef Buskila. Gagne had phone and travel records indicating that Buskila had recently returned to New York and was in contact with Tuito underling Steve Hager. However, no evidence surfaced that Tuito had anything to do with the pills hidden in the antique desks. It's possible he got a cut somewhere along the chain, but he certainly wasn't directing this deal.

62 YORDIM

IN HEBREW, when someone leaves Israel and moves abroad, he is called *yored*—the one that goes down. If it's a group of expatriates, they're called *yordim*. It's a negative connotation and even among Israelis who have lived in the States for decades, many still insist "I will soon be *ole*"—I will ascend, like the others who have returned and are *olim*.

Eshed knew that the Israeli Ecstasy dealers—guys like Tuito, Erez, Koki, Jacob "the Dog" Elchik, and Eddie Sasson—were all *yordim*. Some of them may have paid tribute at some point to mob bosses and crime groups in Israel, but for the most part they were independent drug dealers who had been gone so long from the motherland that they were virtually untouched by Israeli Mafia warfare.

But Eshed had grave concerns about what would happen once the top mafiosos in Israel caught sight of the riches that the *yordim* were making in the Ecstasy trade abroad. Eshed and his colleagues had been cleaning up after the bitter mob rivalries in Israel for years.

63 TRACKING THE WOLF

WHEN GADI ESHED RETURNED to Israel from his assignment in Holland in 1995, he had been promoted to head of the Intelligence section at Tel Aviv's Central Unit, the largest investigations and intelligence unit in Israel. He oversaw about 120 officers in the Serious Crimes division, which handled vice, drug trafficking, murder, and organized crime. A lot had changed while Eshed was away. As Israel was entrenched in defending herself in a seemingly endless border war, internecine warfare was being waged among crime families within her borders.

The American notion of the Mafia, informed by *The Godfather* and *The Sopranos*, conjures warring factions drawn up by generations of family bloodlines. However, organized crime in Israel in the early 1970s was actually drawn up by neighborhoods, so that if a drug dealer grew up in Jerusalem, he would pay tribute to the Jerusalem group. In return, he brought the name of the group's leader, the de facto godfather, to the table as his backing in deals. It was a provincial structure that died out in the 1980s as the gangsters spent more time in jail, meeting their future partners, and then expanding business beyond their villages and cities to national and international venues.

Israeli gangsters fight over control of the typical rackets—extortion, prostitution, drugs, weapons, and gambling—and solutions to Mafia disputes come in several forms. There are arbitrators, often retired bosses, who hold meetings, let both sides air their grievances, and then render a binding decision. (Arbitrators commonly rule in favor of the guy who pays the bigger bribe.) There are leg breakers from the collection-and-protection rackets who exert pressure on one party to pay up. And when it's time to cut to the chase, there are plenty of freelance hit men available to carry out liquidations. Problem solved.

Until 1993, the Israeli mob boss who killed his way to the top and ruled for more than a decade was Yehezkel Aslan. Aslan grew up a poor Iraqi immigrant in the slums of Ha-Tiqwa, a south Tel Aviv neighborhood. He pulled himself up from poverty, first by selling soap at the Central Bus Station, then by injecting heroin into the streets, and finally by controlling the lucrative underground gambling rings in Tel Aviv.

By the late 1980s, globalization and the fall of the Soviet Union had created new opportunities for Aslan and his rivals to combine their loan sharking, extortion, and illegal gambling businesses in Israel with the ownership of legitimate casinos in Turkey and Eastern Europe. They ran package tours, chartering planes to fly Israelis for gambling weekends and vacations. Some six hundred thousand gamblers spent an estimated $4 billion in the Mafia-owned casinos every year. Aslan moved his family to a large gated home in the upscale coastal suburb of Herzliya Pituach—Miami Beach on the Mediterranean.

Aslan was king, and his main business rival, Ze'ev "the Wolf" Rosenstein, was just at his heels. There was plenty of business for the top families below them—the Abutbuls of Netanya, the Alperons of Givat Shmuel, the Abergils of Lod, and the Ohanas of Kfar Saba. But soon it appeared that Ze'ev Rosenstein had decided he preferred a monopoly over a power share.

On February 24, 1993, Yehezkel Aslan was sitting in his black BMW with a twenty-three-year-old woman outside the Pisces restaurant in Tel Aviv. A car pulled up and a masked gunman fired five times, killing the mob boss and injuring the girl. Aslan was forty-three. More than a thousand mourners attended his funeral. Even Ha-Tiqwa heroin junkies praised the crime boss, pointing out to reporters that he was a donor to the local rehab center.

Police lacked the evidence to charge Rosenstein for murder, but it was clear that the Wolf had benefited from the killing. Aslan's death vaulted Rosenstein to the position of number one Israeli mafioso and ignited a fierce war. The Aslan clan wanted revenge. In 1995, Eshed had returned to Tel Aviv from his Hague post in time to wade through the blood feud.

In the summer of 1996, Rosenstein was sitting at a traffic light in the center of Tel Aviv when he was hit twice by gunmen from a passing car. He stepped on the gas, drove himself to a hospital, and survived. Eshed was at the scene when police arrested three suspects, one of whom was Ilan Aslan, the brother of slain godfather Yehezkel. Still, Rosenstein told police he had no idea who would want to kill him.

A few weeks later, a judge granted the three attackers release from custody while the investigation continued. Ilan Aslan vanished without a trace. (The rumor goes that one would have to dig very deep to find Aslan under the giant mall that was being built in the center of Tel Aviv.) A year later, police received an anonymous phone call telling them where to find the body of the second attacker. The third gunman was later tried for murder, acquitted, and then shot to death while leaving a restaurant.

Police had no proof, but they believed the killings to be Rosenstein's work.

In frustration, Yehezkel Aslan's widow, Shoshana, sent a message that spread among underworld hit men that she was willing to pay any sum of money to have

Rosenstein killed. On June 27, 1996, a little before 7:00 p.m., Shoshana was getting home from grocery shopping, bags in her hands, when her eleven-year-old son ran out to greet her and saw a hit man walk up behind his mother and shoot her in the head. Shoshana Aslan became another unsolved murder.

A year later, Eshed and his colleagues received a tip that Meny Aslan, an adult son of Yehezkel and Shoshana, was determined to kill Rosenstein himself in revenge for the death of his parents and his vanished uncle, Ilan. The police made a strategic decision to cover Meny Aslan—they were betting that Rosenstein had already learned about Meny's murderous intent and would move first.

Nearly a hundred officers took part in top-secret 24/7 surveillance. It was a tremendous undertaking, with cops stationed in ambush and surveillance positions covering Meny's daily movements for several weeks. The Aslan house in Herzliya Pituach was on a quiet cul-de-sac and police had to install secret cameras on the block in order to watch the house from vans nearby without being seen by Meny or his neighbors.

Even an old man in a hat and sunglasses who was seen walking his dog past the Aslan residence piqued the officers' suspicions. One astute detective noticed that the man had driven into the neighborhood to walk his dog. On a hunch, police followed him back to Jaffa and discovered he was really an old-school criminal named Jacob Cohen. Eshed knew then that their assumption was correct—preparations for a hit were under way. After all, you can't kill someone without collecting information first: What does the intended victim look like? When does he leave his house? Where are the main entrances and exits? Does he have bodyguards?

On September 10, 1997, the police ambushed two hit men, brothers, outside Meny's office. The fraternal assassins eventually cooperated, giving up the name of the person who sent them; that person cooperated and it went all the way up the chain to a man named Nahman Cohen. And this is where it would end.

Nahman Cohen was a well-known hit man and boss who had previously served seventeen years for murder and was known to run with both Israeli Mafia and criminals abroad—including the *yordim* Ecstasy traffickers. Sources close to Oded Tuito once told Pittsburgh agent Gregg Drews that the Fat Man kept Nahman Cohen on his own payroll as an enforcer.

The Israeli police learned through secret intelligence that Cohen had facilitated the murder contract with a promise of $50,000 for Meny Aslan's head. Cohen's order surely came straight from Ze'ev Rosenstein, but police had no proof. Cohen got fifteen years for the attempt on Aslan's life—and he never gave up the Wolf.

Ze'ev Rosenstein was a master at putting so many layers between himself and crime that police could never charge him for murder, extortion, fraud, or any of the activities that allegedly secured his wealth and position at the top. In fact, he had just one conviction to his name, in 1978, when he was twenty-two, for armed robbery. He liked to tell the press that he was a serious businessman—and that his jealous competitors were trying to dirty up his name with talk of murder and the Mafia.

Intelligence indicated to Eshed that, for now, the criminal networks that ran the Ecstasy trade in America were primarily *yordim*. But while Bob Gagne was focused on Oded Tuito and Sean Erez, Eshed had his eye on the Wolf. Ze'ev Rosenstein was a vicious competitor and Israeli police were already stretched too thin to bridle the power struggles that would arise if the Wolf decided to stake his claim in America's Ecstasy market.

64 NOT A SERIOUS CRIME

GREGG DREWS HAD PUT his Tuito case on the back burner since the French arrest, but on June 17, 1999, a short news item in *USA Today* caught his attention.

Switzerland's Supreme Court had overturned the one-year prison sentence of a man who had been convicted of selling a thousand pills. The tribunal ruled that Ecstasy dealing was "not a serious crime," and that there was no evidence that it posed serious health risks. The tribunal further categorized Ecstasy as a "soft drug" that didn't lend itself to criminal behavior since it was used by "socially integrated people."

Right. Kiddie dope, Drews thought as he read the article. *These people have no clue.* He clipped the item and placed it in Tuito's case file.

65 "YOU'RE UNDER ARREST BY THE DEA"

DEA'S HAGUE REP DON Rospond called Gagne at home on a Sunday morning in June.

"How fast can you get to Amsterdam?"

Erez and Reicherter had been discussing vacationing for several months and were leaving Monday for the French Riviera. It was time.

Gagne needed to get emergency clearance to travel from headquarters, country clearance from the Netherlands, and provisional arrest warrants translated and approved by the Dutch judiciary. With Linda Lacewell's help, they pulled it together at breakneck speed. By 5:30 p.m., he got the green light and rushed to JFK for the next available flight.

Rospond and the Dutch IRT officers met Gagne's plane at Schiphol the next morning, June 21. They ate sandwiches at an airport pub and debriefed Gagne on the arrest plan while they waited for a signal from the surveillance team. The Dutch police could have commandeered the entire takedown and sent a memo about it later, but they trusted Gagne and Rospond and had decided to let DEA take the lead on the American targets. Rospond's boss at The Hague was impressed. This kind of cooperation was unheard of.

By late afternoon, the surveillance unit called: Erez and Reicherter had just left their apartment and would be followed en route to the airport.

Gagne and the arrest team watched the couple check their bags at the Air France ticket counter and pass through airport security. They were early for their 6:10 p.m. flight to Nice, so they shopped the duty-free stores as they slowly worked their way toward the gate.

Once police were certain Erez and Reicherter were alone—and not meeting anyone inside the terminal to do business—Gagne moved in for the arrest. He approached Erez with the casual tone of an acquaintance.

"Sean Erez?"

"Yeah . . ." Erez seemed to be trying to place Gagne's face.

"You're under arrest by the DEA."

"Uh-huh." Erez looked around: a team of plainclothes officers and a pair of uniformed Dutch policemen had encircled them.

"You're under arrest for the distribution and importation of Ecstasy to the United States," Gagne said as the police cuffed Erez and his girlfriend. "These people are executing an arrest warrant on my behalf for the United States."

The couple was transported to a holding location for questioning and their luggage was seized and inventoried. The contents of Reicherter's black suede purse screamed *In Style* summer photo shoot: one Canon Elph camera, one gold Sony cell phone, eight pieces of silver jewelry, Elizabeth Arden makeup, a Cartier wallet with silver and copper foreign coins, Gucci sunglasses, and a brown vial tinged with a white powdery residue. At the Herengracht apartment Dutch police found false-bottom luggage, $10,000 cash, a handful of Ecstasy pills inside a Tic Tac canister, and address books listing numbers for Erez's couriers, for Koki and Hager, and the direct lines for Tunnel and Limelight nightclubs.

Erez's assistant Shimi was arrested on a tram on his way home. The officers escorted him to his apartment for questioning. Gagne had heard Shimi's voice on the wire and knew he was young. But he wasn't prepared to meet a short, scrawny eighteen-year-old.

Shimi came from a good home and a deeply religious family. He still said his morning and evening prayers. So how had he ended up living in Holland, taking orders from a drug dealer, and playing junior Mafia with his girlfriend in tow?

While Erez and Reicherter lived in a luxury apartment in Amsterdam, Shimi and eighteen-year-old Jessica Cusumano were put up in a dull bedroom community in nearby Amstelveen. By day, Shimi ran errands and handled couriers while Jessica stayed home and played with her pet chihuahua, Precious. At night they joined Erez and Reicherter at the casinos. They traveled with the couple to Miami, slept in luxury hotels, got escorted past the velvet ropes into chic nightclubs. Everything seemed exotic to the young couple.

Jessica told Gagne that she knew Shimi was recruiting ultra-Orthodox couriers and delivering money for Erez, and she worried he would get arrested. Shimi told her he was safe because he "doesn't touch anything." He was wrong.

At first, Jessica had looked up to Erez as a Mafia mentor to her boyfriend. But when Reicherter and Erez tried to get her to carry $250,000 in her bag from Miami to Amsterdam, she begged Shimi to help her get out of it. Shimi reminded her that Erez was the boss—he controlled their livelihood. Jessica felt helpless to object.

She was shaking nervous the day of her assignment. When she got to Amsterdam, Erez and Reicherter sent her to a hotel room across from Erez's apartment and told her to wait. She was alone when a tall Dutch man with glasses knocked on the door and took the bag of cash from her. She later identified Michel Denies in a photo lineup: *Yes, that was the man.*

Jessica was not arrested and no drugs or money were found in the couple's apartment. But among the items seized was Jessica's college-lined journal. It was filled with page after page of girlish observations ("I thought my man was cheating on me. But he wasn't"), daily recitations of outfits ("May 4: Today I am wearing a Nelly Hansen sweater with my Fila boots and white DKNY hat"), and recent acquisitions ("Diana gave me a nice shirt . . . and lent me the Monica Lewinsky book"). There was a final entry on the day of her boyfriend's arrest: "So far nothing. His Boss called him and he went to go meet him. I am starving. Cleaned."

Across the top of every single page, scribbled with the obsessive-compulsive will of youth, Shimi had written, "I Love You, Jessica."

66 THE END OF THE SEAN EREZ ERA

IN THE NEXT FORTY-EIGHT hours DEA agents, Customs officials, and police detectives in New York and Florida were on cue, arrest warrants in hand, ready to take down the entire Sean Erez distribution network. With Erez and Reicherter in custody, Gagne called the response groups in Miami and Long Island to give the go. They had to work fast, because Tiny, GQ, and Goombah all knew that if Erez wasn't calling every few hours to harass them about business, he was dead or in jail.

Giacomo "Goombah" Pampinella was arrested in a Burger King parking lot and brought to DEA's Long Island office for questioning.

"Do you know an individual by the name of Sean Erez?" a detective asked.

Goombah said he didn't know anyone by that name. They played a recording of one of his phone conversations with Erez to refresh his memory. The detective asked again if he knew anyone by the name of Sean Erez.

Goombah admitted that he knew Erez, but said he only collected money for him and never touched the pills. They showed him two Western Union receipts they'd found in his car, receipts made out to Erez for $900 apiece—profits from drug sales. One of the detectives asked Goombah what he did with all the money he had made. The twenty-three-year-old dealer said he had just $1,400 to his name. In the last eight months he had spent about $80,000 on vacations, partying, and investing in his family's coffee business.

Erez's twenty-nine-year-old Miami partner, Richard "Tiny" Berman, was arrested as he stepped off the elevator at his Miami Beach apartment building. His Rolodex contained the phone numbers of Erez's entire network. Filed under *D* was a card marked "Drugs" with Steve Hager's number.

When twenty-four-year-old Yves Cesar Vandenbranden III, aka "GQ," was arrested in Miami, his girlfriend made a frantic call to GQ's brother, Eric Vandenbranden. Eric instantly thought of the strange visit he had had from Tiny earlier that morning, when Tiny left a suitcase behind for GQ. Eric rushed into the bedroom to pry open the mysterious locked case. Inside he found thousands of pink and blue pills. He threw the case in his car, drove to the middle of the Rickenbacker Causeway, pulled off, and hoisted the case over the ledge, tossing it into Biscayne Bay. Days later, he would take DEA agents to the bridge to show them where he dumped the pills. A Miami-Dade dive team came up empty-handed.

Back in the Netherlands, Gagne was trying to flip Diana Reicherter. He knew she had helped Erez by secreting pills in rolled-up socks and packing them in couriers' luggage. Erez was always yelling at her to stop getting her fingerprints on everything. If Gagne could get Reicherter to flip, Erez would have to fold, because his girlfriend knew everything about the business. But Reicherter was tough. And terminally pissed off.

"I'm not talking to you guys," she said.

"Diana, it's in your best interests to cooperate now," Gagne said. "If we have to go through all the trouble of extraditing you to the States and then you decide to cooperate, it's only going to be a mark against you."

"I got nothing to say."

"Look, we already know all about your role in the business."

"I know about everything, but I didn't do anything."

"I think you're lying, Diana."

"Fine," she hissed.

Erez, on the other hand, was ready to make a deal.

"I just knew," Erez told Gagne. "I knew this was coming."

The first thing Gagne asked Erez to do was to make recorded phone calls to Ecstasy supplier Michel Denies. Gagne needed to keep his promise to the Dutch police to help them collect evidence against Denies and Lijklema.

67 THE MONEY TRAIL

"YOU DON'T KNOW WHAT a night I went through, oh, my God. I'm in Israel," Erez was calling Denies from a police precinct in the Netherlands.

"Israel?"

"I was on my way to St. Tropez. Missed my flight, and as I'm waiting to get my suitcases back, which I didn't get back until now, I get a phone call from my sister. Her kid got into a car accident and is in a coma."

"Oh, man. Shit," Denies said.

"Shit like you wouldn't believe it."

Gagne was amazed at how easily the lies fell from Erez's lips. *No coaching or nothing,* Gagne thought as he recorded Erez's half-dozen calls to Denies from an undercover phone.

"Don't give this number to no one," Erez bluffed to Denies. "I want to keep it safe."

Erez told Denies he was on his way to Canada, then New York. He tried to coax Denies to visit him in the States. He said he wanted pills, and a lot of them, quickly.

"I would like them landed," Erez said, at Gagne's direction.

Requesting the pills "landed" meant Denies would be responsible for their transportation—and any liability if they were seized—but Erez would pay a dollar or two more per pill upon receipt of the load. Normally, Erez would just give Denies half of the money up front. But there was no way Gagne was going to agree to front Erez any money.

When Erez started cooperating, Reicherter caved. Before he left Holland, Gagne convinced them both to waive extradition, voluntarily return to the States, and cut plea deals. Once Gagne returned home, for the next three days he and Don Rospond orchestrated three-way calls. Rospond would get Erez on the phone in the Netherlands, Erez would call Denies and pretend to be in Israel—and all of their conversations were being routed through and taped in New York.

But in an unexpected change of plans, Ecstasy's Bonnie and Clyde suddenly decided that cooperating wasn't in their best interests anymore. Erez had hired an attorney who thought they could beat the case. Erez shut down. The couple decided the liberal Netherlands prison system was a better deal: Erez could use a cell phone, pay to have steak and lobster brought in for dinner, and enjoy conjugal visits with Reicherter. They vowed to fight extradition.

In the meantime, a federal grand jury in the Eastern District of New York handed up an indictment for Erez and his co-conspirators on Ecstasy charges and money laundering. Judge Fred Block (who, coincidentally, had presided over the Gatien case) signed a restraining order prohibiting the couple from getting their hands on any drug assets subject to forfeiture.

Gagne and Lacewell uncovered evidence that indicated Erez had received about $5 million in Ecstasy proceeds during his eight-month stint in Amsterdam. They tried to seize his money but the trail was tenuous.

Confidential sources told Gagne that Erez hid his money with the help of one or more attorneys in Luxembourg who created paperwork for dummy companies for Erez in the British Virgin Islands. The attorneys would then introduce Erez to private banking reps in Luxembourg and vouch for the legitimacy of his business. Erez would tell the banker that he was in the diamond business or real estate. Once his dummy companies had legitimate bank accounts, Erez was able to deposit cash and move millions of dollars among different accounts to branches in Luxembourg, Israel, Miami, and New York.

Lacewell made formal requests to the courts of Israel and Luxembourg for assistance in procuring Erez's financial records, bank accounts, safe-deposit boxes, and any information on contacts he made with foreign financial officers. She knew it could take years to get that kind of information. She subpoenaed Erez and Tiny's joint bank account records from Florida, and the Federal Reserve Bank for any recorded wire transfers. About $200,000 was discovered in safe-deposit boxes in Miami and Luxembourg. But then, just as they were tracking the rest of Erez's drug money, Gagne and Lacewell discovered Erez had been busy making calls from a Dutch prison. He had already moved $330,000 cash into a bank in Jerusalem and had begun closing his European accounts. He was hiding his money.

As Gagne studied Erez's wire transfer records, he was intrigued in particular by two notations. The first, in April 1999, was for $72,803.58 to his Alcor Bank account by order of a New Jersey yeshiva, or school for religious studies. A second wire in May for $93,000 to Erez's Banque Leu account was by order of a Hasidic yeshiva in Lod, Israel. Why was he receiving funds from religious institutions?

Gagne recalled the time he'd heard Erez arguing on the wire when Goombah refused to body-carry cash. Erez yelled at him, demanding that Goombah pay the

3 percent fee Erez was going to lose by having to send the cash "through the religious guy." They argued about the fee until Erez finally relented and told Goombah in frustration: "Just meet up with the religious guy and finish it up properly."

68 DIRTY MONEY

THE AMOUNT OF MONEY laundered globally in one year, according to the International Monetary Fund, is about 2 to 5 percent of the world's GDP—that's 800 billion to 2 trillion in U.S. dollars. The main sources of illegal proceeds laundered in the United States are drug trafficking, organized-crime enterprises, and white-collar crime.

"Money laundering" is a broad term, but the intrinsic aim of a money launderer is to engage in financial transactions that will disguise the origins and/or the destinations of the money he makes from illegal activities. In other words, it's a way to make dirty money look clean so that law enforcement can't seize it.

Money laundering is the most important phase of the drug business and traffickers employ the classics: offshore bank accounts and front companies in cash-heavy businesses such as strip clubs, restaurants, and Laundromats. Making structured deposits, or "smurfing," is one way traffickers get around the U.S. laws requiring banks to file currency transaction reports for deposits over $10,000. The dealer simply walks into one bank, deposits $9,800 in cash, goes around the corner to another bank, and so on. "Smurfs" are couriers who body-carry just under $10,000 to avoid reporting the cash on Customs forms.

In the mid-1990s, U.S. Customs estimated that at least $10 billion in laundered money flowed through New York City and that drugs generated up to 90 percent of it. Customs agents at JFK, along with their money-sniffing canine partners, had revealed remarkable money-smuggling methods: couriers who swallowed $100 bills rolled in condoms, $7 million in a forty-foot-long refrigerated container, and $6.5 million in twenty-six Colombia-bound canisters that were labeled as containing bull semen.

Drug traffickers face a distinctly unique challenge when laundering money because their profits come in small denominations—and cash is heavy. In 1999, $1 million worth of Ecstasy weighed about 18 pounds, the size of a medium bag of dog food. But $1 million cash, in fives, tens, and twenties, can weigh up to 250 pounds—not easy to stash in a suitcase. When the European Union decided it would issue 500-euro notes, the U.S. Federal Reserve was none too pleased about the effect it would have on money laundering. The $100 note is the highest denomination the United States has printed since 1969, and if criminals had access to the equivalent of $500 bills, then $1 million could weigh as little as 4.4 pounds.

A case study in heavy, dirty money: The largest drug-cash seizure in the world to date was $207 million discovered in a March 2007 raid of the Mexico City mansion of a Chinese businessman and alleged methamphetamine trafficker. The stash was almost entirely in $100 bills and weighed more than two tons. It took three trips to ship the bills to New York, where Bank of America was paid $1.4 million by the Mexican government to count the cash five times and then electronically transfer the money into the Bank of Mexico and the Mexican treasury. It earned $1.6 million in interest in three months.

Some traffickers convert cash into gold or diamonds to lighten the load and evade detection by dogs. In a 1999 case that implicated employees of Metalor USA Refining Corp., one of the largest gold refineries in the United

States, money launderers purchased gold in the States using drug profits and smuggled the gold to South America where it was melted into other forms. From there, the money launderers "exported" the gold back to the States, where it was refined, repackaged in shampoo bottles, and shipped again to South America. Metalor blamed the illegal activity on a few corrupt employees, agreed to pay a fine of $9 million, and pleaded guilty to illegal financial transactions that helped South Americans launder $4.5 million. The investigation began in part after it was discovered that the amount of gold being exported from Colombia in 1999 far exceeded its production capability.

The black-market peso exchange (BMPE) is still one of the most popular laundering methods. The BMPE works in different ways, but at the heart of the system a trafficker in Colombia brings his dirty U.S. dollars to a money broker. The money broker uses the drug dollars to purchase goods in the United States on behalf of Colombian importers who want to evade the Colombian government's tariffs and taxes. The importer then sells the goods in Colombia and pays the broker back in pesos minus a fee, and the broker passes the clean pesos on to the trafficker after collecting a fee. The black-market peso exchange recycles an estimated $5 billion a year.

The repercussions of money laundering have staggering social, economic, and security concerns—most notably the financing of terrorism. In July 1999, the Clinton administration froze $240 million belonging to al-Qaeda and the Taliban in Western banks in response to the 1998 terror attacks on U.S. embassies in Kenya and Tanzania. One lesson the terrorists learned from this was to turn their cash into commodities—gold, tanzanite, emeralds, sapphires, and diamonds—which could easily be transported and then bartered or sold to turn back into cash.

But how did al-Qaeda move its cash? The answer, according to the 9/11 Commission, was *hawala*—an ancient informal banking system based entirely on trust. *Hawala* is the same technique that dozens of Ecstasy traffickers used to move money safely, without risk of detection.

In a typical *hawala* transaction, a client goes to a *hawaladar,* hands him $10,000 in cash, and asks him to transfer the money in, say, rupees to his cousin in India, or shekels to his brother in Jerusalem, or whatever currency is legal tender in the country of the recipient. The *hawaladar* takes about 3 to 5 percent off the top, calls a *hawaladar* contact in the destination country, and has that broker deliver the remaining cash to the recipient. The client does not get a receipt, and no record is made of his individual transaction. *Hawaladar*s keep only a running tab of the amounts owed one another.

Hawala works like a global bank account—no money actually moves, but at some point in time the brokers balance their books and settle the differences with cash or goods. The *hawaladar* doesn't know where a client's money comes from and doesn't want to know. But he will often raise his fee if the transaction *seems* suspicious. For instance, a client who brings a *hawaladar* $100,000 in $20 bills could pay up to 14 percent. The smaller the bills the higher the fee.

Hawala was introduced in India before the onset of traditional Western banking and is primarily used today by migrant workers who need to send money to their home country. *Hawaladar*s have worldwide branches in such places as Dubai, Great Britain, Canada, the Netherlands, Belgium, and such glamour spots as New York, Los Angeles, and Miami. *Hawala* is illegal in India and Pakistan but still exists there.

Because *hawala* is a valued and legitimate form of ethnic banking, it is legal to a point in the States. The Bank

Secrecy Act of 1970 and Money Laundering Suppression Act of 1994 forbade anonymous banking in the United States and forced banks to create anti-money-laundering practices, respectively. While some *hawaladar*s are registered and pay taxes, it's virtually impossible for regulators to know if they are recording every transaction.

Because ultra-Orthodox men may not have physical contact with women who aren't their wives, especially gentiles, Western banking is not an option, and *hawala* within ultra-Orthodox communities has been a legitimate and innocuous alternative for hundreds of years. But any system based on trust is vulnerable and ripe for exploitation by organized crime.

Given that there were no records of Erez's transactions with "the religious guy," it was virtually impossible for Gagne to ferret him out. Gagne learned through confidential sources that Steve Hager too had sent several deliveries of up to $190,000 at a time to a partner in Israel through *hawaladar*s who asked no questions and gave no receipts.

Oded Tuito also was known to launder money through charitable "contributions" to religious organizations. He could drop off cash at 10:00 a.m. at a yeshiva through a rabbi he was friendly with, and by the afternoon one of Tuito's trusted reps could pick up money in the form of a cashier's check from a bank in Israel or Europe, minus 6 or 7 percent—the "donation."

When Gagne called headquarters to have them check on Fedwire's records of financial transactions moving through the yeshivas linked to Erez's bank accounts, he was told that the two schools had moved tens of millions of dollars a year between Israel and the States. But whether any of it was dirty money, he'd never learn. Israel had no money-laundering laws in place at the time, and when Gagne felt out headquarters for assistance, he was told they were shorthanded. At the time DEA was wrapping up several money-laundering operations targeting cocaine and hashish traffickers who used the black market peso exchange. Religious institutions weren't exactly on DEA radar.

Gagne didn't have the time or resources needed to launch an intensive money-laundering investigation on his own, but he believes that it would have been different had he called four years later, when Karen Tandy was appointed to head DEA in a post-9/11 world. Tandy took on money laundering with a passion, changing the focus of DEA and giving agents greater power to chase after the highest-level networks. She put a premium on "revenue denial," hitting drug traffickers where it hurt by taking the money that gave them the power to purchase precursor chemicals, rent stash houses, and pay couriers and soldiers. Every business needs money to make money. The drug business is the same. Tandy set earmarks for cash seizures and DEA reached a milestone in 2007 of $2 billion seized in drugs and cash from trafficking chains. Because DEA operates off a presidential budget that is approved annually by Congress it can't enhance its budget, so the illicit cash goes into the DOJ's asset forfeiture fund, where it's divided up among the assisting city and state law enforcement agencies, drug enforcement task forces, foreign enforcement, and confidential sources whose information directly led to seizures.

Today, America has some of the most sweeping anti-money-laundering laws in the world. For instance, under the Patriot Act, there is a provision that doesn't exist in any other country that allows the American government to forfeit assets from correspondent accounts even if the illicit money was never physically parked in an American bank. Because every single U.S. dollar transaction is wired through New York, no matter what the country of origin or destination, under the American interpretation, once dirty dollars pass through America it's a domestic crime. In other words, if Bank Leumi unwittingly sent $45 million from Israel to Holland at the request of a criminal client, the government could theoretically seize the equivalent amount from Bank Leumi's correspondent accounts in New York if they were proven to be ill-gotten funds. Many sophisticated criminals now do all their transactions in euros to reap the benefits of the stronger currency and to avoid American banking laws.

Erez's money-laundering trail was a whisper of a thread and efforts to freeze his millions in Israeli accounts proved fruitless. Israel had an asset forfeiture law that allowed it to seize property and money that were a direct result of criminal activity. But it wasn't enough—criminals just put assets in the names of trusted family members and assimilated illegal businesses into legal ones to evade detection. Israel was a dream for money launderers. That would soon change.

The Financial Action Task Force (FATF), an influential anti-money-laundering organization made up of thirty-four member countries, reviewed the policies and practices of world governments and their banking centers and placed Israel on a list of fifteen "noncooperative countries and territories" (NCCTs) in June 2000, alongside such financial havens as the Cayman Islands and Lebanon. The Israeli government had begun developing money-laundering laws in 1994, but the threat of international sanctions weighed heavily on the small country, and the Prohibition on Money Laundering Law was quickly enacted, with additional measures to follow that established specific record-keeping procedures for banks and the development of a financial intelligence unit that passed suspicious activity on to the Israeli National Police.

Today Israel's anti-money-laundering, asset forfeiture, and antiterrorism legislation incorporates some of the best aspects of the United States's RICO and drug kingpin laws to fight crime, and FATF removed Israel from its "noncooperative" list in 2002.

But in 1999, Gagne and Lacewell found they could do little to successfully track down Erez's Ecstasy profits. After his arrest he had moved most of it—parked it in Israeli banks where it was likely converted to shekels, awaiting Erez's next directive.

When it was all said and done, the Dutch wiretap recordings helped Gagne and Lacewell freeze just under $1 million in Erez's Luxembourg accounts. Gagne put in a request with DOJ's Asset Forfeiture and Money Laundering unit requesting that the Dutch government receive 40 percent.

Evidence from the Erez case also helped the Dutch to secure convictions on drug trafficking and criminal organization charges for Wyste Lijklema and Michel Denies. (They were not convicted of money-laundering or weapons charges.) Lijklema was sentenced to nine years and Denies got five—the kind of terms that Gagne called "Dutch time."

Erez and Reicherter would fight extradition to the States for nearly three years, using every excuse they could muster, even claiming at one point that they would commit suicide if sent to an American federal prison.

69 THE FRENCH CASE FALLS APART

ON OCTOBER 21, 1999, Gagne got a call from Gerald Graves of DEA's Paris country office. There was a problem with the French case: the charges against Tuito had been dismissed over a technical error.

"How can that be?" Gagne was incredulous.

When the French police had arrested Tuito in February, he had the right to a prompt judicial appearance, within forty-eight hours, just as in American courts. But Tuito gave a fake passport and the police spent several hours just trying to confirm that "Eliyahu Mamo" was in fact Oded Tuito. It seemed that the French prosecutors thought the clock started when they identified Tuito through Interpol fingerprints. By October, when the issue was argued before the French magistrate, it was ruled that the clock had started when he was arrested. Tuito had been arraigned a few hours too late.

The magistrate ordered that the Ecstasy-smuggling charges against Tuito be dismissed—and he would have been immediately released if not for the Israeli authorities, who quickly lodged a detainer for Tuito based on his fugitive status from the 1994 heroin conviction. It was the only thing holding him in jail, and they knew it was weak. Israel wanted the DEA to pursue Tuito's prosecution. They knew the Americans had a stronger case and that Tuito would face stiffer sentencing in American courts.

Lacewell hammered out an emergency extradition request through Interpol and a provisional arrest warrant for Tuito.

Gerald Graves's call came in on a Thursday, and the provisional was written, pushed through DOJ, translated, and put before the French courts by Monday. It was just in the nick of time. The judge dismissed the Israeli warrant, but agreed to hold Tuito in French custody based on the new American warrant.

In November, Gagne and Lacewell had a meeting with Gagne's supervisors and the shot callers at Special Ops Division to discuss the Tuito prosecution game plan. There was no question in Gagne's mind: he wanted to work the Tuito case with Lacewell.

Special Ops decided that New York would pursue Tuito based on evidence from the February Yakov Ariel arrest and Ecstasy seizure at JFK. Pittsburgh would file an indictment based on their case that sprang from the 1997 warehouse raid.

On November 15, 1999, a grand jury in the Eastern District of New York returned a six-count indictment charging the Fat Man with conspiracy in the importation and distribution of Ecstasy from January 1 to February 9, 1998—the period dealing with the Ariel arrest. A month later, Gregg Drews and the U.S. attorney in the Western District of Pennsylvania secured their own grand jury indictment, charging Tuito with conspiracy to distribute cocaine, marijuana, and Ecstasy from 1995 to 1999.

Gagne and Drews were in a race to see who would prosecute Tuito first. But both agents knew that extraditing Tuito to the States to face charges could take years. Bottom line: even if they got their hands on Tuito, it was going to be SOD's call who would try him first, and that honor would go to the district with the strongest case. The sixty thousand Tweety pills that Ariel tried to dump into New York at Tuito's command just weren't enough. Gagne would have to arrest and flip more couriers, figure out how the Fat Man laundered the money, trace his entire network. He knew that going after the heart of Oded Tuito's organization meant getting to Jackie Suarez. She was the linchpin to the New York case.

He would have to work fast, not just to beat Pittsburgh to prosecution but because in seven months Kristen would give birth to their first child. He still needed to get them out of their little apartment and into a home. Everything he had wanted was happening *now*.

Just when he thought things couldn't get any more chaotic, Gagne heard bad news from L.A.: agents had found a dead man in the trunk of a Lexus SUV in Brentwood.

IV THE CHAIN OF TRUST

70 DECEMBER 1999: LOS ANGELES

THE DEAD MAN, Allon David Giladi, had little more than juvenile assault and driving without a license on his rap sheet. But among his peers he was a known leg breaker, formerly associated with the Felix Abutbul Mafia clan in Netanya.

Gagne's confidential sources had scant and conflicting intel on Giladi. Some said he'd gotten killed for trying to shake down Koki and Judy for a cut of their Ecstasy profits. Another source claimed that Giladi and Koki had been allies, not adversaries, and that Koki once paid Giladi $60,000 for knocking around a deadbeat debtor until he coughed up the $180,000 he owed Koki.

Either way, Giladi had been pushing his weight around a little too confidently in Israel and was getting a reputation as an independent strong-arm.

Giladi's fiancée, Keren Azrad, identified his body and told LAPD detectives in a teary interview that Giladi had been in L.A. visiting plastic surgeons because he wanted to fix the scars on his face. The scars, Azrad said, were from two previously failed attempts on his life in Israel. The first attempt to kill Giladi was in April 1999, when the couple was thrown from his Jeep after a car bomb exploded next to them. The second was in August, as they were leaving a wedding party and Giladi was shot by a passing gunman.

Among those who wanted Giladi dead, his former boss Felix Abutbul may have been in the best position to pull it off. And if it was true that the Abutbuls were protecting drug, extortion, prostitution, and gambling operations, then letting a fast-rising soldier such as Giladi venture out on his own would be a mistake. They didn't need any more competition.

Intelligence on the machinations behind Giladi's death has evolved over the years and remains classified. However, early U.S. police reports indicated that Felix Abutbul was believed to have put a $100,000 bounty on Giladi's life and that Nahman Cohen facilitated the hit. Cohen was in an Israeli prison at the time, serving fifteen years for the attempted 1997 hit on Ze'ev Rosenstein's rival Meny Aslan. But prison was no obstacle. All Cohen had to do was inquire among his colleagues. His cellmate, Yossi Harari, who was in custody awaiting trial for a bombing incident, was no stranger to liquidations.

As the leader of the Ramat Amidar gang, Harari and his rival Itzhak Hadif of the Pardess Katz gang (named for their neighborhoods of origin) had been engaged in an endless cycle of vengeance. (Harari's sixteen-year-old nephew had been shot in the head on his way to school after the boy tried to kill Hadif himself. In 1998, Hadif's brother—a rabbi with eleven children—was blown up in his car by a remote-controlled bomb.)

It was never proven that Nahman Cohen asked his cellmate Yossi Harari to help facilitate the hit on Allon Giladi on behalf of Felix Abutbul. But the circumstantial evidence was powerful: Nathan Hanan and Ben Cohen—the two suspects in Giladi's murder who abandoned the SUV in Brentwood—were members of the Ramat Amidar gang and Yossi Harari was their boss.

And when Hanan and Cohen traveled to Los Angeles, it was Ecstasy dealer Judy Ben Atar who made arrangements for their stay.

Judy, Jackie, Hanan, and imprisoned hit man Nahman Cohen were links in a chain of trust. Judy was known to pay tribute to Cohen like a godfather, and

Israeli police suspected that Judy was a dangerous link between the *yordim* Ecstasy dealers who worked in relative peace abroad and the mafiosos from the motherland. But most American law enforcement still hadn't considered that a bunch of love-drug dealers posed a serious threat. Soft-spoken Judy Ben Atar was barely a blip on DEA radar—until a dead body showed up.

Toxicology reports on Allon Giladi came back negative for drugs. An autopsy revealed that his hyoid bone was crushed, and he had suffered blunt-force trauma to the neck with compression—meaning he was strangled to death and perhaps even kicked in the neck by Nathan Hanan, who allegedly boasted of his martial arts training. LAPD Detective Mike Whelan, who investigated the case, got the impression that Hanan had been the leader of the job. After all, phone records indicated that it was Hanan who had called his pal Judy to say he was coming to Los Angeles in November and needed a favor. Based on what Judy had just been through during a recent visit home, it was possible that Judy really owed Hanan that favor.

On September 9, 1999, a few months before Giladi's murder, Israeli police got a call about a suspected armed robbery at a pet store in a busy gas-and-go center at the Mesubim intersection, not far from Ben-Gurion airport. The victim, Jonatan Cohen, was manning the register when he was shot to death by a gunman who escaped on a motorcycle driven by a second assailant.

Eyewitnesses described the killer with a kind of bewildered awe: He entered the pet store with his pistol cocked in the air, stalked to the back of the long, narrow shop to the register counter, and shot Jonatan Cohen several times. As Cohen hit the ground, the killer slowly walked out, got on the back of the bike, and sped off.

He never tried to hide his pistol. The cash in the register was untouched.

Judy Ben Atar and Nathan Hanan had arrived in Israel on a flight from South Africa the morning of the murder. Judy became a suspect when police learned Jonatan Cohen had been harassing Judy's sister Mazal. It was theorized that Judy was the cold gunman who ended the life of his sister's antagonist. Hanan was rumored to be the driver. Judy denied any involvement, but intelligence surfaced about Cohen that led authorities to suspect that Judy and his sister were hiding something.

When victim Jonatan Cohen was thirteen, he discovered he had been adopted. His real parents were the Ben Atars, which meant Judy was his brother and Mazal was his sister. It wasn't exactly news to celebrate.

Lawyers for Judy Ben Atar have plainly described his vicious upbringing in court documents and confidential sources have concurred that Judy was repeatedly beaten and demoralized by his alcoholic father, who used belts, hammers, and anything he could find to throttle his children. Broken bones and bruises were a rite of passage in the Ben Atar home. Judy's mother had tried to take her five children and leave, but she had no means of support. She felt trapped.

When Judy was seventeen, he came home one day to find his mother and siblings lying on the floor, debris strewn about, and his father on a violent rampage. Judy pointed a gun at his dad, pulled the trigger, and missed. After that, every tough on the streets of his Jerusalem neighborhood talked about the kid who had shot at his own father. It was the defining moment that established Judy's reputation for violence.

Jonatan Cohen eventually connected with his sister Mazal and they began living together and running the pet store. All kinds of rumors spread about them, all of which were vehemently denied by Mazal. But it was clear to those who knew her that she was desperately unhappy.

Authorities suspected that Mazal had shared her grief with Judy and that he ended his sister's pain the best way he knew how, by killing his own brother. But there was not enough evidence to truly unravel the complicated relationships. Jonatan Cohen's murder remains unsolved.

A month later, Nathan Hanan called his friend Judy Ben Atar to say he was coming to L.A. and needed a favor. Judy asked his partner Itzhak "Jackie" Cohen to pick up Hanan and Ben Cohen from LAX and put them in a safe house, the vacant residence at 6606 Whitaker Avenue. (Incidentally, none of the Cohens were related.)

The victim, Giladi, and his fiancée, Keren Azrad, had been staying at the Encino apartment of Azrad's uncle, whom Giladi previously knew from Netanya. Giladi also knew his accused killers. He brought them home for dinner four days before he was killed. Giladi told Azrad a mutual friend had introduced him to the men in Israel a month earlier. Azrad thought Hanan was acting nervous and she caught him staring intently at her fiancé.

On November 29, Giladi told Azrad that he had a "private meeting" at a hotel with some business associates. Azrad asked if she could join him, but he refused. She had no idea that it would be the last time she would see him alive.

When Giladi failed to come home, Azrad and her uncle filed a missing-person report.

LAPD Robbery-Homicide Division detectives dug up receipts for the rubber gloves and cleaning supplies that Hanan and Cohen purchased immediately after Giladi's death. They also found bleach stains and a section of carpet missing from the downstairs bedroom of the vacant house. Tests for blood were negative.

Israeli National Police surveilled the two men when they returned to Israel on December 1 and Hanan and Judy were overheard on wiretaps discussing alibis for the period of time that Giladi went missing. They did not speak of murder. Hanan and Cohen were eventually arrested in Israel and charged with manslaughter in 2000. They were each sentenced to seven years.

Hanan and Cohen may have gotten off easy. But after Giladi's murder, no one at DEA would call Ecstasy kiddie dope again, and nothing would be the same for the Ecstasy dealers.

71 OMINOUS SIGNS

GADI ESHED LIKED TO call America the "Sleeping Beauty," and Bob Gagne knew exactly what he meant. It was the kind of place where independent and well-connected drug traffickers could run billion-dollar Ecstasy businesses in Beauty's house while she slumbered, waking now and again to shoo away violent heroin and cocaine dealers, but leaving the love drug in peace.

Oded Tuito had made a fortune spreading his Tweety pills from sea to shining sea—and the Fat Man worked for no one but himself. He needed no backing from crime families in Israel. He was strong and independent—he was *yored*.

But Tuito's success (and Judy's connections) attracted the attention of the big shots back home. Once they put their finances behind the Ecstasy business, they would come to import not only their drugs to America but their Mafia alliances as well. Eshed and his colleagues knew that the overseas mob hit of Allon Giladi in tony Brentwood signaled that a new breed of Ecstasy-peddling criminals had moved into Beauty's house. For guys like Tuito, it wouldn't pose a major problem. But it would for the loose-knit networks of smaller freelance dealers—they would have to pick sides and ask for protection or get out of the business fast.

By the end of 1999, Israeli police encountered a criminal convergence of events that marked the first signs of a shift in the balance of power. Clue number one was the pills.

The very first Israeli Ecstasy seizure was in a nightclub in Tel Aviv in 1992—just 11 pink pills. In 1999, INP seized 464,651 pills—a remarkable 300 percent increase from 1998 figures.

The 1999 release from prison of twenty-nine-year-old murder felon Itzhak Abergil was another catalyst for the shift in the Ecstasy trade. Because he was so young at the time of his crime, Abergil served just twelve years of an eighteen-year sentence and was sent into exile in Europe as one of the conditions of his release—a huge mistake, as it hastened his acquisition of international criminal status. Ecstasy trade was the favored commodity among Dutch and Israeli criminals when Abergil was let loose in Amsterdam in 1999. INP intelligence suggests that Abergil brought his mafioso money and contacts into the fold.

But the most glaring clue to Israeli police that the gangsters at home were dipping into the Ecstasy business came with the arrest of a man named Zvi Fogel.

In late 1999, while DEA was basking in the successful dismantling of Sean Erez's Ecstasy network in Holland, the INP was celebrating its own joint Dutch-Israeli case. The three-year undercover investigation, dubbed Operation Octopus, resulted in the seizure of 1.2 million pills, three Ecstasy labs, a chemical storage space, a field of marijuana, one million Dutch guilders, ten hand grenades, five kilos of TNT, and ten mini Uzis, as well as the October 11 arrest of twenty-five suspects including Maya restaurant owner Eddie Sasson. An Israeli undercover officer had worked with the Dutch for nearly a year to slowly gain the trust of Sasson and infiltrate his Ecstasy network.

One of the suspects arrested in the Octopus case was forty-five-year-old Zvi Fogel, whose crime bio included forgery, conspiracy, receiving stolen property, trafficking in stolen auto parts, burglary, and assault.

Three months before the takedown, INP had received secret intelligence that Fogel was planning a trip to Paris for a drug transaction. The French police agreed to follow him on INP's behalf and Fogel was seen taking meetings in Paris with a former criminal associate named Baruch Dadush, who was wanted in New York for a 1992 charge of conspiring to export stolen vehicles.

Police followed Fogel and Dadush to the Gare du Nord, where the men purchased train tickets to Amsterdam. From there, Dutch police watched Fogel and Dadush meet with a suspected MDMA supplier and a man who made the specially designed false-bottom suitcases. It was not surprising to Israeli police that a lifelong freelance crook such as Fogel appeared to be trying his hand in Ecstasy trafficking. What concerned Gadi Eshed and his colleagues was that Dadush was with him. Baruch Dadush was the right-hand man of top Tel Aviv mob boss Ze'ev "the Wolf" Rosenstein.

When Fogel was later arrested in the Operation Octopus sting in October, he refused to talk and was eventually released for lack of evidence.

Of course, shortly after the Octopus sting, American and Israeli police received the most striking evidence of a shift in power over the Ecstasy trade: the dead man in the trunk of the Lexus in Brentwood. A source would later reveal to law enforcement that Giladi believed he was meeting his accused killers to take part in a $3 million Ecstasy deal.

72 ROUNDING UP TUITO'S SUSAS

ODED TUITO'S BIGGEST WEAKNESS as a business-man was the susas—his mares. Tuito always wanted to meet the women who were going to carry his pills.

Men under the influence of sex and alcohol often spill secrets to the women in their company. Days before he conspired in the deadliest terror attack yet on U.S. soil, Oklahoma City bomber Timothy McVeigh told a dancer in a Tulsa strip club, "On April 19, 1995, you'll remember me for the rest of your life." Years later, several of the 9/11 terrorists spent their last weeks getting lap dances at the Pink Pony in Daytona Beach, Florida, and the Olympic Garden Topless Cabaret in Las Vegas. Strippers are the consummate interlopers between good guys and bad guys—which is why Gagne and his DEA peers know that strippers can be crucial intelligence sources.

Gagne ushered in the millennium by rounding up susas—more than seven arrests in the first few months based on intel from cooperating sources in New York, Miami, Pittsburgh, and Los Angeles and the continued cooperation of "Clare."

Most of the girls were surprised to see DEA at the door because it had been months, for some more than a year, since they'd been to Europe to carry pills for the Fat Man. But every one of them talked. And the more the women revealed, the more Gagne and Lacewell had to enhance Tuito's indictment.

Nikki was a pretty Hispanic dancer at Club VIP in Manhattan who was first approached by Steve Hager in 1998 to mule pills and recruit girls. She made seven trips and recruited a dancer named Jenn.

Jenn took four trips and became a recruiter herself, inviting her roommates Sara and Annie into the mix and pocketing an extra $1,000 for every susa she handed over to Tuito's crew. Jenn identified Tuito in a six-pack photo spread as "Simon," the one with curly black hair, a "big Buddha belly," and scars.

Carlie wasn't a dancer but a photography student who met Steve Hager in 1995 through her sister. One day the budding photographer innocently snapped a still life of Hager's coffee table: a stack of $50 and $100 bills piled ten inches high next to several thin white lines of powder and a bowl filled with cocaine, presumably so abundant as to be left out like candy for the taking. It never occurred to Carlie that Hager was part of an international Ecstasy network.

Carlie took one trip in 1998 and hated it. Gingi put her up in a "rathole hotel" in Brussels. A blond "stripper type" who joined them warned Carlie to stay away from her Israeli boyfriend and then later hit on her in the bathroom. Carlie never took another trip.

Like most susas, Carlie didn't know how much she was carrying. She was surprised when Gagne told her she had smuggled roughly thirty-five thousand pills through JFK. She was later sentenced to three years' probation and a hundred hours of community service.

There were dozens more girls just like Jenn, Nikki, and Carlie, getting picked up and questioned by agents in Miami, Los Angeles, Houston, Boston, and Las Vegas about their Ecstasy courier trips not only for Tuito's network but also for the splinter groups that had arisen in his absence. They had been told by their Israeli handlers to dress like prim angels and to stay calm if they got caught.

Tuito's girlfriend Jackie Suarez wasn't a dancer and she wasn't prim and proper. She was a major player, and she would be stone-cold quiet when they came for her.

73 THE KINGPIN'S GIRLFRIEND

IT HAD BEEN ALMOST a year since Suarez spoke to Tuito; their last conversation had been on her twenty-ninth birthday. At the time, he was hiding out in France, the Germans had arrested Gingi, and couriers were getting knocked off left and right. He told her he wanted to die. She told him she loved him and asked him to call her every day until things calmed down. It was the last time she heard his voice.

In the last twelve months Suarez had gone through devastating lows. Her panic attacks came on so strong she made several visits to the emergency room. Doctors told her that nothing was physically wrong and she began to suspect she was going crazy. A deep foreboding and dread paralyzed her. All the men who used to watch out for her—Tuff Tuff, Gingi, Tuito—had vanished or been arrested. She had no more Israeli connections to reach out to and none of Tuito's phone numbers worked anymore. When Tuito stopped calling she had assumed (correctly) that he was sitting in prison somewhere. She didn't understand why the police hadn't come for her as well. She was alone. She fell into a deep depression and spent a period in complete seclusion sleeping, drinking, and watching soap operas. Her meals, clean clothes, liquor, and drugs were delivered to her door. She was running out of money.

At some point, Suarez began to take inventory of her life. She was almost thirty, well traveled and intelligent, with a bachelor's degree in communications and a head for business. She felt torn, caught between two disparate worlds. She had enjoyed the company of her criminal friends. The men were attentive and funny and dropped cash like bread crumbs. But they had no real skills or formal education. Suarez had a tremendous work ethic. It was her moment to choose which side of the law she wanted to live on. She had never fully committed to a life of crime or to professional ambition. She could excel at either, but her duality pulled her in two directions at once, which left her with nothing. Instead of choosing, she tried to juggle both.

Suarez got a job as a production assistant at an AM talk radio station in New York and found that just giving it a 50 percent effort seemed to please her bosses. On the side, she started reaching out to her old buyers in the club scene to find out if anyone needed help moving Ecstasy. Suarez's Israeli connections were gone, but she found new sources for coke, Ecstasy, and crystal meth. New clients and old lovers rolled into her life. She left her Tenth Avenue studio and moved into a railroad apartment in Hell's Kitchen with a roommate. There were drug-fueled interludes when she stayed up for days with friends, laughing, talking, bullshitting, and playing Scrabble. But she missed Tuito still. And she knew that being a dealer on her own, without her Israeli family, held no meaning for her.

Two days before her thirtieth birthday, Suarez learned that one of her closest friends had died of a heroin overdose in San Francisco. It sent her into black days. She kept it together at work, but at home she was falling deeper into depression and mixing coke, booze, and prescription pills.

74 "YOU KNEW THIS DAY WOULD COME"

"JACKIE, OPEN THE DOOR."

On March 20, 2000, a little before 11:00 p.m., Suarez was in her pajamas brushing her teeth when she heard a knock.

"It's the police," the voice said on the other side. She froze. Her roommate was asleep in the next room.

Another loud knock.

"Jackie, you knew this day would come."

A team of DEA agents stood in her hallway, guns drawn. She was under arrest. They walked right past her and began to secure the apartment.

"What are the charges?" Suarez asked.

"Money laundering and drug trafficking."

She went to her room to change her clothes and swallowed two tranquilizers. She kept her cool, even when her roommate woke up screaming, "What are you doing? Jackie, don't go with them!"

"Call my mom," Suarez mouthed to her as she was escorted away.

In the hallway, the agents cuffed her hands in the front. She plucked a Parliament Light from her jacket pocket and lit it as she was escorted outside. She counted nearly a dozen agents on the street and a line of black SUVs with tinted windows. She was put in the backseat of a small car. The agent in the passenger seat turned and introduced himself.

"Jackie, I'm Special Agent Bob Gagne."

Gagne had been following Suarez's movements for more than a year. He was ready for her. He knew she had played multiple roles in Tuito's organization and had held her own with the men. Ecstasy trafficking— and drug trafficking in general—is a male-dominated business. Someone like Suarez, who was recruiting girls, moving money, and sleeping with the top boss, wasn't the average courier skipping through Brussels with candy pills thinking it's all fun and games. None of the women Gagne flipped had ever touched the money. For the organization to even trust her to carry cash meant she was perceived as credible, tough, and unbreakable.

Girls got used and abused in this business, but as far as Gagne could tell, Suarez was no victim. To break her down, to get her to cooperate, it was going to take a lot more than the condescending "You're in a lot of trouble, missy" speech that some agents leaned on when confronting sweet little couriers, who melted in a puddle of tears once they realized they were pawns for the dealers and now they'd have to be pawns for the feds.

As they rolled through Times Square the tranquilizers began to kick in and Suarez fell into a soporific state, uninterested in Gagne's mundane paperwork questions: *Date of birth? Social?* She said she wasn't answering shit until she talked to her attorney.

"All right," Gagne said. That was fine with him. Gagne needed to accomplish two things before Suarez sat down with her attorney in the morning: he had to earn some credibility with her and he had to show her that prison was a miserable road. Suarez was on her way to Nassau County Jail in Mineola, New York. It was a hellhole, freezing cold even in the middle of summer, fifty-five degrees and no blankets, always packed with drunks whose belligerent, slurred voices echoed through the hall all night long.

A processing agent took Suarez's belongings: leather jacket, boots, socks, and belt. Gagne asked her what she wanted for breakfast and told her he'd bring her cigarettes back when he came for her in the morning. She told him to bring coffee too.

Her cell was dark and smelled like urine.

75 WE FUCKING GOT HIM

OVER THE NEXT TWENTY-FOUR HOURS Suarez was arraigned, handcuffed to a bar, told when she could go to the bathroom and when she had to wait. This was the price: the French Riviera, easy money, good wine—and sleeping on a cold, concrete bench next to a filthy toilet and an itchy crack addict.

Suarez was assigned a public defender and had a chance to meet with her brother at the courthouse. He read through the indictment Gagne had written about his sister: "identified as a drug courier, money courier, and recruiter" for the Oded Tuito network; "responsible for the importation of between 150,000 to 200,000 Ecstasy pills"; "made approximately ten trips" from the United States to Europe and brought Tuito "at least $200,000 in drug proceeds on each occasion, for a total of at least $2 million." Gagne had been tempted to add "major fucking attitude" to the list but thought better of it.

"Is this all true?" Suarez's brother asked.

"Basically," she said.

Gagne had corroborating evidence in Suarez's phone records, travel records, incriminating conversations with sources, and witness statements from couriers. He even had video surveillance of the front of her Tenth Avenue studio, recording the comings and goings of suspected co-conspirators.

She was angry and confused. She hated Gagne and Lacewell and her court-appointed attorney, who agreed that cooperation was her best option. If she went to trial and lost, she was looking at up to fifteen years. But if she pleaded guilty, answered questions about her role in Tuito's network, and agreed to testify, then she could earn a coveted 5K letter, and if the judge was impressed, maybe she'd receive as little as probation. (Named after Section 5K1.1 of the United States Sentencing Commission's guidelines, a 5K motion is a veritable lõve letter from the prosecutors informing the court of a defendant's substantial assistance. It allows the judge to grant lighter sentences.)

Suarez began to tune out the voices around her, but certain words slipped into her consciousness: *Tuito. French prison. Extradition.* It dawned on her that none of this had anything to do with her. The government needed her to nail Tuito. If she refused to cooperate, she'd be throwing herself on the sword to save him. But if she signed a cooperation agreement, she could go home today and maybe never spend a day behind bars. She felt like a dog backed into a corner. Everything was happening too fast. She had secretly held on to the slight hope that Tuito would magically appear and rescue her, but now she knew that wasn't going to happen. She felt as if all her life people had let her down.

Suarez signed the agreement. She was released on bond and would be sentenced at a later date. She wanted to get home and get numb as quickly as possible. But first she had to explain all this to her worried mother.

Back at her apartment, Suarez pulled the last cold beer from the refrigerator as she told her mother that yes, it was true, she had brought millions of dollars to Europe for her boyfriend, who unbeknownst to her was the biggest Ecstasy trafficker in the world. She left out the graphic details of her drug use. Her mother cried. It only made Suarez want to drink more.

On March 23, Suarez took a train to Brooklyn after

work and met with Gagne and Lacewell for her first proffer session. Gagne needed Suarez to talk about the money. Money was the key to a continuing criminal enterprise (CCE) charge. A CCE charge would bring Tuito's potential sentence up to twenty years and help secure New York's position to be the first to try him—before Pittsburgh, Los Angeles, Miami, or any other city where his pills might have landed.

Gagne asked Suarez to go over her entire story: meeting Hager, the first trip to Belgium when she met Tuito, carrying back pills, recruiting girls, working directly for Tuito. And then he got to the money.

Suarez confirmed that she had traveled to Europe on several occasions. Yes, she had brought Tuito cash in false-bottom suitcases. Yes, she had handed the money over to Tuito, and yes, she had seen him hand it directly to members of his organization.

Gagne tried to act casual but felt relief washing over him as she spoke. He looked over at Lacewell briefly. She looked back, also expressionless—but her eyes lit up. They both were thinking the same thing: *We fucking got him.*

"Okay, I'm going to show you some pictures," Gagne said. He gave her his standard legal spiel—a long, cautiously worded instruction meant to avoid any semblance of leading the defendant to a specific photo: "Some of these people you may know, some of these people you may not know. There may be just one person you know in there; there may be a couple people . . ." Suarez hated the cold formality of it, because when he finally laid the six-pack photo spread on the table, she instantly saw Tuito's face. It was overwhelming. She asked for a minute alone with her attorney. Gagne and Lacewell stepped into the hallway.

"What do you think?" Lacewell said.

"I think she's fucking scared," Gagne said.

"No," Lacewell said. "I think she's still in love with him."

"What? No."

"I'm not sure."

"I'm telling you she's scared."

"It's really important that we get her."

"Linda, her attorney would have to be a complete moron to let her walk out of that room right now."

"I don't know, I think she's still in love with him."

"Scared."

"She's probably vacillating," Lacewell said. "You know, going back and forth."

Gagne rolled his eyes. "Yeah, thanks, I figured that out."

Inside the debriefing room, Suarez's attorney was giving her the pep talk: *You're almost done, Jackie. All you have to do is identify Tuito and you're finished for the day. They already have enough evidence to put him away for a long time. If you back out of this deal, someone else will take it. The choice of whether or not to go to prison is in your hands.*

But his words floated past her. Suarez felt nothing.

Gagne and Lacewell came back in. The moment of truth.

"Yeah, I know somebody here," Suarez said.

"You think you want to take a little more time?" Gagne was doing it by the book.

"No."

"Why don't you take a little more time?"

"I don't need time."

"Okay. Do you know anybody in there?"

"Yes."

"Who?"

"Daniel." Suarez had always known Tuito by the name he'd given her when they met, the same name he'd used to escape Israel.

"Why don't you point to him," Gagne said.

She pointed to photo number five.

"Okay," he said. "Anybody else?"

"No."

"Are you sure?"

"*Yes,*" she said with contempt.

Lacewell started to offer kind words. "I know that must have been hard for—"

"Can I leave now?" Suarez cut her off.

As she waited at the Brooklyn Borough Hall subway platform, she fantasized about stepping in front of the approaching train. She decided she didn't have the guts.

Gagne and Lacewell decided Suarez needed help. Lacewell saw pain behind Suarez's vitriol. She tried to be sensitive to her feelings of loss and frustration. Gagne was less sympathetic. Suarez, to him, had taken the tough hand she was dealt as a child—a broken family and absent father—and, instead of learning from it and soldiering on, numbed the pain with drugs. He suspected that as tough as she was in her demeanor, she was that much weaker in her own personal conviction to heal herself.

Gagne had seen the same toughness in his sister so many years ago when she was battling addiction. Gagne had watched Sherrie beat down the pain and emerge stronger than before, comfortable in her own skin. He knew that she'd had to go to hell and back to get there. Suarez hadn't committed to taking that first step to the abyss yet. She needed some pushing.

Under the conditions of Suarez's probation, she was sent to dual therapy for drug abuse and mental counseling. She was ordered to wear a patch that would monitor any drugs she was putting in her system. Suarez kept her troubles to herself. She gave doctors' excuses to her bosses to explain her absences on days she had to be at court hearings and meetings at Lacewell's office.

Her case was eventually assigned to Judge Reena Raggi, who had become the first woman to serve in the roughneck Eastern District of New York after a standout career as a federal prosecutor specializing in narcotics and organized crime.

At Suarez's first appearance, Raggi told her she'd seen a lot of Ecstasy dealers come through her courtroom and act like their predicament was an irritating annoyance. Just because they tended to be more educated and sophisticated than the average crack dealer, they seemed to think they were special. Raggi told Suarez she wasn't special. She challenged her to pull herself together. Sentencing would be in five months. *Stay clean and maybe you'll stay out of jail,* Raggi said.

But Suarez was in too much pain to give up her painkillers—coke, Ecstasy, and alcohol. Her skin patches kept coming up dirty for drugs and she kept denying that she was using. Raggi ordered her to a thirty-day detox at Gracie Square Hospital. Suarez prayed that when it was over her job and her roommate would still welcome her back.

On March 29, 2000, Linda Lacewell filed a superceding indictment on Oded Tuito in the Eastern District of New York, charging the Fat Man with fourteen counts, including Ecstasy importation and distribution, conspiracy, money laundering, and being the head of a CCE, a continuing criminal enterprise.

The new evidence Gagne and Lacewell received from Suarez was the key to the CCE charge. An extradition request had been filed with the French government and Gagne and Lacewell would wait for the French courts to approve it and officially release Tuito to the United States.

If convicted on the enhanced charges, he now faced a mandatory minimum of twenty years in prison.

76 KOKI TAKES THE HELM

ODED TUITO HAD BEEN sitting in a French jail for more than a year, so it was no surprise that authorities noticed a dramatic drop in the number of Tweety pills seized. But total MDMA seizures continued to rise. Tuito's former underling Sean Erez had filled the vacuum of Tuito's absence, and now that Erez was sitting in a Dutch jail, Los Angeles dealer Jacob "Koki" Orgad's business was flourishing.

Koki had visited Erez in Amsterdam in February or early March 1999, back when Erez was just starting out. Erez was making a killing and had no intention of paying kickbacks to his old bosses. Instead of killing Erez, Koki just pilfered Erez's suppliers, stole $30,000 worth of Erez's pills, and then installed his own trusted associates in a $2,300-a-month apartment in Paris. Voilà— Koki was in business.

As always, Ecstasy was devoured by New York, L.A., and south Florida—dubbed "the Party Triangle" by Customs for their tourism and spring break venues—and Koki had plenty of links in the chain to distribute his pills there. He developed a bevy of new distributors, couriers, and partners, as well as some of the old regulars: Judy Ben Atar in Los Angeles, Steve Hager in New York, Meir "Benny" Ben-David, and Yosef Levi in Miami.

The forty-four-year-old dealer split his time among homes in Los Angeles and New York and his Paris apartment on Avenue de Villiers, in a quiet residential neighborhood in the Seventeenth Arrondissement. Koki's close cohort, forty-four-year-old Melissa Schwartz, was one of several partners who worked out of the Paris apartment handling couriers and loads. In return she got about $10,000 a month and all expenses paid.

Schwartz had first met Koki in 1998 in Los Angeles through a mutual friend. She thought Koki was generous and kind. He told her to call if she ever needed a favor. In January 1999, when her Svengali boyfriend, Victor, made her carry ten thousand pills to New York, Schwartz was too scared to say no, so she called Koki.

Don't worry about it, a paternal Koki assured her, *I'll take care of it.*

What happened next depends on who's telling it. Schwartz claimed years later that Koki took the pills off her hands and she was indebted to him. Koki said he persuaded Schwartz to steal the pills and divert them to Steve Hager in New York, who paid her $65,000, and then Koki and Schwartz split the cash. Their stories converged however, when it came to Victor.

When Schwartz got to New York, she called Victor and said her luggage had been cut and the pills were gone—*damn baggage handlers!* Victor wasn't buying it. He kidnapped Schwartz and brought her to a hotel in midtown where a busty blonde was waiting for them. They held Schwartz against her will and threatened to mutilate her and kill her family if she didn't tell them where the Ecstasy was. They eventually took off with Schwartz's jewelry. Terrified, she called Koki in Paris. From then on Koki was her protector and boss. She never heard from Victor again. And Koki never let her forget it. He could be generous and nasty at once.

Agents who surveilled Koki say he was short of stature with big-shot tastes and a hot tub in his bedroom. He drove through Hollywood in his black Mercedes, flashing gold jewelry and designer clothes and enjoying VIP treatment at the nightclubs, where he doled out wads of cash to ensure a constant flow of champagne and girls. He was always talking with his hands and yelling at people. He called his female couriers "toys" and kept company with an entourage of women. Koki had two daughters—an eighteen-year-old and a two-year-old—by different women. According to DEA reports, the mother of his toddler was a woman named Camilla, whom he put up in an apartment near Westwood, California, and bought a brand-new black Range Rover. Sources say he asked Camilla to convert to Judaism for their daughter's sake. He hosted Passover meals. He insisted on eating in kosher restaurants. But Koki's attempts to live a life that pleased God were at odds with his life of crime. He would soon be forced to pick between the two.

Koki sensed in the months before his arrest that importing pills to the States was getting too risky. Instead of getting out of the business, he adapted his stable of mules. Customs began to see an influx of nicely dressed midwesterners and conservative-looking little old ladies who were smuggling Ecstasy. In one case, two couriers posing as a couple brought a mentally handicapped teenager on a smuggling trip. Customs arrested the couple in Houston a week before Christmas in 1999 on a flight from Paris and found two hundred thousand pills concealed in socks in their luggage.

Decoys were paid as much as $2,500 to dress like tie-dye-loving hippie clichés just getting back from a narcotour of Amsterdam. They traveled on the same flight as Koki's mules in a bid to distract Customs agents from the real pill carriers. Koki's lieutenants went to great lengths to prep the mules, taking them clothes shopping for plaid shirts and penny loafers. They would photograph them in their traveling outfits and send the pictures ahead so the airport runner would recognize the pill carrier coming through Customs. Koki's mules got a free vacation to France and $10,000 to $15,000 cash.

77 THE TIPPING POINT

IT HAD BEEN A little over a year since Gagne gave his speech at the Ecstasy summit about the future of MDMA—about the ease of trafficking and the promise of fast, big money that was sure to make it a gangbuster with bad guys and civilians alike. In 2000, that future had arrived. The Israelis still dominated the trade, but demand was so high, everybody tried to break off his own little piece.

In March 2000, Customs agents at JFK were just starting to employ MDMA-sniffing canines when they encountered a disturbing new trend: Ecstasy "internal carriers," aka "swallowers." Swallowers would fill the fingers of latex gloves with dozens of pills, tie the tips to create small pellets, and then choke them down. (Suspected swallowers usually are given a choice: submit to an X-ray or be detained until nature takes its course.) The first Ecstasy swallowers caught at Kennedy Airport in March were two men who had ingested a total of 2,800 pills. Fifteen more swallowers would be caught at JFK by year's end, including a fifteen-year-old boy arriving on a flight from Amsterdam. He had ingested sixty-three pellets containing 2,079 Ecstasy tablets.

In July, Customs agents at LAX seized sixteen boxes marked "clothing" off a commercial airliner. Instead of clothes, they found 2.1 million tablets worth about $41 million. It was the largest single seizure of Ecstasy in history. The complex investigation involved DEA, FBI, IRS, Customs, and law enforcement in Holland, Israel,

Mexico, Germany, Italy, and France. The mastermind behind the network was an Egyptian-born naturalized American citizen named Tamer Ibrahim—a Muslim drug trafficker who partnered with Israeli Jews.

Ecstasy profits had even tempted three cadets from the U.S. Merchant Marine Academy in Kings Point, New York, who had been arrested a year earlier on board the *OOCL Innovation* shortly before its departure from the Netherlands port of Rotterdam on its journey to New York. The men had secreted 50,000 pills onto the ship. Two of them would later plead guilty in New York to smuggling 380,000 pills total into the States.

As demand for pills continued unabated, freelance dealers looking to make a quick buck were starting to ratchet out even greater numbers of fake pills, containing a wide variety of adulterants: methamphetamine, ephedrine, cocaine, mescaline, codeine, and the cough suppressant dextromethorphan, which has PCP-like effects at high doses.

In September 2000, seven Floridian ravers died after unknowingly ingesting paramethoxyamphetamine, or PMA, a hallucinogen that mimics Ecstasy's effects but takes longer to work. They popped what they must have thought were weak E tabs and ingested more, leading to a fatal overdose. The temperature of one victim, an eighteen-year-old girl, shot up to 108 degrees before she succumbed to massive internal bleeding. That made ten total deaths since May 2000 from PMA sold as Ecstasy.

Congress responded to the rising epidemic with the Ecstasy Anti-Proliferation Act. When cosponsor Senator Bob Graham of Florida introduced the bill, he told of *New York Post* reporter Jack Newfield's chilling articles about Jimmy Lyons's death at Tunnel. "Newfield speaks of how the boy tried to suck water from the club's bathroom tap that had been turned off so that those with drug-induced thirst would be forced to buy the bottled water," Graham said in an emotional speech on the Senate floor.

Modified and rolled into the Children's Health Act of 2000, the law enacted stiffer federal sentencing guidelines: trafficking eight hundred pills meant a potential sentence of up to five years (previously up to fifteen months) and eight thousand pills could garner a sentence of up to ten years (previously forty-one months). Also included in the bill was increased funding for scientific research and education programs.

But no story in 2000 did more to put Ecstasy in the spotlight—and emphasize the love drug's links to organized crime—than the headlines from Arizona revealing that former mob enforcer Salvatore "Sammy the Bull" Gravano was heading a major Ecstasy distribution ring in Phoenix. Let the territorial battles begin.

78 "I WANTED MY SON TO BE LEGITIMATE"

IN 1991, SAMMY GRAVANO, underboss of the Gambino crime family and a hit man responsible for nineteen murders, became a federal witness and helped New York prosecutors put thirty-nine top mobsters behind bars, including his former boss John Gotti. For his troubles, Gravano did five years in prison and then he and his family were placed in the Federal Witness Protection Program and quietly moved to Tempe, Arizona, where he took the name Jimmy Moran.

Gravano eventually left the program, sold his memoirs (1999's *Underboss*), bought an eight-bedroom home with a three-car garage and a pool, opened an Italian restaurant called Uncle Sal's, run by his wife, Debra (its motto: "The best-kept secret in Scottsdale"), and started a pool-construction company.

Michael Papa, a close friend of Sammy's twenty-four-year-old son Gerard, was an employee in the pool company. Papa was twenty-three, handsome, physically fit, and a premed student on the dean's list at Arizona State University before he swooned to the Gravano family charm.

By late 1998, Mike Papa and Gerard Gravano were selling pills to ravers in Phoenix nightclubs—a few hundred here, a couple of thousand there. When Sammy caught on, it was a perfect opportunity for the reformed mob soldier to teach the boys a lesson. After all, his former boss, John Gotti, had always pushed the family line:

no drugs. Sammy once even criticized Gotti's pride when his son John junior became a made man.

"I myself would be dead set against it," Gravano said in *Underboss*. "I wanted my son to be legitimate, to have nothing to do with what I did."

But that wasn't Sammy. Instead of discouraging the boys, he mentored them. Soon, Gerard and Papa were carrying guns and using Sammy's name to intimidate other dealers. Sammy even brought his wife and twenty-seven-year-old daughter, Karen, into the business. Gravano's crew became the top Ecstasy suppliers in Arizona. At its height the ring was making almost $1 million a month.

On February 24, 2000, Phoenix state police and DEA arrested Sammy, Debra, Gerard, Papa, Karen, and forty-one others who were named in a 201-count indictment. Pills, guns, and nearly $100,000 in cash were seized. Authorities had been monitoring the business on some eleven wiretaps and bugging devices as part of Operation XTC.

The FBI later learned that Sammy's arrest had saved him from an elaborate revenge-murder plot by two Gambino family soldiers who planned to blast him to pieces with an improvised explosive device. They were apparently furious with the fifty-four-year-old turncoat after he gave an interview to the *Arizona Republic* in July 1999 describing his big, conspicuous life in Tempe, as if he were rubbing it in their faces.

While state prosecutors in Arizona were busy building their case against Gravano, and Gagne had his hands full with Tuito and Erez, Linda Lacewell and DEA agents from the New York Field Division had been busy working a case that would deliver stunning links between Italian and Israeli organized crime.

79 THE BASEMENT TAPES

DEA AGENT SCOTT SEELEY-HACKER, who was tearing up Ecstasy cases out of Gagne's old group D-35 in New York, first became interested in a gang called BTS after reading a December 1998 *Details* article by *Clubland* author Frank Owen. BTS was a *Clockwork Orange*–like crew that operated out of south-central New Jersey, Brooklyn, Staten Island, and Manhattan. BTS was short for "Brooklyn Terror Squad," "Born to Steal," and "Beat, Trash, and Steal"—and they got their kicks by beating and robbing ravers at nightclubs and then selling their own Ecstasy and crystal meth back to them.

Reporter Owen trailed the top members of BTS and witnessed their mayhem at a Manhattan nightclub, where the crew staged a brawl to distract ravers before they robbed them blind.

"When the club finally emptied out in the wee hours of the morning, the signs of BTS's handiwork were obvious," Owen wrote. "The dance floor was littered with items from purses and backpacks the gang had stolen and dumped—driver's licenses, photos, lipstick and mascara."

One gangbanger told Owen that while it *was* true that they sold hundreds of thousands of dollars' worth of fake Ecstasy and that they liked to beat up and rob "candy ravers," it *was not* true that they had sold the fake E that led to the death of a twenty-year-old college student at a rave in the Poconos in April 1998.

"You'd think we were murderers," the guy scoffed, "but all we do is rob people."

The victim swallowed what he thought were three Ecstasy pills that turned out to be a mix of drugs that included horse tranquilizer. A BTS member at the party allegedly passed along the pills. A dozen kids got sick, and the twenty-year-old collapsed in seizures and fell into a coma. His devastated parents had to give doctors the go-ahead to cut his life support system.

The Brooklyn Terror Squad started out as a team of graffiti taggers who called themselves Bomb the Subway in the late 1980s. But as the rave scene grew they got greedy, exploiting suburban naïveté by selling breath mints and niacin tablets as Ecstasy, Epsom salts as crystal meth, and incense as opium that became so popular after they started calling it "Red Rock Opium" that clubgoers asked for it by name and paid $150 an ounce. One BTS member who admitted to climbing through ravers' windows, tying them up with phone cord, and robbing them told Owen he got his start selling real Ecstasy to Lord Michael Caruso at Limelight in the mid-1990s. That was back when clubgoers politely waited in line at Limelight for a free cup of Caruso's Ecstasy punch. Those days were over. As Owen wrote: "[J]ust as the Hell's Angels went to love-ins to prey on '60s hippies, just as Woodstock gave way to Altamont, today's blissed-out teenagers make attractive targets for a pack of predators like BTS. Ecstasy's empathy-inducing effects are great in theory—but only if the person you're sharing your soul with isn't looking to knock you upside the head and jack your backpack."

The *Details* article put BTS on DEA's radar and Seeley-Hacker infiltrated the group through an undercover introduction. Soon he was buying real Ecstasy pills from a founding BTS member, an exotic Italian-Irish-black-Cherokee woman from Sheepshead Bay named Melody

Jones, aka "Miss Melody," who was supplying her crew with X, mushrooms, and cigarettes dipped in PCP. DEA wiretapped Jones's line, pinpointed her supplier, spun off on his line, and by February 2000 had identified the crew's Ecstasy source: an Israeli-born thirty-year-old New Yorker named Ilan Zarger, who had a swaggering style and a laughing-devil tattoo on his chest.

Zarger's phone tap was a bust. He was too sophisticated to talk business on the line. But it didn't matter—Customs had a gold-mine informant, someone who ran a Times Square shop with the typical trinkets and cheap souvenirs. Zarger and his crew liked to use the basement of the store to hang out, bullshit, count money. Agents listened to and watched Zarger on secret videotapes bragging about his connections and telling the informant that he wanted to introduce him to one of his suppliers—a guy named Koki. *That* Koki.

Zarger's phone records confirmed he had been making calls to Jacob "Koki" Orgad. But New York backed down because California was gearing up to arrest Koki and his entire ring.

The dead body in the Lexus in December 1999 had given legs to the L.A. case, and a secret investigation on Koki's network, dubbed Operation Paris Express, was being led by Los Angeles International Airport Customs. The investigation was so expansive, that police, DEA, and Customs agents from L.A., New York, Miami, Las Vegas, Houston, Dallas, Austin, Ft. Lauderdale, Paris, and the Netherlands aided the case. The cop net had to be wide because in just a year's time, from February 1999 to April 2000, Koki and his associates had employed nearly fifty couriers from California, Nevada, Texas, Arkansas, Ohio, New York, New Jersey, and Florida.

Shortly after Gagne and Lacewell secured their enhanced CCE indictment against Oded Tuito, Los Angeles had gotten its own indictment against Koki and several agents flew to New York to arrest him. On April 7, 2000, Koki was picked up outside his three-bedroom midtown Manhattan penthouse apartment as he was returning home from dinner with two women. French authorities raided his Paris apartment. L.A. agents raided the organization's West Hollywood stash house and found cash, handguns, brass knuckles, and a bulk money counter.

Koki was extradited to Los Angeles. As he sat in prison awaiting trial, more than twenty-five suspects in his ring were arrested on Ecstasy trafficking, conspiracy, and money-laundering charges. Some $19.5 million worth of Ecstasy pills, three BMWs, and more than $170,000 cash were seized. Authorities estimated the ring had raked in $34 million in ten months.

But in fall 2000, the L.A. case self-destructed due to a prosecutorial error. The fed attorney was having trouble bringing in out-of-state witnesses to testify and the judge dismissed the case due to the lack of a speedy trial. In a panic, L.A. DEA called N.Y. DEA and said: *You have to do something. Koki's going to walk.*

Lacewell and her colleague AUSA Jed Davis jumped on it, drafting a criminal complaint against Koki and his organization and serving him with an arrest warrant in L.A. before he could even get one foot out the courthouse door.

Koki was eventually extradited from Los Angeles back to the Eastern District of New York, and Jed Davis took over the case. Lacewell already had enough on her plate, working with Gagne on Oded Tuito and with Seeley-Hacker on BTS. In fact, the BTS case had become increasingly complex as its bizarre criminal partnerships began to unfold.

Back when news of Sammy Gravano's February 2000 arrest on Ecstasy charges had first hit the New York tabloids, Ilan Zarger dropped another bombshell in the Times Square basement tape recordings.

"Hey, you saw about Sammy the Bull, he got picked up in Arizona?" Zarger chatted with the informant in March 2000. Lacewell's jaw dropped as she listened to Zarger brag to the informant that he used to compete with Sammy for Arizona and had even sent a soldier to Arizona to stand by, ready to "whack" Sammy—if needed.

Lacewell was savvy. She knew that lots of cons would brag about whacking a guy like Sammy the minute he was safely in jail. But Zarger was dropping names, places, and plots.

In June and July 2000 Zarger, several of his associates, and a dozen members of the BTS crew were arrested. Lacewell and Seeley-Hacker questioned each new cooperator, running down in detail every single piece of potentially incriminating information Zarger revealed in the secret basement videotapes.

Zarger's Arizona distributors were ultimately identified as twenty-five-year-old Ilana Steinberg—a sharp college graduate and daughter of a wealthy Dallas family—and a guy named Jason DePalma. Intelligence confirmed that back in July 1999, Mike Papa beat up DePalma outside a nightclub in Arizona, at Gerard Gravano's bidding, so that DePalma would have no doubt about the pain that was in store if he dared to muscle in on Gravano's Ecstasy territory. Zarger immediately sent a bodyguard named "Macho" to Arizona to shadow and protect DePalma and Steinberg.

Tensions between the rival Arizona crews were high when Gerard suggested they all have a sit-down with his father. Sammy, Gerard, Papa, DePalma, and Steinberg met in the summer of 1999 at Uncle Sal's, his "best-kept secret" restaurant. Sammy took one look at Ilana Steinberg and told her to wait at the bar—he didn't talk business with women. He later invited her back and apologized after learning she was a full partner.

"I own Arizona," Sammy declared. "It's locked down. You can't sell pills here without going through me."

Arguing with Gravano seemed unwise, so DePalma and Steinberg agreed to a lopsided deal instead: Gravano could buy their pills at cost and they'd also have to pay him a kickback of up to $1 for every pill they sold on his turf.

The crime circle was now complete: Koki was selling pills to Ilan Zarger, who was selling them to the BTS crew in New York and to Sammy the Bull in Arizona.

By March 2000, New York Customs and DEA had started a joint investigation against Sammy under the auspices of the Organized Crime Drug Enforcement Task Force. The feds had caught flak for Gravano's cooperation deal against his former bosses back in 1991 when widows of Sammy's victims had been quoted as saying the brutal killer got off with a slap on the wrist. This was the time for the feds to prove they weren't playing favorites. As Lacewell put it: "It was very important that Sammy—who was a lapsed cooperator—be brought to justice not as retribution or vengeance but to show that he wasn't above the law and wasn't getting any special treatment, and that even the district that used him as a cooperator would bring him to justice, that he would be held accountable."

In December 2000, federal arrest warrants went out for Sammy Gravano, Gerard Gravano, and Michael Papa. Sammy Gravano was served at his prison cell in Arizona. All three men were already dealing with state Ecstasy charges in Arizona and now they faced additional federal charges in New York and a maximum of twenty years in prison.

Sammy was later transported to New York for arraignment, where he pleaded not guilty. That day would be burned in Linda Lacewell's mind.

One unresolved question was who would try Sammy first, Arizona or New York. The judge asked Gravano if he had a preference. Sammy paused. He looked over at Lacewell and saw a young prosecutor who was still cutting her teeth on organized crime. She felt like he was sizing her up, and she imagined that he was probably even thinking, *Yeah, I can take her.*

Sammy looked at Lacewell, and then he looked at the judge.

"I'll go to trial here first, your honor," he said.

Okay, Lacewell thought. *That's the way it's going to be.*

BOB GAGNE AND HIS very pregnant wife moved into their new Long Island house on a Saturday in late June 2000. They had been living in Kristen's grandmother's apartment for six months, saving money, when Bob found them a three-bedroom, two-bath Colonial fixer-upper in a quiet family neighborhood at a decent price.

"It needs work, but it's got good bones," Gagne told Kristen.

The previous owners were going through a divorce, and shortly before the house went into escrow, the husband, who had moved to Manhattan, overdosed on painkillers. When Bob and Kristen finally moved in, the place was a mess. There was trash everywhere and animal feces stains on the carpets. Every room needed painting and new carpets. They needed new tile in the kitchen, fencing in the front yard. Kristen was focused on the nursery.

Kristen was a machine through her pregnancy. She read every pregnancy book on the best-seller list and ate crates of strawberries because they were supposed to be good for a developing baby. She worked up until the day she gave birth, and she gained just twenty-three pounds. She was firmly against drugs and wanted an all-natural delivery. Gagne coached her breathing through Lamaze classes. They decided to wait to know the sex of their child, but Gagne knew Kristen dreamed of having a little girl.

Five days after moving into the new house, Kristen

taught a spin class in the morning and in the afternoon she went into labor. It was a long, painful delivery and Gagne held her hand as she screamed and pushed. When the baby finally came out, the first words out of Gagne's mouth were, "You got your girl!"

He stared at their little baby and instantly began to count—ten fingers, ten toes, two arms, two legs. *Okay, good.* Apgar score? Ten out of ten—*good, good.* They were in the clear. He took a breath as the little wide-eyed being, his daughter, was placed in his arms.

Gagne wanted to bring his wife and child home and clean up the place as quickly as possible—wash away the dust and sanding Spackle, get rid of the carpet layers and scratchy-faced men who left their sharp tools lying around.

Gagne thought very little about Oded Tuito that summer. His new family was the perfect distraction. On weekends he worked on the house. He built a barbecue pit in the back and a white picket fence around a verdant front yard. Come six o'clock on weekdays, when his colleagues on Long Island were going out for beers, Gagne couldn't wait to get home to look at his daughter.

81 "HI, I'M JACKIE"

JACKIE SUAREZ HAD ROMANTICIZED her upcoming stint at Gracie Square Hospital, imagining herself standing on a terrace in wraparound black sunglasses and a robe. Then she was hit with the cold reality of the system.

Gracie was a psychiatric care hospital, treating both chemical abuse and mental disorders. The patients looked like shuffling zombies to her, cigarettes were banned, and the nurses wouldn't give her any meds to help her calm down. She rocked herself to sleep that first night and woke up the next afternoon shaky and pale with the chills and red eyes.

Her mother smuggled cigarettes in. Suarez enjoyed them in private in the bathroom and sold a few for $1 apiece. A friend smuggled her a vodka cranberry cocktail and the sweetness made her long to return home. She couldn't understand the ones inside who told her they had entered rehab voluntarily. That was like surrender.

Two weeks later her insurance ran out and she was sent to a federal treatment center in Port Jervis, New York. She traded a private suite at Gracie for a top bunk in a room with three other women. Her roommates were surly heroin junkies with greasy hair and no teeth. Suarez was always a loner, but here in this cramped room she felt painfully alone. The required AA and NA meetings irritated her. She refused to introduce herself as an addict/alcoholic; it was just "Hi. I'm Jackie." She didn't want to share her life story with complete strangers and being told she had to give up partying entirely was ludicrous to her. Why couldn't she just cut back? Suarez resisted the cult of participation—the open weeping, group hugs, serenity prayers. She wanted out.

When her thirty days were up, she came home to find her job and apartment were still hers. She was elated and wanted to start anew; even simple pleasures like walking through Times Square made her happy. After six weeks of sobriety, she decided she had earned a night of treating herself. It would be a private date in her apartment—just Jackie and a gram of coke, some good music, a couple of beers.

It was July 2000 and her sentencing date was in late September. She knew that even with her cooperation agreement, she could get up to seven years or as little as probation. She started to panic as the date approached and she knew her drug patch had to have tested dirty. *Fuck it,* she thought. She figured she deserved a little sympathy for all that time in rehab. But Judge Raggi didn't see it that way.

On July 12, Suarez was arrested when she showed up for a routine meeting with a pretrial services officer. The marshals took her in cuffs before the judge. Her attorney, Gagne, and Lacewell were waiting in the courtroom. Suarez's drug patches indicated she was still using and the judge was remanding her to the Metropolitan Detention Center until sentencing. Suarez felt a wave of nausea overcome her. She seethed with hatred for everyone in that room—the judge, her attorney, Gagne, Lacewell, and especially the scared girl in the handcuffs.

The Metropolitan Detention Center (MDC) was dreary and dehumanizing. She was strip-searched and given a used tan jumper three sizes too big. Her cell was cold and smelly, a thin dirty mattress on a concrete slab. As the weeks at MDC turned into months, Suarez began to suss out the different cliques—the Hispanic women and the Jamaicans, the black girls and the random straggly white women. She had strained visits with her family. Thankfully, she had cigarettes. The bottoming out of her life seemed to erase her desire for drugs. She kept a detailed journal, honing her experiences with raw honesty.

"I could have definitely used some alcohol and some drugs," she wrote of this period in her life. "But the fact that it was impossible lessened my desire to have them. I just put it out of my mind. How pathetic was that, after months of soul searching, rehab, and my trying to curtail my drug use? The only thing that made me stop caring about getting high was incarceration."

Gagne and Lacewell mentioned during a visit that Miami DEA was interested in questioning her about Tuito's soldiers in Florida—Meir "Benny" Ben-David and Yosef Levi. The pair had recently fled to Israel. If Suarez's information strengthened the Florida U.S. attorney's indictment, Judge Raggi might look more favorably on her case at sentencing September 23.

She agreed to go, and by September, Suarez was in Miami. She shared a tiny cell with an angry black woman with gold teeth and cornrows who called her a "red nigga" and farted loudly in her direction. "I'm Puerto Rican," Suarez corrected her.

She spent months waiting for prosecutors to call and her sentencing date had to be postponed to January 26, 2001. She threw herself into the library and the gym. At night, from her tiny cell, she could see downtown Miami and the neon lights of South Beach. It made her miss the nights in Nice with Tuito.

In November, Miami prosecutors finally called for her and she identified Ben-David and Levi from photographs. She retold her story but didn't feel like it meant much to them. She wanted to get back to New York.

When her meeting was over, her attorney took her aside to share some unsettling news: Oded Tuito had been set free.

82 "A VERY BEAUTIFUL AND CLEVER TRICK"

THE FRENCH *LÉGAT* FOR the Department of Justice called Linda Lacewell in October 2000 with an unfortunate development in Tuito's case. Lacewell's first call was to Bob Gagne.

"You're not going to believe this," she said.

Tuito had a team of French lawyers who'd found a loophole big enough for the Fat Man to squeeze through: his Algerian parents.

Under French law, if your parents were born prior to 1959 in Algeria, which was a French colony at the time, then you are eligible for citizenship.

"You gotta be kidding me," Gagne yelled. "This is fucking unbelievable."

Gagne and Lacewell knew Tuito had applied for French citizenship almost a year earlier, but the French prosecutors had assured them it was of little concern.

"They were telling us, '*Eet's imposseeble, eet takes yeerz*,'" Gagne said with disdain. Tuito had somehow managed to get his application on a fast track.

At a hearing before the French magistrate on October 11, 2000, the judge announced that he had two extradition requests in front of him from the United States and Israel. That's when Tuito's lawyer dropped the bomb, presenting the court with a French certificate of nationality, certifying that Tuito had become a citizen.

"Quick work," the judge remarked. He asked for a response from the government.

"Mr. Judge, the government of France does not extradite its citizens," the prosecutor said.

The judge took a recess to think about what he would do next.

DEA Special Agent Gerald Graves and Israeli police officer Etty Yevnin, who were present at the hearing, told the French prosecutor during the break that Israel and America were jointly requesting that Tuito be prosecuted by the French, based on the charges filed in both their extradition requests. Essentially, it meant that both countries were willing to give up their cases and hand all their evidence over in the hope that the French government would try Tuito for them.

Graves and Yevnin knew Tuito was a flight risk and they begged the French prosecutor to ask that he be held in custody pending a French trial. But when the judge returned, he denied the American and Israeli extradition requests and ordered Tuito released.

"You mean, now?" Tuito asked, seemingly confused.

"Yes," his attorney said. "Now."

Tuito was a free man after spending nineteen months in a French prison.

Gadi Eshed called Gagne when he heard. "So, our friend Tuito. I admit that this was a very beautiful and clever trick."

"We can't touch him as long as he stays in France," Gagne said. "But there are no border checks with the new EU, so how are we going to catch him?"

Their best chance at bringing Tuito to American justice was catching him in another country and trying to extradite him again. But if one is going to be trapped within the borders of a nation, Tuito picked well. He put his family up in a white two-story gated home in the suburbs of Créteil, outside of Paris. Then he retook his seat on the throne and set out to reassemble his chain of trust.

Sean Erez was in a Dutch prison; Koki was in jail but the charges might not stick; Meir Ben-David, Yosef Levi, Judy Ben Atar, and Steve Hager were all easily reachable.

Tuito had some calls to make.

83 THE A-LIST

IN THE PAST YEAR, Gadi Eshed had been besieged with phone calls from agents and prosecutors in Houston, Los Angeles, New York, Phoenix—American voices constantly on the line, names he'd never heard, people who introduced themselves by saying: "I've got an Ecstasy case. I've been told you're the expert on the ground in Israel."

If there was one thing Eshed had learned from his four years in the Netherlands, it was the importance of intelligence sharing. When different units were targeting the same suspects yet failing to share information, it only led to folly and missed opportunities. Eshed decided it was time to have INP officers meet their American counterparts face-to-face, to share intelligence and work together to take down the Ecstasy traffickers. He convinced his colleagues at INP to open their files and then he made hundreds of phone calls to his contacts in the States and the American embassy in Tel Aviv.

A date in January 2001 was set. INP officers prepared for months, pulling together every bit of case information they could muster: intelligence reports, photographs, and background information on the suspected MDMA traffickers.

In September 2000, just as the conference schedule and expected attendees was firming up, war broke out in Israel, the Second Intifada. In the ensuing months and years, Israelis' daily lives were marked by a constant threat of terror. Palestinian suicide bombers killed hundreds of innocent Israeli citizens at cafés, shopping malls, and nightclubs and on buses. Israel retaliated with aggressive air strikes and military operations that killed thousands of Palestinian militants and civilians in the cross fire.

When the U.S. Department of State issued warnings that Americans avoid travel to Israel, Gadi Eshed was put in the awkward position of trying to convince dozens of high-ranking American officers to come to Tel Aviv to share investigative intelligence about Ecstasy in the middle of a war. Many agents were told point-blank by their supervisors: *No way, not now, too hot.*

Eshed's boss at the time, Tel Aviv district commander Yosef Sedbon, was welcomed on his first day on the job in 2000 with a terrorist bomb attack on a Dan bus in Tel Aviv. In three years there were thirty terror attacks during his watch. The forty-seven-year-old police commander was in almost daily contact with the Shabak, Israel's internal antiterror unit. Despite the obvious dangers, Sedbon encouraged Eshed to move forward with his conference. He understood that this was an important moment for the Israeli cops to show their cards to the American drug cops for the first time and prove that they were serious about mutual cooperation.

"Gadi, talk with the Americans," Sedbon said. "Take your time."

After several days of relative peace and quiet, Eshed was on the phone with a New York prosecutor, assuring him that it was a safe time to visit. In the middle of their conversation, a bomb exploded at a nearby bus station.

"I think that something just happened," Eshed said. "Let me check it and I'll get back to you."

This is it, Eshed thought. *This conference will never happen.*

But the Americans needed a sit-down with their Israeli counterparts more than ever. The DEA-initiated cases against MDMA violators had more than doubled from 278 in 1999 to 670 in 2000. And it was difficult for the Americans to make sense of the tenuous links between the cases. The agents who knew Eshed went to bat for him, convincing their supervisors that the Israelis were serious about getting together, cop to cop, to unravel the unwieldy trafficking networks.

Finally, a compromise was reached—the Americans could go, but with restrictions. Travel was permitted between the hotel, police station, and American embassy. They were ordered to stay out of shopping malls and cafés, and absolutely no riding on buses.

The conference was held at the Tel Aviv district police station in January 2001. Some three dozen Israeli National Police officers took part in meetings with more than thirty DEA and Customs agents and prosecutors from Miami, L.A., New York, and Houston and a small delegation from DEA Special Ops Division, as well as representatives from Cyprus, Holland, France, and Germany. DEA agent Deanne Reuter, who was helming the Los Angeles investigations, attended, as did Don Rospond, the DEA assistant country attaché in The Hague who'd worked on the Erez investigation in 1999.

Conspicuously missing from the meeting was Bob Gagne. As much as Gagne wanted to put Tuito away, he took one look at his newborn daughter, fragile and perfect, and couldn't leave her behind to spend a week in a war zone. The day he became a father, his brain had reordered the world.

District Commander Yosef Sedbon sat at the head of the table in the conference room at INP. He said a few words, in English, in his gravelly baritone. In the middle of this war, he told them, he was thankful that they had found the time to come and work together, to continue the normal life of fighting crime, to not be terrorized.

Eshed spoke next. It was the first time most of the agents had ever met him, although they had heard his voice many times. He was tall and slender, with light brown hair, blue-green eyes, and a tricky smile. Like them, he was slightly out of place in a suit and tie. In his years working cases around the world, Eshed noticed that Israeli police and American DEA agents dressed exactly alike—jeans, collared shirts, tennis shoes, short hair. But there was something else in their body language, the way they carried themselves—they could always find one another at an airport without ever having met.

Eshed told the agents that he "saluted their bravery."

"I feared it would be just me and Yossi this morning," he joked. "But here in this room are the people with a combination of knowledge and experience—exactly the people who are able to solve the big part of the problems that every individual and every officer is not able to do by himself."

After a round of presentations, the participants would spend the rest of the week in meetings—sometimes fourteen, fifteen hours a day in small working groups, going through hundreds of case files, reviewing suspects' photos, crime records, historical information, and known associates. Dozens of INP analysts and investigators sat in to answer questions, draw out the bigger picture, and refine the agents' understanding of the nuances of the circular chain of trust organized-crime model. A face-to-face meeting with a top-secret informant was arranged.

As the meeting wound down, Eshed and his colleagues stressed to their American counterparts that what they were looking for was full, honest, and professional cooperation in order to bring the Ecstasy targets to justice—whether it be in Israel, the States, or abroad. They had shared information on more than a hundred suspects. But for Israeli police, it was important that by the end of the conference, they devise together a short list of joint targets: the A-list.

The A-list included all the headliners: Tuito, Koki, Judy. But for the Israeli officers, the number one target on their wish list was Ze'ev Rosenstein. Many of the Americans had never heard his name. What evidence did they have that this supposed Mafia boss was even smuggling Ecstasy?

INP believed that Rosenstein was involved in trafficking pills, but they had no arrests or seizures to back up their assumption. They had only surveillance and intelligence reports: Rosenstein's lieutenant Baruch Dadush had been seen meeting with suspected Ecstasy trafficker Zvi Fogel; Rosenstein's ally Nahman Cohen was said to have been involved in deals with Judy Ben Atar and Oded Tuito. But what was any of that? A wisp of proof that Ecstasy traffickers were linked to men who were linked to Rosenstein.

But Eshed stood in front of nearly three dozen foreign agents and said they believed that Ze'ev Rosenstein was financing the importation of millions of pills to the States.

"The intelligence is good," he said. They just needed help building the evidence.

It was done. Rosenstein's name was on the A-list.

84 ZE'EV "THE WOLF" ROSENSTEIN

ZE'EV ROSENSTEIN WAS A stout man, with graying black hair, slack jowls, and meaty legs. He grew up across the street from a police station in middle-class Tel Aviv–Jaffa in a white stucco tenement building, the kind where laundry always hung from the windows. His father had worked forty years for the Dan bus line, sitting at the back of the bus selling tickets. He was said to be partial to his mother, a Bukharian Jew, who had filled their tiny apartment with the exotic aroma of Persian dishes, lamb, and saffron.

Like his former business rival Yehezkel Aslan, Rosenstein had amassed great wealth in the early 1990s by opening casinos in Turkey and sending droves of Israelis on gambling trips abroad. Aslan's 1993 unsolved murder gave Rosenstein even greater riches and power. But in 1998, Turkey's Islamic government banned gambling and ordered the casinos closed. The money flow tightened and many gangsters scrambled, turning their focus toward other parts of Eastern Europe. Netanya mob boss Felix Abutbul opened Casino Royal in Prague. Rosenstein bought a hotel and casino in Bucharest. Some went the way of Internet gambling.

By 2000, the crime families had scrambled to form alliances in order to protect their empires. Ze'ev Rosenstein allied himself with Haniana Ohana and Felix Abutbul. (Abutbul had cemented his underworld reputation in the 1980s after he was caught in a London airport traveling with a box containing a drugged Nigerian diplomat whom he had kidnapped.) On the other side of the war line, the Abergil brothers—Itzhak, Meir, and Jacob—had allied themselves with the Alperon brothers—Jacob and Nissim.

Rosenstein wasn't just an A-list arrest target for the Israeli police, he was also an A-list underworld murder target—the man to dethrone. The Wolf's reputed strategy was kill first. The blood feuds among the warring families would only intensify in the years following Gadi Eshed's 2001 Ecstasy conference.

85 "I'M SORRY"

LEARNING THAT ODED TUITO was free evoked conflicting emotions in Jackie Suarez. She secretly cheered his eleventh-hour escape plan—citizenship. She wondered if he had heard that she sang to the feds. She never feared Tuito would come after her for talking.

In January 2001, her attorney told her they needed to postpone her sentencing again and schedule a psychiatric evaluation. The plan was to play up her tough-luck childhood to engender sympathy with the judge. Suarez didn't like the idea of having her life dissected and her dead father held up as the culprit of her misfortunes. But she was going on eight months behind bars and she didn't have much fight left. Shortly afterward, her mother sheepishly admitted that she had collected Jackie's belongings from her apartment. She would have to live at home with her mother whenever she was released. It was devastating news. In the space of a year, she had lost her best friend to an overdose, her freedom, her job, and now her apartment.

On February 23, the day of her sentencing hearing, Suarez prayed for a favorable outcome. She could get time served and be released right away, or Judge Raggi could make an example of her and give her seven years. Her heart raced as U.S. marshals escorted her to the courtroom.

Linda Lacewell praised Suarez to the judge and said her cooperation had helped secure a more severe indictment against Tuito, including the continuing criminal-enterprise charge. Lacewell's words stung.

Raggi ran down Suarez's list of crimes. She told her that she was an intelligent woman, but if she continued using drugs, it would only lead to more problems. Then she asked Suarez, "Do you have anything to say?"

Her family had been begging her to apologize and act remorseful in front of the judge, but Suarez was still bitter. She was angry about being ratted out, locked up, and losing everything that mattered to her. What was there to say?

"I'm sorry."

Suarez choked up, surprised to hear the words slip out of her mouth.

Raggi sentenced her to a year and a day, with credit for time served. She would be free in about eight weeks. Tears ran down Suarez's cheeks.

86 SEDER IN SPAIN

TUITO WAS A FREE man in Paris. Israel couldn't touch him, he had evaded the Americans, and now the French were calling him one of their own. He rebuilt his Ecstasy network with a new partner in Spain named Michel El Kaiam, a man he'd met in prison in Israel more than a decade ago. He abandoned the old Tweety-stamped pills for testosterone-laden logos: Rolls-Royce, Ferrari, and Armani.

Tuito had long depended on the chain of trust to swiftly move pills and cash without detection. But a lot had changed while Tuito was in prison. The drug cops had finally adapted.

Gadi Eshed's January 2001 conference in Israel heralded a new order for dealing with the Ecstasy traffickers, and Israeli National Police became increasingly active in foreign posts, assisting with international investigations. The quest to capture Tuito took on a new sense of urgency. If the individual countries couldn't catch the dealers on their own, they would do whatever it took to bring them to justice in American courts, where they would face stiffer sentencing. Tuito's partners were being wiretapped and surveilled by law enforcement in California, Florida, and New York and in Israel, Spain, Germany, Holland, Canada, and Australia.

In Spain, a delegation of Israeli officers rotated through posts working alongside Spanish National Police (SNP) who were tapping the phone of Tuito's partner Michel El

Kaiam. The Israeli detectives translated the wires and helped coordinate SNP's casework.

In Tel Aviv, Eshed and his colleagues gained a crucial piece of information—a single landline number—from American DEA agents. That number led them to an apartment in Giv'atayim, in East Tel Aviv, where Meir Ben-David and Yosef Levi were hiding out after fleeing the DEA in Florida the previous fall.

Ben-David and Levi were too savvy to talk business on the landline, but it didn't matter. Surveillance officers caught the men returning again and again to a single pay phone that they were using to make dozens of incriminating calls to Tuito's cell heads in the States and Europe. They spoke in partial code about selling "a half building" (half a million pills) to the "Towers" (New York), while arguing over price schemes and concocting plans to use elderly couriers with fake passports.

In Los Angeles, DEA and Customs were surveilling several suspects who used to get their drugs from Koki and were now buying directly from Tuito. Tuito was sending by UPS shipments of 50,000-pill loads concealed in picture frames to his new L.A. cell heads. DEA started tapping their phones. Soon the agents were listening to the Fat Man bitching about money owed, favors he needed, and the headaches of being the boss. In March 2001, Tuito lost couriers and thousands of pills at increased vehicle border checks when a foot-and-mouth disease outbreak coupled with the resurgence of mad cow disease spread panic through Europe.

"There is a mess over the cows, a serious one, not a joke. It's impossible to get out," Tuito was overheard telling a Los Angeles distributor. "Two friends were caught because of these things."

In New York, Gagne was waiting for Tuito's wanderlust to take hold again—he knew it would only be a matter of time before the Fat Man crossed the French border.

On April 4, 2001, Gagne got the call. The Paris DEA office had just been tipped off by Spanish police: Tuito had snuck out of France and was somewhere in Barcelona. The Spanish police figured it out when they heard Tuito using his Spanish partner El Kaiam's cell phone to call his wife in France.

"Pack up the family and come to Barcelona," Tuito was overheard telling Aliza. "I have a safe place for us to stay."

Tuito advised Aliza to arrive by April 6 so that the family could have Seder together in Spain. Gagne faxed a photograph of Tuito to the Spanish police to help them identify the Fat Man and investigators from Madrid and Barcelona were standing by to arrest Tuito based on the Interpol red notice previously filed by Linda Lacewell. It seemed like an easy enough operation, but there was one problem.

"They missed him," Lacewell told Gagne a week later.

"What?"

"Everybody went home for the holidays."

Like Tuito, the Israeli police translators wanted to be with their families on Passover. They had been away from home for almost three months. Catching Oded Tuito, they decided, was not as important as being with their wives and children on one of the most important Jewish holidays.

With the translators gone, the Spanish police had no idea what was being said on the wires. The Spanish cops were preparing for the Easter holiday, and the units were shorthanded. The operation was abandoned. Oded Tuito enjoyed a quiet Seder with his family and then returned to France, never knowing he had escaped American justice one more time.

Gagne figured Tuito was the luckiest bastard alive. But he couldn't fault the foreign cops. He respected that they chose their families over Tuito. It never would have occurred to Gagne to let a bad guy go. He couldn't even turn his cell phone off, let alone allow a guy to walk.

Every Sunday, when he and Kristen would bring their daughter to her parents' home for dinner, Gagne prayed his cell phone wouldn't ring. But it always did. Kristen would give him the icy look that said: *You are not going to take that.* But he always did. He'd step out to the patio to give his time to an informant, an overseas agent, or whoever needed him in that moment. He'd rejoin the table but he'd be thinking about the call, mulling over the to-do list in his mind. In the car on the way home, he'd be back on the phone. Kristen could see him, sitting right next to her, but she didn't feel his presence.

87 A SECRET MEETING WITH EL KAIAM

IN THE SIX MONTHS since Tuito had been released from prison and resumed his place on the Ecstasy throne, it had been one problem after another for the Fat Man. Competition was stiffer. The police were better connected. He was losing money faster than he could make it.

In late April, Los Angeles DEA agents overheard Tuito making plans to send seventy thousand pills from "the Towers" to "down below." They passed the tip to New York and its neighbor "down below," Florida. The information ultimately led Delaware state police to arrest a pair of drug runners who had 68,456 tablets in the trunk of their rental car. That arrest led to the discovery of Tuito's Miami cell head, a man named Nissim El-al, who was promptly picked up with fifty thousand pills on him.

The succession of hits had the dealers burning up their phone lines: *Who got popped? Did they talk? And what about my money?*

Every load lost was hundreds of thousands of dollars ripped from Tuito's and El Kaiam's pockets. Tuito desperately needed to have another secret meeting with El Kaiam. They had to sit down and root out all the "red yarmulkes," the undercover drug cops, that Tuito suspected were infiltrating his business. Tuito knew he had to stay put in France or face potential arrest. But he had been feeling confident after his Passover vacation and was itching to get out of Paris.

Los Angeles DEA was the first to hear about Tuito's travel plans on a wire intercept. This time, everybody was ready.

In New York, Gagne was holding his breath and waiting for word of Tuito's arrest. Even with the best intelligence, Gagne knew that anything could go wrong. Tuito could slip out a side door while one of the surveilling officers was on a bathroom break. A translator could miss a key piece of information with just one word misunderstood.

Gagne was at home, giving his infant daughter a bath, when he got the call from Chris Kabel of Special Ops: "They got him."

On May 18, 2001, Oded Tuito was apprehended by Spanish police in Castelldefels, a Mediterranean resort south of Barcelona. The official report is that he was captured as he was leaving a hotel. The unofficial report is that it was actually a brothel.

By August, New York, Pittsburgh, and Los Angeles all had filed competing indictments for the thirty-nine-year-old Ecstasy trafficker. Tuito vowed to fight his extradition to the United States.

In the months ensuing, Spanish police discovered that Tuito was still directing Ecstasy shipments from his cell in Madrid's Soto del Real prison by using smuggled cell phones and passing messages through visitors. Instead of confiscating the phones, they intercepted his conversations and let him talk as long as they needed to collect evidence and track down his co-conspirators.

88 HIS OWN LITTLE MAFIA FAMILY

IN THE MIDDLE OF handling the legal business of Oded Tuito's case, Linda Lacewell was also preparing for the upcoming drug conspiracy trial of Sammy Gravano.

In May 2001, Lacewell had filed a thirty-four-page motion detailing Gravano's "other crimes"—evidence she had hoped to introduce to a jury to show how Gravano had used his name and reputation to threaten Ecstasy competitors and maximize his profits. The motion also revealed Gravano's alleged plot to whack his son Gerard's girlfriend. Prosecutors said Gravano was so angry to hear that the girl was bragging to friends about dating "Sammy the Bull's son," that he put a gun to Gerard's head and threatened to pull the trigger—a lesson about disrespecting the family name.

The judge granted Lacewell's motion—all the evidence would be allowed at trial. She also agreed to allow the government to introduce some of its forty thousand hours of secretly taped phone conversations—a collection so broad, it included moments in which Sammy could be heard singing to his dog.

The cards were stacked against Sammy. And days before the trial was to begin, Michael Papa decided to cooperate. Once Papa flipped, Gravano was cooked. He folded and took a plea deal.

On May 25, 2001, Gravano and his son, Gerard, both pleaded guilty to drug charges in New York. The gallery was packed with gavel groupies, reporters, federal prosecutors, and angry women related to men Sammy had killed.

When asked by the judge to state his crime, Sammy said in a monotone: "I lent money to people. They distributed Ecstasy."

Gerard Gravano was later sentenced to nine years and three months and ordered to enter a substance abuse treatment program. The judge had cut his sentence by two years out of pity, noting that he would likely have to spend his entire time in solitary to protect him from those looking to exact vengeance on his father.

Sammy was cocky to the end. He challenged the sentencing enhancements the prosecutors were proposing and demanded an evidentiary hearing. It was a blustering miscalculation on his part, because it gave the prosecutors an opportunity to put on a mini-trial to defend their position. Witnesses were called, and the judge was given a detailed, blow-by-blow account of every crime Sammy was accused of—from threatening to kill his young rivals DePalma and Steinberg to running his own little Mafia family in Arizona.

Judge Allyne Ross sentenced the fifty-seven-year-old Ecstasy trafficker to twenty years—four years above what the sentencing guidelines called for. She told Gravano she wished she could have given him more.

As for Mike Papa, according to at least one DEA report, he followed in the footsteps of his former mentor and entered Witness Protection. Prosecutors would not confirm or deny it.

89 BREAKING TUITO'S CHAIN OF TRUST

BY THE SUMMER OF 2001, Oded Tuito's entire network was under siege. On July 29, Tuito's partner El Kaiam was arrested in Spain and his pill supplier was rooted out in Holland. Two days later, DEA and Customs arrested seven of Tuito's Los Angeles distributors. In August, Israeli police arrested Meir Ben-David and Yosef Levi. Ten months later, after exhausting all appeals, the men were brought back by U.S. marshals to the Southern District of Florida for prosecution.

Israel's legislature, the Knesset, had amended its laws in 1999 to permit the extradition of Israeli citizens to stand trial for crimes committed overseas, as long as they would be allowed to serve out sentences in an Israeli prison. Tuito's Ecstasy traffickers became the road test of the new extradition laws and Ben-David and Levi were the first Israeli citizens to be extradited to America for drug crimes. It was an explicit symbol of the developing cooperation between Israeli and American law enforcement.

Jacob "Koki" Orgad had been in prison for a little over a year when Tuito was arrested. Since then, word had spread among Koki's friends on the outside that Judy Ben Atar was grousing about a $250,000 loan he had given Koki and was still owed.

When it came to money, Judy didn't care if you were friend or foe; he dealt with you the same. But what happened next, according to sources close to both men, went one of two ways. Some say that Judy tracked Koki's daughter down, shoved a gun in her face, and told her that if her father didn't pay, he'd kill her. Others claimed Koki fabricated the entire incident to garner sympathy with prosecutors.

Either way, Koki was said to be so frustrated and helpless behind bars that he pleaded guilty in New York to drug conspiracy charges, told the feds he was fearful that Judy would come after him and his family, and then ratted Judy out.

Judy Ben Atar was arrested shortly thereafter. Like Koki and the others before him, Judy cooperated. He provided important information to Los Angeles DEA in its case against the so-called Jerusalem Group, which oversaw the Las Vegas Ecstasy market and was headed by Israeli expatriate Gabi Ben-Harosh, who was connected to the Abergil crime family in Israel.

For his cooperation, Judy was given a reduced sentence, a little more than five years, and was released in October 2008. Sources say his old Jerusalem associates are waiting for him to dare to return home.

Judy's partner Itzhak "Jackie" Cohen was arrested based on the information provided to law enforcement by his former partners. But Jackie hewed to the code of honor—say nothing. He was sentenced to seventeen and a half years.

Koki, who had started wearing a yarmulke in prison and claimed that he had become a rabbi, was sentenced to six years. As part of his plea agreement he waived his right to fight extradition to France, where he faced additional charges. A French court would later try Koki and twelve members of his ring. Koki served his time, was released early, and last heard was living a quiet life somewhere in Israel.

Koki's former partner, Melissa Schwartz, who helped

run his Paris office, was found guilty of drug charges and sentenced to six years. Schwartz languished alone in a French prison. Unable to speak the language and isolated from friends and family, she hanged herself.

90 "SEAN EREZ MADE EVERYTHING SEEM SO EASY"

WHILE AUTHORITIES ACROSS THE country were breaking down Tuito's chain, Bob Gagne was busy in Brooklyn breaking Diana Reicherter. Erez and Reicherter had fought extradition from the Netherlands for almost three years on the grounds that they were suicidal. They finally landed in Brooklyn in early 2001. The evidence Gagne had gathered from cooperators in the last three years was overwhelming and Reicherter knew it. Once she agreed to cooperate, it was all over for Sean.

Sean Erez's Ecstasy network had fallen hard: some eighteen members of his ring pleaded guilty to importing and conspiracy to import Ecstasy and agreed to cooperate in the case against Erez. It was the largest Ecstasy organization takedown in New York thus far.

Many of Erez's young courier-defendants had stood before U.S. district judge Leo Glasser in a Brooklyn courthouse in the last two years asking for leniency in their sentences. Some seventy members of the Bobover Hasidic community—rabbis and parents in dark garb and somber expressions—had squeezed into the courtroom in March 2000 to support eighteen-year-old Shimon "Shimi" Levita, Erez's Amsterdam assistant.

"Where was the community when all of this was going on?" Glasser asked the gallery. "Where was the family when eighteen-year-old boys were traveling from Paris to Amsterdam, Montreal, New York, and Atlanta . . . Where were the teachers? Who was keeping tabs on these boys who were bringing drugs back and taking money there?"

Shimi was sentenced to thirty months in a federal youth boot camp but got out in eight months for good behavior.

Another Erez recruit, Simcha Roth, had tried to shed light on his actions during his sentencing hearing.

"I'm still searching for answers, wondering how I did what I did," Roth said in court. "I grew up in a very protective environment, and the chance of going to Europe and all that money was like telling a child, 'Don't touch a hot stove.' I just did it without thinking. . . . Sean Erez made everything seem so easy. I was living in a fantasy world."

After dealing for so long with the Sean Erez case and having to sentence so many young yeshiva boys who stood before him, guilty of drug smuggling, Glasser had grown weary of the obligation.

"I've had the misfortune of dealing with this case for the past two years," Glasser said. "This has without any doubt—and I've been sitting in this courtroom for twenty years—been the most painful case I've had to deal with."

On July 11, 2001, Sean Erez pleaded guilty to conspiracy to distribute MDMA. Reicherter, who had also pleaded guilty, was released seven months later.

Erez was sentenced to fifteen years in federal prison, but after five years he was granted his request to serve his time in a Canadian prison. Two months after he arrived, Canada's National Parole Board determined he was unlikely to commit an offense involving violence before the expiration of his sentence and immediately released him.

In 2006, Gagne got a call from Canadian cops. They had just arrested a thirty-six-year-old drug dealer who'd been ripped off and gunned down at an upscale waterfront hotel in Toronto. It was Erez. He was found crumpled and bleeding in an elevator after getting shot three times in the stomach and legs during a botched cocaine transaction. Police told Gagne that Erez had a new girlfriend at his side at the time of the crime.

Erez survived the shooting and would later fight the charges. In October 2008, a jury found him guilty of possession for the purpose of trafficking cocaine, a verdict that could send him back to prison for up to fourteen years. Erez's newly estranged girlfriend was the prosecution's star witness at trial.

91 THE RABBI'S SON

STEVE HAGER'S ECSTASY DEALING had mostly dried up by the time DEA started picking off Tuito's entire crew. He had spent all his money and had to move in with his parents. He never revealed his past or his drug use, and his family didn't ask. The day in 2002 when DEA arrested Hager on the street in Brooklyn, he called his father shortly afterward from a holding cell and finally admitted that he was a drug dealer. His father had little to say. He knew his son was in trouble because DEA agents had just knocked on the door, asking for Hager's diabetes medications. Hager's father was the kind who showed love and disappointment in his face but rarely in his words.

Steve Hager was sentenced to fifty-five months. He quit drugs cold turkey in prison, and once the fog of substance abuse lifted, Hager decided he preferred lucidity. His mother visited every week, bringing money and books and reminders of the pain he'd inflicted on his family.

"If I knew what you were doing," she cried, "I would have gone to the police myself."

Hager's brother Isaac handled so much—making phone calls, lining up attorneys, seeing that he had enough Hebrew books and newspapers to read—that it softened Hager. He felt indebted to his family. They were all he had left to lose.

Hager had heard once that jail was like a revolving door—85 percent go right back to crime.

"I'm going to be from the fifteen," Hager declared. "I won't touch it. I'm not going to sell dope for the rest of my life."

When he got out in 2006, he moved back home again, took small jobs, and took regular drug tests as part of his probation requirements. He had enjoyed cooking meals for Shabbat while he was incarcerated and offered to do the same at the New York synagogue. In the beginning it was ten, fifteen people on Friday nights, but soon he was cooking for up to 120 people. He struck a deal with a caterer to buy up fresh, unused food and spent hours preparing salads, pasta, and fish.

Sometimes, when he thought about his pedestrian existence and living with his parents at the age of forty-six, he would recall his glamorous past—the spacious city apartments, girls who dropped their panties at the sight of an eight ball, piles of money and drugs on his coffee table. But that was over. He was "from the fifteen" now. Mostly, he wanted to be remembered as a nice guy.

92 JACKIE GOES HOME

JACKIE SUAREZ WAS RELEASED from prison on her mother's birthday in May 2001. She stood in the rain just outside the prison gates, holding a box of her belongings, smoking a cigarette, and waiting for her mom to arrive to take her home, whatever that meant. She would have to return to her original family now, and as uncomfortable as it made her feel, she would have to start over and create a new life. (She would also have to go to weekly drug counseling and complete a hundred hours of community service. Judge's orders.)

Shortly before her release, Suarez learned from her attorney that Tuito had been captured in Spain, and it appeared that all his old associates were cooperating against him. It angered her to hear that the tough guys she'd once drawn so much courage from had folded, just like that. She recalled Yosef Levi telling her that cooperation with the authorities was not a viable option. *We live together, we die together,* he had said. Just words.

93 NOT OVER YET

IN JULY 2001, DEA Chief of Operations Joseph Keefe testified before the Senate Governmental Affairs Committee about the "unprecedented level of coordination" among local, state, federal, and foreign law enforcement in combating the nation's Ecstasy epidemic. Keefe stressed the increasing "transnational nature" of MDMA trafficking and recognized Gadi Eshed's Tel Aviv conference as a major step in information sharing and coordinating international efforts to target and capture traffickers like Oded Tuito.

It was a proud moment for Eshed and his colleagues. The Israelis had been instrumental in helping the Americans bring down the Fat Man's Ecstasy empire. But Eshed knew that their work was far from over. Ecstasy dealing had spilled beyond the purview of the *yordim* criminals abroad. The lucrative trade would continue to be dominated by Israeli organized crime until the Israeli police finished the job. Now that Tuito was behind bars, Eshed and his officers were focused more than ever on chasing after their own A-list target, the Israeli Capone, Ze'ev Rosenstein.

NEW YORK MAYOR Rudy Giuliani gestured to the small Lucky Charms–colored tablets laid across a table as he spoke to reporters.

"When you look at these pills," he said, "they look harmless. They are pink and light blue and white, but these are very dangerous substances that can in fact be fatal under some circumstances and do tremendous damage to young people."

Two dealers, David Roash and Israel Ashkenazi, had been arrested the night before when NYPD detectives raided their financial district studio apartment overlooking Battery Park. The place was stash-house Spartan— two futons and a TV set. The cops seized $187,000 in cash and seven hundred thousand pills stuffed inside eight duffel bags and one suitcase. It was the largest MDMA seizure in New York history—450 pounds of mind-altering chemicals, brewed up in a dirty clandestine lab in Holland.

As news of the bust spread, a twenty-six-year-old Israeli drug dealer in Madrid named Mordechai "Flaco" Cohen was desperately retracing his steps, trying to figure out who was the narc and how he got into the chain. Flaco's life was on the line.

"Find out everything," Ze'ev Rosenstein ordered Flaco over the phone. "Why it happened, when it happened."

When was easy, but why was a little more complicated.

95 "A VERY POWERFUL MAN"

FLACO'S TROUBLES BEGAN in early 2001, when he got a call from forty-nine-year-old Shemtov Michtavi, an old friend of Flaco's father, Elias Cohen.

The elder Cohen was an infamous cocaine trafficker who had married into the Medellín cartel family and used his bride's connections to arrange several tons of cocaine shipments from Colombia to the United States and Europe in the early 1990s. Shemtov Michtavi—a squat, hard-edged, and sharp-minded dealer—was one of Elias Cohen's trusted contacts who used to smuggle coke into Russia, hiding it in cans and plastic wrap, disguised as food.

Cohen's son Flaco, the new young drug prince, was fluent in English, Spanish, and Hebrew and his family name gave him credibility and preapproved links to high-ranking drug traffickers. Which is why Michtavi called him. Michtavi had a business proposition, but they would discuss it when he arrived in Spain, not over the phone.

In April 2001, Michtavi flew to Madrid to propose a partnership. He had access to cheap Ecstasy pills; Flaco had connections to buyers in the States. If Flaco provided introductions to his buyers, then Michtavi's associates in New York would take care of the rest.

Michtavi boasted that he was working with Ze'ev Rosenstein, "a very powerful man." Flaco knew who Rosenstein was. His father had also been friendly with the Wolf. A couple of days later, Flaco got a personal call from the very powerful man.

"Don't worry," Rosenstein told Flaco. "Nothing will happen to you." The mob boss promised Flaco that if he got in trouble with competitors, he would have Ze'ev Rosenstein's name as backing.

Flaco started hooking up Michtavi with buyers, they did a couple of deals, and everything was going smoothly—until a narc stumbled into the chain. In July 2001, one of Flaco's Colombian connections passed along the phone number of a man in Florida named "Juan Carlos" who was looking to purchase "CDs"—code for Ecstasy. That man turned out to be a confidential informant for Miami police and DEA.

The sting went down like this: Flaco called Juan Carlos (the Miami narc) and they made a deal for 65,000 pills for $393,000, at Shemtov Michtavi's direction. Juan Carlos said he would send his runner to pick up samples from the organization's New York–based associates and if the pills were good, he would have his runner pay for and collect the rest. Behind the scenes, Miami police had called New York police to arrange for an NYPD undercover officer to play the role of Juan Carlos's drug runner. When the undercover arrived at the prearranged midtown meeting place, it was New York dealers David Roash and Israel Ashkenazi who showed up with the sample pills. NYPD officers followed Roash and Ashkenazi back to their Battery Park apartment and made the arrests. The next day, Rudy Giuliani was calling a press conference to parade the confiscated product—$40 million worth—to the media.

Roash and Ashkenazi pleaded guilty to drug charges but refused to cooperate or say whom they were working for.

96 "PLEASE DON'T LET THIS CASE DIE"

FLACO HAD UNWITTINGLY INTRODUCED an informant—Juan Carlos—into the chain of trust, and Rosenstein was furious. Flaco was now on the hook for Rosenstein's $40 million worth of seized pills and the Wolf warned him that one way or another "someone would be responsible" for recouping his money. Flaco knew that someone would be him. But where was he going to get that amount of money? He started looking over his shoulder, terrified he was going to be killed.

But then Rosenstein made a foolish misstep that gave Flaco leverage: he inveigled Flaco into a murder conspiracy.

Shortly after the debacle over the lost pills, Michtavi called Flaco to ask if he knew any killers who could do a job in Israel. Michtavi didn't say he was calling at Rosenstein's behest, but Flaco knew that the Wolf never made that kind of call himself; he always asked close associates to facilitate hits.

Flaco told Michtavi he happened to know two guys—Colombian hit men—who could do the job. They agreed to speak again soon about money and logistics. Flaco's next call was to Israeli police.

Flaco's defensive strategy was to procure hit men to appease Rosenstein but at the same time secretly feed the valuable information to Israeli police. He knew INP wanted Rosenstein, and in return, Flaco wanted protection from prosecution. He would be a secret informant and play both sides.

Flaco's defection took Gadi Eshed and his colleagues completely by surprise. He gave them the first real piece of evidence that Rosenstein was involved in Ecstasy trafficking—and the murder conspiracy was the cherry on top. Israeli police officers began to work with Flaco out of the Spanish embassy, getting Flaco to tape his phone calls with Michtavi. He collected incriminating conversations with Michtavi about "the brothers" (hit men) and the $40,000 Michtavi was sending to take care of their fees. Rosenstein, however, never called Flaco again nor was his name mentioned.

In late August 2001, two Colombian hit men arrived in Israel and were spotted stepping off the tarmac at the Tel Aviv airport. They had youthful faces, tan smooth skin, and thick dark hair. They wore T-shirts and dark sunglasses, like students on summer break. Their assignment: liquidate brothers Jacob and Nissim Alperon—Rosenstein's rivals. They would pretend to be tourists until the order came down to carry out the hit. Tel Aviv police officers watched the killers' every move for nearly a month.

While the assassins waited for the green light, they partied like freshmen, migrating from one hotel and bar to the next. Rosenstein's aides had to give the killers 40,000 shekels—roughly $11,000—on top of their fee just to cover their extra expenses. After several weeks, Michtavi unexpectedly rang Flaco and told him to call off the dogs. The liquidation order was rescinded; no reason was given.

Eshed could never say for sure, but it seemed as if the men suspected they were being watched. At the same time the hit was called off, Michtavi also started acting strangely. He made friendly overtures to young Flaco to visit him in Bucharest, where Rosenstein had a hotel and casino.

Come take a nice vacation, Michtavi cooed. It reeked of ambush.

Flaco's plan had backfired and now he was in a serious bind. On one side, Rosenstein wanted him dead; on the other, Israeli police were pressuring him to become a full cooperator—to testify against the Wolf. Flaco refused. Nobody had ever dared to face off with the Wolf in court. But what Flaco didn't know was that he was about to be fed to American prosecutors.

The Florida narc, Juan Carlos, had secretly taped his phone calls with Flaco and Miami federal prosecutors were using the evidence to build a drug case against Flaco, Michtavi, Roash, and Ashkenazi. In fact, Miami's case against the Israeli drug traffickers had begun when Gadi Eshed used his own brand of the chain of trust and called in a favor to his old pal, DEA special agent John McKenna.

John McKenna was the twenty-three-year-old kid in a candy store who used to lock up drug dealers in New York's Washington Heights in the 1980s. Eshed had met McKenna in 1991 when they worked together in Eshed's first joint investigation with American law enforcement. It was a DEA heroin case in New York that led to the arrest of Ran Efarin, Eitan Hiya, Johnny Atias, and Yisrael "Alice" Mizrahi, members of an infamous Mafia gang involved in heroin, cocaine, murder, and extortion. (All but Hiya would eventually be killed in mob warfare.) Eshed spent five weeks on Long Island with McKenna working tirelessly day after day, listening to wiretaps and breaking down the network.

That was a long time ago, but Eshed and McKenna had stayed in touch all those years. McKenna was in his late thirties now and recently had been assigned to the Miami office. It was a lucky coincidence for Eshed that one of his closest American colleagues was overseeing the same agents who worked behind the scenes to alert New York police to the deal that led to the Battery Park bust. When Flaco first came to Israeli police with the information that Rosenstein was involved, Gadi got on the phone to Miami to beg his old friend to keep the American case alive.

"John, please don't let this case die at the state level in New York," Eshed had asked McKenna. "Please renew this as a DEA case, a federal case in Florida."

McKenna knew how dangerous Ze'ev Rosenstein was and how important it was to the INP to prosecute him. More important, Rosenstein was a joint Israeli-American target, an A-list suspect.

The Israeli police met with Flaco at the Spanish embassy to give him one last chance. *The Americans are planning to indict you,* they warned him. *Cooperate now and we will try to help you.* Flaco wasn't aware that the two countries had been working together behind the scenes, and he didn't believe the American prosecutors had enough to convict him of drug charges. He also didn't know that two American agents were waiting outside, sent to Spain by McKenna at Eshed's request.

"I will never be a witness against Rosenstein," Flaco told the Israeli officers defiantly. "Only an informant."

Flaco said adios and headed for the door, ready to vanish. An Israeli officer gave the sign for the American agents to move. Flaco was apprehended outside the embassy. He just couldn't win—Rosenstein wanted him dead whether he talked or not and he was facing up to twenty years in prison for conspiracy to import and distribute Ecstasy to the States. After a few days, he finally agreed to cooperate. He was extradited to Florida, where Gadi Eshed interviewed him in depth with DEA and federal prosecutors.

Flaco had a trove of damaging information about the pill deals, but the problem was that Flaco had never met

Rosenstein, Michtavi had never mentioned Rosenstein's name in any of their taped calls, and Flaco's word alone wasn't enough to indict the mob boss. They needed more—another witness who could speak to Rosenstein's crimes.

Shortly after Flaco's arrest and interrogations, John McKenna flew to Colombia and secured a meeting with Flaco's infamous father, Elias Cohen, a known associate of Rosenstein. It ended up being a very short meeting in a hotel room in Bogotá. As McKenna put it: "We were trying to give him a chance to save his son. If he wanted to come on board with us, and whatever he would help us with, we would give credit to his son. But he wanted nothing to do with it. He denied knowing Rosenstein. He lied right to my face and just left his son out there." McKenna walked out shaking his head, thinking, *The kid never had a chance to grow up straight.*

They tried to bend Shemtov Michtavi next.

After U.S. marshals arrested Michtavi in Bulgaria, he was extradited to Florida and Eshed flew out to meet with Michtavi's defense attorney at the federal prosecutor's office. Another short meeting. The attorney opened by telling Eshed that Michtavi "would never say one word against the honest businessman Ze'ev Rosenstein" and that they should just forget about a deal. Eshed started laughing and the attorney wanted to know what was so funny.

"I didn't say a word about Ze'ev Rosenstein," Eshed said. "Maybe I wanted to talk with you about someone else?"

Meanwhile, the Battery Park boys, Roash and Ashkenazi, figured they had gotten off pretty easy in New York—sentenced to just seven years. They were overheard on jail phone lines telling their contacts in Israel that they'd be out of prison in no time—five or six years—and right back home. But the dealers didn't understand that in America, you can be tried by both state and federal courts. They were shocked to learn that their next stop was Florida, where they faced another twenty years of federal time if convicted on drug conspiracy charges. The pressure was on. Both men pleaded guilty and admitted that their boss was none other than Baruch Dadush—the right-hand man to Ze'ev Rosenstein.

It was a huge break for Israeli police. But it still wasn't enough. Roash and Ashkenazi had never met Rosenstein. They insisted they had no knowledge of the Wolf's role in the Ecstasy ring. And Eshed knew they weren't lying. Rosenstein would never touch pills or money. He had people do it for him. Roash and Ashkenazi had only ever dealt with Baruch Dadush and his brother, Ilan.

The feds' case in Florida now amounted to Flaco's phone calls and statements implicating Shemtov Michtavi and Roash's statement implicating Baruch and Ilan Dadush. Nothing on Rosenstein. But Gadi Eshed, whose first name in Hebrew means "luck," had another lucky break four months after the New York seizure.

A secret international investigation had been simultaneously conducted against a ring of Ecstasy traffickers who were taking Dutch-made pills, concealing them in boxes of dried flowers, and driving them to a warehouse in Germany where they were loaded onto freighter ships destined for America and Australia. The smugglers made one tiny mistake: a wire suspect was overheard saying in Hebrew that he would leave an envelope at the reception desk of the Victoria hotel in Germany. German and Israeli police rushed to the hotel. Inside the envelope was a single piece of paper with an address: Geniner Strasse 82.

Police returned the envelope to the reception desk and watched from the shadows as a Dutch trucker later picked up the message. They followed him as he drove to a warehouse at Geniner Strasse 82 in Lübeck, a major port city on the Baltic. The driver was met by two Israelis who loaded the pills into containers, ready to be shipped abroad. Unbeknownst to the smugglers, the warehouse was crawling with surveillance teams and video cameras.

The investigation netted more than 1.6 million Ecstasy pills and the arrest of twenty-nine suspects in Australia, Germany, Holland, and Israel—where Eshed and his colleagues nabbed Zvi Fogel and Baruch and Ilan Dadush. Zvi Fogel was the same man they had arrested in the 1999 Operation Octopus sting and then released for lack of evidence. He was the same man police had spied on taking meetings with Baruch Dadush in Paris and Amsterdam, where they met with the bagmakers. And the pills that New York police seized in the Battery Park bust had originated with Fogel's ring of suppliers, who were arrested in the Geniner Strasse warehouse raid.

Eshed and his colleagues finally had clear evidence that Zvi Fogel was handling the suppliers in Holland and that Baruch Dadush was overseeing the distribution of pills in New York. INP suspected that Ze'ev Rosenstein was the financier—but neither Fogel nor Dadush would say one word. They preferred to sit in jail and wait for a judge to decide their fate.

The Israeli police were stymied again. They had no direct evidence to link Rosenstein to drugs—no taped conversations, and no one who took orders from him who would talk. They had nothing to link Rosenstein to the murder plot because Michtavi had handled the logistics and the Colombian hit men were ultimately called off.

Eshed and his colleagues leaned on Zvi Fogel. But Fogel was a forty-seven-year-old practiced con who'd take prison time without a shrug. ("I'm an old man," Fogel told Eshed. "What do you want from me?") Baruch Dadush, on the other hand, was thirty-four with a wife and children.

The police would wait to see how Dadush's drug case

in Israel played out while simultaneously assisting the American case against Shemtov Michtavi. And when the time was right, Gadi Eshed would ask his American counterparts to help them put pressure on Dadush. Eshed would wait as long as it took to play it right. It would take years.

97 "A PLANE JUST CRASHED"

IN THE SUMMER OF 2001, Bob Gagne was plucked from the Long Island Division Office and sent back to New York, where he was appointed demand reduction coordinator. He wasn't happy about going back to the city. He was getting used to being home in time to play with his cherub-faced one-year-old. He called her his little peanut. Clearly, he was no longer a D-35 meat eater.

As the new head of the Demand Reduction unit, Gagne was the DEA representative in charge of drug prevention programs for the state of New York, which meant public speaking engagements and visits to schools and companies to educate them on drug prevention policies.

Gagne got to know the designated substance abuse prevention and intervention specialists in the city's public schools—often they were teachers who got tagged with the extra job and the title. Gagne found many to be blasé about drug use and poorly informed. For instance, they didn't know marijuana now contained three times more THC than it had when they were toking in high school, they knew much less about Ecstasy, and some still had outdated notions of heroin as a drug that could only be injected, usually with dirty syringes in back alleys. Gagne decided his job was to prepare them to be at least 10 percent smarter than the kids.

"Listen, if I can bring you up to speed, to the point where you know just that much more than they do, then they will believe you when you talk to them about drugs," he would say. "And if they believe you, then you have a chance to help them."

He took courses alongside the specialists to understand exactly what they were learning. He took part in DEA Explorers, a program for youth interested in law enforcement careers, and he mentored about a dozen inner-city teens. His new job was a public role, not the rough-and-tumble fieldwork he preferred, but it supported the larger, loftier mission—protect the children.

In September 2001, Gagne was sent to Marine Corps Base Quantico, Virginia, for an intensive two-week instructor development course—required for anyone spending time in front of an audience. Gagne noticed Matt Germanowski's name on the roster.

The onetime best friends hadn't spoken in a while. Germanowski had just left New York and was preparing for a new post as a DEA Academy instructor, teaching basic agenting skills and such defensive tactics as hand-to-hand combat, ground wrestling, and taking guns off bad guys. There had been a send-off for Germanowski at a local sports bar just a few days earlier. Flaherty had taken off from his family vacation and driven four hours into the city to be there, but there was no sign of Gagne.

"Gags, you stopping by?" Germanowski had finally called to ask.

"No, I can't. We're having cocktails at Kristen's parents' house tonight."

"Right, whatever."

Germanowski felt like Gagne had abandoned his friends once he got married. Gagne had felt the same when he was transferred to Long Island. In fact, he was still hurt that Germanowski hadn't bothered to throw *him* a going-away party. Truth was, there were no cocktails at the in-laws', but Gagne knew it was just the kind of lame excuse that would annoy G. The two tough drug cops were acting like playground rivals. But when each saw the other's name on the class list, both were secretly excited to hang out again.

On the first day of class Gagne and Germanowski arrived early, traded a casual "Hey," and sat next to each other.

At 8:50 a.m., someone walked into the classroom and whispered in the teacher's ear. A five-minute break was called. The teacher returned and made an announcement: "A plane just crashed in New York. We're not sure what's going on."

He turned on an overhead television monitor and the agents tuned in just in time to see United Flight 175 crash into the south tower of the World Trade Center.

"Can you believe this?" Germanowski said.

"No," Gagne said. "We should go back."

The two friends were back in sync, pleading their case for postponing the course so they could get back to New York, where they would be needed most.

"Listen, Superman," the instructor said, "we have four weeks of material to cover in two weeks' time. Let's get back to work."

Quantico went Delta (imminent threat). Young Marines manning tanks mounted with .50-caliber machine guns blocked the entryways. The base was shut down; all commercial U.S. air traffic was grounded. Nobody was leaving.

Gagne tried calling Kristen, but the lines were down. He reached her the next day. She said she was happy to hear his voice. She would stay with her parents for a while until he made it back.

It was good to have Germanowski around. They didn't talk about the past. They studied and played golf and drank beer and made up wild escape-from-Quantico scenarios while fresh news about the terror attacks trickled in like dispatches from a foreign post.

The impact from Flight 77's crash on the Pentagon had shaken the windows of DEA headquarters in Arlington, Virginia, and many DEA employees had a view from their cubicles of the path of destruction. Agents at Gagne's home office, NYFD, located about forty blocks from the Twin Towers, were immediately deployed to the FBI Command Center. They provided technical equipment to help the search-and-rescue teams. The searches turned into body recovery efforts. DEA's Aviation Division transported personnel, equipment, and blood supplies. They provided the Fire Department with airborne video and forward-looking infrared camera systems—thermal imaging technology that could help locate "hot spots" within the World Trade Center buildings so they could determine where to deploy firefighting equipment and extinguish underground fires located near subterranean fuel storage tanks. Security measures at all overseas DEA facilities were upgraded.

Germanowski would later spend a week at the Pentagon, collecting evidence to help identify victims and give families something to bury. He was sifting through bits of hair and charred skin that had melted onto metal and steel when a beautiful woman's face appeared in the ashes. The image was on a photo identification badge, burnt around the edges, but with a name still visible. Michele Heidenberger, a fifty-seven-year-old flight attendant from Maryland, was looking back at him. He never forgot her face.

A week after the terrorist attacks of September 11, Gagne got a call from his sister Susan. They needed him back home in Pawtucket. His brother Ronnie had just been arrested. He was being charged with murdering his drug dealer.

98 RON AND JOE

JOSE BETANCUR'S COLD BODY was received for autopsy by the Office of Medical Examiners of Providence, Rhode Island, in a white plastic body pouch with a yellow plastic lock. Betancur was forty-five years old, 175 pounds, five feet eight inches tall, with brown eyes, short black hair, a black mustache. The medical examiner inspected the trajectory of two gunshot wounds to his body. One bullet had torn away the skin of his pinky finger before entering just under his left elbow, fracturing his humerus, and leaving fragments in his arm and armpit. The second bullet had entered at the left front of his abdomen, taken a path through his skin, muscle, fatty tissue, and small bowel, and sliced through a major artery and vein before it lodged in his lower back. The assistant ME dislodged a large-caliber copper-jacketed bullet from his right flank and marked it with her initials, *JS*.

Bentancur's toxicology report revealed acute cocaine intoxication. But it was the bullet that nicked the arteries that carried blood to his heart that killed him. His abdominal cavity at autopsy was filled with 1.5 liters of blood. He'd hemorrhaged to death.

On the morning of Betancur's death, September 16, his upstairs neighbor in his Pawtucket apartment heard arguing shortly after midnight, then two "popping noises," then sustained silence. She later found Betancur lying on the floor of his bedroom, bleeding to death in a multicolored bathrobe, worn inside out. First responders at the scene noted no pulse or breathing at 12:49 a.m.

Later that day, Ron Gagne got a call from a friend. Cops were at Betancur's place. Someone said he'd been shot. Ron didn't want to believe he was dead. He called him, but it went straight to voice mail, so he left a vague message: *Joe, I heard something happened, I'm wondering if it was you, give me a call.*

The charm and the bother of small-town life is always knowing your neighbors. Two days after Betancur's death, Pawtucket police showed up at Irene Gagne's house looking for Ron. One of the detectives pointed to a photo and asked if it was her son. Irene gave him one of her *Who you kidding?* looks and said, "Yeah—you know him, Scott." The lead investigator, Detective Scott Feeley, had grown up playing hockey and football against the unbeatable Gagne boys. Ron called Feeley as soon as he heard they were looking for him.

Feeley casually questioned Ron about his relationship with Betancur and Ron said he had just finished installing an over-the-stove light and exhaust fan in Betancur's apartment. He had first met Betancur a year earlier through a buddy who fixed cars. Betancur's brother used to take karate at the same place Bobby once taught karate. Betancur had a daughter; Ron had a young son who lived with his mother. They were friendly. That was about it.

"Okay," Feeley said. "I appreciate you calling."

A day later, two more detectives knocked on Ron's door and said they needed to bring him in for more questioning. Ron grabbed his coat, locked the apartment, and called his mother to let her know where he was going.

"Do you want me to come pick you up?" Irene asked.

"I'm sure they'll give me a ride home," Ron said.

At thirty-four, Ron was street-smart and naïve at once. He was an electrician by trade, a little taller than his brother Bob, but a little softer around the edges. Ron was a true-blue, ribs-loving, dues-paying union man. Even as the cops patted Ron down before letting him in the squad car, it never occurred to him that he wasn't coming back home.

At the station it was almost five hours of grilling: *How do you know Joe? When was the last time you saw him? Were you buying marijuana off Joe?*

"Joe doesn't sell marijuana," Ron scoffed. In fact, Betancur had sold cocaine and Ron was a regular customer. But Ron didn't think he had a problem with drugs and he certainly didn't want his brother to ever find out about it.

"You know a girl named Terry Bouyea?"

"Nah, I don't know her," Ron said.

"You sure?"

"Wait a minute. Yeah, I know a Terry, but I don't know her last name or nothing and I ain't seen her in over a year."

Terry Bouyea was a girl who used to date a friend of Ron's until Ron caught her walking into a bar with another man and he told his friend to dump her. Bouyea didn't care much for Ron Gagne. Now she was calling him a murderer.

Shortly after Betancur's death, Bouyea had come forward and said she was at Betancur's place when Ron started banging on the door looking for drugs. She told police she'd hidden in the closet just before Ron busted in and shot Betancur.

"You guys are crazy!" Ron said. "You're out of your mind. She's lying!"

They asked him if he owned a gun. Ron thought about it. He didn't have a permit for that Ruger .22 caliber that was sitting in a Dexter shoe box in a back closet, so he denied it. When they told him he didn't need a permit to keep a gun in his home, Ron confessed, "Okay, I gotta gun," and told them where to find it.

He'd used it a couple of times for target practice in the woods, but it had been so long since he fired it, he couldn't even remember what color it was. It didn't matter anyway—it wasn't the murder weapon. Betancur had been shot with a 9 mm.

Ron told the cops he had been home alone watching 9/11 news and a movie on the night of Betancur's death. He said his truck was parked in the yard the whole time. "Ask my neighbors." He had yelled at them to keep it quiet at about 12:30 a.m. because they were noisily loading their car with flea market wares.

"We never said what time Joe was killed."

"I don't care what time he got killed," Ron said. "I'm just telling you what time I yelled at my neighbors."

The cops told Ron they'd found his personal checks, written out to cash, lying on Betancur's kitchen table. Ron was getting annoyed now.

"What—is that my signature?" he mocked. "Like I'm a serial killer and that's my calling card just in case you were looking for me? . . . Listen, I'm telling you she's lyin'—I don't know how many different ways you want me to tell you.

"You know me, Scott," Ron said to Detective Feeley. "I had nothing to do with it."

Feeley asked Ron if he wanted to take a lie detector test.

Polygraphs are inadmissible in Rhode Island courts and their reliability at determining a person's truthfulness is often called into question because they're meant to measure physical responses such as pulse rate, muscle movements, and blood pressure. Police often use them as an interrogation tool because suspects have been known to confess to crimes, even falsely so, if they think they've been caught by a lie-detecting device. But Ron didn't know—and wouldn't have cared—about any of that.

"Yeah, give me the test. I got nothing to hide," Ron said.

They hooked him up to the monitors, put a mike on his shirt, asked a few baseline questions, and then got to it: *Did you kill Joe Betancur?*

"No."

When it was over, one of the cops spun his laptop around to show Ron the squiggly line that said he was lying.

"Either that machine's wrong or you people don't know how to read it, because I ain't lying!" Ron said. "I didn't kill Joe. I don't know what the hell is going on here!"

The detective dropped an arrest warrant on the table and turned it around for Ron to read. All he saw were the words "Ronald Gagne" and "murder."

"Yeah, this is a joke," Ron said.

"It's not a joke. On your feet."

He was taken to a holding area where he was processed and ordered to remove his belt and shoes.

"Ron, this is the last time I'm going to ask you," Feeley said. "You got something you want to tell me?"

"Yeah," Ron said, "I got something I want to tell you: I didn't fucking do it!"

"We'll see if you change your mind in the morning."

Ron would spend the night in the cage and be transferred to Rhode Island's Adult Correctional Institution (ACI), in Providence, the next morning.

As he curled up to sleep in the cold jail cell that evening, he finally understood that it wasn't a joke. The police were building a murder case around him.

99 "I GOT NOTHING TO HIDE"

GAGNE DROVE STRAIGHT TO Providence as soon as his course ended and he was cleared to leave Quantico. He checked in his gun and badge at ACI and waited in a small room with a table and two chairs. Ron was escorted in a few minutes later by armed guards.

"How you doing?"

"I'm doing great, Bob. Can you get me out of here?"

"I'm working on it," Gagne said. His brother looked tired and disheveled.

"Why did you go with them?" Gagne asked. "Why didn't you ask to see an attorney?"

"Because I didn't do nothing and I got nothing to hide."

Gagne never doubted his brother. Not once. Back in their misspent youth of drunken Friday nights, when everyone was in the parking lot brawling, Ron would be trying to sleep it off in the backseat of a car, fending off a rabble-rouser who was grabbing at his feet through the window. Somehow Ron would end up getting beat up with his own shoe. Gagne saw his brother as the kind of guy who would end up shooting himself if he was trying to shoot someone else.

"I believe you," Gagne said. "I'm going to help you. But you gotta watch your back in here. Don't talk about your case with anyone. Don't trust anybody."

They did not speak about his drug use.

"I'm so sorry if I've embarrassed you." Ron's voice broke and he started tearing up. "It wasn't my intention for this to be spread out in the newspaper for everybody to read. I'm so sorry. I hope this doesn't hurt your job."

"C'mon. Don't worry about me," Gagne said. "You need anything?"

Ron needed a shower, he needed to brush his teeth, he needed to feel human again. They hugged good-bye.

"Thanks a lot for coming and everything. Look, don't worry. I'll be all right."

"Yeah, you'll be all right," Gagne said. He knew this was going to be a long haul.

An hour later a guard called Ron from his cell and sent him to the commissary. When he got there, a care package had been set aside with his name on it. Inside the box was shampoo, soap, a razor and shaving cream, a toothbrush, and toothpaste.

100 A KINGPIN IS CROWNED

WASHINGTON WAS DEVISING ITS 2002 Kingpin list and Oded Tuito was a top contender for inclusion. Linda Lacewell needed Gagne's help pulling a few things together—Tuito's photograph, a summary of his crimes, things they could prove down the line when he was brought to the States.

Under the laws of the Foreign Narcotics Kingpin Designation Act, the president must send to Congress by June 1 each year a list of names of the foreign drug traffickers who present a threat to national security, foreign policy, or the economy of the United States. The drug kingpin list is a who's who of the baddest of the bad—the leaders of the most notorious global trafficking organizations. The Department of Justice's Consolidated Priority Organization Target (CPOT) program later developed its own "CPOT List," an expanded lineup of the most-wanted command-and-control drug traffickers and money launderers.

If you're an agent whose target just got named to one of these lists, it's like being handed a magic pair of scissors that cuts through red tape. Buy money, wiretap budgets, and other resources are made available to you a lot faster.

If your name is on the list, the U.S. government has frozen all the assets you haven't properly hidden and is actively working to freeze the assets of your operatives. The law was designed as a way to deny the top drug organizations access to U.S. banks and trade with U.S. companies.

On May 31, 2002, President George W. Bush released the names of seven new kingpins. The list included five cocaine traffickers from Mexico and Brazil, a Pakistani heroin distributor, and Ecstasy trafficker and French-Israeli citizen Oded Tuito.

Pittsburgh agent Gregg Drews's first reaction when he saw Tuito's name on the kingpin list was "Holy crap."

Tuito had been Drews's first big target at DEA—one small controlled delivery of cocaine that had blossomed into a multiagency international investigation and the naming of an Ecstasy kingpin. The battle over the Fat Man's prosecution had soured Drews on the case in recent months. But even with all the infighting and struggles, after seeing Tuito's name on that list, Drews was satisfied.

101 "DID YOU DO IT?"

GAGNE FOUND A VETERAN Rhode Island defense attorney named Robert Mann to handle his brother's case. Mann was a Yale law grad with twenty-eight years of experience. He had a soothing voice and a round face covered by a beard of cumulus tufts of white hair.

Mann's first impression of Ron was that he "radiated the antithesis of a killer." He was more like a gentle giant. His first impression of Bob was that he was one of those rare people who truly believed in right and wrong. Mann would always recall their first conversation, when Bob told him that if he had thought his brother was guilty he would have done everything possible to help him in prison—make sure he had access to the commissary, advise him on a plea bargain—but he would not have helped Ron to beat the case.

It would have been easy for Gagne to say he couldn't get involved because it might compromise his position with DEA, but Mann never heard him grumble or mention it. In fact, Mann would have welcomed a little breathing room from Gagne.

"Your brother is the biggest pain in the ass I ever met," Mann would tell Ron. "But he knows what he's talking about."

Gagne took an active role in every step of his brother's case and he brought his understanding of drug culture to the table. He analyzed the psychology of the relationships between Bouyea and Betancur, Ron and Betancur. He drew from his own experience as a drug investigator to intuit what the police were thinking during their investigation and what the prosecution's next steps would be. Gagne knew the world his brother had gotten mixed up in, and he knew the language and technical parameters of blood, drugs, and guns.

The more Gagne dug into the facts, the angrier he became. There was no evidence—no murder weapon, no prints, no blood—linking Ron to Betancur's death. Bouyea's story seemed to change with each telling and it didn't add up. She said Ron and Betancur had been standing facing each other when Ron pulled the trigger. But the gunshot wounds, the blood spatter, and the ballistics indicated the gun was fired with a downward trajectory, as if Betancur was lying down or on his knees.

Prosecutors were working on a theory that Ron was so enraged that Betancur wouldn't hand over the coke that he shot him. Gagne's theory was that the cops saw a dead body, saw Ron's name on some checks, and found their answer when a pretty girl who was sleeping with the victim for his drugs said she saw someone else do it.

The checks on the kitchen table made out to cash were another story. Gagne was stunned to learn that his brother not only had had a personal drug dealer, but he had been paying for cocaine with personal checks. It had become that casual. Ron had figured it was just easier than making an ATM stop on the way. When the first check cleared, Betancur was happy to take them. The cops discovered Ron's checks had been cashed all over town.

"Listen," Gagne warned his brother during a jailhouse visit. "There's just as much drugs inside as out of this place. If you fail a drug test in here, you're done. You have to be squeaky-clean."

Ron understood. He was subjected to random urine tests almost weekly. He stayed clean and got a job cleaning tables and pouring coffee in the dining room. He worked out: push-ups and pull-ups on the stairs, lifting buckets of laundry detergent, playing basketball and running in the recreation yard. He got in trouble for swearing once. Another time he slipped up and called one of the guards—a guy he used to play football with—by his first name.

The other inmates liked to watch *Cops* and play cards and Scrabble, but Ron often tired of it and would return to his cell to read or to work on his running list of all the jokes he had ever heard. He missed being able to walk out a door and look at the sky without his every move being studied. He missed his son.

Ron constantly had visitors. His siblings and friends tried to lift his spirits. His mom and sisters helped to keep his personal matters in order and arranged a fundraiser for his defense. Every three days his father would come to see him.

Ron was the only Gagne child who kept a close relationship with René. The day Ron was sent to ACI, René called with one question: "Did you do it?"

"No, I didn't do it," Ron said.

"All right. Then I'm going to help you."

René and his second wife loaned Ron more than $50,000, taking out a line of credit on their home; Ron pulled $27,000 out of his annuity; his mother and sisters helped him with the rest.

His defense and expenses topped out at nearly $90,000. He waited sixteen months for his case to go to court.

102 BOB AND RON

GAGNE HAD SPENT THE last sixteen months visiting public schools, training drug counselors, and telling kids to stay straight and healthy. In the evenings, he'd fight traffic back to Long Island, have dinner with his wife and daughter, and then head to the basement to work on his brother's murder case. Kristen would head to bed alone. Gagne knew he had a small window of opportunity to help Ron, and he feared that he would pay in guilt for the rest of his life if he didn't give his brother's case his full attention. It was the most important casework he had ever done. He discussed it with no one at DEA, not even Germanowski, who was with him at Quantico when he got the news. If he were to try to explain his brother's case to any of the other agents, where would he even start? There would be whispers and gossip about his dysfunctional family. He didn't want to be treated differently.

Sometimes, he'd be alone in the basement, reading through police reports, and he'd forget that it was his own brother he was reading about, the presumed bad guy. Ron had been his best friend and confidant growing up. The scar on Gagne's lip was an ever-present reminder of the time when, as little boys digging for earthworms in the yard, Ronnie tossed a shovelful of dirt over his shoulder and accidentally caught Bobby in the face. The blade gashed clean through Bob's lip and he screamed out in tears. Their father emerged from the garage and threw a pair of pliers at Ronnie. The only thing that hurt Bob more than the stinging gash on his face was the guilt he felt when his father attacked his little brother.

Gagne could always blame his father—the original bad guy—for his brother's troubles, but deep down, he felt a measure of culpability. He'd been so busy chasing drug dealers and trying to create a healthy home for his own family that he hadn't even noticed his brother was in trouble.

He decided to put his mind on problems that were fixable and clear-cut. He focused on his brother's trial, and eventually he mustered his courage and turned to Linda Lacewell as a discreet sounding board.

Lacewell was sympathetic. In the four years she had spent working alongside Gagne she found that fairness characterized his work. It was imperative in their cases together that they were certain they were bringing the right person to trial, and she knew that he was vexed that the case against Ron seemed held together by a single, dubious eyewitness. Gagne searched for inconsistencies in her statements to police and obsessed over the grand jury testimony of the detective who was present when Bouyea identified Betancur's killer. It was a single word in the detective's testimony, a slip of the tongue that jolted Gagne. The officer said he had presented the photo spread to Bouyea and then "we" picked Ron as the person she saw.

Gagne felt like championing the rights of every murder suspect who was ever railroaded into a false conviction. But that was one more obligation he didn't need. He was juggling so many responsibilities—Tuito's trial, Ron's trial, demand reduction coordinator, student mentor, husband, and father. A lot of people depended on him and letting any one of them down was not an option. Sometimes he felt like he was barely holding it together.

In the summer of 2002, Gagne was sent back home to Long Island to work as a street agent again. Kristen was glad for it. She was pregnant with their second child.

103 MURDER IN THE FIRST DEGREE

RON GAGNE'S TRIAL BEGAN on a Monday in late January 2003. He was transported to the courthouse in shackles and a waist chain. He changed into a suit and tie in his holding cell.

His case was heard in one of the smallest courtrooms in the state: one door to get in, the jury box immediately to the right, two or three tables for the lawyers, and three rows of benches in a gallery that seated twenty-five to thirty spectators.

Ron's childhood friends, parents of friends, his siblings, and his parents all sat close in the aisles next to local reporters. Gagne watched the trial from the back row with a notepad and pen.

The charges against him were first-degree murder and use of a firearm while committing a crime of violence. He faced two consecutive life sentences if convicted of both counts. Eight men and four women were seated as jurors. For the next nine days they heard from neighbors, detectives, ballistics experts, forensic investigators, the medical examiner, and the two opposing star witnesses—Terry Bouyea and Ron Gagne.

In addition to the neighbor who had found Betancur's body, another neighbor testified that he had heard a man and a woman arguing the night of Betancur's death. He heard banging against a wall, as if someone was being roughed up, and then gunshots. He looked out his windows and saw a dark-haired girl, Bouyea, leaving the front of the building, shoving something down her pants, and running down the street.

Prosecutors theorized that Ron had escaped out a back window, cut through a field, and run home, a little over a mile away. They had even recovered a fingerprint on a window screen. To call it a possible statistical match required that at least eight points on the print were identical to Ron's prints. The forensic examiner admitted during cross-examination that because the window print had only six matching points, he couldn't say it was Ron's.

Betancur had been paranoid and awake for days on a binge when Terry Bouyea came to see him. Bouyea told the jury that she wanted drugs and Betancur wanted sex, so she gave it to him. While they were in bed, she said, Ron came banging on the door. She begged Betancur not to let him in, but he didn't listen. She said she hid in a closet while they argued, and then she saw Ron shoot Betancur and leave without taking the drugs. Bouyea admitted that she stole a bag of coke from Betancur's shorts before she left the apartment. She spent the evening with a boyfriend and eventually called police. Bouyea had initially denied knowing Ron Gagne, and she explained to jurors that she had lied because she was scared he'd come after her.

Now it was time for Ron to give his side. The prosecution had portrayed him as a drug-crazed murderer and he knew he would have to answer difficult questions on the stand. He testified candidly for about three hours over two days.

Ron said he had been buying cocaine from Betancur for more than six months. He had been depressed about his girlfriend leaving with their son, so he spent more time partying with friends. In the beginning, he'd do a little coke on a Friday or Saturday night but never during the week. Pretty soon, his drug use was on a predictable cycle: go to work, come home, nothing on TV, call the dealer, spend $100, party, go to bed, get up, go to work, nothing to do, call Joe. Ron called Joe more than three dozen times in the month leading up to his death and bought coke from him at least once a week.

Ron admitted to jurors that he had a drug problem, but he didn't have it in him to kill anyone.

"I had nothing to do with his death," he said.

The trial would come down to a case of he said, she said—a battle of credibility.

"At the end of the day you have to decide if you will convict Mr. Gagne based on [Bouyea's] testimony," Mann told the jury in his closing arguments. He noted that, by Bouyea's own admission, Betancur was still breathing when she rifled through his pockets, stole his drugs, and called her boyfriend rather than calling 911. "She should be on trial," Mann said.

Prosecutor Russell Sollitto urged jurors to give Bouyea credit for telling the truth, "even when it was bad for her."

The jury began deliberating at about 1:00 p.m. on a Thursday. Ron was led back to a holding cell in the courtroom. He loosened his tie and sat down. He was emotionally exhausted. He'd had a lot of time to think about his life the last 498 days in prison. He heard that some of the detectives, guys he grew up playing sports with, were bragging about their strong case and how they were going to put a Gagne boy away. It felt personal to him. Yet he kept coming back to the same obvious conclusion: if he hadn't been doing drugs, the cops never would have seen his checks on Betancur's table, linked him to the murder, and forced him to recount every detail of his drug use to his family and the community. It was embarrassing, but not nearly as bad as murder. At thirty-five, he felt like he had come clean about everything. It was up to the jury now to decide if he was going home or going back to his cage for the rest of his life. He'd eased back to take a nap when a deputy walked in.

The panel had reached a decision in about two hours. Ron was weak and shaky as the officer led him down the corridor and back into the tiny courtroom. Mann was nervous too. Despite his objections, the prosecutors had been allowed a jury instruction, which stated that if they could not agree on first-degree murder, they had the option of finding Ron guilty of second-degree murder. Mann warned Ron: *When the first verdict is read, don't react. Wait for the next verdict—the second-degree charge.*

Ron looked into the gallery at his parents and siblings, braving smiles but clearly on tenterhooks. Bob, however, had left. After sitting through the entire trial, Gagne was confident that his brother had been his own best witness on the stand. He saw it on the jurors' faces. He was so certain his brother would be freed that he said his good-byes and started the long drive home before the reading of the verdict. Gagne figured there would be tears and celebrations afterward, and he wasn't a parade guy. He could get people dressed and ready for the parade and get them there on time, but he preferred to slip out before the cheering and flag waving. He needed to get back home to his pregnant wife and try to return to normalcy. He was tired.

Defendant, please rise.

The jury foreman announced that they had reached a unanimous decision. The judge reviewed the verdict form, handed it back to the deputy, and asked the foreman to read it aloud to the court.

We the jury in the case of the State of Rhode Island versus Ronald Gagne, in the charge of murder in the first degree, find the defendant . . . not guilty.

A gasping sigh shot through the gallery like a rumble of electricity. Ron stood stony as a statue, squeezing the defense table to keep from passing out.

"Have you reached a verdict in count one?" the judge asked.

Yes . . . We the jury find the defendant, Ronald Gagne, in the charge of murder in the second degree . . .

Ron swore he saw the foreman turn and say those last words just to him: *not guilty.*

He collapsed into his chair, put his face in his hands, and wept.

104 THREE MONTHS LATER

ODED TUITO WAS RETURNING to America. By the spring of 2003, after two years of fighting extradition, Tuito had exhausted his appeals and the Spanish authorities were ready to hand him over. Gagne got a call from a U.S. marshal, checking in to see what kind of suspect they'd be dealing with.

"He's dangerous. Don't let your guard down and stay focused," Gagne said.

Around the same time, Linda Lacewell handed Gagne a laundry list of to-do items—preparations in their case against the Fat Man. It was time for him to start dialing up cooperators. There were about a dozen names on his list, mostly couriers. Finding Yakov Ariel—the first Tuito courier he had arrested at JFK—was going to be tough. Ariel was in Israel, but no one knew where he was living. Gagne called Gadi Eshed for help.

"All right," Eshed said. "I will get back to you."

Eshed called back within forty-eight hours. Not only had he found Ariel, he had already called to prep him for Gagne. Ariel still sounded surprised to hear Gagne's voice on the line. It had been four years since his arrest. His cooperation agreement obligated him to testify, Gagne reminded him, and the U.S. government would pay for his flight to New York—if they needed him.

When Gagne caught up with Jackie Suarez, she was typically cold to him, but he could hear a lightness in her voice. She was working for an Internet-based gourmet food company and had been traveling on business around the country. Things were good at home. She sounded clean and in control.

"We may call you to testify when Tuito comes back," Gagne told her. "It's possible he could plead out. But I'm just calling because I have to let you know."

"How is he?" she asked. The question threw Gagne. He had no answer.

On April 15, 2003, U.S. marshals took custody of Oded Tuito in Spain and transported him on a commercial flight to JFK without incident. He was scheduled for arraignment in federal court in Brooklyn the next morning.

"You're going to be there, right?" Lacewell asked. She seemed nervous and Gagne enjoyed antagonizing her.

"Linda, you know my wife is super pregnant right now?" Gagne said. "Like, ready to give birth any minute?"

"Okay, but you're going to be there, right?"

On April 16, Lacewell stood at the prosecution table in the courtroom of U.S. magistrate judge Cheryl Pollak. A public defender took the defense table. Gagne sat behind Lacewell in the front row of the gallery.

Oded Tuito's name was called. He wore a khaki prison uniform and slip-on shoes. He was unshaven and jet-lagged. He glanced around the courtroom. It was the first time Gagne and Lacewell had seen him in the flesh. Gagne and his DEA partners across the country had been chasing Tuito and his underlings for more than five years. To finally see him in shackles and standing before an American judge was a tremendous relief. Gagne was surprised at how small Tuito looked—thinner than in the old photographs. He seemed worn down.

The forty-one-year-old Ecstasy kingpin smirked as Judge Pollak summarized the counts against him: conducting a criminal enterprise, importation of Ecstasy, distribution of Ecstasy with the intent to import it, related drug conspiracies, money laundering.

"Everything you told me I know," Tuito interrupted. He pleaded not guilty and requested a kosher meal for Passover. He would receive chicken with horseradish and a box of matzos for Seder in federal prison.

In classic cowboy parlance, SAC Anthony Placido of DEA New York announced that day that Oded Tuito's arrest and extradition "will not only serve to disrupt the flow of millions of dosage units of illegal drugs into our country, it also sends the unmistakable message to criminals that they can run, but they cannot hide."

Tuito faced twenty years to life in prison and $2 million in fines if convicted. He was ready for a fight—he wanted to go to trial. New York had the strongest case and would try Tuito first. Gagne and Lacewell had yet to locate his assets, but because of his kingpin status, if he wanted to hire a private attorney he'd have to prove he wasn't paying with drug proceeds.

They'd finally gotten him. Still, Gagne had a vague feeling that Tuito had more tricks up his sleeve. He had masterfully manipulated the courts abroad for years. Gagne knew they would have to stay one step ahead, anticipating his next possible move.

Later that same day, Kristen went into labor. Like the first time, the couple had opted to wait until delivery to learn their child's gender. Around 7:30 p.m., Gagne met his son.

He had been nervous, thinking about what it would mean to be a father to a little boy. Beyond the coaching, hockey games, and Little League, raising a boy felt like more responsibility, heavier territory. He wanted to be a good father.

As he watched his son sleeping, swaddled in a blanket, Gagne was overwhelmed with emotion, a sense of accomplishment and pride. His family felt complete now.

It was a good day.

V "THE AMERICANS ARE INVOLVED?"

105 THE NEW RULES OF ENGAGEMENT

RETIRED ISRAELI NATIONAL POLICE detective Amram Edri is a compact, muscular man who chased after Jerusalem's most notorious gangsters back in the 1970s when he was a little swifter of stride. During his twenty-five years of service, Edri's car was burned, his tires were slashed, his home was ambushed, and his two young sons escaped kidnappers who tried to drag them into a car. Even now, as a rough-around-the-edges septuagenarian, Edri has retained his Charles Bronson–esque mystique. Bad guys cross the street to avoid crossing his path.

Edri was holding court in a Jerusalem hotel lounge one January morning while Gadi Eshed and a few INP colleagues sipped from dainty coffee cups and revisited the evolution of the Mafia wars with the elder states-man. The rules of organized crime in the 1970s had been very clear, Edri said. The families had fought to control their geographic territories and if you dared to cross the border you would be killed. But by the time Eshed and his colleagues began targeting the modern organized crime families, the rules as Edri knew them had changed. Families still fought to protect monopo-lies over illegal ventures, but now they also fought over legitimate businesses such as recycling, egg production, vegetable markets, and casinos abroad. If one family puts its tentacles into a new legitimate frontier, you don't dare to cross into that territory.

The methods of control have also evolved. The old

gangs were uneducated and rarely planned out their attacks. They'd be sitting around when someone—usually Edri's rival, Micha "the Lion" Levi—got the bright idea, "Hey let's go ambush Edri's house," and off they went. Levi even knocked on Edri's door once as a prelude to an ambush.

The new generation, however, is treacherous and sophisticated. They carefully plan every step, waiting months or years to assassinate rivals. They hire savvy attorneys. They know their rights and they exploit the vulnerabilities of the anti-crime and anti-money-laundering laws.

The tools of liquidation have sharpened. In Edri's day it was bare hands, pistols, and kidnappings. The height of technology was a hand grenade placed under the victim's car clutch, set to go off within seconds of releasing the pedal. Today's mafiosos install remote-controlled bombs in the headrest of the driver's seat and shoot at rivals with light anti-armor weapon (LAW) missiles—shoulder-launched, high-explosive anti-tank long-range rockets.

Increasingly aggressive weaponry meant the mobsters had to secure heavier armor. By 2000, Ze'ev Rosenstein was never seen without bodyguards—at least two in front and two behind. He had a special Mercedes S320, 3,200 cc, custom built with an armored chassis, armored windows, and bulletproof tires.

Edri's life is simpler now that he's off the streets and has time to play with his grandchildren. But retirement doesn't come with any such guarantees for the bad guys. Not even for an old man like Edri's rival, Micha "the Lion" Levi, who was shot in the back on June 27, 2003, while vacationing in Eilat. Three days later, in a totally unrelated attack, Ze'ev "the Wolf" Rosenstein almost joined the Lion.

106 THE TRAVEL AGENCY

THE TEL AVIV DISTRICT police station on Dizengoff Street sits on a well-manicured thoroughfare alive with café culture, family-run shops, bohemian youth, glitter, and grit—the Sunset Boulevard of Tel Aviv.

Gadi Eshed was at the station on the morning of June 30, 2003, in a meeting with Avi Noyman, head of the investigation department at the Tel Aviv Central Unit, when a bomb blast shook the station windows.

"Not again," Noyman said. The officers were certain it was a terrorist attack. But then a dispatcher barked out the address of the explosion: "Ha' Taarouca 3."

"Rosenstein!" Eshed and Noyman shouted in unison. Ha' Taarouca 3 was the headquarters of Rosenstein's tourist agency, about one kilometer from the police station. They ran toward the site. The smell of smoke and the sound of crushed glass underfoot intensified as they approached the agency. The first thing Noyman could make out in the haze was the front office doors, mangled and burnt. People covered in blood were staggering in a daze. Sirens blared.

He's dead, Eshed thought. *There's no way Rosenstein could have survived this*. But through the smoke, there was the Wolf, hearty and unfazed, a couple of spots of blood on his shirt.

During the night, assassins had driven a car outfitted with a remote-controlled bomb into the open parking lot and parked it in such a way as to maximize damage to the front entrance of Rosenstein's office. Rosenstein arrived the next morning in his armored Mercedes, accompanied by two Skoda cars with up to four armed bodyguards in each car. As usual, the guards checked the area first before opening Rosenstein's door. One team entered the office, and Rosenstein followed, with another team behind him.

But as he had reached the door, Rosenstein's cell phone rang—a call from a business associate—and in the milliseconds before the assassins flicked the bomb switch, Rosenstein had turned and stepped no more than two feet away from the door, out of the trajectory of the explosion.

The blast was so strong it crushed the armored front door and traveled through the office, destroying everything in its narrow path. Nearly twenty people, including Rosenstein's bodyguards, were injured. The Wolf suffered a cut pinky finger.

Police had a single piece of evidence—a small black remote control box, about the size of a pack of cigarettes, which had been found across the street by an elderly woman. As the respective heads of the intelligence and investigation departments, Eshed and Noyman worked in lockstep on serious crimes. After several months of investigation, Eshed and Noyman's teams discovered that the remote was made for a specific type of model airplane. They tracked down the model shop and learned the remote control had been purchased two years earlier along with nine others. The man who bought them had used a fake ID, but police were still able to track him down. Police ultimately discovered that the remotes had been paid for by the Abergil clan—Rosenstein's rivals. But none of their sources would testify, and Rosenstein refused to cooperate in the investigation of his attackers. It was the sixth attempt on the mob boss's life.

107 "THIS MAN IS A LIAR"

DRUG COPS WILL TELL you that every country has its share of organized crime. Sophisticated organized crime groups operate like sovereign governments, establishing laws and codes of conduct outside their nation's laws. They carry out capital punishment among their members and regulate the crime economy and illicit trade markets. If left unchecked, factions will thrive and infiltrate legitimate government, installing their own leaders and proxies into local and state political positions to further their own interests.

Organized crime breeds when law enforcement is weak—weak from a lack of police manpower and resources, from inefficient crime laws, from failures in support among the agencies and courts that uphold the laws.

Israeli police had been so consumed with dealing with Palestinian terror attacks that the organized crime groups were slowly engaging in a brash escalation of the mob wars. The most visible wars involved six main families, including bitter rivals Ze'ev Rosenstein and Itzhak Abergil.

Rosenstein was the man to kill if one was aiming for the top spot. Abergil and his allies were suspected in a series of assassination attempts against Rosenstein; in one instance, there were two attempts in a single day. Ironically, the police surveillance that so irked Rosenstein saved his life on several occasions when officers had thwarted would-be attackers. Rosenstein's allies Haniana Ohana and Felix Abutbul (the notorious diplomat kidnapper) were not as lucky.

In 2002, Abutbul was gunned down in Prague at the entrance to his Casino Royal—allegedly in revenge for the recent killing of Itzhak's brother Jacob Abergil. About four months before Rosenstein escaped the bomb attack at his office, Ohana was shot to death in front of his wife and child in a parking lot. One of the two assailants, Yoni Elzam, agreed to cooperate and had been expected to implicate Itzhak Abergil in the Ohana hit. But Elzam was mysteriously poisoned to death in his prison cell on the eve of his testimony. An autopsy revealed traces of cyanide.

Elzam's death underscores a complicated vulnerability in the Israeli justice system: there is no witness protection program. And in a country the size of New Jersey, where would one hide a cooperator? Mob bosses knew that only a dead man would dare to testify. But there have been exceptions.

Two months after the Wolf's office was bombed, a convicted murderer from the north named David Attias claimed he had had a secret meeting with Rosenstein years earlier during a weekend furlough. (Israeli prisoners, even those serving a life sentence, may apply for a "vacation" every three months—a benefit many Israeli police officers find troubling.) Attias said the mob boss had personally asked him to whack the brothers Jacob and Itzhak Abergil. Rosenstein was arrested based on Attias's confession. The media were rabid: this was it, the papers proclaimed—police had finally caught the Wolf.

But Eshed, Noyman, and their boss, district commander Yosef Sedbon, were skeptical from the start. The police had been watching the mob bosses for so long, they knew their codes and business practices—and Rosenstein would never deal directly with a hit man. Even meetings between the big bosses, for instance, are carefully arranged. Bodyguards check each other first before the CEOs arrive. They don't like to sit inside; they prefer to walk and talk, especially along the beaches in Tel Aviv. And when they talk, they keep their faces toward the Mediterranean, to avoid any potential lip readers with binoculars watching from hotel windows. Rosenstein seemed distinctly paranoid. He would hand cash to employees wordlessly and walk on, as if handing a ticket to a bus driver.

Eshed and Avi's teams pulled up Attias's cell phone records and ran down the facts of his story. It didn't add up. Attias was sounding more like a prisoner who was trying to earn benefits. When confronted, Attias admitted he had made the whole thing up. Rosenstein was freed after spending two days in police custody.

The most surprising part of the Attias episode for Eshed and Noyman was that Rosenstein had talked. Suspects in Israel, like in the United States, have the right to remain silent. On previous arrests, when Rosenstein was brought in for questioning, he would simply write on a white sheet of paper: "My wish is not to say a word." Police would sit with him for hours, peppering him with questions, and day after day he said nothing. He'd simply tap an index finger on the paper or hold it up in response. It would drive the detectives crazy.

But when he was picked up over the Attias accusations, Rosenstein was unusually vocal.

"This man is a liar," he told the officers. "I have never met him. Bring him before me. I will confront him."

Of course, he was right. But within days of Rosenstein's release, the assassins were back on his tail. Attempt number seven would set a new bar for recklessness in the mob wars.

108 THE CAT WITH SEVEN LIVES

THE ARMORED CONVOY PULLED up to the currency exchange shop on Yehuda Halevi Street at lunchtime on December 11, 2003. Rosenstein was a regular customer at the boxy little money store located on a busy sidewalk lined with cafés, a hardware store, and a tailor.

Rosenstein entered with his bodyguards, went up to the window to change his money, exchanged a few words with the owner, and then turned to leave. As Rosenstein approached the front glass door, someone watching from a safe distance hit the switch of a remote control. A powerful blast ripped through the shop, sending shrapnel flying, demolishing several storefronts, collapsing the second-floor concrete balcony above the money changer, and shattering windows along Yehuda Halevi. Rosenstein sustained only minor injuries to a hand and a leg.

Police later theorized that assassins who had been tracking the Wolf's routine had surreptitiously installed a bomb on the change shop's awning. But Rosenstein— who possessed either keen intuition or uncanny luck— realized that he had forgotten to say something to the shop owner. He turned back inside the store, away from the path of the bomb blast, just seconds before the explosion.

At least eighteen people were injured and three died— innocent bystanders who were walking past as Rosenstein stepped into the kill zone. Among the dead was the change shop owner's son.

* * *

The per capita murder rate in Israel in 2003 was just 3.01 murders per 100,000 inhabitants. (The U.S. rate was 5.7; in the Netherlands it was less than 1; Ecuador's was 15.) Israel handled 163 murder cases that year, not including an additional 213 murders from Palestinian terror attacks. (A comparably populated American state, Georgia, reported 656 non-negligent homicides.) Israelis enjoy relative peace despite the constant threat of terror attacks. But as Police Chief Sedbon puts it: "In Israel, the media and the people suffer terrorist attacks, they suffer deaths from car accidents, of which there are maybe ten or more per week. But they cannot suffer criminal warfare that kills one innocent person."

In 2003, criminal warfare resulted in the deaths of ten innocent bystanders. The change shop attack on Rosenstein—attempt number seven—was a turning point in the Mafia wars, and a new phrase was coined: "criminal terror attacks." Newspaper editorials across Israel questioned whether police were up to the job of fighting them.

In response, Prime Minister Ariel Sharon ordered the internal security minister, Tzahi Hanegbi, to "use all measures to stop this dangerous development." INP officers embarked on a wide crackdown on the business of organized crime, closing down some four hundred illegal gambling dens and three hundred brothels.

But as the bomb smoke cleared and the trauma of the event faded from memory, a shift in perception was building among younger Israelis: Ze'ev Rosenstein slowly gained cult figure status as the boss who couldn't be killed. He was strong, famous, rich, and untouchable.

When the tabloids caught on to Rosenstein's growing underground popularity, he was dubbed in headlines as "The Israeli Gotti" and "The Cat with Seven Lives." His son's wedding hit the gossip pages. He was seen on the street having coffee with a famous singer/comedian, Nansi Brandes, and youngsters ran up to ask for an autograph, not from Brandes but from the Israeli Gotti.

Gadi Eshed's colleague Avi Noyman had followed Rosenstein's rise to power since joining the police force in 1987. Noyman has a shaved head, blue eyes, a gruff throaty voice, and an angular face that brings to mind those stony Moai monoliths of Easter Island. In his years of chasing mobsters, Noyman felt fear on the job just once, in the late 1980s, when he was part of a team of officers watching Yehezkel Aslan—the man whose murder outside Pisces restaurant in 1993 vaulted Rosenstein to top boss. Police had been trying in vain to arrest Aslan, even pulling him over at night just to see if they could get him on drunk-driving charges. Aslan quickly wearied of the hassling.

"I'm very pleased to know you, Mr. Noyman," Aslan said one evening. "I'm sure you have very cute kids that you love. I wish you to continue to love them."

Years later, Noyman was having a quiet Shabbat meal with his family when his inquisitive seven-year-old son asked him out of the blue: "Dad, what about Rosenstein?"

Noyman was taken aback. For twenty years, his family had rarely asked about his work. But it seemed like every child in Israel knew the name Ze'ev Rosenstein. If he'd run for office—he was a registered Likud party member—he could have won. The public loved him, and some reporters began to ask why the police were hounding Rosenstein.

The police believed Rosenstein murdered his way to the top—but they hadn't been able to pin any criminal activity on him since his armed robbery conviction in 1978.

Rosenstein's denying any knowledge of his attackers

only played into his mythology. "I do not wish it on any-one to go through what I'm going through now," he said in an interview with *Yedioth Ahronoth*, the most widely circulated Hebrew paper in Israel. "One blow after an-other and I don't know where it's coming from."

Eshed and Noyman felt a special responsibility to the Rosenstein case. They had spent hours each day care-fully planning their investigations, determining what targets they would intercept, and identifying weak links in the chain. They worked together in a style that Eshed liked to call a "salami system"—a sliced-up, step-by-step plan, carried out in small pieces. And like Al Capone with taxes, if they couldn't get the Wolf on the crimes of murder, extortion, bribery, or illegal gambling, then they would go for the Ecstasy connection.

109 "NO DEAL"

BARUCH DADUSH WAS A car dealer who'd met Ze'ev Rosenstein in downtown Tel Aviv in the mid- to late 1990s. The two became fast friends, business partners in a car wash, and eventually partners in Ecstasy deals. But for the last two years, Baruch Dadush and his brother, Ilan, had sat in prison for their roles in the Lübeck warehouse seizure that netted 1.6 million Ecstasy pills. In April 2004, Tel Aviv district court judge George Kara found the brothers guilty of international drug trafficking.

Baruch's attorney paid a visit to Eshed and Noyman after the guilty verdict to obliquely suggest that Baruch might have information to trade for a reduced sentence. His client had sensitive information, the attorney said. Not to testify to, but to share. Intelligence about "the big guy."

"Who is the big guy?" Eshed asked, slightly amused.

The lawyer continued his cloak-and-dagger routine, telling Eshed that Baruch could provide him with "the real big building."

"Listen," Eshed said, "you want big buildings, short buildings, small buildings—are we talking about Ze'ev Rosenstein?"

Baruch's attorney smiled proudly but would not repeat the name. Eshed cut to the chase.

"I know you're a very important and busy attorney and I don't want to waste your time," Eshed said. "My answer is no."

Shaking off the sting of insult, the lawyer suggested to Eshed that he take the offer to his boss before making any hasty decisions.

"Ah, but in this case I'm the boss. No deal."

It was hard to say no to intelligence. The pressure to strike Rosenstein's organization was overwhelming and the press was getting nasty. A columnist for *Yedioth Ahronoth* began badgering Eshed by name, claiming he had fabricated the case against Rosenstein in order to foster his international connections and take trips, "Eshed Tours," to the United States.

Tel Aviv district commander Yosef Sedbon retired in 2004 after thirty-one years on the force. His stint at the Central Unit had begun with a terrorist bomb blast and ended with the criminal terror bomb blast at the change shop. Eshed and Noyman's new boss, David Tsur, would inherit the negative press over the Rosenstein investigations. Tsur, who looked more at home in a leather jacket on top of a motorcycle than in his starched blue police uniform behind a desk, had a long history of crime fighting under his belt. A major general, from 1992 to 1995 he had commanded Israel's elite civilian counterterrorism unit, the Yehidat Mishtara Meyuhedet or Yamam, a paramilitary force renowned for hostage rescue, SWAT operations, and undercover police work. In 1996, he spent a year in Atlanta, Georgia, as a consultant on counterterrorism and security during the Olympic games. He came home to more high-ranking police positions.

As commander of the Tel Aviv district, Tsur was aware that organized crime represented an infinitesimal percentage of INP's caseload. Car thefts and robberies were the crimes that affected people's daily lives. But the crime families had become so powerful that the press was reporting on Rosenstein's every move and the Tel Aviv district was spending a disproportionate amount of time and resources watching mob bosses. Tsur understood that the media needed to sell papers, but he abhorred the romanticization of Ze'ev Rosenstein.

Tsur was attacked by some reporters for giving Eshed his full support. He was even told by one newspaper publisher that it was a career-ending move to go after Rosenstein. The barbs seemed relentless and came at a time when Tsur was dealing with his own personal struggles, watching his beloved wife battle terminal cancer. Still, he stood by Eshed.

110 FOUR DAYS IN FLORIDA

IN SEPTEMBER 2004, Gadi Eshed flew to Florida for the Ecstasy trial of Shemtov Michtavi. Authorities in the Southern District of Florida had built strong cases against the traffickers involved in the Battery Park seizure and almost every one of the defendants had pleaded guilty—including Roash, Ashkenazi, and Mordechai "Flaco" Cohen. But Shemtov Michtavi took a gamble and took his case to trial. The wry con man was so certain he would be found innocent, he told Eshed when he saw him in the courtroom that they should shake hands.

"In a few days, you will see that I will be free," Michtavi said. He told Eshed that he was a man of God, and that God would help him.

"If you trust God," Eshed said, "I think in this case you will be disappointed."

Flaco was a powerful witness against Michtavi, describing the pill deals, the $40,000 he received for the hit men, and his own fears of a bloody retaliation for his missteps in the deal. But the real showstopper was Shemtov Michtavi, who delivered fantastic, overarching dramatics on the witness stand.

Michtavi insisted he had never been involved in Ecstasy smuggling and he reimagined the entire hit-man plot, starring Shemtov Michtavi as the hero. The way Michtavi told it, Flaco's infamous coke-dealing father, Elias Cohen, was the one who had hired the Colombian hit men in a conspiracy to kill the Wolf. Michtavi said he sent Flaco the $40,000 to call off the hit men, establish a truce, and save his good friend Ze'ev Rosenstein. The jury wasn't convinced. After a four-day trial the panel found Shemtov Michtavi guilty. He was sentenced to twenty years. Another piece of Eshed and Noyman's plan had been sliced up and carried out.

111 "I SEE YOU FOLLOW ME?"

A FEW WEEKS AFTER the trial, Gadi Eshed was sitting on a lounge chair inside the Habanos Brill Cigar shop on Dizengoff Street, a cozy nook with a floor-to-ceiling selection of eclectic tobaccos and Cuban cigars. It was early afternoon, and Eshed was having an espresso and working on a cheap Dutch cigarillo—a small respite before heading back to the office. Shemtov Michtavi's conviction was heavy on his mind. He and Noyman were at a crucial juncture in their plan to catch Rosenstein, but it was still too soon to move. There was one more piece.

From Eshed's seat near the cigar shop window, he saw the convoy pulling up. There was always a sense of foreboding when the Wolf was on the streets. Crowds parted from his path as if bombs could go off at any minute and he'd be the only one left standing.

Rosenstein and his entourage walked right past the cigar shop and into the pharmacy next door. On his way back, Rosenstein saw Eshed through the shop window and made a detour to say hello to his antagonist. He walked up to Eshed and put out his hand. They shook. Eshed didn't get up.

"So. This is the place where you have a drink and smoke a cigar?" Rosenstein said as he looked around the shop.

"Yes," Eshed said. He gestured to the pharmacy next door. "And this is the place where you get your medicines for your problems with your stomach?"

"I see you follow me?" Rosenstein said.

"It seems to me," Eshed replied, "that you follow me."

Rosenstein laughed as he walked out, his lackeys trailing behind.

In the time they had been talking, the cigar shop had quietly cleared out.

112 THE LAST SLICE

IN OCTOBER 2004, the district court in Tel Aviv sentenced Baruch Dadush to twenty years—eighteen for the drug charges and two for tax evasion. His brother, Ilan, received the same. It was more than Eshed and Noyman had expected and it positioned them exactly where they needed to be when Baruch Dadush's lawyer came calling again.

Baruch was still a young man, just thirty-six. Ilan was twenty-nine. They had wives and children at home who needed their fathers. Baruch sent his attorney to try to hammer out a trade—intelligence for benefits, maybe more vacation time. Eshed welcomed the attorney into his office at INP, said he'd been planning to call him.

The attorney opened the negotiations by making the same demure suggestions that Baruch had valuable information that Eshed and Noyman would be very interested in—information about a weapons stockpile that might belong to "someone."

The attorney was about to feel the knife of the salami system. The pieces had been cut just so. Baruch was the last slice.

"First of all, as to your proposal," Eshed said, "my answer is, no way. We don't need any intelligence against your big building Rosenstein. But I am happy you are here."

Eshed handed the defense attorney a business card for Ben Greenberg, an AUSA in the Southern District of Florida.

"Please call this prosecutor," Eshed said. "He will explain that your client is going to face a new case, an American case, and we are ready to arrest him for extradition."

Eshed added up the bill: Baruch was looking at eighteen years in Israel for the drug charges, plus another two years on tax evasion, and—if Shemtov Michtavi's trial was any measure—another twenty years for the American drug case.

"I believe that in forty years, your client will be free," Eshed said.

Baruch's lawyer was speechless. These were the new rules of the game. The Americans would no longer stand by as Ecstasy traffickers conspired to bring drugs to the United States, and the Israelis were ready to work with their American counterparts if it meant bringing their own crime bosses to justice.

Eshed told Baruch's attorney he didn't need any big buildings. He said he wanted "the whole neighborhood."

113 THE AMERICANS MAKE AN OFFER

AFTER FLACO, MICHTAVI, and all the others, now it was Baruch Dadush's turn. For the first time he realized he was going to suffer. Michtavi had gotten twenty years in federal prison—the price for keeping his mouth shut about Rosenstein. Baruch was angry about being backed into a corner. He arranged to meet with Eshed face-to-face.

"What, are you crazy?" he asked Eshed. "Is twenty years here not enough?"

He wanted more time to think things through. The police wanted him to turn against a man who had been his boss and mentor for years. A man he knew was capable of murder.

An American law enforcement delegation—including DEA agent John McKenna and AUSA Ben Greenberg—was swiftly dispatched to Tel Aviv to meet with Baruch, his lawyer, the district attorney, and Ministry of Justice lawyers to iron out the details. They laid down the specifics for Baruch: He was facing serious drug conspiracy charges in Florida and he was still wanted on the 1992 New York case of conspiracy to export stolen vehicles. He was looking at a good twenty years if convicted. They wanted his full cooperation in the American drug case against Ze'ev Rosenstein.

Baruch was facing tremendous pressure. The Americans made an offer to Baruch and his brother to try to sweeten the deal: upon release, they'd be admitted into the Federal Witness Protection Program with their families. But it would mean leaving the motherland forever, as there was no way to guarantee their protection from retaliation if they remained in Israel.

After several weeks of negotiating on the parts of the two governments—and soul-searching for the Dadush brothers—Baruch agreed to cooperate. But the families decided they could not live under the confines of the Witness Protection Program. The Americans would have to find another way.

114 PROTECT EVERYONE

ISRAELI POLICE HAD TO get the Dadush brothers and
their families out of the country—and fast. The moment
Rosenstein learned that Baruch was on Team America,
revenge would be certain. The logistics to secure their
safety required dizzyingly precise maneuvering.

The families were moved first, swept out of Israel on a
commercial flight to Ft. Lauderdale, Florida. It was an
emotional transition. None of the Dadush kin spoke
English. John McKenna and his team ended up babysitting the wives and their children in a hotel in Ft. Lauderdale. It was a chaotic and cramped existence for the
families until the agents could help them find new
homes. DEA helped them obtain S-visas, special visas
granted only to aliens who help U.S. law enforcement to
investigate and prosecute crimes and terrorist activities.

Rosenstein's safety also became a major element in the
covert choreography. His prime rival, mob boss Itzhak
Abergil, was reportedly crazed over the public's adora-
tion of the Wolf. Secret sources told INP that Abergil
wanted to be number one and would do anything to
achieve that position. While Eshed and Noyman carefully protected Baruch and Ilan, who were still in jail, officers on the street secretly watched Rosenstein to make
sure he didn't flee the country or get killed. District commander Tsur feared that if Rosenstein was assassinated
at the height of his popularity—before they could bring
him to justice—he would be lionized as the golden
Mafia hero who'd never been caught. Noyman lay

awake at night, sleepless with worry. They were so close, a few documents, a few signatures away.

In early November 2004, Baruch and his brother were quietly flown out of Israel, escorted by INP officers, and taken into custody by DEA agents the minute they touched ground in Florida. The provisional arrest warrant for Ze'ev Rosenstein on the American drug charges had been signed and submitted. It was time to collect the Wolf.

115 "WHAT ARE YOU DOING HERE?"

A PHONE CALL CAME in at the INP press center a little before midnight on November 7, 2004, the eve of the INP's secretly planned arrest operation. The journalist on the line said he was writing a story for the next morning's paper—a tip had come in that the police were about to arrest Rosenstein for extradition to the United States on drug charges. He wanted a comment. What he got instead was a reminder that a court order prohibited the press from publishing any information that might jeopardize the case.

Avi Noyman knew that if just one reporter was aware of their plans, then Rosenstein was minutes from discovering it. Sources had earlier confirmed to police that Rosenstein was persistently snooping to find out if Baruch Dadush was talking about him. They couldn't take any chances; they would arrest Rosenstein that night.

A surveillance team had been following the Wolf twenty-four hours a day, protecting him from potential assassins, and the unit leader called Noyman a little after midnight to report Rosenstein's position. He had just entered a small hotel in Tel Aviv with a pretty nineteen-year-old girl. They would report back the minute he left the hotel.

At about 2:30 a.m., Noyman got the call: *Rosenstein just walked out. He looks tired but happy.*

"Follow him," Noyman ordered. They were ready.

The surveillance unit watched as Rosenstein's armored convoy rolled down Ben-Gurion Street toward

Dizengoff. As the black Mercedes approached the intersection, it was held back in a dead-stop traffic jam. Rosenstein looked out his window to see a police blockade along the entire intersection. He had a bored expression on his face, as if he had registered the annoying holdup as another routine traffic checkpoint. But then he saw Noyman approaching his car window.

"Noyman," Rosenstein called out. "What are you doing here?"

Rosenstein knew Noyman was a high-ranking officer, not the kind of cop who would be out after midnight on traffic patrol.

"Rosenstein, this is it," Noyman said. "It's done."

The Wolf had been through the cop-stop routine before. But when he looked at Noyman, he must have known this time was different. He had one question.

"The Americans are involved?"

"Yes," Noyman said.

Rosenstein turned pale; the color completely left his face. Noyman, without thinking, reached down and pinched Rosenstein's cheek, as one would with a sad child. Later at the police station, as Rosenstein was being processed, he told Noyman that the one thing he would regret was missing his son's bar mitzvah.

"When is the date?" Noyman asked.

"Four months from now."

Rosenstein was in the prime of his career—a cocky, gum-chewing forty-nine-year-old boss who hadn't been in prison for almost three decades and had never been held in police custody for longer than a week or two. He knew he had been caught. Noyman felt sorry for him for the first time. Just for a moment.

At a press conference the next day, Gadi Eshed revealed the details of the case against Rosenstein, which had been shrouded in secrecy up until his arrest.

"This is the result of extraordinary American and Israeli cooperation," Eshed said. "It's only the first piece in the puzzle. The next one will be the extradition and the final piece will be his conviction."

The Israeli media was unaware of the extensive behind-the-scenes casework between the two countries and a reporter made the swipe that INP couldn't catch their own Israeli Gotti—they had to call the Americans to do the job.

"I'm willing to cooperate with the Chinese, with the Iraqi police—I just want him to stay in jail," Avi Noyman said. "I don't care who is involved and who took part in this investigation. The only important, significant fact for me was that the name Rosenstein will be no more in the headlines."

After the conference, the officers moved into a separate room and pulled out a couple of bottles of champagne they had been holding on to for several years. They didn't notice the cameraman shooting them. The next day's news featured footage of Eshed and Noyman and their colleagues smiling, corks exploding, and cheers all around as TV reporters gave their own take on the Wolf's arrest: *Police have already opened the champagne bottles, but Rosenstein will be released as usual and Gadi Eshed and his team will regret this early champagne celebration.*

"What do you think about this behavior?" a reporter later asked district commander David Tsur. "Isn't it too early to be celebrating when Ze'ev always gets out?"

"Yes, I called Gadi personally and told him I was very disappointed," Tsur said. "I told him, 'How do you dare to arrange this ceremony and forget to invite me?'"

Tsur arranged a second celebration and brought top-quality whiskey. He chided his officers for drinking cheap champagne.

116 A CAGED WOLF

ZE'EV ROSENSTEIN WAS EXTRADITED to the Southern District of Florida on March 6, 2006. He was charged with two counts of conspiracy to import and distribute Ecstasy in the United States, based on the 700,000-pill bust in Battery Park City. He faced a maximum of forty years in prison.

"Rosenstein has orchestrated the delivery of hundreds of thousands of Ecstasy tablets into American neighborhoods," DEA administrator Karen Tandy said in a statement. "Today, we answer his crime with the consequence criminals fear most: extradition to the United States. DEA stands firmly with our Israeli partners in this battle against drugs, and we will not relent until drug traffickers, from the kingpins to the street dealers, are behind bars."

As the Wolf paced in his cage, his former lieutenant, Baruch Dadush, sealed his fate. In his intelligence debriefings with Gadi Eshed, Dadush revealed the genesis of Ze'ev Rosenstein's foray into Ecstasy, a partnership officially struck in 1999 when Dadush and Rosenstein met with Zvi Fogel at a hotel on the beach in Tel Aviv. The Ecstasy trade had become competitive and vicious and Fogel realized he could no longer be an independent trafficker. Fogel made a proposal to Rosenstein that day: "If you invest the money and give me your name as protection, I will be responsible for the way"—for the transportation of the drugs from Holland to the United States.

It had been a crucial moment in Ze'ev Rosenstein's criminal career. He knew that Tuito and Koki and the networks of *yordim* had made small fortunes trafficking Ecstasy. But Rosenstein was a purported billionaire from his casinos and gambling package tours and presumably from his illegal rackets. He wasn't known as a drug trafficker and had no financial need to get involved. But informants had long ago revealed Rosenstein's greatest weakness to police—the Wolf was greedy to a fault.

Rosenstein accepted Fogel's offer that day in 1999, and he put Baruch Dadush in charge of their new business venture. They had agreed to share in Fogel's profits, taking up to 60 percent in some transactions. Dadush installed Roash and Ashkenazi in the Battery Park apartment to receive and distribute pills. The new organization had two successful test runs in 1999, moving nearly half a million pills overland from Holland to Germany—hiding the drugs in copper scrap, computer parts, and a vehicle—before sending them by freighter ship to the States.

Dadush confirmed to prosecutors that Rosenstein had financed the deals. Rosenstein didn't know who supplied the pills (that was Zvi Fogel's job), he didn't know who bought them (Dadush and the Battery Park dealers handled that part), and he didn't want to be bothered with the details. He should have kept it that way. But in the spring of 2001, the traffickers had suffered from a paucity of buyers, and Rosenstein made a call to his longtime friend Shemtov Michtavi to ask him to find buyers in the States. Michtavi called Flaco, and Flaco called his Colombian connection, who called the narc. That's when the trouble for Rosenstein began.

Authorities seized about 2.3 million pills total in the Lübeck and Battery Park busts, but when Eshed added up the statements of all the defendants, nearly 5 million pills had been distributed by the Ze'ev Rosenstein organization in a three-year period. For Eshed it was a huge relief. He had stood in front of three dozen foreign law enforcement officers at his conference in 2001, describing the mountain of drugs that INP believed Rosenstein was financing. If Dadush had said they had only smuggled a few hundred thousand pills, it would have been damaging not only to Eshed's reputation but also to the Israelis' relationships with the Americans.

After a miserable year in solitary confinement, Rosenstein pleaded guilty.

Although suspected of numerous crimes in Israel, Rosenstein was brought to justice in America only on the Ecstasy charges. He was sentenced to twelve years, to be served in Israel under the laws of the extradition treaty.

Baruch Dadush's twenty-year sentence was eventually reduced to ten years in return for his extensive cooperation. His brother received forty-six months.

Rosenstein left Miami in March 2007 on a heavily guarded El Al commercial flight back to Israel. He was cuffed on both hands and feet and wore a bulletproof vest. An armored convoy took him from the airport to Ayalon Prison.

In a symbolic victory for the Israeli police, Rosenstein's plea agreement required that he make a public confession of his criminal acts. In June 2007, he stood in a Tel Aviv courtroom and admitted that he had hired the Colombian hit men in an attempt to assassinate the Alperon brothers. His innocent businessman charade was over.

The mob wars would continue without Rosenstein. The Alperons and Abergils—once thought to be close allies—soon became entangled in a fierce competition over bottle recycling, a $5-million-a-year industry, according to police and environmental groups.

The chain of trust between American and Israeli authorities would also continue. Just as Israeli police worked with Miami prosecutors to arrest and extradite Ze'ev Rosenstein, in August 2008, INP executed federal arrest warrants from Los Angeles for Itzhak Abergil, his brother Meir Abergil, and six alleged co-conspirators who are suspected of Ecstasy trafficking, money laundering, and murder. Abergil and his network are accused of forming an Ecstasy distribution alliance with the Vineland Boyz, a Latino gang in the San Fernando Valley, and hiring a member of the gang to carry out a 2003 revenge murder of a dealer who tried to steal a shipment of Ecstasy pills.

Like Rosenstein before him, Abergil has denied the charges. At last call, he was fighting extradition to America.

117 "YOU CAN'T DO NOTHING BEHIND THE GOVERNMENT'S BACK"

AS ODED TUITO SAT in jail awaiting trial, DEA began to tally up the results of the investigations into the Fat Man's syndicate. By 2004, the nationwide, multiagency investigations dubbed Operation Rave I and II had netted 247 arrests and the seizure of 7.5 million pills, $2.7 million in cash, and $1.9 million in other assets. During the course of the operations, seventy-one wire intercepts were utilized in Europe and the United States.

If seizure and arrest data are any measure, MDMA availability hit its peak in 2001 and then decreased significantly—hitting a high of 5.47 million dosage units submitted to DEA labs in 2001 and dropping to 1.47 million by 2003. In 2001, DEA made 2,015 Ecstasy-related arrests. By 2006, the number had dropped to 690.

Ecstasy also lost some of its candy-coated glamour with American youth. At MDMA's peak in 2001, some 9.2 percent of twelfth graders, 6.2 percent of tenth graders, and 3.5 percent of eighth graders reported having used Ecstasy in the previous twelve months, according to the University of Michigan's annual Monitoring the Future study. By 2005, the numbers had fallen by more than half to 3.0, 2.6, and 1.7 percent, respectively. Reported first-time MDMA use by Americans age twelve and older declined from 1.2 million in 2001 to about 600,000 in 2005. Perception of the hug drug also changed. In 2006, 59.3 percent of high school seniors perceived "great risk" in taking Ecstasy just once or twice, up from 33.8 percent in 1997.

But researchers also noticed a trend of "generational forgetting," causing the numbers to increase slightly by 2007. It seems that while 58 percent of high school seniors viewed MDMA as harmful, just 30 percent of eighth graders shared that view—a sign that communication about the dangers of MDMA use needs to be consistent and continuing.

The prevalence of Ecstasy in America appears to wax and wane as new distribution routes are forged. Now, instead of the Israelis dominating the trade from the Netherlands and Belgium, it's Canadian-based Asian traffickers who smuggle the pills by car into the U.S. northern border states. But Ecstasy has never regained the level of production or purity it once held. And the Israeli traffickers appear to have mostly abandoned the trade.

Former Ecstasy trafficker Steve Hager believes that the high-profile arrests of Israeli dealers had a direct impact: "The Colombians didn't know nothing about Ecstasy, the blacks never knew about it, the Dominicans never knew about it. But the Israelis had the connections to get it from Europe and bring it to the United States. And Israelis knew from the beginning—this would bring very big profits. But now? Not worth it no more. You can't do nothing behind the government's back. Always—the government will get you."

118 TUITO'S LAST MOVE

AFTER FOURTEEN YEARS of chasing bad guys in the streets of New York, Bob Gagne was ready for a new challenge. He reached back to his early military training and remembered how much he enjoyed flying planes, before his time in Snowcap. As the Oded Tuito investigation wound down, Gagne renewed his pilot's license and joined a police flying club out of Long Island. In 2004, DEA's pilot out of Long Island retired and Gagne successfully lobbied for the job. Being a DEA pilot let Gagne take his street work to the skies, conducting air surveillance, posing as a drug-smuggling pilot, and sometimes just transporting warm bodies.

Meanwhile, his partner Linda Lacewell had been tapped by the Department of Justice to work on loan with the high-profile Enron Task Force in Houston. Lacewell helped secure guilty pleas from Enron CFO Andrew Fastow and his wife, Lea Fastow. However, her other defendant, Oded Tuito, wasn't so quick to plead out. Preparations for a 2005 drug conspiracy trial were well under way when the Ecstasy kingpin played his last move.

Linda Lacewell was sitting in a Houston courtroom checking her BlackBerry one morning in June 2004 when she received an e-mail from a duty assistant at the U.S. attorney's office in New York: *I got a call from the marshal's office. A defendant of yours, Oded Tuito, has died.*

Lacewell typed back: *Says who, and where is he?*

She stepped outside the courtroom to call Gagne. She was sure Tuito had scammed the guards and was laughing at everyone as he jetted off to his next foreign destination.

"What?" Gagne said. "Let me call you back."

For the next two hours, Gagne was on the phone with the U.S. marshals, the warden at the Metropolitan Detention Center, and the FBI—who had already begun an investigation.

"Linda, it's not a scam this time," Gagne said when he got back to her. "Tuito's dead."

"Are you sure?"

"I just talked to the FBI. I read the report."

"Okay, but are you sure?"

"Yeah. I didn't check his pulse. But I'm sure."

Around 7:30 a.m. on June 20, Oded Tuito went to work out in the prison yard. His new prison routine of running and lifting weights had helped him shed his portly Fat Man physique. He was in the best shape of his life.

When Tuito returned from the yard, he told his cellmate he was having chest pains. Thinking it was muscular, he rubbed Ben-Gay on his chest and lay down on the bunk. His cellmate left for breakfast and by the time he had come back, Tuito was still in bed, unresponsive and not breathing. The prisoner yelled for the block manager's help. They gave him CPR while waiting for emergency services.

Tuito was transported to Lutheran Medical Center in Brooklyn and pronounced dead at 11:50 a.m. from a heart attack. No autopsy was required, because no foul play was suspected. His body was immediately returned to his family in Israel for a proper Jewish service. He was forty-two years old. He was buried under a black marble headstone in one of the largest plots in the modest cemetery in Zerufa, the village where he grew up.

Whispered rumors and innuendo followed Tuito's death. Some said he'd gotten so used to living the good life that he'd killed himself rather than face the prospect of spending the next twenty years in prison. But there was no evidence of suicide. In fact, in one of Tuito's last appearances in court, his attorney had told the judge they were looking forward to bringing the case to trial.

"I just wanted to tell you that you're not going to have to testify against your friend," Gagne informed Jackie Suarez over the phone.

"Oh . . . ?" Suarez said. It had been more than a year since she'd heard Gagne's voice and it was never good when he called.

"He had a heart attack, Jackie. He's dead."

Suarez was speechless. She wanted to tell Gagne that she'd never had any intention of testifying against Tuito. Instead she thanked him and hung up.

Suarez thought back on her time with Tuito, his sweetness to her, and how he had changed her life. She didn't want to believe she'd never see him again. She preferred to entertain an alternative ending—that this was his crafty escape, a faked death. Suarez imagined Tuito back on the French Riviera, salty and free, out on that fishing boat he had always wanted.

Gadi Eshed called Gagne when he heard the news.

"It's a strange way to win this game," Eshed said. "Now he will say in heaven—or for him maybe hell: 'You see, I was never found guilty in this case. I am innocent. I win.' "

" 'Innocent' is a relative term," Gagne said.

For all legal intents and purposes, Oded Tuito died an innocent man. Linda Lacewell decided she was fine with that. Tuito had been a star among his peers, the original Ecstasy kingpin, who smuggled millions of pills to America with seeming impunity. But his arrest and extradition to the States had been a sign to Ecstasy traffickers worldwide that the American justice system would make them accountable for their crimes.

For Gagne, it was a bittersweet end. He had been chasing Ecstasy dealers for nearly a decade. He had wanted to see Oded Tuito brought to justice. But at the same time, Gagne knew Tuito had died alone in his prison cell, without his family and his children by his side, and perhaps that was a far worse price to pay.

A NOTE ON SOURCES

All of the names in *Chemical Cowboys* are real with a few exceptions. DEA neither confirms nor denies the identities of its confidential informants, who are identified in case files only by a CI or CS number. I have used pseudonyms for informants (in quotation marks on first reference) instead of numbers. I have used real names if an informant has previously been identified in the press or I have been able to identify the person through other means.

In one case, a DEA informant I've referred to as "Clare" is actually a composite of three different individuals who shared sensitive information with DEA at the risk of grave danger. I have taken some creative liberty in combining the identifying details of these sources in order to further protect their identities.

The events depicted in *Chemical Cowboys* are based on reporting and research conducted between 2004 and 2008. At the approval of DEA headquarters, I was given unprecedented access to review and take notes from the materials in DEA's New York and Pittsburgh Ecstasy case files, which provided me with vivid case reports, facts and figures on evidence and seizures, confidential DEA memos, interviews with informants, audiotapes of phone conversations, lab reports, operational plans, agents' handwritten notes, and other invaluable materials. What I could not find in case files, I culled from police records, court documents, trial transcripts, and congressional testimony. I also conducted hundreds of hours of interviews with DEA agents and employees, Israeli police and intelligence analysts, attorneys, defendants, informants, and others involved in Ecstasy casework—all of whom are mentioned in the Acknowledgments, with the exception of those sources who have requested anonymity.

When possible, I met with sources in person and also traveled to the sites of enforcement operations, drug-dealing activity, and Mafia warfare detailed in the book. This led me to such far-flung places as Amsterdam, Amstelveen, and The Hague in the Netherlands; Brussels, Belgium; Créteil and Paris, France; Bucharest, Romania; Jaffa, Herzliya Pituach, Jerusalem, Netanya, Tel Aviv, and Zerufa in Israel; the former San Fernando Valley neighborhoods and haunts of Tuito's Los Angeles crew; DEA headquarters in Virginia and offices in Brussels, The Hague, Los Angeles, Long Island, and New York City; the former nightclubs and residential sites associated with the New York Ecstasy operations; and a visit to the Gagne clan in Pawtucket, Rhode Island.

There are many informative Web sites for those seeking more information on Ecstasy and club drugs. I frequently relied on information provided by the Drug Enforcement Administration (http://www.usdoj.gov/dea/concern/mdma .html), the National Institute on Drug Abuse (http://www .drugabuse.gov/NIDA_Notes/NN0060.html), and the Office of National Drug Control Policy (http://www .whitehousedrugpolicy.gov/drugfact/club/club_drug_ff .html). I also turned to an Ecstasy advocate organization, the Multidisciplinary Association for Psychedelic Studies (http://www.maps.org/mdma), for its comprehensive information about ongoing research, as well as copies of the original legal briefings, letters, testimony, and documents from the 1984–1988 government hearings on the scheduling of MDMA.

Clubland, by Frank Owen; *Party Monster: The Shockumentary,* produced and directed by Randy Barbato and Fenton Bailey; and the Michael Alig Club Kids' fan site (http://www.michaelaligclubkids .com/) provided rich detail on Club Kid life and lore.

I relied on countless articles, books, government materials, and reports to confirm and supplement my own reporting. Many of these are listed in the bibliography.

While there is no seminal book specific to Israeli organized crime, Naím Moisés's *Illicit* and Misha Glenny's *McMafia* provide compelling illustrations of the ominous political and social implications when nations are unable to fight or contain the burgeoning transnational organized crime networks that have flourished under increasing globalization.

BIBLIOGRAPHY

"A novelist's son pleads in stolen property case." *New York Times,* Jan. 21, 1998.

"Brooklyn haredi sentenced for recruiting Ecstasy smugglers." *Jerusalem Post,* Mar. 30, 2000.

Barnes, E. "Ecstasy in Arizona: A cop and bull story." *Time,* Jun. 5, 2000.

Bastone, W. "Gatien's last dance?" *Village Voice,* Jan. 12, 1999.

———. "Peter's pad? Pal: Gatien bribed an NYPD detective." *Village Voice,* July 29, 1997.

Beck, J., and M. Rosenbaum. *Pursuit of Ecstasy: The MDMA Experience.* Albany: State University of New York Press, 1994.

Bennett, D. "Dr. Ecstasy." *New York Times,* Jan. 30, 2005.

Ben-Tal, D. "Mafia explosion." *Jerusalem Post,* Dec. 19, 2003.

Blickman, T., D. Korf, D. Siegel, and D. Zaitch. "Synthetic Drug Trafficking in Amsterdam." In *Synthetic Drugs Trafficking in Three European Cities: Major Trends and the Involvement of Organised Crime.* Amsterdam: Transnational Institute/Gruppo Abele/The Institute for Studies on Conflicts and Humanitarian Actions, 2003. http://www.tni.org/detail_page.phtml?page=books_synthetic.

Bumiller, E. "Sparse crowds and hard times for Peter Gatien, club owner, who maintains his innocence." *New York Times,* June 21, 1996.

Butterfield, F. "Violence rises as club drug spreads out into the streets." *New York Times,* Jun. 24, 2001.

Califano, J. "It's drugs, stupid." *New York Times,* Jan. 29, 1995.

Continetti, M. "Money, mobsters, murder: The sordid tale of a GOP lobbyist's casino deal gone bad." *Weekly Standard,* Nov. 28, 2005.

Council on Foreign Relations. "Backgrounder: Shining Path, Tupac Amaru (Peru, leftists)." Nov. 2005. http://www.cfr.org/publication/9276/shining_path_tupac_amaru_peru_leftists.html.

De Kort, M. "The Dutch cannabis debate, 1968–1976." *Journal of Drug Issues,* 1994; 24 (3). http://www.drugpolicy.org/library/dekort2.cfm.

Derfner, L. "A scary place called Pardess Katz." *Jerusalem Post,* Jan. 30, 1998.

———. "The outlaw allure." *Jerusalem Post,* Oct. 9, 1998.

Drug Enforcement Administration. "Biographies of DEA Agents and Employees Killed in Action." http://www.usdoj.gov/dea/agency/10bios.htm.

———. "Operation Red Tide." Nov. 2000. http://www.justice.gov/dea/major/redtide.html.

———. "The hallucinogen PMA: Dancing with death." Drug Intelligence Brief, Oct. 2000. http://www.erowid.org/chemicals/pma/pma_dea_intellbrief.pdf.

———. "Heroin traffickers used puppies to smuggle drugs." Press release, Feb. 1, 2006. http://www.justice.gov/dea/pubs/pressrel/pr020106.html.

Drug Enforcement Administration: A Tradition of Excellence 1973–2003. Washington, D.C.: U.S. Department of Justice, 2003.

Dudkevitch, M. "Israeli agent key to huge Dutch drug bust." *Jerusalem Post,* Oct. 13, 1999.

"The Ecstasy Anti-Proliferation Act of 2000." *Congressional Record,* May 23, 2000 (Senate), S4317–S4318. http://frwebgate.access.gpo.gov/cgi-bin/getpage.cgi?position=all&page=S4317&dbname=2000_record.

Eisner, B. *Ecstasy: The MDMA Story.* Berkeley, CA: Ronin, 1989.

Farah, D. *Blood from Stones: The Secret Financial Network of Terror.* New York: Broadway Books, 2004.

Federal Bureau of Investigation Uniform Crime Reports. *Crime in the United States 2003.* http://www.fbi.gov/ucr/03cius.htm.

Feuer, A. "Club owner pleads guilty in mob murder case." *New York Times,* Oct. 14, 2000.

———. "Going out with a mobster's son? Follow the code of silence." *New York Times,* May 20, 2001.

———. "Gravano and son are to enter guilty pleas in ecstasy case." *New York Times,* May 25, 2001.

———. "Gravano and son plead guilty to running ecstasy drug ring." *New York Times,* May 26, 2001.

Foderaro, L. "Psychedelic drug called Ecstasy gains popularity in Manhattan nightclubs." *New York Times,* Dec. 11, 1988.

Freudenmann, R., F. Öxler, and S. Bernschneider-Reif. "The origin of MDMA (Ecstasy) revisited: The true story reconstructed from original documents. *Addiction,* 2006; 101 (9). http://www.mdma.net/merck/ecstasy-mdma.pdf.

Fried, J. "Jury to decide whether clubs doubled as drug supermarkets." *New York Times,* Jan. 11, 1998.

———. "Club operator created 'drug supermarkets,' prosecutor says." *New York Times,* Jan. 15, 1998.

Galtney, S. "One man banned." *Time Out New York,* Feb. 12–19, 2004.

Geist, W. "The beat goes on, inside their home." *New York Times,* Dec. 1, 1984.

George, L. "Bright lights, medium-size city." *New York,* May 21, 2006.

The Geraldo Rivera Show. Transcript of Jan. 9, 1997, broadcast: "The Party's Over." Executive producer Jose Pretlow.

Gilbert, M. *The Routledge Atlas of the Arab-Israeli Conflict.* New York: Routledge, 2005.

"Gold shampoo washed money: Refiner pleads guilty in U.S.–South American laundering." *Washington Post,* Jan. 9, 2004.

Gordon, M. "Little big man." *New York,* Jan. 5, 1998.

Harnden, T. "Seedy secrets of hijackers who broke Muslim laws." *Telegraph,* Oct. 5, 2001.

Hayes, S. "Strippers, hookers, and terrorists." *Weekly Standard,* Oct. 16, 2001.

Heller, A. "Rival underworld gangs battle in Israel." *Oakland Tribune,* July 23, 2007.

Holland, J. *Ecstasy: The Complete Guide.* Rochester, VT: Park Street Press, 2001.

Humphreys, A. "Dealer's reduced term irks U.S., Canadian police." *National Post,* July 6, 2006.

Itim. "Man found shot in mob-style hit." *Jerusalem Post,* Feb. 25, 1997.

———. "Five remanded in probe of mob-style murder plots." *Jerusalem Post,* Oct. 9, 1997.

"Jailed mob boss admits hiring hit men, escapes longer sentence." *Haaretz,* June 7, 2007.

Jost, P., and H. Sandhu. *The Hawala Alternative Remittance System and Its Role in Money Laundering.* Interpol General Secretariat, Lyon, Jan. 2000. http://www.interpol.int/public/financialcrime/moneylaundering/hawala/default.asp.

Katz, Y. "Hiding witnesses no easy task here." *Jerusalem Post,* June 6, 2004.

———. "Kosher nostra." *Jerusalem Post,* Nov. 12, 2004.

———. "For Abergils of Lod, crime is a family affair." *Jerusalem Post,* Sept. 10, 2004.

Kaufman, J. "Come to our party, whoever you are." *Wall Street Journal,* June 21, 1984.

KCET's Life and Times. Transcript of Feb. 15, 2002, show on Ecstasy and the death of Jimmy Lyons. http://kcet.com/lifeandtimes/archives/200202/20020215.php.

Kolker, R., and E. Brown. "Unmade man." *New York,* Apr. 10, 2000.

Korten, T. "Goon over Miami." *Miami New Times,* Dec. 23, 1999.

Krauss, C. "New York's violent crime rate drops to lows of early 1970's: Analysts increasingly credit new police efforts." *New York Times,* Dec. 31, 1995.

Lefkovits, E. "Going after the godfathers." *Jerusalem Post,* Dec. 19, 2003.

Lefkovits, E., and H. Krieger. "The man they couldn't kill." *Jerusalem Post,* Dec. 12, 2003.

Leland, J. *Hip: The History.* New York: HarperCollins, 2004.

Levy, C. "Impresario of the night." *New York Times*, July 31, 1994.

Lipton, E. "Love of adventure leads to death of DEA agent." *Washington Post*, Sept. 4, 1994.

Maas, P. *Underboss*. New York: HarperCollins, 1997.

Malkin, M. "Back in the Limelight." *Time Out New York*, Feb. 4–11, 1999.

Marcus, R. "Reputed gang lord gunned down in car." *Jerusalem Post*, Feb. 25, 1993.

———. "Widow of underworld kingpin murdered." *Jerusalem Post*, June 28, 1996.

Marzulli, J. "Matzo for a humbled kingpin." *Daily News*, Apr. 17, 2003.

McCann, U., M. Mertl, V. Eligulashvili, and G. Ricuarte. "Cognitive performance in 3,4-methylenedioxymethamphetamine users: A controlled study." *Psychopharmacology*, 1999; 143 (4).

Meislin, R. "Body of U.S. drug agent believed found in Mexico." *New York Times*, Mar. 7, 1985.

Moisés, N. *Illicit: How Smugglers, Traffickers, and Copycats are Hijacking the Global Economy*. New York: Anchor Books, 2005.

Monitoring the Future. *National Results on Adolescent Drug Use: Overview of Key Findings 2007*. http://www.monitoringthefuture.org.

Morrison, D. "Ecstasy: From overseas to our streets." *Newsday*, Jan. 16, 2001.

Mozingo, Joe. "Racketeer loses his swagger." *Los Angeles Times*, Dec. 29, 2006.

National Commission on Terrorist Attacks upon the United States. *The 9/11 Commission Report*. July 22, 2004. http://govinfo.library.unt.edu/911/report/911Report.pdf.

National Drug Intelligence Center. *National Drug Threat Assessment 2008*. http://www.usdoj.gov/ndic/pubs25/25921/index.htm#Top.

The National Institute on Drug Abuse. *Ecstasy: What We Know and Don't Know About MDMA: A Scientific Review*. 2001. http://www.nida.nih.gov/PDF/MDMAConf.pdf.

Newfield, J. "Club king can't fix facts of teen's drug death." *New York Post*, Mar. 14, 1999.

———. "It took kid's death to stop Gatien; drug tragedy dooms empire." *New York Post*, May 9, 1999.

———. "Tragic mom hits club king Gatien with rackets suit." *New York Post*, Oct. 26, 1999.

O'Connor, K. "Gagne found innocent." *Pawtucket Times*, Jan. 31, 2003.

Oreck, A. "The Jewish Virtual History Tour: Belgium." *Jewish Virtual Library*. http://www.jewishvirtuallibrary.org/jsource/vjw/Belgium.html.

Owen, F. *Clubland: The Fabulous Rise and Murderous Fall of Club Culture*. New York: St. Martin's Press, 2003.

———. "Club buster." *Village Voice*, Dec. 30, 1997.

————. "Death of a disco dancer." *Village Voice*, Feb. 16, 1999.

————. "Ecstasy bandits." *Details*, Dec. 1998.

Peers, A. "Studio 54 it's not, but it does have Elly May Clampett." *Wall Street Journal*, Aug. 5, 1991.

Peterson, H. "King of clubs gets dealt an acquittal." *Daily News*, Feb. 12, 1998.

Peterson, H., H. Kennedy, and A. Kornblut. "King of clubs is busted: Designer drugs in the Limelight." *Daily News*, May 16, 1996.

Quinton, M., and B. Yamamoto. "Causes and consequences of methamphetamine and MDMA toxicity." *American Association of Pharmaceutical Scientists Journal*, 2006; 8 (2).

Rashbaum, W. "Drug experts report a boom in Ecstasy use." *New York Times*, Feb. 26, 2000.

————. "Two men arrested as police seize one million Ecstasy tablets." *New York Times*, July 19, 2001.

————. "Gravano's arrest saved him from murder, officials say." *New York Times*, May 16, 2003.

Ravo, N. "Two nightclubs linked to drugs are shut down." *New York Times*, Aug. 24, 1996.

Romero, D. "Sasha Shulgin, psychedelic chemist." *Los Angeles Times*, Sept. 5, 1995.

Ronson, J. "Conspirators." *Guardian*, May 5, 2001.

Room, A. *Placenames of the World*. Jefferson, NC: McFarland, 2006.

Rosenbaum, M. "Ecstasy: America's new 'Reefer Madness.' " *Journal of Psychoactive Drugs*, 2002; 34 (2).

Rosenbaum, M., and R. Doblin. "Why MDMA should not have been made illegal." In *The Drug Legalization Debate*. Edited by J. Inciardo. Thousand Oaks, CA: Sage Publications, 1991.

Rubenstein, J. "The X-files." *Details*, Sept. 2001.

Schmued, L. "Demonstration and localization of neuronal degeneration in the rat forebrain following a single exposure to MDMA." *Brain Research*, 2003; 974 (1–2).

Ser, S. "Married to the mob." *Jerusalem Post*, May 4, 2007.

"Shadow of a gunman." *Expatica*, Nov. 2, 2005. http://www.expatica.com/nl/life_in/feature/shadow-of-a-gunman-24978.html.

Shapiro, S. " 'I wanted to be an actor since "Rumpelstiltskin" at PS 138,' says the real-life detective." *Newsday*, Sept. 20, 1993.

Shelah, O. "Israeli mob war hits the streets of central Prague." *Jewish Daily Forward*, Aug. 6, 2004.

Shyovitz, D. "The Jewish Virtual History Tour: Netherlands." *Jewish Virtual Library*. http://www.jewishvirtuallibrary.org/jsource/vjw/netherlands.html.

Simpson, L. "The kids are alright." *Time Out New York*, Mar. 12–19, 1998.

Spapens, T. "Interaction between organized crime and law enforcement: The case of Ecstasy production and trafficking." Centre for Information and Research on Organised Crime,

Sept. 2007. http://www.ciroc.nl/nieuwsbrieven/en_nieuwsbrief
%20sep07.pdf.

The State of Israel—Ministry of Justice. *Money Laundering Prohibition: The Israeli Struggle Regarding Money Laundering and Terror Financing.* July 2, 2004. http://www.justice.gov.il/mojENG/Halbanat+Hon/Publications.htm.

Statement by Joseph Keefe, DEA Chief of Operations. Senate Governmental Affairs Committee, July 30, 2001. http://www.usdoj.gov/dea/pubs/cngrtest/ct073001.htm.

Statement of Karen Tandy, DEA Administrator. House Appropriations Committee, Mar. 24, 2004. http://www.usdoj.gov/dea/pubs/cngrtest/ct032404.htm.

Steinhauser, J. "After fabulousness, an age of intimacy." *New York Times,* Feb. 12, 1995.

Stoil, R. "Rosenstein returns from U.S. to serve remainder of sentence." *Jerusalem Post,* Mar. 29, 2007.

Stutman, M., and R. Esposito. *Dead on Delivery.* New York: Warner Books, 1992.

Tantum, B. "Heaven on earth." *Time Out New York,* Sept. 18–25, 2003.

Thornton, K. "Family remembers soldier of drug war." *San Diego Union Tribune,* Feb. 8, 2005.

Tobar, H., and C. Martínez. "The $207-million question in Mexico." *Los Angeles Times,* July 17, 2007.

Tooher, N. "Truth about polygraphs: They're still around." *Massachusetts Lawyers Weekly,* June 19, 2008.

Tugend, A. "The rise and fall of an unlikely drug smuggling ring." *Los Angeles Times,* Oct. 19, 2001.

"Two draw 20-year terms for killing club denizen." *New York Times,* Oct. 2, 1997.

United Nations Office on Drugs and Crime. *Ninth UN Survey of Crime Trends and Operations of Criminal Justice Systems, 2003–2004.* http://www.unodc.org/documents/data-and-analysis/CTS9_by_indicator_public.pdf.

United States Sentencing Commission. *MDMA Drug Offenses: Explanation of Recent Guideline Amendments.* Report to Congress, May 2001. http://www.ussc.gov/r_congress/mdma_final2.PDF.

U.S. Customs and Border Protection. "U.S. Customs sees growing number of Ecstasy swallowers." Press release, Dec. 19, 2000. http://www.customs.gov/hot-new/pressrel/2000/1220–01.htm.

———. "U.S. Customs Service operation dismantles international Ecstasy smuggling organization." Press release, June 14, 2000. http://www.cbp.gov/hot-new/pressrel/2000/0614–00.htm.

U.S. Department of State. "Money laundering and financial crimes." *1998 International Narcotics Control Strategy Report.* http://

www.state.gov/www/global/narcotics_law/1998_narc_report/
ml_intro.html.

———. "Europe and Central Asia." *1999 International Narcotics Control Strategy Report.* http://www.state.gov/p/inl/rls/nrcrpt/1999/925.htm.

U.S. General Accounting Office (GAO) Report to Congressional Requesters. *The Drug War: U.S. Programs in Peru Face Serious Obstacles.* Oct. 1991.

———. *Drug Control: DEA's Strategies and Operations in the 1990's.* July 1999.

Van Meter, J. "Party boy in a cage." *New York,* Nov. 27, 2006.

The White House. *Fact Sheet: Foreign Narcotics Kingpin Designation Act.* May 31, 2002. http://www.whitehouse.gov/news/releases/2002/05/20020531–9.html.

"Why did Walter die?" *Time,* Dec. 26, 1969.

Wohlgelernter, E. "Israeli underworld surfaces as gang warfare hits street." *Jewish Daily Forward,* Aug. 15, 2003.

———. "Mob violence spurs crackdown on organized crime." *Jewish Daily Forward,* Dec. 19, 2003.

Wren, C. "Business schemes change dynamics of the drug war." *New York Times,* May 5, 1996.

———. "Seizure of ecstasy at airport shows club drug's increase." *New York Times,* Oct. 29, 1999.

Ze'ev Rosenstein v. The State of Israel. The Israeli Supreme Court's Nov. 30, 2005 decision on Rosenstein's extradition appeal. http://elyon1.court.gov.il/files_eng/05/960/045/o06/05045960.o06.HTM.

Zohar, A. "A primer of Israeli crime." *Haaretz,* Jan. 13, 2006.

ACKNOWLEDGMENTS

Writing *Chemical Cowboys* was a crazy endeavor that required endlessly coaxing information from people who had no good reason to talk to a reporter. Luckily, just about everyone agreed to talk, and I owe them my deepest thanks and a drink next time I'm in town.

To start, *Chemical Cowboys* would have never been possible without the support of New York Field Division's Special Agent in Charge John Gilbride. Gilbride provided key introductions, assured my access to case files, and arranged for guided tours of NYFD facilities. He was an invaluable resource on countless topics that are covered in the book. Most important, he encouraged me to take my time getting to know the agents as human beings. I can't thank him enough for his generosity and his faith in me as a writer.

The story of how the DEA and law enforcement worldwide came together to take down the Ecstasy trafficking networks would have been a mundane case study if not for Bob Gagne. Gagne's adventures, achievements, and struggles are the heart of the book. His ability to soldier through when others quit is inspiring. Getting him to talk about his family and his feelings was no easy task, but I'm grateful for his courage and his trust in me to tell it right.

Very special thanks to Matt Germanowski, now a DEA supervisor in Birmingham, Alabama, who shared vivid details about agent life, his casework in New York, and some vintage B-side metal. Germanowski is a true good guy and a good friend.

Thanks to Jay Flaherty for providing leads to important

sources abroad and colorful details about his exciting years working Ecstasy cases.

Gregg Drews was generous in his assistance and his candor, and he shared important information about Oded Tuito's Pittsburgh connection. His support was invaluable.

The unfailing Erin McKenzie-Mulvey provided invaluable assistance at every step of the book and I'm ever-grateful for her help.

DEA's Dan Anderson, Roger Bach, Peter Breslow, Lou Cardinali, Peter Carpanini, John McKenna, Gary O'Hara, Scott Seeley-Hacker, Jack Toal, John Trustey, and Robert Yoos provided colorful details about the New York Field Division's history, culture, confidential source system, building security, and undercover Ecstasy operations. Edward Manning led me on a private tour of DEA's Northeast Regional Laboratory and let me observe (from a distance, it must be noted) as bench chemists analyzed an Ecstasy sample. Special thanks to Michael Guidetti and Glen Glover for an informative walk-through of the Title III Operations Center and the old listening rooms where Gagne and his partners worked the Ecstasy wires. Thanks to Leonard Lerner, who always made me feel welcome at NYFD, and to James Li, who showed me how to take apart a Glock in three easy steps.

I am grateful to Irene Gagne and her children, specifically Sherrie, Susan, and Ron, for their hospitality and openness in discussing the challenges and benefits of growing up a Gagne. I wish I could have gone into more detail in the book about what a uniquely supportive clan they are. Pawtucket's finest.

Steve Hager was an invaluable source for passages dealing with Oded Tuito's New York crew and the reasons why Israelis dominated the Ecstasy trade. Hager kept me honest, and I wish him a life filled with the things he cherishes most: love and family.

Jackie Suarez graciously shared her insider's perspective and her personal writings to help me better understand her relationship with Oded Tuito and her conflicted feelings about her involvement in his organization. I can't thank Suarez enough for helping me to present him as a human being, and not just a name on a kingpin list. It's been a pleasure getting to know such an intelligent, loyal, and empathic woman.

In Arlington, Virginia, I owe a tremendous debt of gratitude to Mary Irene Cooper, chief of congressional and public affairs at DEA headquarters, who green-lighted DEA's cooperation with the book, and to the ever-helpful public affairs officer Garrison Courtney for facilitating that process. Steven Robertson and Michael Sanders were generous with their time and provided important information about case law, asset forfeiture, T-III procedures, and DEA's use of confidential sources, as well as a tour of the DEA museum. John McKenna provided me with fascinating details about the Rosenstein case and was a consistent and reliable source on Israeli organized crime.

In Los Angeles, DEA's Michele Figura Dyer and Deanne Reuter and LAPD Robbery-Homicide Division's Mike Whelan provided important information and insights for the chapters dealing with the murder of Allon David Giladi and the Los Angeles Ecstasy investigations. DEA agent Jose Martinez and Robbery-Homicide detectives George Diaz, Dennis English, Ron Ito, and retired detective William Cox also provided valuable help and guidance.

Special thanks to DEA's Linda Miller Davis and Michael Sanders for their firsthand insights on Operation Snowcap. I am also grateful for the time and expertise of DEA's Edward Alvey, Ken Dinino, Gerald Graves, Steve Luzinski, Mike Mancuso, Andrew Petyak, and Don Rospond as well as AUSA Ben Greenberg of the Southern District of Florida, and Judith Friedman at the Department of Justice's Office of International Affairs.

Linda Lacewell has a lot better things to do now that she's on the executive staff to New York Attorney General Andrew Cuomo, serving as counsel for economic and social justice. So I'm grateful to her for taking my early-morning phone calls and late-night e-mail queries.

Thanks to Defense Attorney Ben Brafman for his graciousness while indulging my pointed questions about a case that's more than a decade old.

Thanks to Defense Attorney Bob Mann and his cocounsel Dana Harrell, as well as retired prosecutor Russell Sollitto for digging into their memory banks about the murder trial of Ron Gagne.

My sources abroad were many, but in particular, I'd like to give thanks to Chris Kabel, Chris Urben, and Sandra Radice at DEA's Brussels office. In The Hague, country attaché Jeffrey Boobar and agents Kevin Flood and David Larson provided important insights about DEA's role in the Netherlands, as well as that country's privacy laws, drug policies, policing challenges, and Ecstasy investigations.

It was my greatest fortune that DEA supervisor John McKenna introduced me to Israeli National Police commander Gadi Eshed, head of the research division at the intelligence section of the intelligence and investigations department. Eshed facilitated crucial interviews and was my tireless guide to the criminal underworld, providing informative tours of the sites of police operations, Mafia warfare, and historical locations that I've described in the book. Eshed and his wife, Anat, also showed me the beauty of the Israeli countryside and coastline, endearing me to their home in a lasting way.

A very special thanks go to Eshed's partners, the men and women of the Israeli National Police. Commander Avi Noyman of the central unit, central district, provided riveting details about police operations on the Israeli gangsters and about his private struggles as he and Eshed chased after Rosenstein and his cohorts. Retired major general Yosef Sedbon took time out of his busy schedule as vice president of Ramat-Gan College to meet with me and discuss the challenges he faced as the Tel Aviv district commander during the Second Intifada. Retired major general David Tsur, the former Tel Aviv district commander and a veritable action hero who has held some of the most dangerous military positions in Israel, provided thoughtful insights about the mechanisms of organized crime. Retired Israeli police officer Amram Edri regaled me with cinematic stories of the early days of Israeli gangster warfare. I'm thankful to have been able to highlight a fraction of Edri's adventures in the book.

I'd also like to offer my deepest gratitude for the time and expertise of Chief Superintendent Dvir Shai Bareli, head and public order coordinator of the research division intelligence section; Chief Superintendent Alon Magen, head of the intelligence section of the Tel Aviv central unit, Tel Aviv district; Chief Superintendent Orit Shapira-Heiman, head of the criminal research section; Superintendent Yifat Steinberger, assistant to the head of the intelligence branch; and Superintendent Yehuda Twersky, head of the money laundering squad, investigations and intelligence department.

There are many people who provided constructive guidance on the writing and editing of *Chemical Cowboys*. I am beholden to Will Murphy, my editor at Random House, who believed in the project from the start and worked diligently to try to keep me from boring my readers. Special thanks to Lea Beresford, who provided excellent notes on early drafts, and Courtney Turco, who patiently guided me through the final drafts. The supremely talented Catherine Quayle made tremendous editorial contributions and helped me to refine the work.

I am most fortunate to have Kathy Robbins and the folks at the Robbins Office on my side. Many thanks to Rick Pappas for his keen legal mind, to Kate Rizzo for spreading the word and the work far and wide, to Ian King for his astute editorial suggestions, and to my eloquent agent David Halpern, a wise guide and a cherished friend.

Speaking of friends, I would be remiss if I did not mention those who provided so much counsel and encouragement. Namely, Dan Stockenberg for his belief in me and the book when I wasn't so sure; Dennis Mukai for his artistry and empathy; Carol Pogash for being my sounding board and intellectual inspiration; Catherine Elsworth for her infectious laughter; Lara Lenington for always seeing the good; Michele O'Donnell for being my closest confidante; Janet Wexler for being generous of heart and ever-present in my thoughts; Efrén García and Efraín Talavera for their translations of Peruvian news reports and for nourishing me with sangria and ceviché; Jeff Gomez and Mark Pensavalle of Starlight Runner for their early and ongoing support of me in this project; and Judith Crist, my beloved mentor, a woman of style and wit.

Without family, there is no reason. I am grateful to my mother, Bodie, for instilling in me a sense of wonder. To Ron and Jenny Sweetingham for their love and support. To Stephen Strum for nurturing my early curiosity. To Bill Rendall for his kindness. To Adam Strum for being a poet and a gangster. To Wolf Rendall for reminding me to chase adventure.

Finally, I relied on several anonymous sources who have, at times, lived on the wrong side of the law. They know who they are. Thank you for your trust.

There are countless publications and case studies about the Drug War and drug addiction in America. How we move forward on both fronts deserves thoughtful and evolving discourse. I have chosen to not engage in the debates in *Chemical Cowboys*, deferring to those who live and work on the front lines. But I do hope that the experiences of the men and women who shared their personal struggles with drug abuse for this book serve to illustrate at least one important point: an imperative step on the long road to overcoming addiction is mending and nurturing the bonds to one's own family and community.

INDEX